# Dynamics of Long-Life Assets

Stefan N. Grösser · Arcadio Reyes-Lecuona
Göran Granholm
Editors

# Dynamics of Long-Life Assets

## From Technology Adaptation to Upgrading the Business Model

Springer Open

*Editors*
Stefan N. Grösser
School of Management
Bern University of Applied Sciences
Bern
Switzerland

Göran Granholm
VTT Technical Research Centre of Finland Ltd.
Espoo
Finland

Arcadio Reyes-Lecuona
E.T.S.I. de Telecomunicación
Universidad de Málaga
Málaga
Spain

ISBN 978-3-319-45437-5 ISBN 978-3-319-45438-2 (eBook)
DOI 10.1007/978-3-319-45438-2

Library of Congress Control Number: 2017932015



Printed on acid-free paper

This Springer imprint is published by Springer Nature
The registered company is Springer International Publishing AG
The registered company address is: Gewerbestrasse 11, 6330 Cham, Switzerland

# Foreword

The recent global financial crisis has underlined the importance of the real economy and a strong industry with industrial activities integrated in rich and complex value chains, linking multinationals to small or medium enterprises across sectors and countries. Economies with a solid manufacturing base focusing on high-tech or medium-tech activities and with integrated value chains have proved to be more resilient to the economic downturn and better placed to achieve higher growth in times of rebound.

A strong industrial base is of key importance for Europe's economic competitiveness. With scarce natural and energy resources and ambitious social and environmental goals, EU companies cannot compete on low price and low quality products. They must turn to innovation, productivity, resource-efficiency and create high value-added in order to compete in global markets. Europe's comparative advantage in the world economy lies and will continue to lie in high value-added goods and services. And for this, it will have to rely on innovation and technological advancement as its main source of competitiveness.

Use-it-Wisely, a EUR 8.6 million industrial project supported under the European Commission's Seventh Research and Innovation Framework Programme over the last 39 months, has attempted to achieve this. It has investigated tools and methodologies to help industries adapt to an environment characterised by constant change. The approach has built on the idea of a continuous, incremental upgrade process based on close collaboration between involved actors throughout the product life cycle. Managing this process requires a holistic understanding of the causal effects of various factors to support strategic decision making regarding technology upgrades, service development and introduction of novel business models. Solutions based on virtual and augmented realty and 3D scanning technologies were applied.

The tools and models developed in this project were implemented and tested in six different industries. They comprised service inspection of power turbines, modular upgrades of mobile rock crushers, space applications engineering, production systems in truck production, marine vessel data management, and office furniture supporting a radical, circular economy approach.

The project's diversity has proved to be its particular strength: interacting with seemingly unrelated fields of industry has contributed to an unprecedented transfer of knowledge, experience and technological know-how amongst the involved researchers and industrial practitioners, providing fertile ground for new ideas and solutions.

The European Commission is happy with this project's outcomes and as the official responsible for the monitoring of this project's activities I recommend the study of the material contained in this book.

January 2017

Dr. Erastos Filos
European Commission
Directorate-General for Research and Innovation
Brussels, Belgium

# Acknowledgements

This work was made possible through a collaborative research project jointly funded by the European Commission through the contractual public–private partnership (PPP) on Factories of the Future (FoF), and the twenty organisations participating in the project. We want to thank all project partners for their genuine engagement, enthusiasm, and collaborative effort. Special thanks go to the contributing authors and to all researchers, engineers, and other staff making possible the results reported in this book. Moreover, we are indebted to Paul McDonnell and Stephen Walker of Carr Communications for their magic abilities to alter and improve figures in the chapters. Finally, we would like to thank the Project Officer Dr. Erastos Filos and Project Technical Adviser Dr. Marco Sacco for their valuable insights and assistance throughout the project. The research leading to these results has received funding from the European Community's Seventh Framework Programme under grant agreement No. 609027 (Project Use-it-wisely).

# Contents

# Contributors

**Susanna Aromaa** VTT Technical Research Centre of Finland Ltd., Espoo, Finland

**Valter Basso** Domain Exploration and Science Italy—Engineering, Thales Alenia Space, Turin, Italy

**Katri Behm** VTT Technical Research Centre of Finland Ltd., Espoo, Finland

**Jonatan Berglund** Product and Production Development, Chalmers University of Technology, Gothenburg, Sweden

**Tim Bosch** Department Sustainable Productivity & Employability, TNO, Leiden, Netherlands

**Eric C.B. Cauchi** SEAbility Ltd., Athens, Greece

**Michele Cencetti** Mission Operations and Training, ALTEC, Turin, Italy

**Stefano T. Chiadò** Vastalla, Turin, Italy

**Maria Cuevas-Rodriguez** DIANA Research Group, Departamento de Tecnología Electrónica, ETSI Telecomunicación, Universidad de Málaga, Malaga, Spain

**Susana Flores-Holgado** Materials and Life Management, Tecnatom, San Sebastián de los Reyes, Spain

**Nikos Frangakis** I-SENSE Research Group, Institute of Communication and Computer Systems, Zografou, Greece

**Liang Gong** Product and Production Development, Chalmers University of Technology, Gothenburg, Sweden

**Daniel Gonzalez-Toledo** DIANA Research Group, Departamento de Tecnología Electrónica, ETSI Telecomunicación, Universidad de Málaga, Malaga, Spain

**Göran Granholm** VTT Technical Research Centre of Finland Ltd., Espoo, Finland

**Stefan N. Grösser** Institute for Corporate Development, Bern University of Applied Sciences, Bern, Switzerland

**Kaj Helin** VTT Technical Research Centre of Finland Ltd., Espoo, Finland

**Robert J. Houghton** Human Factors Research Group, University of Nottingham, Nottingham, UK

**Dominic Hurni** Institute for Corporate Development, Bern University of Applied Sciences, Bern, Switzerland

**Björn Johansson** Product and Production Development, Chalmers University of Technology, Gothenburg, Sweden

**Stefan Katz** Institute for Corporate Development, Bern University of Applied Sciences, Bern, Switzerland

**Alyson Langley** Human Factors Research Group, University of Nottingham, Nottingham, UK

**Simo-Pekka Leino** VTT Technical Research Centre of Finland Ltd., Espoo, Finland

**Luis Molina-Tanco** DIANA Research Group, Dpt. Tecnología Electrónica, ETSI Telecomunicación, University of Málaga, Málaga, Spain

**Tiina Pajula** VTT Technical Research Centre of Finland Ltd., Espoo, Finland

**Vangelis Papakonstantinou** International Naval Survey Bureau, Piraeus, Greece

**Mauro Pasquinelli** Domain Exploration and Science Italy, Engineering, Thales Alenia Space, Turin, Italy

**Harshada Patel** Human Factors Research Group, University of Nottingham, Nottingham, UK

**Arcadio Reyes-Lecuona** DIANA Research Group, Departmento de Tecnología Electrónica, ETSI Telecomunicación, Universidad de Málaga, Malaga, Spain

**Elina Saarivuori** VTT Technical Research Centre of Finland Ltd., Espoo, Finland

**Magnus Simons** VTT Technical Research Centre of Finland Ltd., Espoo, Finland

**Vassilis Stratis** OCEAN Boatyard Company OE, Attica, Greece

**Hanna Sundström** Product and Production Development, Chalmers University of Technology, Gothenburg, Sweden

**Saija Vatanen** VTT Technical Research Centre of Finland Ltd., Espoo, Finland

**Karin Verploegen** Gispen, Culemborg, Netherlands

**Carlo Vizzi** Technology Research Advanced Projects & Studies, ALTEC, Turin, Italy

**Gu van Rhijn** Department Sustainable Productivity & Employability, TNO, Leiden, Netherlands

# Abbreviations

| | |
|---|---|
| ALTEC | Aerospace Logistics Technology Engineering Company |
| API | Application Programming Interface |
| APS | Actor-Product-Service |
| BIM | Building Information Model |
| BoL | Beginning of Life |
| BOT | Behaviour Over Time |
| BPM | Business Process Modelling |
| BYOD | Bring Your Own Device |
| CAD | Computer Aided Design |
| CAE | Computer-Aided Engineering |
| CAS | Complex Adaptive Systems |
| CAVE | Cave Automatic Virtual Environment |
| CCM | Causal Context Models |
| CE | Circular Economy |
| C-LCA | Circular Life Cycle Analysis tool |
| CoP | Community of Practice |
| COTS | Commercial Off-The-Shelf |
| CX | Customer Experience |
| DEVICE | Distributed Environment for Virtual Integrated Collaborative Engineering |
| DHM | Digital Human Model |
| ECSS | European Cooperation for Space Standardization |
| EoL | End of Life |
| EPD | Environmental Product Declaration |
| FMEA | Failure Mode and Effect Analysis |
| FRP | Fibreglass-Reinforced Plastics |
| GDP | Gross Domestic Product |
| GHG | Greenhouse Gas |
| GPRS | General Packet Radio Service |
| HFE | Human Factor/Ergonomic |

| | |
|---|---|
| HMD | Head-Mounted Display |
| HR | Human Relations |
| HS | High Season |
| I/O | Input/Output |
| ICT | Information and communications technology |
| IMS | Intelligent Manufacturing Systems |
| INCOSE | International Council on Systems Engineering |
| IP | Intellectual Property |
| IPCC | Intergovernmental Panel on Climate Change |
| IPSS | Industrial Product Service System |
| ISECG | International Space Exploration Coordination Group |
| IT | Information Technologies |
| JSON | JavaScript Object Notation |
| LADAR | Laser Detection and Ranging |
| LCA | Life Cycle Assessment |
| LCI | Life Cycle Inventory |
| LCIA | Life Cycle Impact Assessment |
| LS | Low Season |
| MBSE | Model-Based Systems Engineering |
| MDA | Model-Driven Architecture |
| MoL | Middle of Life |
| NPAPI | Netscape Plug-in API |
| NR | New Request |
| OECD | Organisation for Economic Co-operation and Development |
| OEM | Original Equipment Manufacturer |
| PCR | Product Category Rules |
| PDM | Product Data Management |
| PLM | Product Life cycle Management |
| PM | Plenary Meeting |
| POV | Point of View |
| PSS | Product Service System |
| QRM | Quick Response Manufacturing |
| R&D | Research and Development |
| RC | Request Web Configurator |
| RoRo | Roll-On/Roll-Off |
| SD | System Dynamics |
| SDL | Service Dominant Logic |
| SE | Systems Engineering |
| SLM | Service Life Cycle Management |
| SME | Small- and Medium-sized Enterprise |
| SoS | System of Systems |
| SSM | Soft System Modelling |
| SysML | The Systems Modelling Language |
| TAS | Thales Alenia Space |
| TAS-I | Thales Alenia Space Italia S.p.A |

| | |
|---|---|
| UIW | Use-it-Wisely |
| UML | Unified Model Language |
| VE | Virtual Environment |
| VP | Virtual Prototyping |
| VR | Virtual Reality |
| VSM | Value Stream Mapping |
| WebGL | Web Graphics Library |
| XMI | XML Metadata Interchange |

# List of Figures

# List of Tables

# Part I
# Introduction and Setting the Scene

# Dynamics of Long-Life Assets: The Editors' Intro

**Göran Granholm, Stefan N. Grösser and Arcadio Reyes-Lecuona**

**Abstract** The manufacturing industry is changing. Driven by a number of concurrent trends, including economic and political development, technological breakthroughs and social connectivity, the impacts on industry in general are fundamental. Companies need to find ways to adapt to this change in collaboration with actors across their value networks. For long-life industrial assets, i.e., industrial product-service systems, both economically and environmentally sustainable solutions become an imperative supported by new business models-based collaborative value creation. In an EU-funded research project twenty organisations including three research institutes, four universities and thirteen companies studied, developed and demonstrated ways to deal with the dynamics of long-life assets. The main findings are summarised in this book. This chapter provides a brief introduction to the topic and presents the structure of the rest of this book.

**Keywords** Digitalisation · Business model · Industrial product-services system · Technology adaptation · Asset · Dynamics

G. Granholm (✉)
VTT Technical Research Centre of Finland Ltd., Espoo, Finland
e-mail: goran.granholm@vtt.fi

S.N. Grösser
Institute for Corporate Development, Bern University of Applied Sciences, Bern, Switzerland
e-mail: stefan.groesser@bfh.ch

A. Reyes-Lecuona
DIANA Research Group, Departmento de Tecnología Electrónica, ETSI Telecomunicación, Universidad de Málaga, Malaga, Spain
e-mail: areyes@uma.es



S.N. Grösser et al. (eds.), *Dynamics of Long-Life Assets*,
DOI 10.1007/978-3-319-45438-2_1

# 1 Introduction

Digitalisation transforms industries globally. Companies, products and people have become increasingly connected and constantly accessible regardless of time or location. Combined with new technology innovations this gives rise to completely new products and services capable of adapting to specific customer needs. However, the demand for fast delivery of personalised solutions cannot be met by traditional, rigid supply chain structures. Instead, agile supply networks of highly specialised companies are emerging, adopting new, innovative business models. The growing technological complexity and speed of development requires a high level of specialisation. This emphasizes the need for collaboration on research and development between relevant actors to complement gaps in knowledge and innovation capacity, and to share risk and resources, especially in small and medium sized companies (Romero and Molina 2011). In a recent survey (KPMG 2015), more than three-quarters of the respondents said that partnerships will form the basis of innovation for their company.

In search of efficiency and flexibility, firms are driven to both form vertical and horizontal alliances, which in turn require a more strategic approach to integration and networking (Rothwell 1994). This extends to new ways of sharing revenues through the value network. Enabled by the digital transformation, a new performance economy is emerging, shifting the focus from selling products and services to selling measurable outcome and results, a change that will redefine the base of competition and industry structures (World Economic Forum 2015). Technology platforms and ecosystems of partnerships will take over large parts of the current business in the near future. For instance, the emerging Industry 4.0 supplier ecosystem is expected to reach €420 billion in value and ICT-based services are expected to account for more than 75% of all industrial services, amounting to nearly €17.5 billion in revenues by 2020 (Frost and Sullivan 2015). Knowledge has been seen as an asset for coping with the increasing complexity of inter-organisational value chains. Thus, continuous learning within and between organisations has become a key strategic requirement for building and sustaining future competitiveness (Bessant et al. 2003).

In parallel with technological development there is a growing concern about human impact on the environment and the limits of the global ecological capacity. This has led to political decisions and global agreements aiming at reducing ecological footprints. Research into key enabling technologies, such as new materials and manufacturing technologies, help reduce ecological footprints and comply with tightening regulations to, for example, reduce global warming or the use of non-renewable resources. Closed-loop life-cycles and circular economy business models appear as a viable solution to reduce environmental impacts. The European Commission has adopted an ambitious Circular Economy Package, which includes revised legislative proposals to stimulate Europe's transition towards a circular economy (European Commision 2015). A prerequisite for circular life-cycle models is a shift from a business logic based on products as the main bearer value to models based on life-cycle value shared through the value network (Tukker 2013). This requires new forms of collaboration and focusing on product based services to create end user benefit.

An industrial product-service system (IPSS or $IPS^2$) is an integrated product and service offering that delivers values in industrial applications, characterized by the integrated and mutually determined planning, development, provision and use of product and service shares (Meier et al. 2010). The majority of companies that have adopted the concept of industrial product-service systems offer the use of a product, but not the ownership of the respective product (Guidat et al. 2014). In business models where user value is based on system outcome instead of ownership OEMs are more prone to design for total life-cycle cost, which in turn tend to lead to longer life spans and focus on sustainable solutions (Sundin and Bras 2005). This includes better end-of-life management but also the dynamic adoption of changing customer demands and improved provider abilities along the life cycle (Meier et al. 2010).

High-investment industrial product-service systems face new challenges in this dynamic and highly competitive business environment. Due to high initial investment costs such systems are usually designed for relatively long life spans. Sustainability goals call for further extension of system life-cycles. At the same time personalised, targeted solutions and improvements based on new technologies push in the opposite direction (EFFRA 2013). Extending systems life-cycles require careful planning and close collaboration with end-users to ensure both ecological, economic and technical sustainability. Processes for continuously improving IPSS need to match the specific IPSS characteristics and value network structures (Schweitzer and Aurich 2010). Continuous performance monitoring and information exchange processes need to be established case by case.

Innovation has been identified as the most important asset for creating business value. Focus has already shifted from the own R&D department as the main source of innovation to include other in-house functions, and is now extending beyond corporate borders to involve other actors of the value chain, including end-users and other stakeholders. In the future, innovation will depend heavily on emerging ecosystems. This, again, requires new forms of collaboration, which includes also competing companies.

Efficient strategies must be developed to upgrade legacy product-service systems to meet new requirements and enable economically and ecologically viable system life-cycles. This requires new ways of collaboration and a comprehensive approach building on the combined knowledge of the actor network, exchange of knowledge between researchers and practitioners, and learning across industry domains.

## 2 Future-Proofing Industrial Product-Service Systems

In July 2013, twenty organisations representing research and industry across Europe signed an agreement with the European Commission to undertake a research project focusing on upgrading of capital intensive product-services to meet future demands of efficiency, performance and fitness for purpose. The project called "Innovative continuous upgrades of high investment product-services" was funded under the European Commission's seventh Framework Program theme [FoF.NMP.2013-5] *Innovative design of personalised product-services and of their production processes based on collaborative environments*, short named *Use-it-Wisely*, and was part of the Factories of the Future public-private partnership in 2009. Public-private partnerships (or PPPs) were launched by the European Commission (executive of European Union or EU) as part of European Economic Recovery Plan presented in 2008.

The general objectives of the Factories of the Future PPP are to (EFFRA 2013):

- increase EU industrial competitiveness and sustainability in a global world through R&I activities for the timely development of new knowledge-based production technologies and systems;
- promote EU 2020 targets of a smart, green and inclusive economy;
- support EU industrial policy targets (EC industrial policy communication October 2012); and
- underpin EU trade and investment policy.

To meet these targets, the Use-it-Wisely (UIW) project set out to develop tools and models to help industry deal with change. The project focuses on continual improvement of products and services through a continuous upgrade activity based on a comprehensive approach involving multiple actors in a collaborative effort to improve product and services through small innovative upgrade increments.

The project targets industries dealing with high-investment products and services in general, not limited to any particular industry sector. The definition of 'high-investment' is therefore more linked to the rate of return than on the absolute value of the initial investment. A common characteristic of such systems is therefore a relative long operational life-cycle. During their life such systems must be maintained and regularly upgraded to meet requirements that were not known or anticipated when they were first designed.

Tools and methods developed in the project were implemented and tested in six separate pilot cases representing different industries: power turbines inspection, machinery, space mission, manufacturing lines, shipping and office furniture.

## 3 Content of the Book

The book is organised in three main parts. Part I gives an introduction to the specific challenge addressed in the book (Chapter "The Challenge") and presents the foundations of the UIW-approach (Chapter "The Use-it-Wisely (UIW) Approach"). Part II goes into more detail in some of the key topics of the approach: innovation management (Chapter "Innovation Management with an Emphasis on Co-creation"), systems and complexity management (Chapter "Complexity Management and System Dynamics Thinking"), environmental impact (Chapter "Managing the Life Cycle To Reduce Environmental Impacts"), virtual reality (Chapter "Virtual Reality and 3D Imaging to Support Collaborative Decision Making for Adaptation of Long-Life Assets"), human-centred design (Chapter "Operator-Oriented Product and Production Process Design for Manufacturing, Maintenance and Upgrading"), virtual communities (Chapter "Fostering a Community of Practice for Industrial Processes"), and system modelling (Chapter "Extending the System Model"). Part III describes six actual use cases where tools and technologies have been implemented and tested in the six different industry clusters: Service inspections power plant turbines (Chapter "Collaborative Management of Inspection Results in Power Plant Turbines"), upgrade business models of mobile rock crushers (Chapter "Rock Crusher Upgrade Business from a PLM Perspective"), collaborative information management in space systems development (Chapter "Space Systems Development"), adaptation of high variant automotive production systems (Chapter "Adaptation of High-Variant Automotive Production System Using a Collaborative Approach"), actor collaboration in maritime passenger vessel design (Chapter "Supporting the small-to-medium vessel industry"), and sustainable furniture business based on circular economy (Chapter "Sustainable Furniture That Grows with End-Users"). Finally, different upgrade business models defined based on an analysis of the pilot cases (Chapter "Comparing Industrial Cluster Cases to Define Upgrade Business Models for a Circular Economy").

The chapters can be read independently but for understanding the concept of the approach is advisable to first read Sect. 1. References to relevant chapters inside the book will be given when needed. The book is linked to online resources maintained by the UIW-virtual community accessible at http://use-it-wisely.eu.

**Acknowledgements** The research leading to these results has received funding from the European Union's Seventh Framework Programme (FP7/2007-2013) under grant agreement no 609027. The results are based on close collaboration between the 20 partners of the UIW-research project.

## References


Bessant, J., Kaplinsky, R., & Lamming, R. (2003). Putting supply chain learning into practice. *International Journal of Operations & Production Management, 23*(2), 167–184.

EFFRA. (2013). *Factories of the future: Multi-annual roadmap for the contractual PPP under Horizon 2020*. Publications Office of the European Union.

European Commision. (2015). Closing the loop—An EU action plan for the circular economy. Communication from the Commission, COM (2015) 614 final.

Frost & Sullivan. (2015). Industry 4.0 business ecosystem—Decoding the new normal.

Guidat, T., Barquet, A. P., Widera, H., Rozenfeld, H., & Seliger, G. (2014). Guidelines for the definition of innovative industrial product-service systems (PSS) business models for remanufacturing. *Procedia CIRP, 16*, 193–198.

KPMG. (2015). Global Manufacturing Outlook: Preparing for battle - Manufacturers get ready for transformation. Retrieved from https://home.kpmg.com/xx/en/home/insights/2015/05/preparing-for-battle.html

Meier, H., Roy, R., & Seliger, G. (2010). Industrial product-service systems—IPS2. *CIRP Annals—Manufacturing Technology, 59*(2), 607–627.

Romero, D., & Molina, A. (2011). Collaborative networked organisations and customer communities: Value co-creation and co-innovation in the networking era. *Production Planning & Control, 22*(5–6), 447–472.

Rothwell, R. (1994). Towards the fifth-generation innovation process. *International Marketing Review, 11*(1), 7–31. http://doi.org/10.1108/02651339410057491

Schweitzer, E., & Aurich, J. C. (2010). Continuous improvement of industrial product-service systems. *CIRP Journal of Manufacturing Science and Technology, 3*(2), 158–164.

Sundin, E., & Bras, B. (2005). Making functional sales environmentally and economically beneficial through product remanufacturing. *Journal of Cleaner Production, 13*(9), 913–925.

Tukker, A. (2013). Product services for a resource-efficient and circular economy—A review. *Journal of Cleaner Production, 97*, 76–91.

World Economic Forum. (2015). *Industrial internet of things: Unleashing the potential of connected products and services*. Retrieved from http://www.weforum.org/reports/industrial-internet-things.

# The Challenge

**Arcadio Reyes-Lecuona**

**Abstract** Industries involved in manufacturing and providing services for high-value, long-life products must address challenges related to upgrading their products once they are in operation. The aim of this chapter is to present some of those challenges, which have been addressed in the Use-it-Wisely (UIW) project using the tools and methods presented in this book. To outline these different challenges and how they are interrelated, an imaginary company is assumed, a European manufacturer producing high-investment equipment for customers worldwide. Their products are complex machinery with a long life cycle, and thus, an important part of the business is focused not only on manufacturing but also on inspection, maintenance, refurbishing, upgrading, and retirement. This chapter presents a brief description of its activities and business areas to highlight the main challenges that this company has to address in the current context of globalization, rapid change and high restrictions, together with other companies and stakeholders that define a value network. Finally, the chapter outlines how these challenges have been organized to discover key elements for addressing them. This organization is a result of the UIW-project.

**Keywords** Product lifecycle · High-investment products · Long-life products · Product upgrades · Product maintenance · Product reutilization · Customer involvement · System modelling · Business modelling · Technological support of collaboration

---

A. Reyes-Lecuona (✉)
DIANA Research Group, Departmento de Tecnología Electrónica,
ETSI Telecomunicación, Universidad de Málaga, Málaga, Spain
e-mail: areyes@uma.es



S.N. Grösser et al. (eds.), *Dynamics of Long-Life Assets*,
DOI 10.1007/978-3-319-45438-2_2

# 1 Introduction

The Use-it-Wisely (UIW) Project gathers several important companies grouped into six industrial clusters, together with universities and other research institutions. They work in vastly different industries with the common goal of investigating new business models and opportunities based on innovative methods of managing continuous upgrades in different industrial product-service systems. These are high-investment, long-service-life, one-of-a-kind or highly customized products such as working machines, ships, trucks, power plant equipment, spacecraft or long-life furniture. These companies are facing important challenges due to global off-shoring, rapid business environment change, shrinking investment budgets, and environmental pressures (Schuh et al. 2011). These challenges can be addressed by creating added value by augmenting their products with agile knowledge-based, environmentally friendly post-manufacturing services. This was outlined in the Factories of the Future roadmap for Horizon 2020 (EFFRA 2013) and other platforms and networks focused on innovation in production, such as Manufuture (2006) or the Intelligent Manufacturing Systems (IMS) project (2011).

During the execution of the UIW-project, the industries involved worked together to describe common interests, visions and approaches to face the aforementioned challenges. Each of them has contributed specific solutions to their problems. Although these problems are specific, there are many commonalities that were captured during the UIW-project. To structure those contributions, we assume an imaginary company in which all these challenges are present. It is important to highlight that the challenges outlined are not the challenges of a single company. A whole network of stakeholders is implied in each of them, whose role is relevant. We have named this imaginary company "Eutopia[1] Ltd." and present these challenges in the next section.

# 2 Presenting the Challenges: A High-Investment Product Manufacturer

Let us imagine Eutopia Ltd., a global manufacturer based in Europe that produces high-investment equipment for customers worldwide. Eutopia is a large company with several thousand employees working in several plants in Europe and provides service to customers throughout the world. Its products are complex machinery with a long life cycle, and thus, an important part of the company business is focused on

[1]The name Eutopia is used as a combination of Europe and Utopia, from ancient Greek: "ou" (non) + "topos" (place), coined by T. More (and used as title of his book, 1516, about an imaginary island enjoying the utmost perfection in legal, social, and political systems). The word eutopia can also be understood from ancient Greek as "eu" (good) + "topos" (place). Eutopia would therefore be a desirable place to be, whether it exists or not.

the inspection, maintenance, refurbishing, upgrading, and retirement of their products as well as their manufacture. Its customers are companies running large facilities, which are subject to strict regulations and operate in a highly competitive environment with rapidly changing conditions. Moreover, many other companies provide products and services to Eutopia's customers, and collaboration and information sharing among them is necessary.

To be able to adapt to the high diversity and rapid changes in market conditions, Eutopia must tackle various problems in the entire product life cycle that involve different stakeholders and other associated companies that define a value network. The next paragraph summarizes these challenges.

## 2.1 Challenge 1: Involving Customers in Early Stages

Due to the high diversity of customer needs and the need to adapt to different environments, interaction with customers for ordering new units must be very flexible and allow a high level of customization. Moreover, some of the products produced by Eutopia are one-of-a-kind products specifically designed for one customer. Therefore, the company needs methods and tools for gathering high-level requirements from the final customers and enhancing the communication among all relevant stakeholders involved in the value generation process, including customers and other service companies.

Therefore, they must develop applications to enhance communication between stakeholders including customers because the first interaction is with them when a product is ordered. The basis of this system should be a product model that is built following a reference data model (meta-model) to store and interchange information about the product design, configurations, data for calculations and simulations. With this approach, the system could provide support for the initial choices among different design and configuration possibilities and associated prices. In Chapter "Space Systems Development", a similar challenge in the space industry, maintaining communication with the customer from the early stages in commercial space service development, is addressed.

This approach is so generic that this improvement in product modelling can serve as a standard for storing and interchanging any industrial information in multiple types of industries, e.g., large series, small series, or one-of-a-kind products (Eigner et al. 2014). Furthermore, Chapter "Extending the system model" describes extending the models to support different project activities throughout the product life cycle and maintaining control of system consistency.

## 2.2 Challenge 2: Factory Upgrading

A rapidly changing market leads to the necessity of continuously adapting and developing production systems (Lindskog et al. 2013). Therefore, factory upgrading as a mechanism to adapt to customer needs is another challenge Eutopia must address. However, modifying a manufacturing system requires complex plans and necessarily involves contributions from actors across the entire organization and beyond (Lindskog et al. 2016). All of the involved actors must collaborate and share a common understanding of the design, functions and performance of the current and future manufacturing systems.

One tool for supporting engineers in preventing mistakes and misunderstandings when working in redesigning an existing factory is virtual representation of products and manufacturing systems (Becker et al. 2005). Therefore, Eutopia is interested in developing applications to store technical information for the production system (3D models of the factory, live production data, etc.) and improving current work activities with a collaborative focus. Its goal is to improve the communication between actors from different departments to make technical decisions including positioning, allocation of work, maintenance, and planning of production-related activities using this information. Chapter "Virtual Reality and 3D Imaging to Support Collaborative Decision Making for Adaptation of Long-Life Assets" contains a more detailed elaboration of the use of virtual representations to improve understanding of existing systems and for facilitating collaboration and decision making in this context.

A particular challenge for a global manufacturer such as Eutopia is to harmonize and standardize the production processes within operations in multiple locations and markets to ensure best practices and the most efficient way of working. Hence, with virtual representations of their production sites, together with a rich collection of associated metadata, the upgrading process can be easily shared among different factories. This allows considering their multiple experiences to improve the collaborative decision making process that is required in modifying a manufacturing system. Chapter "Adaptation of High-Variant Automotive Production System Using a Collaborative Approach" presents an industrial case in a truck factory that addresses a similar challenge.

## 2.3 Challenge 3: Maintenance Management

Once the equipment is sold and in operation, periodic maintenance management is an important business area. Maintenance operations can be undertaken by Eutopia itself or through other service companies that are part of its network. Again, collaboration among the actors involved, which could include the customer, inspection companies, the manufacturer and other maintenance companies for repair or refurbishing depending on the inspection results, is a key challenge of paramount importance (Reyes-Lecuona et al. 2014).

In the case of inspections, the results for each unit sold that is in operation should be stored in Eutopia's information systems and linked to a product realization model built based on the aforementioned meta-model. There, all of the information relevant to the system context is identified and structured. In addition, it is necessary to develop collaborative applications to share and manage this information. Here, it is convenient to link all this information to the 3D geometry of the product.

This challenge has additional implications. In many cases, the product consists of a physical assembly of parts defining the product geometry. This assembly is usually hierarchical, with several levels of sub-assemblies. Maintenance work is usually focused on one sub-assembly or a specific part, and different maintenance services may be conducted different parts of the product or over an area or volume defined within the product geometry. Providing a user-centred design of the 3D interaction mechanisms is essential for a collaborative decision making tool (González-Toledo et al. 2015).

Chapter "Collaborative Management of Inspection Results in Power Plant Turbines" presents an industrial case in which a company working on inspections of power plant turbines addresses a similar challenge and a collaborative tool that has been developed to improve the decision-making process among the actors involved.

## 2.4 *Challenge 4: In-Operation Upgrades Demanded by Customers*

Once Eutopia's products are in operation, customers might require different upgrades to the equipment during its operating life, sometimes after a long operation time with possible unknown modifications. This is another challenge as well as a business opportunity. The challenge is to create modular upgrade solutions so that the same parts can be reused in many product models. The company must develop pre-engineered modules for these upgrades so it will be able to provide a machine upgrade service as a new business model [see Leino (2015) for a similar case description].

However, delivery of upgrade modules for physical assets in operation for a long time is not an easy task. It is necessary to build tools and methods to evaluate compatibility between upgrades and machines, prior to design, customization and delivery of upgrade offerings to customers. As the machine has possibly undergone modifications affecting its geometry after a long time in operation, it is necessary to track these changes to ensure that an upgrade module is compatible with a specific machine. This is not easy, as these products might not be under the producer's control after the sales process. In general, as in previous challenges, improvement of communication between actors is essential to interchange commercial and technical information as well as recording the actual state of each unit sold, including possible geometric changes.

Chapter "Rock Crusher Upgrade Business from a PLM Perspective" presents a similar industrial case in which novel digital technology is used to enable a new business model for upgrading old machines in the mining and construction industry. There, the innovative business model is based on clever engineering design solutions of the upgrade products and on digitalization of information flows for upgrade projects.

## 2.5 Challenge 5: Upgrades Driven by Changes in Regulations

There are many more reasons for upgrading equipment that is already in operation. Eutopia's products are subjected to strict regulations. Changes in these regulations, operational data, post-delivery inspections and surveys may lead to a decision that upgrading is necessary. In these cases, the actors involved in this process should have access to an information-rich technical metafile that includes all aspects of the product, including initial customer specifications, designs, trial data, inspection results, and required regulations that may change over time, necessitating an upgrade to extend the operating life of the product (Frangakis et al. 2014). Here, communication among different actors, including regulatory bodies, is essential.

Therefore, the upgrading process requires the company to develop tools and methods to improve the information flow and communication between actors and to exchange technical and legal information. The products should be transformed into meta-products that are accompanied by an information-rich environment.

Chapter "Supporting the Small-to-Medium Vessel Industry" presents an industrial case focused on the manufacture of small craft passenger vessels made of composite materials, which poses a similar challenge. This challenge is addressed by developing a set of tools that enables the storage of information on all aspects of a vessel's life cycle.

## 2.6 Challenge 6: Business Modelling Simulation and Innovation

Current rapid market changes force Eutopia to constantly generate new business models or adapt current business models to innovative ideas. To address these challenges, the company works on innovation management such as business model innovation using system dynamics simulation modelling (Groesser and Jovy 2016; Martinez-Moyano and Richardson 2013; Sterman 2000). Their objective is to produce estimations of costs and updates, thus following market dynamics in the context of increasing the duration of the life of the equipment in service. Such business model analyses allow the company to evaluate the effectiveness of various policy options under varying circumstances and to improve management decision-making.

In addition, such business model analyses could be extended with quantitative simulation models for estimation in the context of business model innovation (Rahmandad and Sterman 2012; Groesser and Jovy 2016). Simulating business cases in a systematic and reliable manner would allow for informed decisions to be made on which upgrades should be conducted.

Chapter "Complexity Management and System Dynamics Thinking" presents how to address this challenge using causal context models and how to extend them with quantitative models for performing estimations.

## 2.7 Challenge 7: Retirement and reutilization

Retirement of old equipment and reutilization of old components in new products is another challenge for Eutopia to achieve flexibility, adaptability, and modularity in its product designs as well as a high level of material reuse and hence sustainability. To achieve high levels of returned material, a new business model should be developed through new product-service strategies based on the Circular Economy (CE) paradigm (Tukker 2015; Lieder and Rashid 2016). In addition, Eutopia must respond to constant market developments and adjust their products, services, processes and business model while accounting for the required sustainability and flexibility of products. In this context, one question is how to retain the highest value of its investments.

To address this challenge, Eutopia has developed a causal context model (Groesser 2012) in which different variables and their relationships are identified (see Chapter "Complexity Management and System Dynamics Thinking"). The causal context model builds the foundation for a simulation-based business model analysis that can be used to simulate the effects of important business model decisions. This is done using a business simulator based on system dynamics modelling to reflect its product and service portfolio using CE scenarios.

Further, the company's approach is to develop a CE Check to support a modular, adaptable product design, creating the possibility of adapting (by upgrading, retrofitting or remanufacturing) the product while in use at the customer site, to prolong the lifespan of the product and meet changing final customer needs. A special focus is on modularity aspects that support the re-use of parts within and between product lines.

Chapter "Sustainable Furniture that Grows with End-Users" presents an industrial case in which this challenge is addressed in the context of sustainable furniture production.

## 3 Addressing the Challenges

The challenges we have presented as those faced by Eutopia Ltd. can be structured in a generic model around the upgrade initiation process. To manage and address these challenges, we can differentiate them into three domains: (1) innovation management and business models, (2) collaboration and data visualization, and (3) Actor-Product-Service modelling. Figure 1 shows the three domains related to the upgrade initiation process.

Market and data analysis using business forecasting models and tools can, from a strategic decision, initiate the upgrade of its product/service or business model. This decision can be supported by business simulation, made by management directly or be the result of a collaborative process to analyse simulation outputs. As an example, a simulator application could be used to study new product-service strategies based on the CE model or to allow the customer to be informed of the costs involved in different possible upgrades. In both cases, the outputs of these simulators will be the base upon which to choose what upgrades should be initiated.

The decision to initiate an upgrade could also arise from technical analysis of the situation. Collaboration management via models and applications that support this collaboration and the knowledge of product status through enhanced visualization can also drive an upgrade decision. As an example, a collaborative application that includes discussion management could help technicians to determine when initiation of an upgrade is necessary.

Both sources for an upgrade decision, based on strategic market estimation or the result of collaborative technical work, should rely on effective Actor-Product-Service models and tools to support decision making. These three domains are described in more detail below:

- **Actor-Product-Service Modelling domain**. Company applications must handle large amounts of information from different sources (3D scan data, CAD models, ad hoc process databases, etc.) A reference meta-model would provide a set of rules to develop specific Actor-Product-Service Models. This meta-model would contain recommendations on how to model information on product and services so that interfaces between different formats and tools are easier to maintain. Information about customers and other actors in the value network can also be included. This meta-model is general enough to serve as a standard for storing and interchanging any industrial information in multiple types of industries.
- **Collaboration and Data Visualization domain**. As noted in the previous section, a recurrent challenge is to improve the communication between different actors involved in the life cycle of products or services. To that end, several methods and tools might be implemented inside the collaboration management domain. These tools would be focused on enabling information flow, promoting collaborations in technical developments, and providing an easy and efficient method for making decisions. As mentioned before, the Actor-Product-Service model organizes all of the information related to the

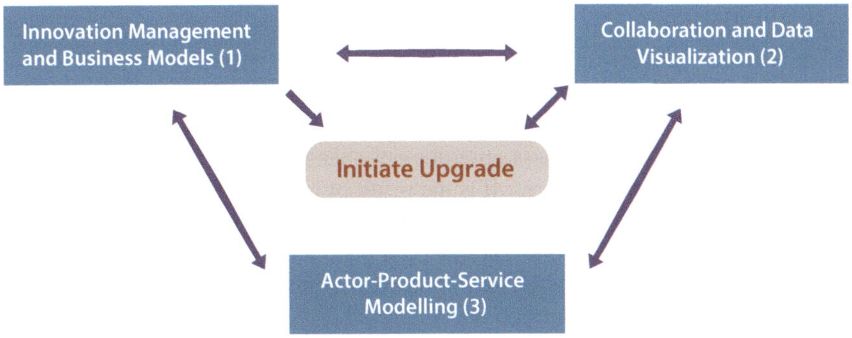


**Fig. 1** The three UIW challenge domains and their relationship with the upgrade initiation process

product/service. This information can be used by the applications contained in this domain to offer: a collaborative environment (in which many actors can interchange technical, legal and commercial information), decision making support (providing a discussion management mechanism) and visualization of the product/service (using 3D models and specific diagrams). The collaboration management domain has two roles. First, this domain can work as the upgrade originator. In this case, actors use the collaboration management tools to study the problem and decide if it is worth initiating the upgrade or not. Second, this domain appears when an upgrade has been initiated and different actors must make technical decisions regarding modifications to the system of interest.

- **Innovation Management and Business Modelling (market and data analysis) domain**. Some of the aforementioned challenges require producing applications and models to perform predictions in the context of business innovation in a systematic and reliable manner to subsequently make decisions about which upgrades should be carried out. To model applications related with the market and data analysis, some generic structures must be defined (Lane and Smart 1996; Lane 1998; Paich 1985; Ulli-Beer et al. 2010). Some of these generic structures, which are basic structures of System Dynamics models, were created during the UIW-project. First, generic business model structures include major business elements with generic values. Then, using an inductive process, other generic structures can be extracted from causal context models. These generic structures should illustrate a basic understanding of upgrading and its effects for the company as well as for the users of upgradable assets. Generic structures are the first element of any System Dynamics model and allow practitioners to model their own upgrading challenges using the generic structures as a stepping stone for a more specific model applied to their challenge (Groesser and Jovy 2016).

# 4 Conclusion

This chapter introduced the main challenges that companies involved in producing, maintaining, and operating high-investment, long-life products must address due to global off-shoring, rapid business environment change, shrinking investment budgets, and environmental pressures. It is the result of an analysis conducted with the industrial partners of the UIW-project and has been presented as the unified story of an imaginary company, Eutopia Ltd. The idea behind this chapter is to present the challenges that have been addressed during this project in developing and testing new tools, methods and business models that build the remaining elements of the book. Companies with similar needs to those presented here as Eutopia's challenges could discover that the tools and methodologies presented in the remainder of this book are applicable to their business.

To address these challenges, actors should be involved in a collaborative process for producing upgrade innovations. In the next chapter, a generic framework for managing these system upgrades is formulated. This framework goes beyond the three-domain model outlined here and is designed to address the challenges presented in this chapter using an adaptation mechanism to manage factors influencing the upgrade design, a system model definition that integrates actor, product and service data, and a virtual collaboration environment to facilitate the interaction between actors.

# References

Becker, M. C., Salvatore, P., & Zirpoli, F. (2005). The impact of virtual simulation tools on problem-solving and new product development organization. *Research Policy, 34*(9): 1305–1321.

Cagnin, C., & Könnölä, T. (2011). The challenge of global foresight: Lessons from scenario and roadmapping process on intelligent and sustainable manufacturing systems. In *Proceedings of the Fourth International Seville Conference on Future-Oriented Technology Analysis*, Seville, May 2011.

EFFRA. (2013). Factories of the future 2020 roadmap. Research roadmap produced by the European factories of the Future Research Association, 2013.

Eigner, M., Dickopf, T., Apostolov, H., Schaefer, P., Faißt, K. G., & Keßler, A. (2014). System lifecycle management: Initial approach for a sustainable product development process based on methods of model based systems engineering. In *Product lifecycle management for a global market* (pp. 287–300). Berlin: Springer.

Frangakis, N., Stratis, V., Papakonstantinou, V., & Cauchi, E. (2014). Vessel information-rich meta-file to increase the life cycle of small craft passenger boats. In *Proceedings of the 5th Advances in Human Factors and Ergonomics (AHFE) Conference* (pp. 83–88), Krakow, July, 2014.

González-Toledo, D., Cuevas-Rodríguez, M., Garre, C., & Molina-Tanco, L. (2015). A tool for collaborative decision making on service information linked to 3D geometry of complex hierarchical products. In *Proceedings of EuroVR2015*, Lecco, October, 2015.

Groesser, S. N. (2012). Co-evolution of standards in innovation systems: The dynamics of voluntary and legal building codes. Heidelberg: Springer.

Groesser, S. N., & Jovy, N. (2016). Business model analysis using computational modeling: A strategy tool for exploration and decision-making. *Journal of Management Control, 21*(1), 61–88.
Lane, D. C. (1998). Can we have confidence in generic structures? *Journal of the Operational Research Society, 49*, 936–947.
Lane, D. C., & Smart, C. (1996). Reinterpreting 'generic structure': evolution, application and limitations of a concept. *System Dynamics Review, 12*(2), 87–120.
Leino, S. P. (2015). *Reframing the value of virtual prototyping*. Ph.D. dissertation, VTT Science, 89.
Lieder, M., & Rashid, A. (2016). Towards circular economy implementation: A comprehensive review in context of manufacturing industry. *Journal of Cleaner Production, 115*, 36–51.
Lindskog, E., Berglund, J., Vallhagen, J., & Johansson, B. (2013). Visualization support for virtual redesign of manufacturing systems. *Procedia CIRP, 7*, 419–424.
Lindskog, E., Vallhagen, J., Berglund, J., & Johansson, B. (2016). Improving lean design of production systems by visualization support. *Procedia CIRP, 41*, 602–607.
Manufuture High Level Group. (2006). Manufucture strategic research agenda: Assuring the future of manufacturing in Europe, Report of the High Level Group, September 2006, European Commission, Luxembourg. http://www.manufuture.org/documents.htm
Martinez-Moyano, I. J., & Richardson, G. P. (2013). Best practices in system dynamics modeling. *System Dynamics Review, 29*(2), 102–123.
Paich, M. (1985). Generic structures. *System Dynamics Review, 1*(1), 126–132.
Rahmandad, H., & Sterman, J. D. (2012). Reporting guidelines for simulation-based research in social sciences. *System Dynamics Review, 28*(4), 396–411.
Reyes-Lecuona, A., Molina-Tanco, L., González Toledo, D., Flores, S., Frutos, E., Patel, H., et al. (2014). Design, maintenance and refurbishment of turbines in a collaborative environment. In *Proceedings of the 5th Advances in Human Factors and Ergonomics (AHFE) conference*, Krakow, July, 2014.
Schuh, G., Aghassi, S., Orilski, S., Schubert, J., Bambach, M., Freudenberg, R., et al. (2011), Technology roadmapping for the production in high-wage countries. *Production Engineering, 5*(4), 463–473.
Sterman, J. D. (2000). Business dynamics: Systems thinking and modeling for a complex world. Boston, MA: McGraw-Hill.
Tukker, A. (2015). Product services for a resource-efficient and circular economy—A review. *Journal of Cleaner Production, 97*, 76–91.
Ulli-Beer, S., Gassmann, F., Bosshardt, M., & Wokaun, A. (2010). Generic structure to simulate acceptance dynamics. *System Dynamics Review, 26*(2), 89–116.

# The Use-it-Wisely (UIW) Approach

Göran Granholm and Stefan N. Grösser

**Abstract** Industrial products and services must be continually upgraded to meet changing demands of enhanced functionality and performance. The digital transformation of industry, together with new emerging technologies, enables improved solutions but at the same time cause increasing complexity and interdependence between system components. New forms of collaboration across the value chain are necessary to deliver sustainable solutions to satisfy current and future needs. The UIW-approach builds on the idea of a continuous incremental upgrade process carried out in collaborative effort between actors and stakeholders with the common objective to achieve a sustainable project life-cycle. Based on this approach a conceptual framework is defined. The UIW-framework includes an adaptation mechanism designed to account for the diverse influence factors affecting the upgrade design, a multi-disciplinary system model definition integrating actor, product and service data, and a virtual collaboration environment to facilitate the interaction between actors and a collection of tools and methods to support the collective efforts. The UIW-framework is used as a template for system implementations in installations in various actor networks.

**Keywords** Industrial product-service system · Collaborative innovation · Innovation network · Circular economy · System upgrade · Business model · Systems engineering

G. Granholm (✉)
VTT Technical Research Centre of Finland Ltd., Espoo, Finland
e-mail: goran.granholm@vtt.fi

S.N. Grösser
Institute for Corporate Development, Bern University of Applied Sciences, Bern, Switzerland
e-mail: stefan.groesser@bfh.ch



S.N. Grösser et al. (eds.), *Dynamics of Long-Life Assets*,
DOI 10.1007/978-3-319-45438-2_3

# 1 Introduction

The speed of technological development in concurrence with global economic development and short-term market volatility force companies to find new strategies to compete in the marketplace. The competitiveness of manufacturing firms will be increasingly linked to their ability to rapidly transfer developments in science and technology into their processes and products as well as adopting ideas developed both internally and externally (UNIDO 2013). Foresights of future markets and operating environments (Müller and Müller-Stewens 2009) become crucial when making decisions about investments in innovation and R&D of products and services that need to create value in the long-term.

The digital transformation of industry is profoundly changing the manufacturing of products, provision of services and structures of value creation in general and of individual businesses in particular. Advances in wireless communication combined with embedded sensor and computation technologies have changed the way humans and machines interact, shaping the concept of cyber-physical systems (Rajkumar et al. 2010). At the same time increased awareness of the effects of human activity on the environment has become an important factor affecting the design of new products as well as upgrade solutions. New business models based on the circular economy vision are being adopted in order to minimise waste and save resources through efficient reuse of material (Parker et al. 2015). A common denominator of much of the current development is the need for closer ties between the involved actors. This is driven both by the growing demand for customised products and services, and the increasing complexity of technical systems requiring cooperation between large numbers of experts and sub-contractors. To stay ahead in the competition, companies increasingly turn to innovation-led strategies and focus on improving R&D efficiency and value (OECD 2015). In a complex and highly interdependent business environment innovation involves a wide range of actors, including firms, entrepreneurs, foundations and non-profit organisations, universities, scientific institutes, public sector agencies, citizens, and consumers, often working in close collaboration. Managing this collaboration becomes an important target (see also Hurni and Groesser, Chapter "Innovation Management with an Emphasis on Co-creation" in this book).

## *1.1 System Obsolescence and Decay of Use Value Require Change*

Systems are designed based on available knowledge to fulfil current and future needs. The objective is to produce value during the system life-cycle to cover investment costs and profit expectations. To sustain their value when markets and user needs change, products and services need to be continually maintained, upgraded and improved. High-investment assets with long payback periods, e.g., a production system for a car manufacturer, can provide specific challenges as complete replacements are infrequent and the value of using the system (use value) might become significantly reduced. The capability of suppliers to retain or increase the use value of the asset throughout its planned service life becomes an important, perhaps even decisive, factor for customers' investments decisions.

All technical systems will face a gradual decay of their use value over time. This value degradation is due to both internal factors, such as wear and tear leading to increasing maintenance costs and interrupted operation, and external factors, such as changing market demands, new technologies, and alternative solutions. A further external factor is component obsolescence, i.e., the redesign required as replacement components become obsolete. To account for such obsolescence, systems undergo major upgrades (Engel and Browning 2006).

Technical solutions are often designed to meet current requirements without emphasizing enough that systems inevitably evolve with time (Schulz and Fricke 1999). Moreover, factors that are difficult to measure or deal with are often neglected due to time or cost pressures. Fink et al. (2004) have identified three main traps to avoid when planning for the future: (1) suppression of uncertainty, (2) suppression of complexity, and (3) suppression of change. Avoiding dealing with difficult issues may speed up decision making, but does not eliminate risk, and shifts more difficult decisions to a later point in time. Thus, delaying decisions makes it impossible to manage risks in a systematic and effective way.

Investment decisions have to be made based on information about the future that is inherently uncertain. Managing risk and uncertainty associated with design solutions requires considerable effort. Systems thinking and tools for modelling complexity and causal dependencies (e.g. Anderson and Johnson 1997) may be used to help strategic planning and management by building a common understanding of the implications on the design task and possible future developments (see also Groesser, Chapter "Complexity Management and System Dynamics Thinking" in this book).

## *1.2 Adapting to Change in Markets and Environment*

Companies need well-defined strategies to ensure effective adaptation to change. According to Schulz et al. (2000), the major drivers of future development are marketplace dynamics, technological evolution, and variety of environments. Marketplace dynamics can be observed as new markets emerge and existing ones change or converge with others. On the supplier side, new actors appear introducing new offerings, often by employing new, most often digital, business models. On the customer side demands for individualised solutions call for a higher degree of responsiveness and customer adaptation, which in turn require increased agility of design and production processes. Fast technological evolution brings up new opportunities, but also introduces challenges when system life-cycles are longer than the life-cycles of technologies that the systems are built on. This is especially the case for industrial product-service systems (IPSS) (cf. the definition in Chapter "Dynamics of Long-Life Assets: The Editors' Intro" of this book), and leads to increasing maintenance costs and expensive upgrades replacing old technologies with new ones. Variety of environments refers to the increasing variety and complexity of technical systems where individual components must be able to adapt to operate as part of different system compositions, i.e., systems of systems (Schulz et al. 2000).

Changes to end products frequently also require changes to the production lines and manufacturing systems, while service changes may require adopting new business models. Thus, changeability requirements may have to target simultaneously the product or service, the way it is manufactured, and the complete value network delivering the value added. Sharing of tasks and resources across various forms of collaboration networks can provide improved capacity to change due to smaller, more agile operators and flexibility of the collaboration network itself. Efficient operation of the supplier network requires a flexible information architecture that supports decentralized collaborative processes (Gunasekaran et al. 2008).

In order to meet future change demands, changeability features must be premeditated and built into the IPSS. Different technological approaches have been developed for this purpose. A quantitative method to model adaptability cost and value fluctuations of given system architectures has been proposed by Engel and Browning (2006).

In parallel with system properties that allow for future change, a streamlined process to support effective adaptation is required to achieve agile adaptation. Companies are increasingly moving from linear product life-cycle process with decoupled supplier and customer views (Fig. 1) to an integrated product-service life-cycle based on a continuous collaboration between actors (Fig. 2).

In the linear product-based process ownership is handed over in a delivery-acquisition transaction, which causes a disruption in the flow of product life-cycle data. This can be due to incompatibility between product data management systems or practices, or because of unwillingness to share data between customer and supplier organisation. In addition, direct personal communication and

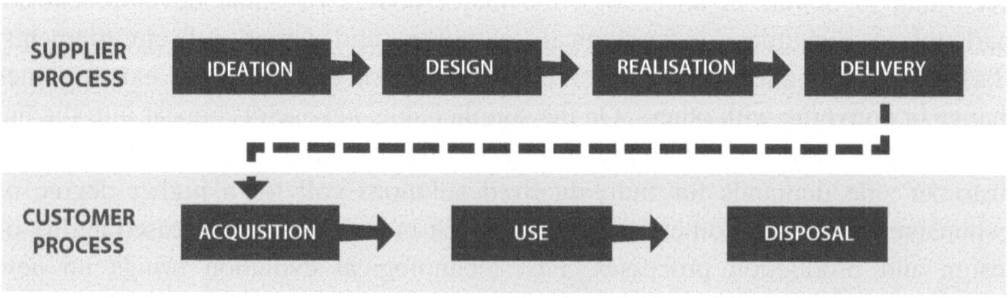


**Fig. 1** Linear product life-cycle process with decoupled supplier and customer views

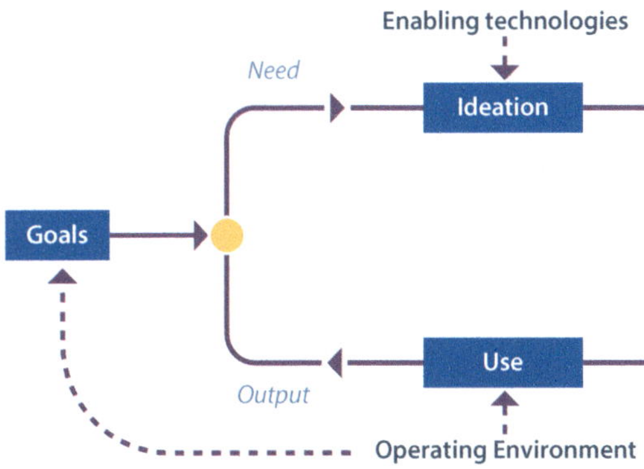


**Fig. 2** Integrated customer-supplier product-service life-cycle process

exchange of tacit product knowledge between individuals across company borders is reduced in a life-cycle product model.

Figure 2 shows an integrated collaborative product-service life-cycle process. The main aim of the supplier is not to maximise profit in a single product delivery but to deliver end-user value, for instance as guaranteed up-time or system output. This requires business models focused on the sharing of revenues between the actors contributing to generating the output. As such models are typically based on service provision instead of transfer of ownership, delivery and acquisition sub-processes have been removed. Focusing on end-user value instead of product value creates a shared interest among the actors to maximise the output and to reduce life-cycle costs. This motivates systematic maintenance and continuous adaptation to change: alterations in the operating environment, such as increased production cost, changed market demand and new competition, force the user to set new business goals. The gap between current output and the new goals creates a need to modify the system.

The integrated collaborative product-service life-cycle process model builds on sharing of data across the actor network. Ideally all life-cycle data is accumulated in a shared database. The information on change in system status as well as changes in operating environment or user needs are available as input for successive system updates. This requires closer ties between customer and supplier, and provides a basis for defining structures for networked collaboration for continuous adaptation of industrial product-service systems.

## 1.3 *The Use-it-Wisely Project*

The Use-it-Wisely (UIW) research project focuses on continuous upgrade of high-investment industrial product-services (IPSS). The goal of the project was to develop an approach to support systematic adaptation to changing needs by developing business models and technologies to support collaborative efforts to sustain and improve high-investment IPSS. This chapter describes the research methodology used and the fundamental principles of the approach.

### *1.4 Structure of the Chapter*

The chapter is divided into four parts: the introduction in Sect. 1 describes the background including the need and main drivers behind the Use-It-Wisely project idea. Section 2 describes the research methodology applied in the project. Section 3 discusses the main principles of the approach. Section 4 presents an outline of the solution nurtured with brief introductions to six pilot cases.

## 2 Research Methodology

The research was based on a continuous dialog between theory and practice. Theoretical knowledge and science-based methodologies were applied to analyse actual pilot cases. The project took place from September 2013 until November 2016. Feedback and results from practical implementation and testing was recorded and analysed. Six different industries were included in the research, each with a different upgrade case. The gradual progress of the pilot cases was presented and discussed in ten meetings and several workshops within the project. Sharing information and experience between seemingly unrelated pilot cases from different industries served to identify similarities especially in the problem space. The research setting was based on the assumption that creativity is fostered by exposure to groups of people with apparently unrelated tasks and knowledge. This assumption is supported by numerous studies showing that people connected across groups are more familiar with alternative ways of thinking and new ideas emerge from selection and synthesis across the structural holes between groups (Burt 2011). The following outlines the research setting and the research process applied in the UIW-project.

### *2.1 Research Setting*

The focus of research was the transition from a linear product-service delivery process to an integrated, continuous process of small-step incremental upgrade innovations based on close collaboration within value chains. The research hinges on two basic assumptions: small upgrade increments and actor collaboration. The reasoning for both is presented in Table 1.

**Table 1** Rationale behind the main research assumptions

| Assumption | Rationale |
|---|---|
| Small upgrade increments | Reduced financial risk due to smaller investment<br>Reduced technical risk due to smaller changes<br>Shorter disruptions<br>Shorter implementation time leading to faster response times and enhanced upgrade agility<br>Reduced environmental impact due to extended use of major system parts |
| Actor collaboration | Important system knowledge exists outside of the corporate borders, on multiple levels<br>System defect, deficiencies and changing user needs are communicated directly and proactively across the network<br>Sustained actor involvement leads to deeper engagement and firm actor networks, building trust and loyalty between partners |

**Table 2** Industrial clusters included in the study and their primary research target

| Cluster | Industry sector | Primary research target |
|---|---|---|
| 1 | Energy production | Turbine service inspection |
| 2 | Heavy machinery | Upgrade service for mobile rock crushers |
| 3 | Aerospace | Integrated system data management |
| 4 | Automotive | Production line configuration |
| 5 | Shipbuilding | Value chain collaboration |
| 6 | Furniture | Circular economy business model for office furniture |

To ensure a wide applicability of the results, companies from six different industries were included in the study: energy production, heavy machinery, aerospace, automotive, shipbuilding and furniture. For each of the six industries, a cluster was formed, consisting of two to four organisations representing parts of the value network. One organisation responsible for technical and scientific research was included in each cluster. The clusters defined their own use cases based on identified needs or foreseen business potential. The use cases included specific research targets including maintenance inspection, upgrade service development, model-based systems engineering, and circular economy. Table 2 presents the industry sector and primary research target of the six clusters. The cluster cases are presented in more detail in Section III of this book.

We included these industries not because of their differences, but because of their commonality. Common between the six industry clusters and their use cases was the focus on IPSS. Another commonality was that the product-services could be classified as "high-investment", at least in relation to the size of client businesses, or to the expected rate of return on investment in the system. This definition of high-investment product-services implies relatively long life-cycles, due to long repayment periods and relatively small financial assets available for complete system recommissioning. In some cases, the push towards long life-cycle solutions was due to potential risks and complications associated with complete system replacement, such as incompatibility with connected legacy systems or unacceptably long service disruptions. The need to further extending life-cycles could also be caused by environmental motives, driven by user requirements or societal push. Inherently long system life-cycles and the push for further life cycle extension motivate the need for repeated system upgrades.

Within each cluster the viewpoints of a broad range of actors, such as design engineers, service personnel, sales staff, managers, decision makers, and end users, were taken into account to create comprehensive systems views. The broad scope of the study allowed for applications supporting both a horizontal integration, i.e., through the life-cycle, and vertical integration, i.e., "shop-floor to top-floor". In addition, the collaboration between research and practice as well as between seemingly unrelated industries proved beneficial and provided new viewpoints to identified problems (Fox and Groesser 2016). This observation is in line with previous research supporting the hypothesis that good ideas emerges from the intersection of diverse social worlds, i.e., across "structural holes" in knowledge networks (Burt 2011).

The research setting, including the six industry clusters, different research targets and multiple actor viewpoints, provided the material to study applications on two different levels: first, on a generic level to analyse commonalities across the clusters and conceptually develop the UIW-approach for dealing with shared issues. And second, on a cluster-specific level to analyse individual use cases to provide bespoke solutions based on the tools and methods of the UIW-framework. This two-level approach was designed to ensure the applicability and practice-orientation of the UIW-approach and the transferability of specific solutions to other industries facing similar challenges.

## 2.2 Research Process

The research followed an iterative approach. The cluster cases were analysed to identify specific challenges and business opportunities and to extract commonalities. The goal was to apply a holistic approach to discover latent mechanisms and causal dependencies that could affect the outcome of introduced change, and eventually the success of suggested upgrades. Rich pictures were used to facilitate communication between actors on different levels and to create a shared view of the target case. Business perspectives were analysed using causal context models and system dynamics (SD) modelling to be able to identify influence factors and causal relationships (see Groesser, Chapter "Complexity Management and System Dynamics Thinking" in this book).

In successive iterations analysis was refined and tools for further enhancing collaboration and data management were developed. Virtual and augmented reality techniques were selected to develop collaboration applications facilitating communication between various actors. To deal with upcoming research or development issues of interest across clusters, dedicated task forces were set up as needed.

The topics of these task forces ranged from overall system architecture and implementation mock-ups to data modelling, simulation and use of individual software tools. The task force concept provided improved agility to work in a result-oriented way on defined topics on their own schedule. The iterative approach applied in the project enabled a continuous interplay between conceptual and empirical methods. It also facilitated a continuous collaboration between researchers and practitioners in different stages of development.

The results of the iterative development process were collected and reported by each of the clusters. The generic tools and methods used for the analysis of the use cases and the experience from applying specific technologies in the implementation of technical solutions targeting concrete development needs were collected to form the foundation of the UIW-approach to support innovative upgrades of high-investment product-services. The final stage included a sequence of on-site demonstrations of the pilot cases. The final UIW-approach is described in detail in Sect. 4.

Figure 3 shows the research process covering areas of theory and research, cross-domain collaboration and knowledge creation, and application in specific industry networks.

The research covered three main areas of activities: research (A), collaboration (B), and application (C). Research activities targeting the general approach (A.1) deal with the basic, theoretical foundation of UIW and strived to ensure that methodologies applied in various activities are founded on scientific evidence. They also aimed to facilitate the transfer of new knowledge to practice. The principles of the general approach are presented in Sect. 3. Based on relevant general research topics, a number of focus areas were selected (A.2) to support the development of shared knowledge, tools and methods (B.2) and to populate the Use-it-Wisely "tool box". Current focus areas and corresponding tools are described in Section II of this book. A community of practise (B.1) consisting of project partners was engaged with collaboration across industry and between research and practice. The community maintained collaboration across selected focus areas and contributed to developing shared knowledge and tools (B.2). With the help of the community of

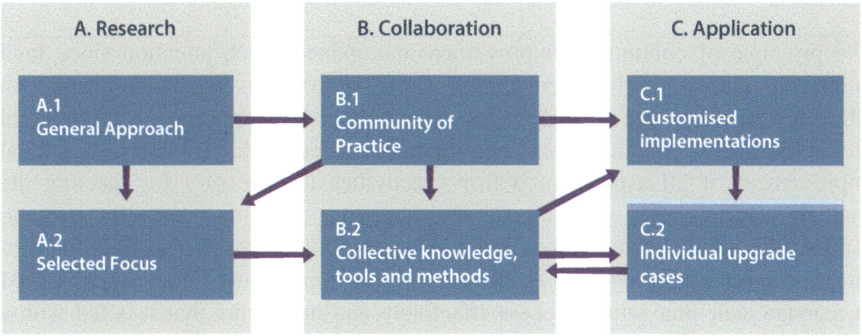


**Fig. 3** Research process for the UIW-project

practice and the generic tools and methods were customised and implemented to meet the needs of specific actor networks (C.1). The adapted tool-box was then used in individual upgrade development cases (C.2).

## 3 Principles of the UIW-Approach

In the following, we introduce six principles which provide a foundation for the UIW-approach.

### *3.1 A Holistic System View*

Transitioning from a product-based economy to models based on provision user value or output requires new forms of collaboration. Instead of focusing on revenues from individual sales transactions along the value chain service-based models must find ways to maximise total end-user value. This requires a thorough understanding of the business drivers and implications of both the end user and of the contributors in the value network. It also requires an understanding of the technical components of the system and of new emerging technologies that may impact future system implementations, markets and competitors. Making the right decisions with regard to system design, upgrade interventions and business model development must be based on a holistic systems view. Creating and evolving a comprehensive, shared view requires the combined efforts of the involved actors. Various tools can be used to model causes and effects of alternative decisions. These are described in more detail in Chapter "Complexity Management and System Dynamics Thinking" of this book.

### *3.2 Continual Improvement*

The principle of continuous improvement has gained much attention since Imai introduced the approach called Kaizen (Imai 1986). This approach focuses on efficiency based in the identification, reduction and elimination of sub-optimal processes based on continuous and immediate feedback. However, continual improvement of all aspects of a firm's activities is necessary for meeting the challenges of evolving environments and changing customer needs (Bessant and Caffyn 1997). This includes the capability to continually renew and improve product and service offerings. To enable continuous improvement organisations need to manage their innovation process effectively and make sure that it is fed with a constant steam of good ideas and solutions (Brennan and Dooley 2005).

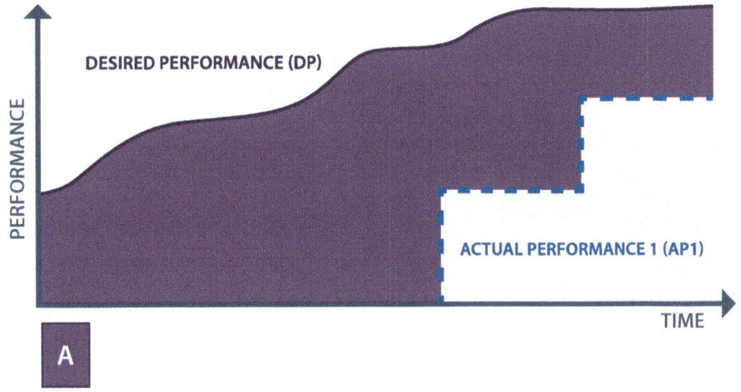


**Fig. 4** Meeting increased performance demands through discrete upgrade increments

The idea behind a continual upgrade strategy is to initiate and implement relatively small but frequent change increments to minimise the gap between customers' desired performance and the actual system performance (Fig. 4).

Figure 4 shows two curves: desired performance (DP) and actual performance 1 (AP1). DP is the performance of an IPSS as desired by the owner or user of the IPSS. This performance increases over time in waves. Reasons are new technological developments or new demand and requirements of final customers. AP1 is the performance the current installed IPPS can provide. AP1 is improved by two stepwise increments. The decision to improve the actual performance, i.e., the decisions to upgrade the assets by investing depend on multiple factors; for example, ease of upgradability of the asset, the direct cost and benefits of upgrading, and the (more indirect) potential loss in customer and market share, if the IPSS is not upgraded. Figure 4 shows a large area A which represents the "area of loss" due to not upgrading frequently. In the figure, it is assumed that the two upgrading increments cannot improve the performance to the latest DP but that there is a significant gap.

With the UIW-approach, the IPSS can be upgraded more frequently as Fig. 5 shows. The objective of the UIW-framework is to minimize the area of loss, i.e., the area between the DP and actual performance by using continual, i.e., more frequent and smaller improvements. As Fig. 5 indicates, AP2 is much closer to DP as AP1. The previous "area of loss" A could be reduced to the area A'. In other words, the UW-approach aims to avoid the loss of area B.

## 3.3 *Integrative Flexibility*

Due to the continuously changing settings and the variety of networks firms will have to be involved in, it is not possible to develop a fixed solution capable of meeting all needs. Therefore, the solution must be flexible. It must be capable of adapting to various scenarios and it must be capable of evolving over time.

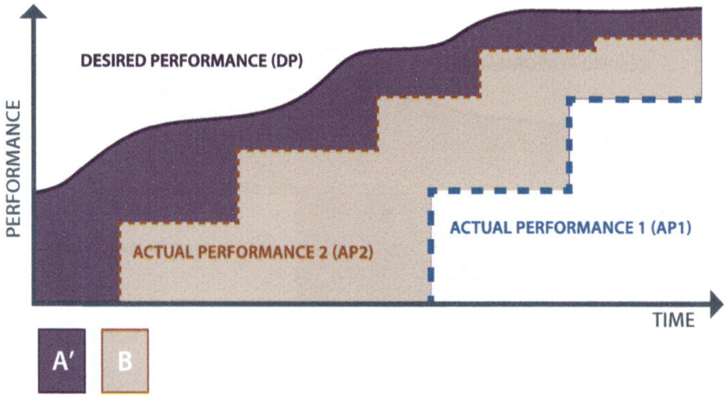


**Fig. 5** Meeting increased performance demands through more frequent discrete upgrade increments

The UIW-approach is aiming to serve a wide range of industries and diverse upgrade needs. The approach is by design generic to provide sufficient flexibility to adapt to different use cases and scenarios in manufacturing industry at large. The tools and methods described in the approach are selected to serve a variety of user groups in each application case. This is necessary to enable actors across the value network to contribute effectively to the upgrade process bringing in knowledge and experience beyond what is available in traditional R&D teams.

The UIW-approach is also designed to cover a broad range of functions, including business development and decision making, engineering data management and life cycle support. Thus, it supports an integration of functions both horizontally across the life-cycle and vertically "from shop-floor to top-floor".

### *3.4 Collaborative Innovation*

The capacity to innovate determines a firm's capability to survive in the global competition and meet the challenges of changing markets. In search for competitive strength firms have developed new strategies involving external resources in product design and customer adaptation. This is based on the insight that important knowledge about the product, and especially of its use, resides outside of the corporate boundaries.

End-user collaboration is frequent in consumer products and services where users are asked to provide feedback on designs, or mobilised in collaborative ideation about future products or services. This goes beyond traditional requirements management processes based on an elicitation of user needs and specified sets of requirements. Hienerth et al. (2014) have studied the efficiency of user vs. producer innovation and found that even an uncoordinated group of users can be as or more efficient than the specialized producer innovators. Companies can also seek increased innovation capacity in collaboration with each other. However, collaborative innovation is more common in radical innovation than in continuous improvement (Chapman and Corso 2005).

The need for increased collaboration across the value network is also a direct consequence of the shift towards a service-dominant business logic where value is determined by the consumer and produced as a collaborative effort of the value network (Vargo et al. 2008). Opening parts of a firm's innovation process to external actors is a strategic decision with important implications on, for instance, operational cost, value and knowledge creation, intellectual rights management. The decision should therefore be guided by careful analysis of technical and financial viability of different types and levels of collaboration. However, open, collaborative innovation models are fundamentally different from traditional organisation centred ones especially with respect to where in the network knowledge is accumulated and innovation created (Lakhani et al. 2012). This requires a new mode of thinking where shared knowledge is regarded as a competitive advantage of the collaboration network instead of a strategic in-house asset.

## *3.5 Sustainability*

Increasing awareness of human activities on nature as a global habitat, as well as the depletion of natural resources has put increasing pressures on manufacturers to ensure environmental sustainability of their products and services. The requirements are enforced by public opinion driving market forces, and by international treaties and legislation. As a result, sustainability turns from a cost driver to an opportunity for companies leading the development.

The trend of sustainable product development is shifting from reduce, reuse and recycle to include also recover, redesign and remanufacture, and leading to the implementation of multiple generation life-cycle products (Go et al. 2015). This defines a transition from linear life-cycle process to a process based on a circular economy (Ellen MacArthur Foundation 2013). More details can be found in Pajula et al. in Chapter "Managing the Life Cycle to Reduce Environmental Impacts" of this book.

Environmental sustainability is a driver for new products and markets based on new environmental friendly technologies. On the other hand, sustainability goals also motivate life extension of existing systems (EFFRA 2013). Thus, sustainability improvement becomes an important upgrade objective.

Extending operational life cycles contribute to ecological values by postponing energy- and material-intensive system renewals, provided that the system can be operated in an environmentally sustainable manner.

### 3.6 Model-Based Engineering and Data Management

The growing complexity of technical systems calls for high levels of specialisation. Complex, interlinked systems of systems (SoS), therefore, have to rely on a close collaboration between a large number of actors across the value chain. Managing complex engineering processes involving multiple actors requires a systematic approach and efficient data management. The quantity of system documentation generated over the life-cycle of complex engineering artefacts quickly becomes unmanageable for human operators and may lead to design errors, expensive rework and added risk. Model-based systems engineering (MBSE) approaches aim to reduce and eventually replace document-centred system data management. Transitioning from human-readable text based information to model-based representations makes it possible to automate design tasks and ensure data consistency. Human readable (e.g. graphical) system modelling notations may also help communication across diverse design disciplines and between actors with different native languages (Vitech Corporation 2011). System data must also be managed in a reliable way while ensuring security and confidentiality of sensitive data from various collaborating parties. Chapter "Extending the System Model" of this book deals in more detail with the question of system modelling in complex design environments.

## 4 The UIW-Approach Supports Continuous Upgrades

To deal with the challenge of meeting the changing needs of an increasing group of customers requesting personalized solutions and life-cycle support, a generic approach for managing system upgrades of IPSS has been developed. The purpose of the approach is to facilitate a life-long upgrade process of IPSS aiming to extend the profitable service-life by enabling continuous adaptation to changing requirements. The approach combines theory knowledge, best practice and supporting tools and technologies.

The underlying idea is that successful IPSS upgrades require a comprehensive approach where the design of individual upgrade steps is not only based on single customer needs and feasibility analysis, but on a holistic understanding of the system in relation to the dynamic environment. This requires capturing extensive system knowledge form a wide spectrum of actors, including customers, end users, designers, operators, and marketing staff. The approach combines this comprehensive system knowledge with theory knowledge of experts with access to relevant tools, methods, and technologies for system analysis, decision making and process support.

The UIW-approach supports a collaborative innovation and design process in which each upgrade step is based on close interaction and knowledge sharing between involved actors. Through this collaboration, knowledge about the systems performance as well as changes to the operating environment, market changes, and other external factors are systematically collected and shared. At the core of the collective knowledge base is a generic representation of an upgrade innovation process (Fig. 6). The process supports collaborative and concurrent upgrade innovation. Collaborative innovation involves engaging actors, such as workers, designers, end uses, managers and sales staff, in a collaborative effort to solve identified problems. In the first phase problem solving involves identifying problems and their root causes, and finding possible solutions through creative ideation. The purpose of the ideas is to take the system from its current state ("as is") to a desirable future state ("to be").

The collaborative ideation produces ideas and suggested solutions to transform the system from the current state to a desirable future state. The proposed solutions are tested in the analytic cycle using simulation and analysis tools. The results of the simulations may show that the ideas are insufficient to transform the system to the target state. The discrepancy between the target future state and the simulated future state provide input to further ideation and refinement of proposed solutions. The simulations may also show that the future target state is unrealistic, given the existing system parameters, in which case a re-evaluation of possible target stages is necessary.

The process described in Fig. 6 applies two separate modes of thinking: the ideation cycle represent the fast, intuitive and associative "System 1" thinking and the analytic cycle represents the slow and analytic "System 2" (Kahneman 2011). Separating the two modes of thinking aims to enable, on the one hand, a creative ideation process free from the restrictions of premature analysis and rejection, and on the other hand an analytic cycle with an abundant flow of input in the form of new ideas. The ideation and analytic cycles, although separated, run in parallel forming a concurrent engineering environment where solutions and ideas are thoroughly tested before proceeding to production and implementation. The integration of key actors in the process ensures that upgrade solutions are not only tested for technical and economic feasibility, but also evaluated against the needs and system knowledge of end users.

The UIW-approach comprises three main elements: the UIW-framework; the UIW-web platform, and; the UIW-virtual community. These are introduced next.

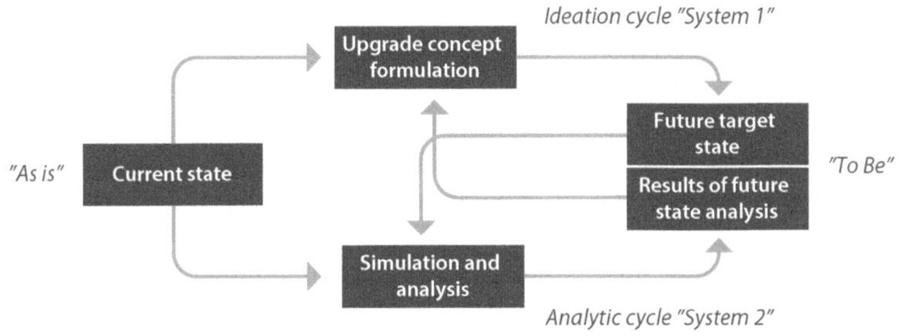


**Fig. 6** Collaborative upgrade innovation process

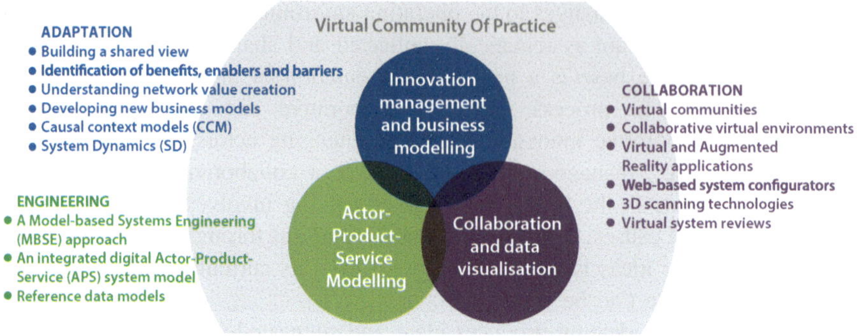


**Fig. 7** The UIW-framework

## *4.1 The UIW-Framework*

The purpose of the UIW-framework is to support a comprehensive approach to a continuous innovation process for a life-long adaptation of industrial product-service systems by outlining a generic solution to be further specified and implemented in actual use cases. The framework covers three main areas: adaptation, collaboration and engineering. Reflecting the analysis of the imaginary industrial company in Chapter "The Challenge", the UIW-framework describes three complementary sets of modelling solutions targeting the application areas. A number of tools and methods are suggested in each of the model categories. Figure 7 shows a schematic overview of the UIW-framework indicating tools and methods associated with the different sections.

Established actor networks select the best tools on a case-by-case basis to set up a dedicated upgrade innovation platform for a specific IPSS. The tools are then adapted, modified or extended to meet the specific needs in each case. Both the use and the adaptation of the tools may require special skills which may be offered by members of the Community of Practice. New, modified or extended tools are returned to expand the platform and to serve future needs. The following sections describe the model categories in more detail.

### 4.1.1 Innovation Management and Business Modelling

The purpose of innovation management and business modelling is to support the continual adaptation of the system in order to find optimal upgrade solutions to meet changing needs and exploit new opportunities. The key element is a shared understanding of the business dynamics of the upgrade case. This includes identifying influential actors, their motives and capabilities, and understanding how value is created and shared within the network. Rich pictures, Causal Context Models (CCM) and System Dynamics (SD) simulation can be used as tools (see Groesser, Chapter "Complexity Management and System Dynamics Thinking" in this book). The model emphasizes a shared effort between the actors to learn about system dependencies and the effect of change. A comprehensive, shared view on actor roles and interests, as well as an understanding of the effects of potential future development, help establishing new competitive business models. The adaptation model can later be used to identify and simulate the effects changes in the business environment, thus supporting decision making in later stages of the systems life-cycle.

The UIW-web-platform includes resources for constructing a bespoke adaptation model, in the form of a selection of model exemplars. These exemplars can be extended and configured to meet specific requirements of actual upgrade cases. The platform also provides resources in the form of expert support on setting up and working with the models.

### 4.1.2 Collaboration and Data Visualisation

One of the key elements of the UIW-approach is a close and continuous interaction between involved actors. This is supported by digital tools for collaboration and data visualisation. Collaboration between diverse groups of actors with different interest, motives and professional background differs substantially from collaboration between individuals of in-house R&D teams or other established networks of a more stable nature. In addition to social or professional distribution actors may also be spatially distributed, separated by distance, time zones or language barriers. To enable efficient communication and active collaboration between network actors the framework suggests various tools for shared virtual system representations based on Virtual Reality (VR) and Augmented Reality(AR) and tools for retrieving the and presenting necessary 3D information. Current internet-based communication solutions offer multiple options for establishing collaboration networks capable of operating effectively regardless of physical distance. VR and AR technologies can be used to provide users with a realistic and interactive virtual representation of target system or the operating environment, making it possible to try out and comment on suggested upgrade solutions. The use of visualisation techniques based on virtual and augmented reality to create shared views is presented in Chapter "Virtual Reality and 3D Imaging to Support Collaborative Decision Making for Adaptation of Long-Life Assets" and was implemented in several pilot cases presented in Part III of this book.

In addition to technological solutions the UIW-framework also contains guidelines for establishing and maintaining active actor communities or virtual Communities of Practice (CoP). CoPs are seen as an efficient way to foster a continuous dialog between actors to share knowledge and support the generation of new ideas. The collaboration model should enable an ongoing exchange of information through the system life, also between individual upgrade increments. Principles for establishing successful CoPs are treated in Chapter "Fostering a Community of Practice for Industrial Processes".

### 4.1.3 Actor-Product-Service Modelling

Designing complex product-service systems require the combined efforts of large engineering teams and a diversity of different domain experts. When the system undergoes repeated upgrades during their life-cycle a well-managed engineering process is necessary. The UIW-framework strongly supports the use of shared digital system models to capture all system life-cycle data to enable efficient collaborative engineering based on MBSE principles. An extension of the product-centric data model is proposed. The extended actor-product-service (APS) system model includes data relating to actors and product-based service. Reference data models have been developed, but actual implementations must be designed separately in each case to account for specific needs and requirements of individual actors. Especially technical restrictions or incompatibility issues between different data systems used by various actors may limit the implementation of an optimal shared APS system model. Transitioning from a document-based design process to a MBSE approach promises to facilitate automation of design information by introducing a more generic, symbolic system representation, overcoming the limitations of written text is described in Chapter "Extending the System Model".

## 5 The UIW-Web Platform

The purpose of the UIW-web platform is to work as a public front-end combining the outcomes of the project and making them available to external audiences. The platform also provides access to expert knowledge and services related to the implementation of the tools and models in future upgrade cases and hosts a virtual community of practice within which members can share their experience and generate new knowledge in a continuous collaboration process.

UIW-web platform acts as a broker of information and services relating to the upgrading of industrial product-service systems. The platform website is available at http://use-it-wisely.eu.

## 6 UIW-Virtual Community

The UIW-virtual community brings together suppliers, customers, engineering experts and researchers focusing on upgrades of high-investment product-services. The community combines theory and practice knowledge across various fields of industry, and presents tools and methods applied in documented reference cases. The purpose of the virtual community is to ensure continuous development of the UIW-framework and to contribute to the accumulation of shared knowledge and resources. The combined resources generated through the sustained activities of the multi-domain collaborative community of practice are collected in a pool of collective knowledge, tools and methods accessible through the UIW-web platform. The community also provides access to information or expert services relating to the application of the various methods.

## 7 Reference Cases

The UIW-framework is an abstract building on the main idea of involving actors in a collaborative effort to sustain and create IPSS through upgrading. Practical implementation of the framework is supported through a community platform that provides access to knowledge and tools as well as expert advice to assist companies set up their own collaboration networks and toolsets to specific needs. The community platform is maintained at http://use-it-wisely.eu. The localised implementations of the framework may target a single product-service development case, a specific business area or build on the collaboration of a network with a shared interest looking for new opportunities. The objective may be technical improvement, taking advantage of new technology opportunities of business model innovation. Thus, all implementation instances will have their own characteristics with different adaptation systems, APS system models and virtual collaboration spaces. The use of the framework in dedicated update innovation projects improves existing tools and models, and generates new knowledge. Voluntary sharing this generated knowledge through the community platform contributes to the common knowledge base and promotes cross disciplinary learning shared across industry domains. Part III of this book presents implementation of the UIW-framework in six industry clusters.

## 8 Conclusions

Global competition in manufacturing industry and industrial services increase as emerging economies enter the market, and communication and logistics channels develop. Customers take advantage of the new opportunities and require solutions adapted to specific needs at competitive costs. Environmental sustainability becomes a high priority driven by legislation and social pressures. Companies need to find new ways to maintain their competitive advantage in the changing business landscape.

One way of approaching the challenges is to shift focus from tangible products to customer benefit. Rather than just offering add-on services there is a shift towards service-dominant business models where value is provided primarily as services or resources. This shift of business logic has important implications on how firms collaborate with the customer and other actors. The creation and utilisation of knowledge outside of traditional corporate boundaries becomes a prime target.

The volatile market with fast moving market entrants and a continuous stream of new technologies poses specific challenges to well established industries supplying high-investment products with high long expected life-cycles. To meet changing requirements in different phases of the operational life, these systems need to be continually upgraded. Efficient maintenance and upgrade services may also enable an extended life-cycle, which brings savings to customers and contribute to environmental sustainability objectives.

In the UIW-project, co-funded by the European Commission and twenty companies, universities and research organisations, a generic approach was developed for enabling effective upgrade innovation and customer adaptation. The UIW-approach is based on close actor collaboration, a shared, holistic system view and effective information management to support life-cycle sustainability based on frequent, demand-led upgrade increments. Based on this approach a conceptual framework was created to help companies develop their upgrade innovation processes. The UIW-framework builds on three corner stones: an adaptation mechanism, consisting of tools and methods for a holistic view of influence factors and causal dependencies to support decision making and creation of upgrade strategies; an actor-product-service system model, integrating product and actor data with a model-based systems engineering approach for a comprehensive and up-to-date digital system representation throughout the life-cycle; and a collaborative virtual environment, to support upgrade innovation by connecting actors in a collaborative effort independent of location.

The UIW-framework is supported by a collection of selected tools and methods, best practice information and selected reference cases made available through a community web site. The site is maintained by a virtual community bringing together practitioners and researchers in a continuing effort to further develop tools and methods and build on the collective knowledge of the community. The framework does not describe a strict process or prescribe specific tools to be used. Instead, it proposes a number of viewpoints and suggests tools and methods to support analysis, decision making and collaboration based on the previous research knowledge and practical experience from the pilot cases. This makes the framework agile to adjust to upgrade cases beyond those treated in the current project and to other sectors of industry. The framework itself is intended to be extended and upgraded based on resources and experience gained from future case studies.

The approach and related tools were tested in six clusters representing a broad variety of industries. Some examples of the tools and their use in the process are presented in Part II of this book. Industrial implementation cases are presented in Part III.

## References

Anderson, V., & Johnson, L. (1997). *Systems thinking basics: From concepts to causal loops*. Waltham, Massachusetts: Pegasus Communications Inc.

Bessant, J., & Caffyn, S. (1997). High-involvement innovation through continuous improvement. *International Journal of Technology Management, 14*(1), 7.

Brennan, A., & Dooley, L. (2005). Networked creativity: A structured management framework for stimulating innovation. *Technovation, 25*, 1388–1399.

Burt, R. S. (2011). Structural holes and good ideas. *The American Journal of Sociology, 110*(2), 349–399.

Chapman, R. L., & Corso, M. (2005). From continuous improvement to collaborative innovation: The next challenge in supply chain management. *Production Planning & Control, 16*(4), 339–344.

EFFRA. (2013). *Factories of the future: Multi-annual roadmap for the contractual PPP under Horizon 2020*. Publications Office of the European Union.

Ellen MacArthur Foundation. (2013). *Towards the circular economy* (Vol. 1). Available at: http://www.thecirculareconomy.org

Engel, A., & Browning, T. R. (2006). Designing systems for adaptability by means of architecture options. *INCOSE International Symposium, 16*(1), 237–258.

Fink, A., Siebe, A., & Kuhle, J.-P. (2004). How scenarios support strategic early warning processes. *Foresight, 6*(3), 173–185.

Fox, S., & Groesser, S. N. (2016). Reframing the relevance of research to practice. *European Management Journal, 34*(5), 457–465.

Go, T. F., Wahab, D. A., & Hishamuddin, H. (2015). Multiple generation life-cycles for product sustainability: The way forward. *Journal of Cleaner Production, 95*, 16–29.

Gunasekaran, A., Lai, K. H., & Edwin Cheng, T. C. (2008). Responsive supply chain: A competitive strategy in a networked economy. *Omega, 36*(4), 549–564.

Hienerth, C., von Hippel, E., & Berg Jensen, M. (2014). User community vs. producer innovation development efficiency: A first empirical study. *Research Policy, 43*(1), 190–201.

Imai, M. (1986). *Kaizen: The key to Japan's competitive success*. New York: Random House.

Kahneman, D. (2011). *Thinking, fast and slow* (1st ed.) New York: Farrar, Straus and Giroux.

Lakhani, K. R., Lifshitz-Assaf, H., & Tushman, M. (2012). Open innovation and organizational boundaries: The impact of task decomposition and knowledge distribution on the locus of innovation. *SSRN Electronic Journal*.

Müller, A. W., & Müller-Stewens, G. (2009). *Strategic foresight*. Stuttgart: Schäffer-Poeschel.

OECD. (2015). *The innovation imperative: Contributing to productivity, growth and well-being*. Paris: OECD Publishing.

Parker, D., et al. (2015). *Remanufacturing market study*. European Remanufacturing Network.

Rajkumar, R., (Raj) et al. (2010). Cyber-physical systems. In *Proceedings of the 47th Design Automation Conference on—DAC'10*, p. 731.

Schulz, A. P., & Fricke, E. (1999). Incorporating flexibility, agility, robustness, and adaptability within the design of integrated systems—Key to success? In *Gateway to the New Millennium. 18th Digital Avionics Systems Conference. Proceedings (Cat. No. 99CH37033)* (Vol. 1/17, pp. 1–8).

Schulz, A. P., Fricke, E., & Igenbergs, E. (2000). Enabling changes in systems throughout the entire life-cycle—Key to Success ? In *Proceedings of the 10th Annual INCOSE Conference, July 2000, Minneapolis, USA*.

UNIDO. (2013). *Emerging trends in global manufacturing industries*. Report of the United Nations Industrial Development Organization. Vienna. Retrieved from http://www.unido.org/fileadmin/user_media/Services/PSD/Emerging_Trends_UNIDO_2013.PDF

Vargo, S. L., Maglio, P. P., & Akaka, M. A. (2008). On value and value co-creation: A service systems and service logic perspective. *European Management Journal, 26*(3), 145–152.

Vitech Corporation. (2011). *A primer for model-based systems engineering*.

# Part II
# Tools and Methods

# Innovation Management with an Emphasis on Co-creation

**Dominic Hurni and Stefan N. Grösser**

**Abstract** Innovation management is a means of supporting an understanding of an organisation's operating environment and enables the organisation to create and manage innovations more systematically throughout a system's life-cycle. This chapter introduces innovation management and co-creation in general, and details the methods of design thinking and business model canvas, thereby enabling organisations to professionalise their collaboration with customers and manage complex supply chains. Through co-creation organisations potentially improve their ability to innovate, optimise processes, adapt products and services to customer's actual needs, encourage stronger customer buy-in, hence creating a more sustainable market position through a more flexible organisational culture

**Keywords** Innovation management · Co-creation · Design thinking · Business model canvas · Open innovation · Management tools

## 1 Introduction

Innovation management is about rapidly transforming good ideas and inventions into innovative products or services. It is this commercialisation which the German Federal Ministry of Education and Research seeks to promote in its high-tech strategy for European industry published in 2015 (Bundesministerium für Bildung und Forschung 2015a). Although industry in Europe faces new technology such as "Industry 4.0" (Bundesministerium für Bildung und Forschung 2015b) and more intense global competition (Lusch and Vargo 2015), even more challenging seems to be enabling employees to remain agile in fast-changing business environments.

D. Hurni · S.N. Grösser (✉)
Institute for Corporate Development,
Bern University of Applied Sciences, Bern, Switzerland
e-mail: stefan.groesser@bfh.ch

D. Hurni
e-mail: dominic.hurni@bfh.ch



S.N. Grösser et al. (eds.), *Dynamics of Long-Life Assets*,
DOI 10.1007/978-3-319-45438-2_4

According to the report "Fast Forward 2030" (Fast Forward 2030 2014), 50% of current occupations in corporations will fundamentally change in the next ten years. It is possible that European industry with its "zero-defects principle" finds itself locked-in this culture, focusing exclusively on optimizing existing products and thereby missing these other changes (Divernich 2007). Executives in Europe are aware that different approaches to innovation management are required. Often companies set up innovation projects free from the constraints of normal production to speed up the innovation process (Assink 2006). However, this separation fosters the creation of sub-cultures in the company and has to be avoided. Another crucial requirement to run projects successfully is user involvement (CHAOS Manifesto 2013 2013). Companies which have a rapid in- and outflow of relevant knowledge have a higher internal innovation rate (Chesbrough et al. 2005). But the implementation of open structures in companies appears to be challenging. Innovation management in general, and co-creation in particular, are approaches to address these.

Such challenges are also addressed by the Use-it-Wisely (UIW) project (see Reyes, Chapter "The Challenge", and Granholm and Groesser, Chapter "The Use-It-Wisely (UIW) Approach" in this book). In this chapter, we detail several approaches to innovation management and thereby offer a rich source for practitioners and researchers to innovate process, products, services, and subsequently business models.

This chapter is structured as follows: Sect. 2 provides both a definition of innovation management and a generic overview. Then, Sect. 3 details the general approach of co-creation and examines in detail "design thinking" methodology and the method "business model canvas". Section 4 discusses and concludes the chapter.

## 2 Generic Overview of Innovation Management

This section provides an overview of innovation management and includes discussions of various definitions that have been proposed within the field. This section aims to provide a theoretical foundation for the subsequent section on co-creation and design thinking in practice.

### *2.1 Definition of Innovation Management*

Innovation management has arisen as a logical consequence of Schumpeter's (1934) concept of creative destruction. Innovation management is the process of handling the development of a product or service including successful market launch. Invention represents the creative act of developing a product or service and is the logical first step of an innovation. There are multiple definitions of innovation management; for example Edison's et al.'s (2013) literature review found more than

40 definitions of the term and declared Crossan's and Apaydin's (2010, p. 1155) as the most complete: "Innovation is: production or adoption, assimilation, and exploitation of a value-added novelty in economic and social spheres; renewal and enlargement of products, services, and markets; development of new methods of production; and establishment of new management systems. It is both a process and an outcome." Therefore, innovation refers not only to product, service or market development, but also to organisational development. Consequently, innovation management is the discipline of planning, executing, steering, and controlling a systemic process (Bergmann and Daub 2008; Hauschildt and Salomo 2011; Müller-Prothmann and Dörr 2009; Vahs and Burmester 2005) in an interdisciplinary team (Bergmann and Daub 2008; Hauschildt and Salomo 2011; von der Oelsnitz 2009) to create innovation.

## 2.2 *Management of Innovation*

According to Gassmann and Sutter (2011), innovations and technologies have to be managed at the normative (Fig. 1—blue rectangle), strategic (Fig. 1—white rectangle), and operational level (Fig. 1—development funnel) which are indicated in Fig. 1. Simply supervising technology development is not sufficient for innovation management. On the normative level, for instance, values and cultural norms of society influence the vision and mission statement of an organisation as well as the market and technology development in general. One normative question is: How should we use and control "artificial intelligence" in our organisation? It has to be answered congruently with the internal and external self-image of the organisation otherwise its credibility and also the trust in its strategy suffers.

From the perspective of strategy, innovation is both a strong source for short-term reduction of costs and for long-term sustainable competitive advantage. When technology is a source of an organisation's core competences, the protection

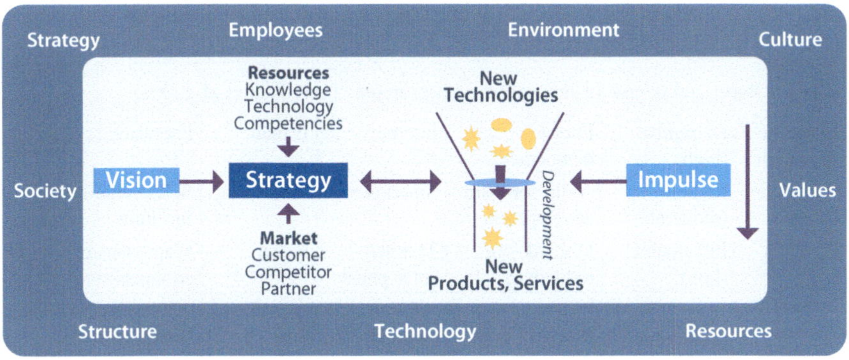


**Fig. 1** Innovation management (taken from Gassmann and Sutter 2011, p. 8)

of intellectual property (IP) rights becomes crucial. From an R&D perspective, the issue of the protection of IP rights becomes especially critical in countries where legal frameworks are unsupportive. The strategic-level of innovation management builds the link between more abstract normative-level and highly detailed operational-level management. Moreover, the strategic-level has to position the company internally with regards to employees as well as externally with regards to customers and partners (Fig. 1). Operational-level management focuses on innovation processes which use methods and tools to control performance, quality, costs, and time.

### 2.2.1 Objects and Degrees of Innovation

Often it is recommended to use innovation portfolio tools to obtain an overview of current innovation projects. Tidd et al. (2001) provide one example of such an innovation portfolio tool. They distinguish four potential innovation objects and three degrees of innovations. The object is the thing being innovated and is categorised as a process, product, service, or business model (Table 1).

Degrees of innovation can be understood in several ways (Crossan and Apaydin 2010; Edison et al. 2013) and a scale of innovation degrees which fits our purposes here stems from Damanpour (1991). Incremental innovation represents variation in existing routines and practices. Radical innovation induces fundamental changes and is a clear change of existing organisational practices. Disruptive innovation changes not only organisational practices, but whole markets by creating new market opportunities as well as value networks and probably displacing established market leaders and alliances (Bower and Clayton 1995). The higher the degree of innovation, the larger the potential influence on the market and the more significant the challenge is likely to be for a company. As Nünlist (2015) stated when talking about competition: "We are not afraid of our competitors, rather more of a sudden game changing start-up that set new market rules." But why are large enterprises with more resources than start-ups not disruptively innovating themselves? One reason is that such companies might not be able to adjust to fast changing market needs with a workforce of, say, 2500 employees compared to a start-up with only 8

**Table 1** Object and degree of innovation with examples from Tidd et al. (2001)

| | | | | | |
|---|---|---|---|---|---|
| Degree of innovation | Disruptive (high) | Direct democracy | Internet | E-mail | Freeware |
| | Radical (moderate) | Agile software development | Smartphone | Telealarm | Self-assembly of furniture |
| | Incremental (low) | Discard redundant forms | Thinner solar panels | Faster food delivery | Maintenance contracts for dishwasher |
| | | Process | Product | Service | Business model |
| | | Object of innovation | | | |

employees—it is as comparing the manoeuvrability of oil tankers with speed boats.: Speed and flexibility is an advantage of start-ups.

### 2.2.2 Innovation Inhibitors

New technologies can change markets. Given that the market defines what is needed from companies, those companies that can adapt to market needs will survive and others will perish irrespective of their company size. One prominent example is Nokia that missed the changing market demand for smartphones (Lääperi and Torkkeli 2013; Lindholm and Keinonen 2003). But why did this happen? Assink (2006) examined factors that impair companies' ability innovate in a disruptive manner. Figure 2 summarises these barriers to identify disruptive innovation.

- **Path dependency (Field 1)**: Companies which focus on their successful dominant product and service designs tend to concentrate exclusively on incremental innovation (Paap and Katz 2004). With this strategy, companies fail to recognize the emergence of important enhancing technology in their field (Divernich 2007). Nokia, which was slow to react to the emergence of the smartphone concept, is one example (Lääperi and Torkkeli 2013).
- **Inability to unlearn old patterns, logic, and methods to adapt to something fundamentally new (Field 2)**: Companies are forced to change mental models and their theories-in-use to be able to adjust to market dynamics. This requires a learning organisation in which employees master their own development which includes unlearning of old patterns and learning new ones (Senge 2011). Sinkula and Baker (2002) distinguish three innovation drivers which have an influence on a learning organisation: first, management-driven which is mainly incremental; second, market-driven which is also predominantly incremental; and third, engaged generative learning driven which leads to radical or disruptive innovation.

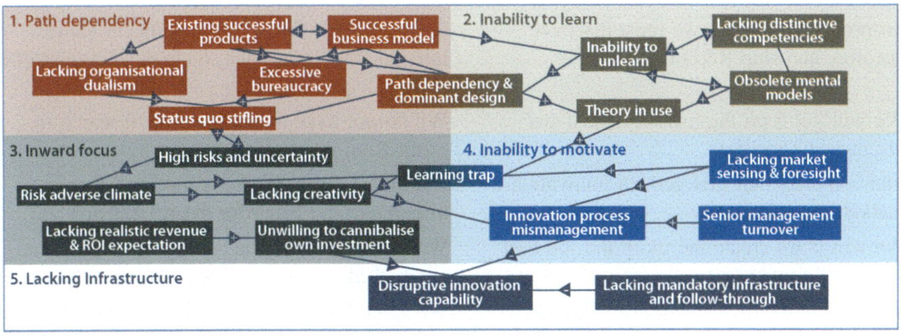


**Fig. 2** Model of limiting factors for disruptive innovation (Assink 2006)

- **Inward focus (Field 3)**: Companies are occupied with internal risk optimisation and stabilisation. Required external changes do not register on the company's risk radar. The company exists in a bubble, oblivious to required changes from the outside world. New challenges are tackled by routine processes that have been successful in the past. This leads to biases and distorts realistic revenue expectations, often combined with reluctance to write-off previous unsuccessful investments. All of this severely hinders the development and exploration of disruptive ideas or proactive behaviours (Sandberg 2002).
- **Inability to motivate employees for innovation (Field 4)**: Companies lack the ability to motivate or attract creative and innovative employees with ground-breaking ideas (Stringer 2000). Often these companies observe the market with conventional methods which then result in incremental innovations (Trott 2001).
- **Lacking infrastructure (Field 5)**: Companies might lack the necessary infrastructure, for instance, the transfer of computer files changed drastically with the introduction of internet and wide-area networks (Paap and Katz 2004). It is also possible that there is an insufficient support of infrastructure (Innovatie in Nederland 2003).

Reflecting on the factors which limit disruptive innovation, Chesbrough (2006a) introduced the open innovation approach.

### 2.2.3 Open Innovation

Open innovation assumes that organisations can use external ideas and externally created paths to market as well as their own pre-existing internal mechanisms.

**Table 2** Closed versus open innovation (Chesbrough 2006b)

| Closed innovation | Open innovation |
|---|---|
| The smart people in the field work for us directly | Not all the smart people work for us directly. We need to collaborate with smart people inside and outside our company |
| To profit from R&D, we must discover, develop, and ship R&D ourselves | External R&D can create significant value; internal R&D is needed to claim some part of it |
| We will get it on the market first, if we discover it ourselves | We do not have to originate the research to profit from it |
| The company that first gets an innovation to market wins the race | Building a better business model is more important than being on the market first |
| We win if we create the most and the best ideas in the industry | We win if we make the best use of internal and external ideas |
| We should control our intellectual property (IP), so that our competitors do not profit from our ideas | We should profit from others using our IP and we should buy others' IP whenever it advances our business model |

Research shows that companies which employ open innovation principles are more likely to create radical or disruptive innovations and tend to sell a greater number of new products (Innauen and Schenker-Wicki 2012). Table 2 compares the characteristics of open and closed innovation (Chesbrough 2006b).

The awareness of opening a company's doors to co-create with outside stakeholders is a crucial factor to the innovation process. The top-management team of a company needs to establish the required framework and space to innovate processes, products, services, and business models. This is not easy, as Google demonstrates. Larry Page and Sergey Brin admitted in Google's IPO Letter for investors 2004, "We encourage our employees, in addition to their regular projects, to spend 20% of their time working on what they think will most benefit Google. This empowers them to be more creative and innovative. Many of our significant advances have happened in this manner." This famous 20%-policy often falls victim to productivity ranking tools designed to appraise management efficacy. These tools force managers to focus on the "here and now" rather than allocating time to more "out there" ideas which do not currently contribute to the bottom line (Ross 2015). Implementing a culture of innovation can take many years. However, a beneficial starting point is moderated pilot projects in heterogeneous groups with stakeholders from the supply chain outside the company. This helps to unfreeze the mind-sets of employees (Lewin 1947).

## 3 Co-creation in Innovation Management

The reality of innovation management is that data gathering for new products or services in fledgling markets often focuses on internal capabilities and on quantity of data, not on data quality (Kohn 2006). Furthermore, the insight produced from market data is often limited since it can only describe patterns about how customers use already existing products; the data seldom indicate the motivation behind the actual usage of products or the deeper needs of customers. Co-creation fills this gap by involving customers or stakeholders directly in product or service design. In the last ten years, the role of knowledge about users and their respective needs has advanced from specifying functional, usability, and performance requirements alone to also capturing deeper, more affective needs (Schütte et al. 2004). For instance, Apple does not only understand the functional needs of their customers, but also knows the lifestyle, wishes, and emotional states of their clients. Unlike traditional waterfall models of software or product development, user-centred design approaches, e.g. design thinking, uncovers these affective demands. It defines phases in developing innovations by observing stakeholders and eliciting feedback about their state of mind. ISO 9241-210 is a generic example of user-centred design processes for specific technologies including collaborative work systems (Wobbrock et al. 2009). When customers not only provide feedback, but are also integrated in the development process as partners to produce a valued outcome it is called co-creation (Prahalad and Ramaswamy 2004b).

In a supply chain context, this can be seen as co-creation between customer and product or service provider. Co-creation is an approach to value creation through interactions between stakeholders across and even from outside the supply chain to shake up existing, rigid collaboration patterns. Crucially, these stakeholders include the customer who had hitherto been regarded as simply someone to be offered a value proposition (Prahalad and Ramasawamy 2004a, b). From a human factors perspective, collaboration and not only contribution within the supply chain requires skills such as communication, community, shared spaces and open thinking has to be anchored in a company's culture to create mutual benefit. It is a change management challenge to work together as partners instead of a supplier-customer relationship. Design thinking goes even further by placing one partner in the position of naïve apprentice in order to learn from other partners within and also outside the supply chain. The objective is to obtain feedback about a project from a person in the natural setting of the product or service application. Take the example of post-it of Minnesota Mining and Manufacturing (3M) Company: In 1968, Spencer Silver intended to invent the strongest glue ever—but his result was only a weak removable adhesive that failed the goal. In 1974, Art Fry, a friend of Spencer, got annoyed because his little notepapers fell out of his choir book. He asked Spencer to use the removable adhesive to fix his notepapers. The notes adhered without damaging the music sheets when they were removed and so Post-It's found their final purpose through a stakeholder who was not a part of the supply chain (3M 2005). A closed approach may well seek to limit this seemingly unauthorised use, whereas an open co-creative perspective would invite these new users to explain how they are using the product and to possibly build their requests into future iterations, provide schematics, or make the product easier to adapt. A further example of harnessing the ideas of users for product developing is the computer game industry: it actively cultivated fan forums to develop and beta-test their games. Mutual value is therefore created by the company locating interest and therefore a new market and the consumer a new requested game experience.

Design thinking is both a methodology and a mind-set for designing innovations by means of a co-creational process thus bringing a culture of innovation to companies. The change of existing mind-sets starts when participants realise the potential success of the design thinking approach and start to question habitual processes in their company (Brown and Martin 2015). Co-creation and design thinking are gaining more awareness and traction in the business world. More and more large organisations have started collaborating with external parties. Procter and Gamble, for instance, has created the position of "Director of External Innovation". Based on open innovation, new collaboration forms emerged, through which engagement and compelling experiences, new ideas and approaches from various internal and external sources are integrated in a platform to generate new value for customers (Lee et al. 2012). Brown (2008) describes first experiences with design thinking as a methodology of meeting people's needs and desires in a technologically feasible and strategically viable way. In iterative loops visualised assumptions in the form of prototypes are verified by stakeholders or customers.

Osterwalder and Pigneur (2010) created the business model canvas as a supportive tool to visualise prototypes of a business model for iterative development.

"If three people get together, you get the wisdom of not just three, but that of ten people". This Japanese saying shows the power of co-creation, where people with different knowledge and experiences come together to solve a problem (Fast Forward 2030 2014). "Co-creation is the joint, collaborative, concurrent, peer-like process of producing new value, both materially and symbolically" (Galvagno and Dalli 2014, p. 644). Their framework of co-creation (Fig. 4) provides an overview of existing literature on value co-creation. The framework originated from the fields of service science, marketing and consumer research, and innovation and technology. It is organised into two topics: first, theory of co-creation that contains four areas to outline and define co-creation approaches: Service Dominant Logic (SDL), co-creating value through customer experience and competences, online and digital customer involvement, and development of service science. And second, collaborative innovation in new product development which comprises two approaches applied in co-creation: Service innovation and individual consumers and communities, collaborating with companies (Fig. 3).

"Theory of Co-Creation" and "Collaborative Innovation in New Product Development" are described in more detail in the following:

- **Service dominant logic (SDL)**: In SDL, Vargo and Lusch (2008, p. 7) state that "service is the fundamental basis of exchange". This perspective allows a car seller to support the customer with much more than just the car. Now, security support such as driving insurance, or exercises to prevent back pain on long journeys add possible value. Over the last decade Vargo and Lusch (2016) have developed various SDL axioms and premises. Their model envisages co-creation as customers working with companies to build a shared future. Therefore methods, techniques, and tactics to engage productive dialogues need to be developed; additionally, research into motivation for co-creation is overdue and should be carried out (Lusch and Vargo 2015).

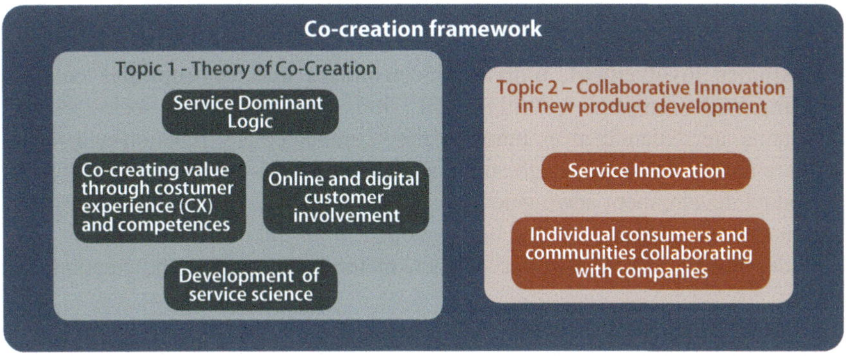


**Fig. 3** Value co-creation topics and respective areas (Galvagno and Dalli 2014)

- **Co-creating value through customer experience (CX) and competences**: Customer experience is "the cognitive acknowledgment or perception that follows from stimulated motivation of a customer who observes or participates in an event. Such acknowledgment or perception consequently enhances the value of products and services" (Chen and Lin 2015, p. 41). Verhoef et al. (2009) proposed a conceptual model of the determinants which influence a customer's experience.
- **Online and digital customer involvement**: Nambisan and Nambisan (2008) formulated five different virtual customer roles for innovation and value co-creation: product conceptualiser, product designer, product tester, product support specialist, and product marketer. Brodie et al. (2013) highlight the importance of enhancing loyalty, satisfaction, empowerment, connection, emotional bonding, trust, and commitment of virtual community members.
- **Development of service science**: Maglio and Spohrer (2008, p. 18) defined service systems as "configurations of people, technology, value propositions connecting internal and external service systems, and shared information (e.g., language, laws, measures, and methods). Service science is the study of service systems aiming to create a basis for systematic service innovation." In an attempt to integrate service research from different disciplines to meet complex business and societal challenges, four core principles are described by Maglio and Spohrer (2013, p. 669). First, service system entities dynamically configure four types of resources: people, technologies, organisations, and information. Second, service system entities compute value given the preferences of multiple stakeholders. Third, the access rights associated with entity resources are reconfigured by mutually agreed value propositions. And finally, service system entities plan and coordinate actions with others through symbolic processes of valuing and symbolic processes of communicating.
- **Service innovation**: "Service innovation is a new service or a renewal of an existing service which is put into practice and thus providing benefit to the organization that has developed it; the benefit usually derives from the added value that the service innovation provides the customers." (Toivonen and Tuominen 2009, p. 893). Snyder et al. (2016) propose four emerging themes out of 43 service innovation categories: degree of change, type of change, newness, and means of provision.
- **Customer involvement, individual consumers and communities collaborating with companies**: Within SDL, it is recognised that socio-technical systems are dynamic in as much as they simultaneously function and reconfigure themselves (e.g., Vargo and Lusch 2011). It is also recognised that typical product development stage-gate plans are of limited use when something such as a system adaptation has to be developed in an unknown way and involves predominantly tacit knowledge. Rather, methods that enable the creation of a

shared experience are seen as more effective. The UIW-adaptation system (Chapter "The Challenge" and "The Use-It-Wisely (UIW) Approach" of this book) involves collaboration and self-organisation in the concurrent design of goods, services, business models, and production processes based on evolving and interoperable human and machine knowledge.

In the next section we introduce the methodology of design thinking.

# 4 Deep Dive 1: Design Thinking

## *4.1 Purpose of the Methodology*

The design research community has yet to clearly defined design thinking (Dorst 2011), but according to Brown (2009), "design thinking functions within a framework of three intersecting 'constraints.' They are 'feasibility', which is what can be done; 'viability', what you can do successfully within a business; and 'desirability', what people want or will come to want." The principle underlying the intersection of desirability, feasibility, and viability is an iterative process. This process includes the development of visualized prototypes, then demonstrating them to customers and observing the customers to learn what they really desire (Maurya 2012). Although this process leads to more failures than successes, it tent to reveal customers' current needs (bootcamp bootleg 2015). To navigate through this process requires a different mind-set and also a high level of empathy for people, hence a human centred approach. The objective of design thinking is to improve the rate at which successful product, service, and business model innovations are brought to the market (Harvard Business Review 2015).

## *4.2 The Application Process*

Even though different design thinking processes are in use (SAP 2016; Tschimmel 2012), all of them apply an iterative exploration and learning process following the 'trial and error' principle. Trial and error is understood as learning by unearthing assumptions and falsifying them in the real world by means of iterations until a sufficient match between problem and solution is found. Figure 5 shows a typical design thinking process. It is the amalgamation of the processes suggested by d. school (bootcamp bootleg 2015) and the Hasso Plattner Institute (2016). The iterative process ceases when the resulting prototype fulfils both people's needs, is technical feasible, and economically viable. The process consists of the six phases: understand, empathise, define the problem, ideate, prototype, and test the solution (Fig. 4).

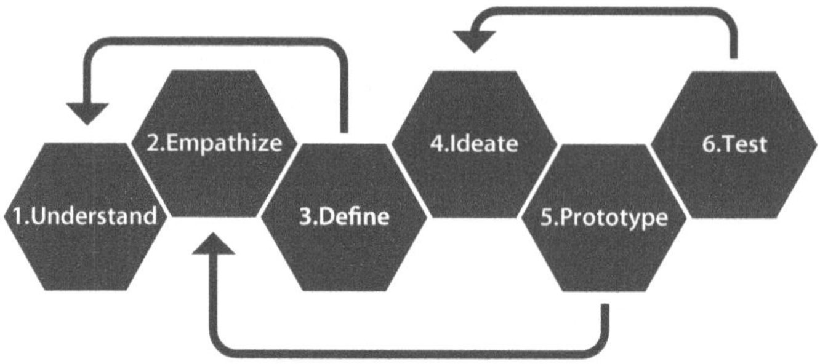


**Fig. 4** Amalgamated design thinking process

In the following, we look at these phases in more detail and provide guidance for concrete applications. Here, we do not provide specific techniques for each phase. The interested reader should consider the following references for more details (Curedale 2016; Stickdorn and Schneider 2014).

Before we consider the design thinking process, a short word on the design team. In general, a heterogeneous design team produces a brother range of insights and ideas, but suffers of misunderstandings because different use of expressions. Team setup depends on the type and degree of innovation project (Table 1).

### 4.2.1 Phase 1: Understand

The phase 'understand' first defines the design scope within a number of actors interact with each other in certain places, and it is within this scope that the design team carries out its search for innovation. Secondly, it helps the design team to communicate their knowledge with mental pictures about actors, places, and reasons in such rather chaotic situations to build up a common understanding in the team. For instance, the design scope for the case of public transport: A design team member shares his knowledge that on average, a commuter (actor) arrives 5 min before boarding a train on the platform in the train station (place) to make sure not to miss the train (reason). The design scope is not fixed. In case new insights emerge in the following phases, the design scope can be adjusted. For example, at the beginning the design scope about public transports includes only trains and buses. Then, through insights from iterations the team includes the last mile and a bicycle sharing in the design scope. Within the design scope, a team elaborates their initial assumptions about a topic leading to a common understanding about actors, places and reasons. This is similar to the boundary of the context used in requirement engineering (Hull et al. 2011).

Hint: Team members often share they knowledge related to existing products or services that can be collected as existing solutions or hints for existing problems. In business, the customer explains his problem based on that a **design challenge**. For example: How can we make public transport for passengers smarter?

### 4.2.2 Phase 2: Empathise

The goal in this phase is to empathise with people especially target stakeholders to understand their physical and emotional needs and to visualise them. The guiding principle is to walk in the shoes of others. One way is to shadow target stakeholders in their everyday life. For instance, the actor Dustin Hoffmann spent time with Kim Peek, an autistic person, preparing himself for his role in the movie "Rainman". In the example of smart mobility in public transport this could require following different stakeholders, e.g. commuters, bus drivers, bicycle parking clerks, ticket collectors, disabled passengers, but also extreme users such as fare dodgers, football hooligans, or carnival bands. These groups should be observed not only at the train station or bus stop, but also on their way from home to their destination. Besides participatory observation of their behaviour, taking pictures and videos of problematic or challenging situations is also useful. Another possibility is interviewing people about their positive and negative experiences while using a product or a service. If they feel functionality or information is missing it is known as a "pain point". If they experience satisfaction, this is called a "gain point". An important aspect in this phase is to approach uninvolved people and to listen to their stories naively, i.e., without using your previous knowledge. Assume a state of a neutral observer and reporter. Then, create fictive stories that summarise the gained insights during the empathising phase. This helps to convey them to the design team. For instance, Peter (WHO) commutes every day and has to look for a free seat on the train every day during rush hour gets annoyed (WHAT) because he loses ten minutes working time because of this search time (WHY). While WHO and WHAT are visible, some WHY's are formulated by the stakeholder, but some motives are latent and have to be assumed by the design team. For instance, commuter Peter mentions he needs a seat to work in the train. But latently, he needs to go from A to B and able to work on his laptop during this time. Therefore, the seat is not necessarily a part of the solution to fulfil this needs. Latent motives partly surface in this phase or during phase 3. The team members can imagine such story-based situations and are able to add their comments. For this purpose, team members can visualise their stories on flipcharts. This phase ends, when all obtained stories are communicated and discussed.

Hint: Use story-telling. Every team member has one minute per story to communicate to the team the task in the journey as well as pain and gain points of the stakeholder. Then, the team asks questions and provides feedback to formulate insights within four minutes. An insights for the commuting case is, for example, that a seat is not necessarily needed.

### 4.2.3 Phase 3: Define

The 'define' phase develops a problem statement with a clear **point of view (POV)**. A POV is the formulated perception of a chosen stakeholder group, about their behaviour and their needs/requirements and motives within the design scope based on the analysis of stories and insights from the previous phase. The analysis consists of discussing and clustering information of the story or insights to reveal latent motives and solution requirements. The following is a possible template: **Who** (stakeholder A) needs **what** (requirement) to do **what** (task) to fulfil **what** (motive). For instance, Peter **needs** a calm place with electricity supply and place for his laptop **to** work in the train **to** reduce his workload to gain time (motive) **to** feel that the time has used meaningfully (latent motive). This POV has once again to be validated by the chosen stakeholder group. Especially the reaction of the stakeholders by confronting them with the latent motive might lead once again to new insights. One example, what else besides work brings a feeling of use time meaningfully in train?

Hint: Technique to reveal latent motives are also called and described as "job to be done" (Silverstein et al. 2012). Another technique is "persona" that describes ab archetype of a stakeholder group.

In principle, the define phase ceases when an accurate definition of a POV exists. However, it might be that new insights emerge during the remaining three phases which require the POV to be reformulated and re-explored. Since this is possible, the speed by which the remaining three phases are executed becomes crucial. It is feasible to have a full-fledged POV within three or four days, when the team has expertise about the design scope. By formulating the POV the working mode of design team changes from formulating customer's needs to finding solution for those needs. For our example: How might we support Peter in working efficiently while he is travelling home from workplace during rush hour? The POV forces the team to focus. Without this focus the team finds itself in an ongoing search without any result, therefore moderation within the design thinking process is recommended.

### 4.2.4 Phase 4: Ideate

This phase generates ideas for solving the design challenge. A design team may use the technique brainstorming to post ideas on an empty pinboard. A standard brainstorming session consists of three steps under time pressure: First, the design team answers the design challenge by collecting all thoughts and ideas that come to mind without criticizing them (7 min). Second, the team sorts and clusters the ideas and provides headlines (10 min). During this process, new, complementary, or lateral ideas are welcome. And finally, the design team evaluates and rates clusters to decide which solution to prototype in the next phase (8 min). Another way to find novel ideas besides brainstorming is to image how a fictional person might face the POV needs. For instance, what spell would Harry Potter use so that Peter finds space to work while travelling home from work?

The criteria to evaluate and select which idea should be prototyped emerges from the verified requirements of phase 3, for instance, calmness to concentrate or electricity supply. If the idea does not fulfil these validated motives, it should not be prototyped. But ideas should not be rejected too fast; sometimes wild ideas open a new view on the design scope and therefore open up new opportunities. Sometimes it is true that the wilder and newer the idea, the fewer people have thought about this. In our example, if Peter is placed on the top of the train in a glass dome his needs might be fulfilled.

### 4.2.5 Phase 5: Prototype

In the prototype phase, ideas get visualised in a form that stakeholders can interact with. This may be, for example, a drawing, a business canvas, a storyboard, a cardboard construction combined with role-play, or a LEGO model to allow a "walk through". It is crucial in this phase that the design team focusses on functionality instead of appearance. It is not important how the prototype looks as long as it is recognized as one and the test persons recognise the functionality. However, prototypes can create barriers to progress. Often, the longer a person works on a prototype, the more the person defends it, which is likely to be counterproductive from a learning perspective. It is recommended that the team formulates what they want to explore or test with a prototype before they visualize the function in a most rapid and cost-efficient way. Uebernickel et al. (2015) list several types of prototypes according to the state of the project. In our example the team might construct a cardboard prototype of a train carriage with a plastic dome, showing how it could be accessed.

### 4.2.6 Phase 6: Test

In this phase, you solicit feedback from your stakeholders about the prototype to learn about the context and gain new insights. Ideally, the prototype is shown without any explanation and creates an experience for stakeholders. The experience is more intensive in an appropriate location. For example, the glass dome prototype is likely to receive more accurate feedback on a noisy train track platform than in a calm restaurant because it is an authentic environment. In the role of a naïve reporter (phase 2) using the technique "5 why's" to inquire about cause-and effect relations to reach a profound level in the test. Perceiving verbal and non-verbal feedback to gain new insights. These new insights might result in reframing the design scope (phase 1) and start a new iteration of the design process. It is important to work through all of the six phases quickly to prevent too much frustration resulting from failing prototypes. After several, sometimes hundreds of, rounds of prototyping, a fitting solution to a problem or even an innovation may be found. Moreover, the design team should have gained a lot of knowledge about the design scope.

## *4.3 Expected Results of Applying the Methodology and Limitations*

Design thinking is a methodology which seeks to reveal unknown opportunities for innovation because neither the designer nor the test person nor the stakeholder knows the outcome of a design project. Design thinking is a human-centred approach and therefore suitable for every human interaction with products, services, processes or proof of concepts development. Design thinking is meant to be used for radical or disruptive innovations. It is less useful in contexts of incremental innovation projects, because it reveals and focuses on unknown or latent needs of stakeholders. IDEO's example of the first computer mouse for Apple is exemplary for a radical innovation. Financial resources alone are not sufficient for successful design thinking projects. What is required is a mind shift of team members, who learn to deal with failing by focusing on generating insights and learning, instead of being correct in their assumptions. Design thinking helps to transform companies into learning organisations (Senge 1996).

Pangaro (2012) describes design thinking as an improvement over analytical thinking in business. But he also states that design thinking will not solve problems, because it is neither a discipline nor a methodology and hence lacks clear process descriptions. He rather sees design thinking as a set of techniques. Meinel, Plattner and Leifer address this lack and establish a design thinking research program to improve and describe design thinking in more detail (HPI—Stanford 2016). Initial research into performance measurement of design thinking in co-located and business teams has been published (Meinel et al. 2012), and their results show that, amongst other things, the concept of mind shift or strengthening the development of epistemological viewpoints (POVs) improve in participants while performing design thinking projects. HPI provides further examples of the impact of design thinking in practical applications (HPI 2016).

## 5 Deep Dive 2: Business Model Canvas

Business model is one of the four types of innovation (Table 1). The following section outlines the business model canvas, which is relatively quick and simple way of capturing nine important elements of a business model. These nine elements are clustered into the revenue and expense section of the table thus reflecting more profoundly the relationship between customer profile and value proposition (Fig. 5).

### *5.1 Purpose of the Method*

To keep up with this pace of change, tools are required to assemble and visualise the most important facets of potential business opportunities. The business model canvas (Osterwalter and Pigneur 2010) is one such tool used to analyse and develop business models. It focuses on the most important elements to obtain a quick overview of an organization's business model, thereby providing a basis for discussions. The canvas method was developed to create a common understanding and thus increases the effectiveness of teams. The business model canvas specifies nine elements and follows a clear procedure, which will be dealt with in section "Applying the method".

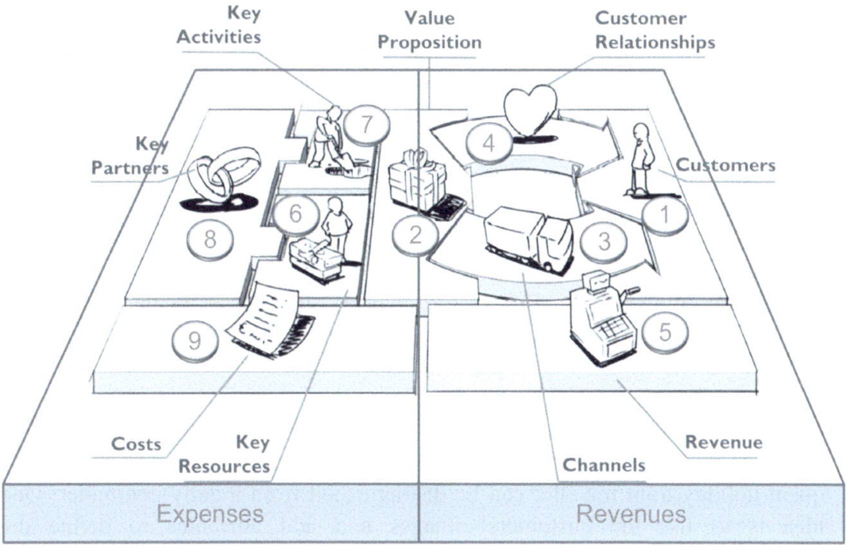


**Fig. 5** Elements of business model canvas (Osterwalter and Pigneur 2010)

## 5.2 *Applying the Method*

When following the business canvas method, we recommend copying the template (Abb. 4.5) to a flipchart, providing the team with markers and using Post-It's to describe each element with content in the provided field. A team workshop typically requires 45 min. The process of describing the nine elements (3 min for each element, in total: 27 min) is followed by a phase for sorting and discussing the intermediate results (13 min) and ends with a wrap-up phase (5 min) to finalize the canvas. This section briefly describes the process, guiding questions, and recommendations for each element.

1. **Customers**: Customers pay for the offered value proposition and they are segmented for the purpose of the canvas. For whom are we creating value? Potential customer segments are listed. The level of detail in the segmentation depends on the type of market (e.g., niche vs. mass market). In the creation of a business model for new products and/or services, it is important that the team identifies and empathises with promising customers, as described in first deep dive about design Thinking. For instance, commuters with an ICT affinity, who work with laptops on their way home.
2. **Value Proposition**: The value proposition is not necessarily a product or a service, it can be any added value. For instance, commuting by train is not just the physical transfer but there is also the ecological life style aspect, which certain customers will value. What value do we offer to our customers? A list with monetary, emotional, environmental or sustainable values is created. To

avoid confusion, we recommend choosing only the most promising customer segments for which the value proposition is then defined. One example is the working ICT affine commuters, who are concerned about their ecological footprint. The match between customer and value proposition is essential as we explain later in more detail.

3. **Channels**: How does our value proposition reach the customer? Both current and potential information and distribution channels are listed here. It is helpful to imagine a typical customer journey and concentrate on the points of contact with the customer. It is important that the selected channel fits to the customer's expectation of the value. Hence, the channel supports or enables the value proposition. For instance, ecological ICT affine commuters might identify a glossy brochure as a waste of paper.
4. **Customer Relationship**: What is the relationship to our customer? The answer depends on how the company segments its customers. The relationship to a key customer may be different than to a sporadic customer. The needs of an infrequent holiday train traveller can be distinguished from a daily commuter. One idea is to use the customers' images and add attributes to define the relationship. For instance, the personalised customer's image of a railway company might be a conductor in uniform who emits reliability and kindness. This picture changes or solidifies through experience with the railways.
5. **Revenues**: What are the revenue streams? All revenues streams the organization can possibly generate should be listed. It is best to distinguish between unique payments, licencing royalties, rental payments or membership fees to estimate recurring revenues. For instance, Swiss National Railways offers annual cards (allowing "free" travel or half price), monthly cards or day/return/single tickets. In addition Swiss National Railways is a partner of a bicycle renting company located at train stations, where travellers can rent bicycles.
6. **Key Resources**: What is needed to create the value? Resources required to create the value proposition have to be detailed. Key resource might be infrastructure resources (trains and tracks), human resources (conductor), knowledge resources (research reports, intellectual property rights.
7. **Key Activates**: What has to be done to create the value? List all the activities that resources from the previous element have to fulfil. A mental walkthrough through the value creation process is the best way to discover these important activities. Resources without any activity in the value creation process are eliminated. Moreover, activities without any internal resources should be outsourced to partners. In our case of the commuter example this would be the train wagon interior equipment and services offered for commuters during the train ride.
8. **Key Partners**: What key partner do we need to guarantee the key activities? Reflect on the partners needed to create the value and to complete the tasks we cannot complete internally. Consider the additional transaction costs of external partners. Cooperation also results in interdependency by asymmetrical information. An advantage however is that the organization obtains expertise and external resources to actually produce the high quality value. For instance, the

core business of the Swiss National Railway is to transport people not to support them with ICT services. Therefore, the railway might cooperate with an ICT service provider.

9. **Cost**: What are the costs associated with creating the value? Activities, resources, and costs of using partners have to be summarized. Distinguishing between fix and variable costs helps to estimate the recurring costs.

The business model canvas contains the described nine elements and should be elaborated in this order. Additionally it is partitioned in two sections: A revenue section which contains the elements #1 to #5, and a cost section which contains the elements #6 to #9. Figure 5 shows both sectors. The comparison of these two sectors results in a rough estimation of the viability of the developed business model and provides a basis for discussion. The business model canvas was criticised of its rather superficial guidance for defining the value proposition. Hence, Osterwalder et al. (2015) provided a more detailed approach, which is shown in Sect. 5.3.

## *5.3 Customer Profile and Value Proposition*

A better understanding of the customer allows us to create a more appropriate and sophisticated value proposition. The two arrows in the middle of Fig. 6 indicate the essential question: Does the product or service fulfil the jobs of the customer? What function eases the customer's pains? What function increases the customers' gains?

Osterwalder et al. suggest interviews or observations to collect information about customers' jobs and their pains and gains to create a customer profile. For instance, Peter commutes every day by train from home to work. Compared to driving with the car, he can work on his computer in the train (gain), but gets annoyed by the noise in a train wagon (pain). Peter in the example, is a fictional person and represents the customer segment "working commuters".

Then, the design of a value proposition can be used to create the answer to what product or service might ease the pains and increase the gains for this customer segment. For instance, the Swiss National Railway might offer Peter a train to commute from home to his office (service) and in the train they offer him a working space with bench and table and also an electricity socket for his laptop (gain creator). Finally, they label a train wagon with "Business Wagon" where only silent working is aloud (pain killer). The match between customer profile and value proposition has to be verified by customer tests. In iterative loops customer profile and value proposition have to be adjusted till test customers approve the match.

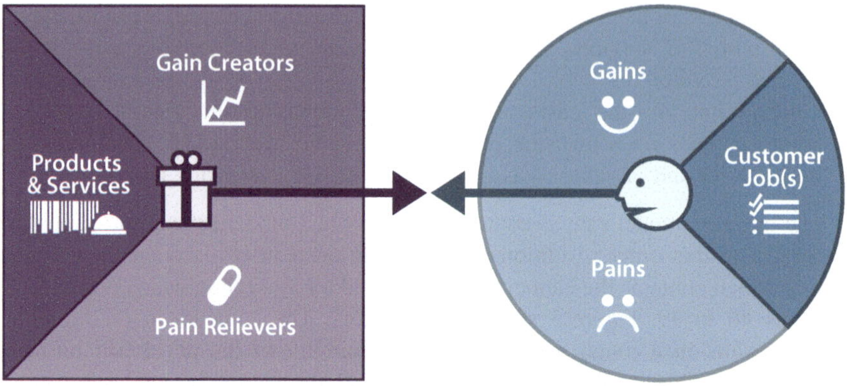


**Fig. 6** Match of value proposition and customer profile (Osterwalder et al. 2015)

## *5.4 Expected Results of Applying the Methods and Its Limitations*

The business model canvas forces the author to focus on the important nine elements of a business model. The business model canvas is a method that allows, within a short time, the user to gain an overview of a business model and builds a basis for discussion. The tool is also beneficial for prototyping. However, these nine elements only consider the business meso-level. To allow for a more general overview, Osterwalter and Pigneur (2010) have been working on a business macro-level model consisting of four elements: Market forces, industry forces, key trends and macro-economic forces. However, the business canvas model does allow a profound understanding of the relationship between customer and value proposition on a micro-level provided by defining the customer profile in accordance with the value proposition (Osterwalder et al. 2015).

Currently the business model canvas is predominantly used in an early phase of the business model development to develop a common understanding within the development team and to communicate ideas. It can be used as a basis for discussion to reveal misunderstanding and gaps. The business model is however less suited to analysing the internal or external dynamic consequences of a new business model. One possible way to overcome these limitations is to use system dynamics simulation to quantify the relevant elements of a business model as suggested by Groesser and Jovy (2016) and also Groesser in Chapter "Complexity Management and System Dynamics Thinking" in this book—in which the strengths of simulation methodologies when designing business models are discussed.

## 6 Conclusion

The maxim *survival of the fittest* seems to apply to most established companies operating in fast-changing markets prone to disruptive entry by start-ups. Companies are forced, through permanent contact and interaction with their market environment, to constantly adapt their offerings. This adaption happens not only in R&D departments but also throughout whole companies (Gassmann and Sutter 2011). To manage innovation we recommend creating an innovation portfolio which differentiates in object (process, product, service, or business model) and degree of innovation (incremental, radical, or disruptive). Interaction with, and adaption to the market environment lead to fundamentally new forms of collaboration for innovation; this is known as co-creation (Galvagno and Dalli 2014). Established enterprises fear disruptive innovations emerging from start-ups which change the whole market. Despite resources and methods like design thinking (Brown 2008) or business model canvases (Osterwalter and Pigneur 2010), companies, especially large enterprises, suffering from inhibiting factors (Assink 2006) and difficulties regulating open innovation (Chesbrough 2006b) that decelerates the speed of adjustment to the market or exploitation of new technologies. As a stop gap, while attempting to evolve into learning organisations (Senge 1996), companies are scanning the start-up market for take over opportunities or implementing separate organisational entities such as innovation centres (Lee et al. 2012).

## References

3M. (2005). *Post-it Haftnotizen feiern Geburtstag*. Retrieved April 7, 2016, from http://presse.3mdeutschland.de/buero-kommunikation/Post-it_Haftnotizen__2005-02-21_14_50_20

Assink, M. (2006). Inhibitors of disruptive innovation capability: A conceptual model. *European Journal of Innovation Management, 9*(2), 215–233.

Bergmann, G., & Daub, J. (2008). *Systemisches Innovations- und Kompetenzmanagement*. Wiesbaden: Gabler.

bootcamp bootleg. (2015). *d.school*. Retrieved from https://dschool.stanford.edu/wp-content/uploads/2011/03/BootcampBootleg2010v2SLIM.pdf

Bower, J. L., & Clayton, C. M. (1995). *Disruptive technologies: Catching the wave*. Boston: Harvard Business Review.

Brodie, R. J., Illic, A., Juric, B., & Hollebeek, L. (2013). Consumer engagement in a virtual brand community: An exploratory analysis. *Journal of Business Research, 66*, 105–114.

Brown, T. (2008). Design thinking. *Harvard Business Review, 86*(6), 84–92.

Brown, T. (2009). *Change by design*. New York: HarperCollins.

Brown, T., & Martin, R. L. (2015). *Design for action*. Harvard Business Review.

Bundesministerium für Bildung und Forschung. (2015a). *Die neue Hightechstrategie*. Retrieved from https://www.bmbf.de/de/die-neue-hightech-strategie-86.html

Bundesministerium für Bildung und Forschung. (2015b). *Zukunftsprojekt Industrie 4.0*. Retrieved from https://www.bmbf.de/de/zukunftsprojekt-industrie-4-0-848.html

CHAOS Manifesto 2013. (2013). *Vision one*. Retrieved from https://www.versionone.com/assets/img/files/CHAOSManifesto2013.pdf

Chen, S. C., & Lin, C. P. (2015). The impact of customer experience and perceived value on sustainable social relationship in blogs: An empirical study. *Technological Forecasting and Social Change, 96*, 40–50.
Chesbrough, H., Vanhaverbeke, W., & West, J. (2005). *Open innovation: A new paradigm for understanding industrial*. Oxford: University Press.
Chesbrough, H. W. (2006a). *Open innovation: Researching a new paradigma*. Oxford: Oxford University Press.
Chesbrough, H. W. (2006b). *Open innovation—The new imperative for creating and profiting from technology*. Cambridge: Harvard University Press.
Crossan, M. M., & Apaydin, M. (2010). A multi-dimensional framework of oragnizational innovation: A systemic review of the literature. *Journal of Management Studies, 47*(6), 1467–6486.
Curedale, R. (2016). *Design thinking process and methods*. Topanga: Design Community College.
Damanpour, F. (1991). Organizational innovation—A meta-analysis of effects of determinants and moderators. *Academy of Management Journal, 34*, 555–590.
Divernich, F. E. P. (2007). *Pfadabhängigkeit im Management*. Stuttgart: W.Kohlhammer.
Dorst, K. (2011). The core of 'design thinking' and its application. *Design Studies, 32*(6), 521–532.
Edison, H., Bin Ali, N., & Torkar, R. (2013). Towards innovation measurement in the software industry. *The Journal of Systems and Software, 86*, 1390–1407.
Fast Forward 2030. (2014). *CBRE*. Retrieved from http://www.cbre.com/research-and-reports/future-of-work
Galvagno, M., & Dalli, D. (2014). Theory of value co-creation: A systemic literature review. *Managing Service Quality, 24*(6), 643–683.
Gassmann, O., & Sutter, P. (2011). *Praxiswissen Innovationsmanagement*. München Carl Hanser.
Groesser, S. N., & Jovy, N. (2016). Business model analysis using computational modeling: A strategy tool for exploration and decision-making. *Journal of Management Control, 21*(1), 61–88. doi:10.1007/s00187-015-0222-1
Harvard Business Review. (2015). *The evolution of design thinking*, from https://hbr.org/product/harvard-business-review-september-2015/BR1509-MAG-ENG
Hasso Plattner Institute. (2016). *School of design thinking*. Retrieved January 31, 2016, from http://hpi.de/en/school-of-design-thinking.html
Hauschildt, J., & Salomo, S. (2011). *Innovationsmanagement*. München: Vahlen.
HPI. (2016). *Design thinking research program*. Retrieved June 13, 2016, from http://hpi.de/de/dtrp/programm/uebersicht.html
HPI—Stanford. (2016). *Design thinking research program*. Retrieved June 6, 2016, from http://hpi.de/en/dtrp/program/overview.html
Hull, E., Jackson, K., & Dick, J. (2011). *Requirements engineering*. Heidelberg: Springer.
Innauen, M., & Schenker-Wicki, A. (2012). Fosterin radical innovations with open innovation. *Journal of Innovation Management, 15*(2), 212–231.
Innovatie in Nederland. (2003). Voorburg: Centraal Bureau voor de Statistiek.
Kohn, K. (2006). Managing the balance of perspectives in the early phase of NPD: A case study from the automotive industry. *European Journal of Innovation Management, 9*(1), 44–60.
Lääperi, A., & Torkkeli, M. (2013). *Case study: Challenges in innovation management through paradigm shifts in the mobile phone and smartphone markets*. Paper presented at the ISPIM—The International Society for Professional Innovation Management, Manchester.
Lee, S. M., Olson, D. L., & Trimi, S. (2012). Co-innovation: conver genomics, collaboration, and co-creation for organizational values. *Management Decision, 50*(5), 817–831.
Lewin, K. (1947). Frontiers in group dynamics: Concept, method and reality in social science; social equilibria and social change. *Human Relations, 1*, 5–41.
Lindholm, C., & Keinonen, T. (2003). *Mobile usability: How Nokia changed the face of the cellular phone*. New York: Mc Graw-Hill.
Lusch, R. F., & Vargo, S. L. (2015). *The service-dominant logic of marketing: Dialog, debate, and directions*. London: Routledge.

Maglio, P. P., & Spohrer, J. (2008). Fundamentals of service science. *Journal of Academic Marketing Science, 36,* 18–20.
Maglio, P. P., & Spohrer, J. (2013). A service science perspective on business model innovation. *Industrial Marketing Management, 42,* 665–670.
Maurya, A. (2012). *Running lean.* Sebastopol: O'Reilly.
Meinel, C., Plattner, H., & Leifer, L. (2012). *Design thinking research: Measuring performance in context.* Berlin: Springer.
Müller-Prothmann, T., & Dörr, N. (2009). *innovationsmanagement - Strategien, Methoden und Werkzeuge für systematische Innovationsprozesse.* München: Carl Hanser.
Nambisan, S., & Nambisan, P. (2008). How to profit from a better 'virtual customer enviornment'. *MIT Sloan Management Review, 49*(3), 53–61.
Nünlist, S. (Producer). (2015, April 30). Vernetzte Welten. *Swisscom User Experience Day.* Retrieved from https://www.swisscom.ch/de/about/innovation/open-innovation/cx-day-april-2015.html
Osterwalter, A., & Pigneur, Y. (2010). *Business model generation.* Hoboken: Wiley.
Osterwalder, A., Pigneur, Y., Bernarda, G., & Smith, A. (2015). *Value proposition design.* Frankfurt: Campus.
Paap, J., & Katz, R. (2004). Anticipating disruptive innovation. *Research Technology Management, 47*(3), 13–22.
Pangaro, P. (2012). *Limitations of design thinking.* Retrieved May 28, 2016 from https://vimeo.com/42136543
Prahalad, C. K., & Ramaswamy, V. (2004a). Co-Creating unique value with costumers. *Strategy & Leadership, 32*(3), 4–9.
Prahalad, C. K., & Ramaswamy, V. (2004b). Co-creation experiences: The next practice in value creation. *Journal of Interactive Marketing, 18*(3), 5–14.
Ross, A. (2015). *Innovating professional services: Transforming value and efficiency.* Farnham: Ashgate.
Sandberg, B. (2002). Creating the market für disruptive innovation: Market proactiveness at the launch stage. *Journal of Targeting, Measurement and Analysis for Marketing, 11*(2), 184–196.
SAP. (2016). *Introduction to design thinking.* Retrieved January 31, 2016, from https://experience.sap.com/skillup/introduction-to-design-thinking/
Schumpeter, J. A. (1934). *The theory of economic development.* Cambridge (MA): Harvard University Press.
Schütte, S. T. W., Eklund, J., Axelsson, J. R. C., & Nagamachi, M. (2004). Concepts, methods and tools in Kansei engineering. *Theoretical Issues in Economics Science, 5*(3), 213–214.
Senge, P. M. (1996). *The fifth discipline and the infrastructures of a learning organization [Videocassette (VHS)].* Waltham, MA: Pegasus Communications.
Senge, P. M. (2011). *Die fünfte Disziplin - Kunst und Praxis der lernenden Organisation.* Stuttgart: Klett-Cotta.
Silverstein, D., Samuel, P., & DeCarlo, N. (2012). *The innovator's toolkit.* Chichester: Wiley.
Sinkula, J. M., & Baker, W. E. (2002). Market orientation, learning orientation and product innovation: Delving into the organization's black box. *Journal of Market-focused Management, 5*(1), 5–23.
Snyder, H., Witell, L., Gustafsson, A., Fombelle, P., & Kristensson, P. (2016). Identifying categories of service innovation: A review and synthesis of the literature. *Journal of Business Research. 69,* 2401–2408.
Stickdorn, M., & Schneider, J. (2014). *This is service design thinking.* Amsterdam: BIS.
Stringer, R. (2000). How to manage radical innovation. *California Management Review, 42*(4), 70–88.
Tidd, J., Bessant, J., & Pavitt, K. (2001). *Managing innovation: Integrating technological, market and organizational change.* Chichester: Wiley.
Toivonen, M., & Tuominen, T. (2009). Emergence of innovations in services. *The Service Industries Journal, 29*(7), 887–902.

Trott, P. (2001). The role of market research in the development of discontinuous new products. *European Journal of Innovation Management, 4*(3), 117–125.

Tschimmel. (2012). *Design thinking as an effective toolkit for Innovation.* Tschimmel 2012.

Uebernickel, F., Brenner, W., Pukall, B., Naef, T., & Schindelholzer, B. (2015). *Design thinking—Das Handbuch.* Frankfurt: Frankfurter Allgemeine Buch.

Vahs, D., & Burmester, R. (2005). *Innovationsmanagment—Von der Produkt Idee zur erfolgreichen Vermarktung.* Stuttgart: Schäffer-Poeschel.

Vargo, S. L., & Lusch, R. F. (2008). Service dominant logic: Continuing the evolution. *Journal of Academic Marketing Science, 36,* 1–10.

Vargo, S. L., & Lusch, R. F. (2011). It's all B2B...and beyond: Toward a systems perspective of the market. *Industrial Marketing Management, 40*(2), 181–187.

Vargo, S. L., & Lusch, R. F. (2016). Institutions and axioms: An extension and update of service-dominant logic. *Journal of Academic Marketing Science, 44,* 5–23.

Verhoef, P. C., Lemon, K. N., Parasuraman, A., Roggeveen, A., Tsiros, M., & Schlesinger, L. A. (2009). Customer Experience creation: Determinants, dynamics and management strategies. *Journal of Retailing, 85,* 31–41.

von der Oelsnitz, D. (2009). *Die innovative organisation.* Stuttgart: Kohlhammer.

Wobbrock, J. O., Ringel Morris, M., & Wilson, A. D. (2009). *User-defined gestures for surface computing.* Paper presented at the CHI'09 Proceedings of the SIGCHI Conference on Human Factors in Computing Systems New York.

# Complexity Management and System Dynamics Thinking

**Stefan N. Grösser**

**Abstract** With the dawn of the internet, mobile technology, cloud computing etc. our socio-technical environment has become ever more intertwined and hyper-complex. The field of complexity management tries to devise methods and methodologies to cope with the challenges arising from complexity. This chapter provides a brief overview of the field of complexity management. More specifically, it defines in detail the terms complexity and dynamic complexity. Dynamic complexity is most relevant for high impact decisions and I examine two methods First, causal context modelling (CCM). This is an integrative, qualitative, transdisciplinary approach which creates a qualitative description of a system including key variable interdependencies and system boundaries. The second methodology I explore is system dynamics (SD). Here I provide examples from a project carried out within the Use-it-Wisely project which helped the companies involved understand and deal with the dynamic problems facing them.

**Keywords** Systems thinking · Causal context model · Context analysis · Qualitative method · Simulation method · Quantitative method · System dynamics · Mixed-methods · Integrative design · Complexity management · Dynamic complexity

## 1 Introduction

Leonardo Da Vinci said "simplicity is the ultimate sophistication" (Gaddis 1955; Granat 2003). Most managers would agree. Nobody would deny that the world has become more complex during the past decades due to technological change and globalization. With digitization, the interconnectivity between people and things has rapidly increased. Dense networks now define our technical, social, and

S.N. Grösser (✉)
Institute for Corporate Development, Bern University of Applied Sciences, Bern, Switzerland
e-mail: stefan.groesser@bfh.ch

 
S.N. Grösser et al. (eds.), *Dynamics of Long-Life Assets*,
DOI 10.1007/978-3-319-45438-2_5

particularly, business environments. The idea of applying complexity science to management was first discussed in the 1990s (Straub 2013). Popular literature propagated the ideas of complexity theory—in particular, the notion of the "butterfly effect" by which a small event in a remote part of the world could trigger a chain of events that would add up to a disruptive change in the whole system. Managers' eyes were opened to the reality that organizations are not just complicated but complex.

This growing complexity is why many management thinkers have been urging businesses to embrace complexity to become, in effect, system thinkers rather than reductionists. However, Straub (2013) states that complexity is not something managers need to embrace, merely something executives need to accept and manage. In fact, complex issues are often made worse by organizations themselves, especially by the approaches they adopt to deal with these issues (Isanda 2014). Managers and other business leaders seem to be vaguely aware of complexity's existence, and those that know of its existence do not know how best to deal with it —usually resorting to wishing it away or using models that give simplistic solutions that cannot be applied in turbulent and complex environments.

If you ask managers for the major business challenges within the next ten years, you will get the answer "complexity" quite frequently. It is a reoccurring theme in annual reports, analyst calls, and public speeches (Satell 2013). Failing to manage complexity causes high transition and overhead costs as well as frictional losses, inefficiencies, and difficulties in overall strategic orientation or incomprehensibility of the value chain. In particular, the challenge of managing high value assets has become ever more complex (see the challenges in chapter "The Challenge" in this book). It is therefore all the more important that decisions makers develop a deep understanding of complexity.

In this chapter, I provide a brief background on complexity and tools for its management. I define different types of complexities and then focus on dynamic complexity. Thereafter, I introduce causal context modelling (CMM) a specific method to structure messy problems. Then, I introduce the simulation methodology of system dynamics (SD). Both methods are highly useful when addressing the challenges resulting from the maintenance and upgrading of high-investment, industrial product-service systems (IPSS).

## 2 Background on Complexity and Tools for Its Management

Complex systems can be found anywhere multiple actors interact, are subject to feedback dynamics, and are influenced by time delays between cause and effect (Sterman 1994, 2002; Groesser 2014). Section 2 details six systems approaches that can help to understand and manage complex systems. These are soft system modelling (SSM), viable system model, mental models of dynamic systems, and group model building. Additionally in Sects. 3 and 4, I detail the methods of CMM and SD. But first, let us take a look into the underpinnings of complexity theory.

## 2.1 Selected Background on Complexity

The field of complexity theory or complexity science is vast and I do not intend to cover it comprehensively in this chapter. Rather, I briefly introduce complex adaptive systems (CAS) because they can be considered a theoretical background to many methods developed in the field of complexity management. More comprehensive overviews are available (Anderson 1999; Lewin 1999; Phelan 2001; Schwaninger 2009a, b).

"Adaptive social systems are composed of interacting, thoughtful (but perhaps not brilliant) agents. [...] What it takes to move from an adaptive system to a complex adaptive system is an open question and one that can engender endless debate. At the most basic level, the field of complex systems challenges the notion that by perfectly understanding the behaviour of each component part of a system we will then understand the system as a whole" (Miller and Page 2007: 3). Miller and Page refer to the difficulty of including aspects of complexity in a definition such as this. Simon understands CAS as "a large number of parts that have many interactions" (Simon 1997: 230). This definition corresponds with Gell-Mann (1995) who speaks of a CAS as an information processing system that "acquires information about its environment and its own interaction with that environment, identifying regularities in that information, condensing those regularities into a kind of 'schema' or model, and acting in the real world on the basis of that schema. In each case, there are various competing schemata, and the results of the action in the real world feedback to influence competition among those schemata" (Gell-Mann 1995: 117).

As Levy (1994) states, CAS can be found in a number of fields, including ecology, medicine, international relations and economics. In each case there are nonlinear and network feedback systems that handle information in a similar way. Gell-Mann (1995), Stacey (1995), Beinhocker (1997) and Pascale (1999) assert that the behaviour of CAS is at the root of the science of complexity. An illustration is provided by Bonabeau and Meyer (2001) who cite the example of ant colonies. In these colonies, interacting ants (agents) in an open-system are guided by simple rules. On an individual level, the behaviour of the ants seems to be random and unpredictable. However, on the macro-level, the collective behaviour that emerges out of the interactions between the ants exhibits a distinct pattern, resulting in a nonlinear growth of efficiency in the system—the ants' behaviour is characterized by flexibility, robustness and self-organization (Bonabeau and Meyer 2001). A similar example is provided by Kupers (2000) who observes that a group of door-to-door sales persons use random feedback loops to exchange information with each other on how to increase sales (i.e. how to increase the efficiency of the system). These feedback loops and exchanges of information lead to nonlinear and jumpy growth in sales (i.e. nonlinear increases in the system's efficiency). Thus, small causes of change can possibly have enormous effects on the outcome (the butterfly effect), through the non-linear amplification from feedback loops. Even a simple feedback system may result in (deterministic) chaos with an unpredictable outcome (Holbrook 2003). Anderson et al. (1999) suggests four elements that characterize [CAS] models that have particularly interesting implications for organizational theorists.

- **Agents with schemata**: Anderson's first element entails the idea that an organization's higher-level outcomes are produced by a system of agents at a lower level of aggregation such as individuals, groups or coalitions of groups. The agents act according to a schema, i.e., a cognitive structure that determines what action the agent takes at time *t*, given its perception of the environment at time *t* (or at an earlier time, if theoretical considerations suggest applying a delay). The schemata are often modelled as a set of rules, but they can also be represented by a neural network that consists of a set of connected nodes where a signal from one node leads to a specific activation of the other. This understanding seems to be similar to Gell-Mann's (1995) depiction of CAS processes.
- **Self-organizing networks sustained by importing energy**: The second key element characterizing CAS is seen in the self-organization in such systems, where pattern and regularity emerge without the intervention of a central controller. There are three important notions behind the concept of self-organization: First, self-organization is the natural result of nonlinear interaction between simple agents. Nonlinear interaction in this context refers to self-reinforcing feedback cycles that can lead to self-amplifying behaviours. One condition for the existence of self-reinforcing feedback cycles is that interaction takes place between a large numbers of components. However, there is niether a lower boundary of interactions for self-organization nor also an upper one. Second, if interaction takes place between too many organizational actors, self-organization does not lead to pattern formation. In real human systems, however, agents only act on information available in their immediate environments: from those few agents connected to them in a feedback loop. And third, self-organization only occurs in open systems such as human organizations when energy is imported from the outside. The pattern, or dissipative structure, can only be sustained when the members contribute energy to make, break or maintain their ties to others.
- **Coevolution to the edge of chaos**: The third element is represented in the model of a "fitness landscape". This is a metaphorical map of a mountain region, where agents act to increase their payoff or fitness, i.e., their altitude (Epstein and Axtell 1996). The landscape continually shifts because it is affected by the agent's actions. Also, the individual fitness functions of agents affect each other as each individual trajectory is adjusted according to the successes of its neighbours (Eberhart et al. 2001). In this sense, agents usually co-evolve at a local level. The co-evolvement leads to a dynamic equilibrium in the system which might be thought of as teetering on the edge of chaos (Beinhocker 1997). Small changes in the actions or the behaviour of agents can have small, medium,

or large impacts on the system as a whole. If the system is in chaos, i.e., beyond the edge, then small changes in behaviour lead to widely different fitness levels, systems can reach extraordinary fitness peaks, but cannot remain on them. The slightest change in behaviour will send the system tumbling off its peak, perhaps plunging into a region of very low fitness. On the other hand, if small changes in behaviour lead only to small cascades of co-evolutionary change, the system's performance can never improve much.

– **Recombination and system evolution**: The fourth element is that every aspect of a complex adaptive system—agents, their schemata, the nature and strength of connections between them, and their fitness functions can change over time. That is, new agents and new schemata can be introduced to the system, and ties between agents emerge, break and are sometimes re-established. To model an organization, it is important to consider that the relationship between variables (or agents) is not fixed (as in traditional causal models).

## *2.2 Definition of Complexity*

After this brief examination of the theoretical background of complexity research, let us move our attention to practical side of things and concentrate on the management of complexity and the tools used. Research on the management of complexity and complex systems is particularly considered in technological and natural sciences (Bleicher 2004; Kastl and Schmid 2008). Since the 1960s, the social sciences have repeatedly analysed the steering of complex systems within the field of management theory (Malik 2008). In both the realms of scientific research and society in general, there is still no uniform understanding and consensus on the concept of complexity. Equally, it is not possible to find a consistent and generally-accepted definition of complexity. Depending on the pursued research goal or which method is applied, definitions and interpretations differ substantially (Kirchhof 2003; Scherf 2003; Rall and Dallhöfer 2004; Kersten et al. 2012).

Ulrich and Fluri (1992) define complexity in terms of situations that contain a high diversity of influencing factors and numerous mutual interdependencies which prevent structural decision-making. However, complexity must be distinguished from complicated systems. The difference between complex and complicated issues is determined by the degree of predominant uncertainty. Results in complicated systems are predictable due to the linear behaviour of their variables (Simon 1962).

Casti (1994) determines complexity by means of specific criteria. Complex systems do not possess a central control centre but rather consist of numerous, communicating units. Furthermore, feedback relationships between variables and delayed cause-and-effect are present within the complex system. The most prominent feature, however, is the characteristic of irreducibility, i.e., the system as a whole is greater than the sum of its parts and exhibits dynamic, emergent patterns.

Klabunde (2003) describes complexity through the characteristics of variety, connectivity and dynamics. Variety concerns the number and type of elements in a system, whereas connectivity deals with the number and type of the relationships between the variables. The characteristic "dynamic" captures the uncertainty and unpredictability of complex systems (Denk and Pfneissl 2009; Schoeneberg 2010).

Groesser (2015a, b, c) and others create the distinction between simple, complicated, complex, and hyper-complex (i.e., chaotic) systems. These four types of systems can be divided into a four-field matrix representation (Fig. 1), which is spanned by the system characteristics "variety/diversity" (y-axis) and the "variability/momentum" (x-axis).

- A **simple system** is characterized by a low number of components, which are not subject to variability themselves. An example is a simple process of predetermined steps in a production chain. In a simple system it is possible to estimate the progression of effects since they are stable over time.
- A **complicated system** comprises many combinatorial possibilities that arise due to the large number of components in the system and the array of possible combination between them. This complexity is also referred to as "detail complexity" or "combinatorial complexity". Everyday decisions are complex if a large number of different elements have to be considered for decision-making. One example is an antique church bell. The mechanical system is highly complicated. However, in principle the stages of each element can be known, moreover, how they interact is definable and thus limited. Moreover, the progression of these interactions is relatively stable.
- The defining characteristics of a **complex system** are its high variation in the elements and their relationships in a system, i.e., their variability, momentum, or behaviour. This leads to the concept known as "dynamic complexity" (Richardson and Pugh 1981; Senge 1990) which is the ability of a system to be able to develop into different states over time. For a complex system, it is still possible to understand the interrelations and development ex-post. The amount

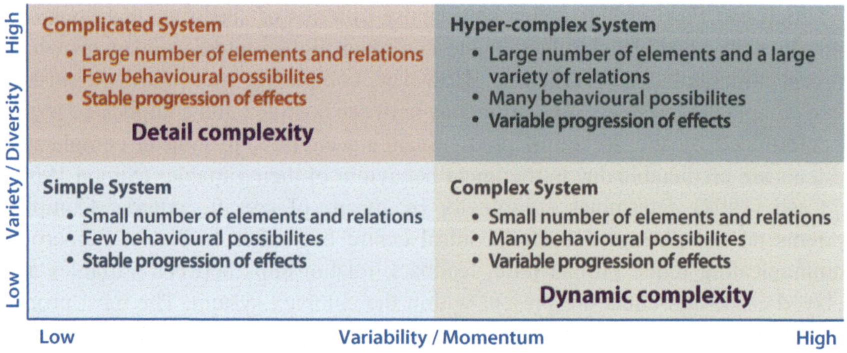


**Fig. 1** System types from simple, to complicated, to complex (Ulrich and Probst 1991; Groesser 2015a, b, c)

of variables and interconnections is moderate; the amount of interconnections can be large.

- A **hyper-complex (chaotic) system** comprises of a large amount of different variables which have a large number of interconnections. Understanding the development of the system over time is not feasible due to the many interacting and changing variables. From a management science perspective, it is only of little use to try to detail the inner workings of such hyper-complex systems since they cannot be inspected and clearly analysed or only with large estimation errors.

Table 1 details the definition of simple, complicated and complex systems based on the system's characteristics: number of elements, similarity of the elements, variability of the elements over time, the number of relationships and the connectedness of the relations. The characteristics of hyper-complex systems are not detailed here. They can be derived from the characteristics of complicated and complex systems.

Complex systems, as defined in Fig. 1 and Table 1, can exhibit dynamic complexity. Dynamic complexity is the label given to a system whose characteristics do not follow direct and simple (i.e., linear) cause-effect relationships. Dynamic complexity results from temporal interactions and interrelationships of system elements. It is considered to be caused specifically by delays, feedback, accumulations and nonlinearities. Dynamically complex situations are essentially not transparent for a decision-maker. He or she has no means of intuitively detecting the connection of circular causality and way of modelling and predicting them exactly. The decision-maker must expect surprises, side effects and unintended effects of decisions in different parts of the system.

**Criteria for dynamic complexity**: A system is dynamically complex if the following, but not necessarily all, criteria are met:

**Table 1** Comparison of simple, complicated, and complex systems

| Characteristics | Simple systems | Complicated systems | Complex systems |
|---|---|---|---|
| Number of elements | Few | Large | Moderate |
| Similarity of the elements | Identical in all characteristics | Partly or entirely different | Partly or entirely different |
| Variability of elements over time | No | No | Yes |
| Number of relationships | Few | Moderate/large | Large |
| Connectedness of relations | Few | Moderate/large | Large |
| Example | Pendulum | Car, engine | Business ecosystem |

1. **Dynamic**: The system develops or changes over time. What seems to be fixed, varies over a longer time horizon.
2. **Close connection of the system elements**: The system elements or agents in the system interact strongly with each other.
3. **Feedback**: Systems are controlled by feedback. This coupling between system elements actions and events can react upon themselves.
4. **Non-linearity**: Non-linearity exists when at least one element in the system interacts with another in a non-linear way. Non-linearity is graphically expressed as a curved, e.g., exponential or quadratic line. In particular, "non-linear" means that an effect is seldom proportional to its cause.
5. **Past dependent**: Past dependent means that the decisions, which must be made by an agent, depend on the decisions already taken in the past. Structure in any system is the product of past actions (interactions).
6. **Self-organizing**: The dynamics of the system are formed by self-organization and spontaneous consequence of its internal structure.
7. **Adaptive**: Adaptive means that a system itself changes as a result of experience. Thus, the skills and decision rules of agents change in a complex system over time.
8. **Counterintuitive**: Decision-makers cannot capture causes and their effects only relying on intuition. The behaviour of the system is often against, i.e., counter, the behaviour the decision-makers expect. This is because causal relationships are often not sufficiently understood since it is often neglected that causes may have different intended and unintended effects.
9. **Intervention resistant**: The complexity of the system, in which an agent is embedded, overwhelms his or her ability to understand the system. Consequently, implemented solutions often fail in a complex system or even aggravate the situation. Interventions do not produce obvious (expected) effects or even lead to unintended consequences.
10. **Temporal balancing decisions (trade-offs)**: time delays result in a system in which the long-term effects of an intervention are often different from the short-term effects.

## *2.3 Short Overview of Some Tools for Managing Complexity*

After introducing the foundations of different types of complexity, I will now briefly look at several tools from the field of complexity and systems theory which have been developed to cope with the ever growing situations of complexity. We will not concern ourselves with the methods of CCM and SD in this section since they are introduced later in detail in dedicated subchapters.

### 2.3.1 Soft System Modelling

SSM incorporates an interpretive perspective of social settings (Lane and Oliva 1998). With a focus on action-research, SSM practitioners do not attempt to describe the real world, rather they use several models, i.e., ideal types, to explain a problem from different perspectives. The ultimate goal is to gain insights and changes by comparing ideal types with the real world problem. The models themselves are represented by a mapping technique which results in "rich pictures" of the problematic situation (Fig. 2).

### 2.3.2 Cybernetic Models

The cybernetic view of socio-technical systems is suitable for diagnosing and de-signing organizations. Stafford Beer's viable system model (Beer 1979, 1981) is one of the most wide-ranging theories in this discipline (Fig. 3). Despite its applicability to any human or social system, it has primarily been used to describe the viability of organizations. An underlying proposition is that an organization is only viable if it has a set of management functions and interrelationships as specified by the theory (Schwaninger and Ríos 2008). Differences between the

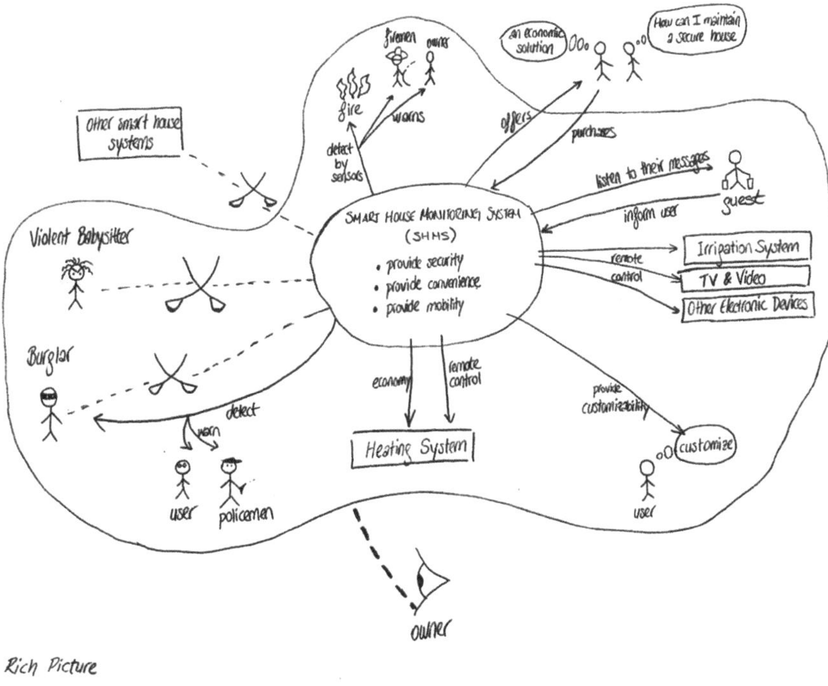


**Fig. 2** Rich picture as used in the SSM (Checkland 2001)

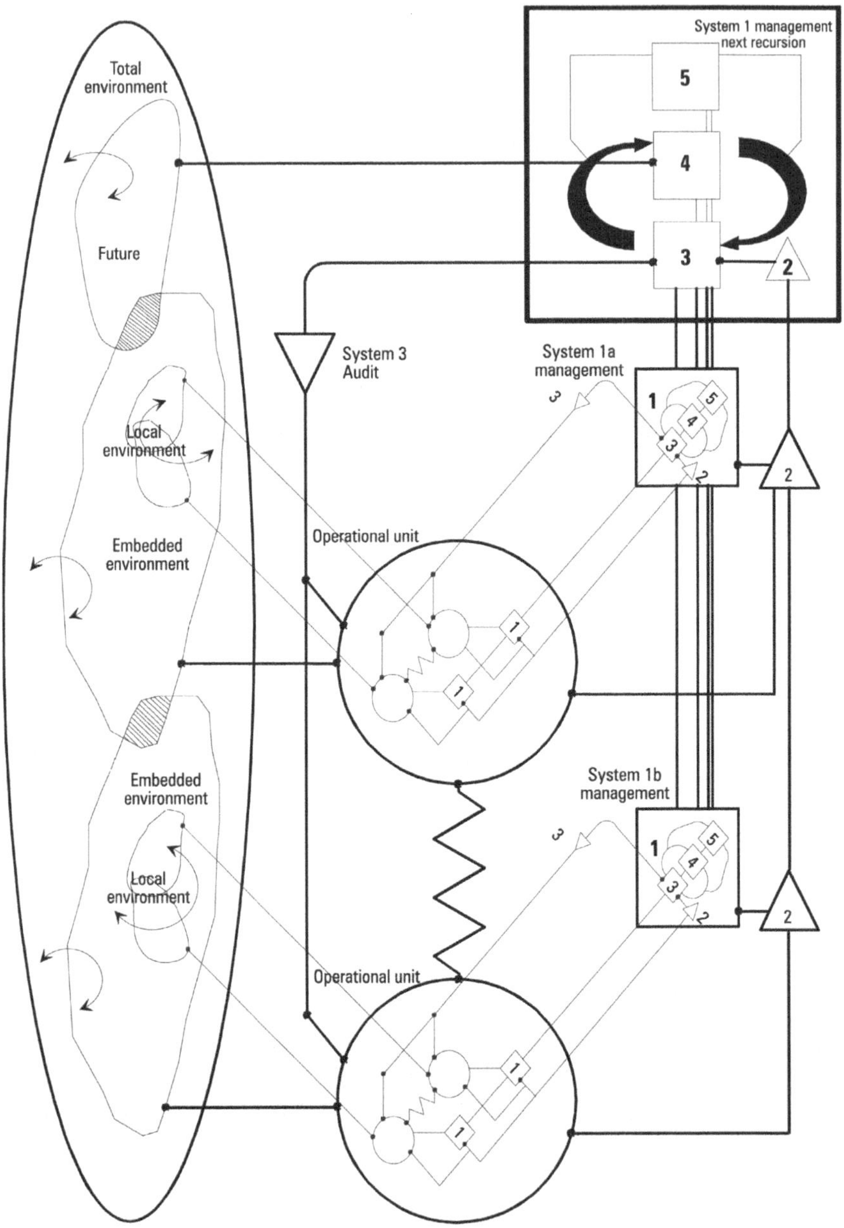


**Fig. 3** Viable system model (Beer 1981)

elements and links of the real system and the elements and links as proposed by the Viable System Model result in a possible threat to the viability of the organization.

### 2.3.3 Mental Models of Dynamic System

An anthropocentric approach focussing on humans' ability to reason is the concept behind mental models. It has been shown that humans' ability to perform in dynamic complex settings is limited and biased. Therefore, improved mental models which account for accumulation processes, time delays, and feedback loops are required (Groesser and Schaffernicht 2012). The mental model approach to dynamic systems has been developed to elicit managerial cognitions about dynamic situations to represent these cognitions, and to analyse the mental models with the objective of improving decision-making. The most recent methods of elicitation and comparison can be found in (Schaffernicht and Groesser 2011; Groesser and Schaffernicht 2012; Schaffernicht and Groesser 2014).

### 2.3.4 Group Model Building

Group modelling is a process which is expected to adapt mental models and foster the implementation of decisions (Rouwette et al. 2011). This process is based on involving different actors, e.g., clients and experts, who provide particular knowledge about contents or techniques (Vennix 1996). The goals of group model building are versatile. By means of group model building, the individual and group mental models can be aligned. This improves the clarity and efficiency between different system actors.

# 3 Deep-Dive I: Causal Context Models

## *3.1 Purpose of Causal Context Models*

This section provides details about CMM. A CCM is a qualitative word-and-arrow diagram, i.e., a graphical representation that details the cause-and-effect relationships between variables in a system. A CCM follows, in principle, the method of a causal (loop) diagram (Richardson and Pugh 1981; Sterman 2000; Lane 2008; Groesser 2016). It emphasizes the interdisciplinary interaction between technological, social, legal, and natural spheres when high-value IPSS, and other systems, are managed (see chapter "The Challenge" of this book for the challenges of upgrading and managing IPSS).

The objective of a CCM is to explain the behaviour of technical- and business-level variables which are key to an organization's objectives. In doing so, a good model will reveal the network of influences that impinge on those variables. Before one can start to use CCMs some prerequisites are helpful: (1) openness to a new qualitative method, (2) thinking in variables and how they are interconnected, (3) a mind-set open to crossing disciplinary boundaries to connect different fields of thought (e.g., engineering, informatics, and business). A CCM helps those involved to evaluate the impact of changes to their business-level objectives and compare various these scenarios using behaviour over time charts. To do this, the user imagines changing the value of a relevant variable in the model and then traces the consequences through the model to see if the desired and expected outcomes are achieved. This is done in a qualitative, imaginative way of reasoning.

## *3.2 Elements of a Causal Context Model*

A CMM consists of variables and directional causal links that have one of two possible polarities. A link marked positive (+) indicates a positive causal relation and a link marked negative (–) indicates a negative causal relation.

- A **positive** causal link (+) means the two variables, which are connected by this causal link, change in the same direction. In other words, if the initial variable decreases, the other variable also decreases. Similarly, if the variable, in which the link starts, increases, the other variable increases as well.
- A **negative** causal link (–) means the two variables, which are connected by this causal link, change in opposite directions. In other words, if the initial variable increases, the other variable decreases and vice versa.

It is common for CCM to have closed chains of causal links known as feedback loops (Sterman 2000). A feedback loop can either be reinforcing or balancing.

- A reinforcing feedback loop (R) is a closed causal chain in which the effect of a variation in any variable propagates through the loop and returns to the variable thus reinforcing the initial deviation. In other words, if a variable increases in a reinforcing loop the effect through the cycle will return an increase to the same variable and vice versa. An example of a reinforcing loop is the word of mouth dynamics. In reaction to any questionable statement or activity of an organization, social media users can create huge waves of outrage within just a few hours. These so-called online firestorms pose new challenges for marketing communications—reinforcing feedback dynamics.
- A balancing feedback loop (B) is the closed causal chain in which the effect of a variation in any variable propagates through the loop and returns to the variable a deviation opposite to the initial one. In other words, if a variable increases in a balancing loop the effect through the cycle will return a decrease to the same variable and vice versa. An example of a balancing loop is the actions executed by managers to prepare and avoid online firestorms, as described above. The company's capabilities are built-up until the management is satisfied. Then, no further investments are executed. A balancing feedback loop leads to goal-seeking dynamics of the respective system.

A CCM explicates the assumptions and helps thereby to reveal how things are connected to each other within a system. The example in Fig. 4 shows an example of a CCM developed for an organization taking part in the UIW-project. The figure should provide an indication of how a CCM looks; I do not intend to detail or explain the CCM here. It shows the *technical-level* (e.g., total construction time or number of vague regulations) and **business-level objectives** (e.g., return on investment), scenario variables (e.g., number of future regulations issued or effectiveness of future regulations), and feedback loops (B1 to B4).

In addition to the causal, structural model, a CCM requires that at least one behaviour over time chart (also known as a BOT or a time chart) of an important variable is developed. The variable has to be an element of the CCM (see Fig. 5).

## 3.3 Causal Context Model Development

CCMs are developed to create comprehensive causal maps, i.e., models that include different perspectives on a challenge that needs to be managed. For instance, all companies that participated in the UIW-project (see Part III of this book) established CCMs that show the relationships between technical-level objectives and business-level objectives. The CCM supports the definition of the problem to be addressed as well as helping elaborate possible solutions. The generic process of CCM development follows six steps:

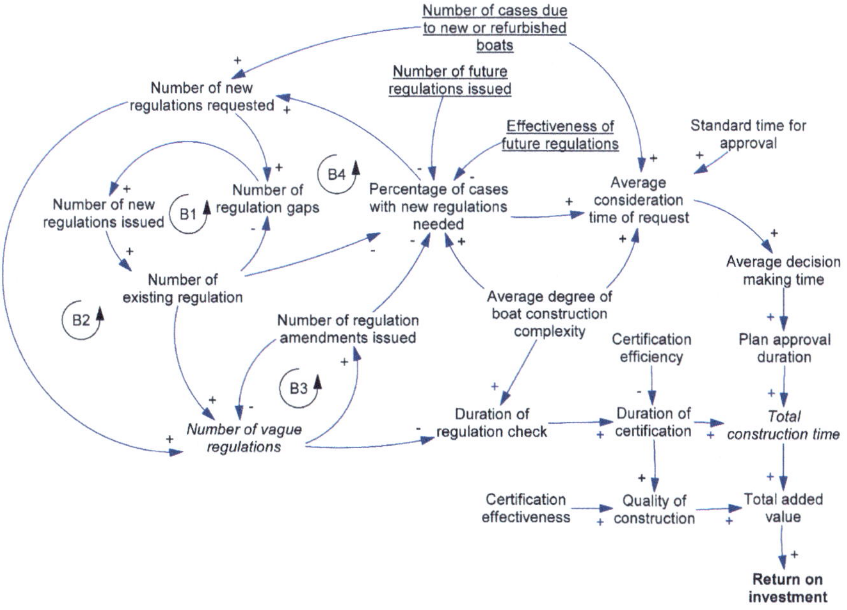


**Fig. 4** Example of a causal context model

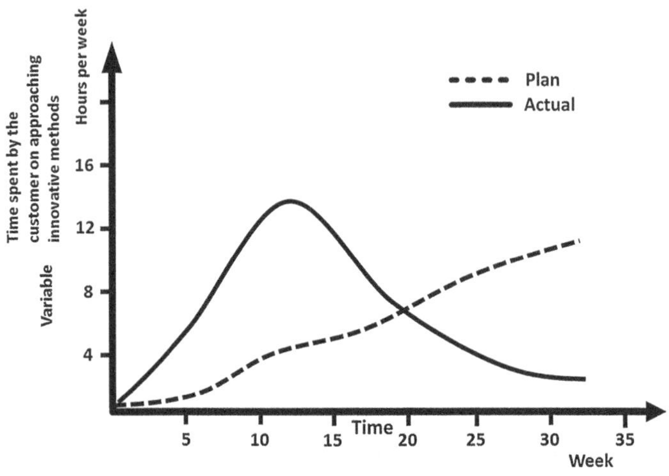


**Fig. 5** Example of a behaviour over time (BOT) chart

1. **Define the reference behaviour in technical-level objectives by means of behaviour over time charts**: the reference behaviour is the over time development of an important technical variable, e.g., availability of relevant information to project team. This variable shows problematic behaviour, e.g., that the level of relevant information the team has access to does not conform to the intended level. One, or ideally, several such reference modes in technical-level variables should be defined. The tutorial https://www.youtube.com/watch?v=ktKGrDds3No provides additional information about step 1.
2. **Define the reference behaviour in business-level objectives by means of behaviour over time graphs**: Then, perform step 1 now for business-level objectives. Develop behaviour over time charts for variables that show business-level objectives. Examples of such variables are market share, revenues, customer satisfaction, or throughput time. The business-level objectives are then: to have a higher market share, increased revenues, higher customer satisfaction, or lower throughput time (see the charts in Fig. 4).
3. **Develop the causal model**: in order to develop a causal model the next step is to connect the technical-level and business-level variables by means of causal links. One will certainly have to include new variables about relevant aspects of the system being modelled to create the causal paths between the different variables. Only include variables and causal links that exist in the system. All the relevant variables have to be included in the final model so as to sufficiently explain the behaviour of the objective variables in steps 1 and 2.
4. **Define scenario variables**: After the causal model is completed, ensure that the model includes important scenario variables. A scenario is a description of possible external developments in the future. A scenario variable, e.g., requirements for energy efficiency, operationalizes these possible developments by embedding these clearly in the causal model. Scenario variables assume

different values, e.g., legal requirements for energy efficiency might be change. The CCM helps the user to think about the following developments:

- If the scenario *variable X* increases (or decreases respectively), how will the technical-level objectives develop?
- If the scenario *variable X* increases (or decreases respectively), how will the business-level objectives develop?

5. **Define policy variables**: A policy is a set of basic principles and associated guidelines, formulated and enforced by the governing body of an organization, e.g., a decision maker, to direct and limit his or her actions in pursuit of long-term goals. In other words, a policy is a decision rule that defines how available information is used for decision making. One example is a hiring policy: it guides the each (monthly, annual etc.) decision about how many people should be hired. Polices are operationalized by policy variables which are under the control of the decision maker. This step should ensure that the relevant polices, i.e., measures a decision maker can influence, to achieve the technical-level and business-level objectives are included in the CCM.
6. **Continuously validate the model being created**: Validation activities occurs continuously during the model creation process. For more information on this, see Groesser and Schwaninger (2012) who go through the modelling process (both qualitative and quantitative) in more detail (see also Barlas 1996; Forrester and Senge 1980; Schwaninger and Groesser 2009). The modeller has to ensure that the resulting CCM only features variables and causal links with polarities. Other concepts are not used in CCMs.

The process of developing a CCM is a learning process for the participating organization. For each iteration, the CCMs are expanded with new variables, causal relationships, scenario and policy variables. Discussions about different meanings of specific variables as well as different causal relationships foster understanding between participants and also nurture learning about the context in which the decisions on the technical and business-level are made.

CCMs offer several benefits: first, different perspectives, e.g., economic, technical, and social aspects, can be integrated into one holistic model; second, CCMs are statements about causes and consequences. Such a causal model becomes a tool with which concrete actions to overcome challenges can be found. A CCM is, however, a qualitative model. The next step of analysis would be do develop a quantitative simulation model. The advantage of such a simulation model is that the participants cannot only identify positive and negative effects, but also by how much the changes can impact their technical-level objectives and their business-level objectives. Furthermore, the rigor a simulation model requires leads to a more intense and in-depth thought process regarding the different causalities and values as well as the expansion of the model boundary. This is what I address next.

# 4 Deep-Dive II: System Dynamics Simulation Modelling

## 4.1 *Purpose of System Dynamics Modelling*

System Dynamics (SD) is one of the most popular, widespread and validated simulation (computational) methodology and cannot be overlooked when discussing decision making tools and complexity management. In this Sect. 1 will briefly address SD simulation methodology and address in more detail how it can be useful when managing real world complexity. The more curious reader will benefit greatly from the references supplied here.

The basic idea of SD is to capture the underlying characteristics of complex dynamic systems to understand them better and foster desirable developments (Schwaninger and Ríos 2008; Schwaninger and Groesser 2008). To capture all these characteristics SD-models must represent nonlinearities, long-term patterns and the internal structure of a system. This is technically achieved by mapping the system's stock- and-flow structure. Jay Forrester, the founder of SD, devised the means of modelling any dynamic situation by means of stocks and flows. The process of building an SD model is a continuous learning process consisting of formulating hypotheses, testing, and revising formal and mental models. SD captures essential characteristics of management reality, for instance, nonlinear behaviours, accumulations, delays, and information feedback, which are not systematically taken into account by existing methods (Sterman 2000; Schöneborn 2003; Morecroft 2007; Warren 2008). A computational modelling approach is most helpful in providing insights about the type and magnitude of interaction in high value asset system and allows an integrated evaluation and thereby complements the existing methods in the analysis of such systems.

## 4.2 *System Dynamics Modelling Process*

When creating a System Dynamics model, a six step modelling development process is used: (1) selection of the dynamic problem, (2) conceptualization, (3) formulation, (4) scenario and policy analysis, (5) selection of policies and implementation planning, and (6) implementation (Fig. 6).

### 4.2.1 Step 1: Selection of the Dynamic Problem

The first step of the modelling process is to identify the issue and the relevant stakeholders. This enables modellers to identify from whom to draw expertise when developing the model as well as from where to collect data in the latter stages of the process. The development of a model will require the collaboration between the

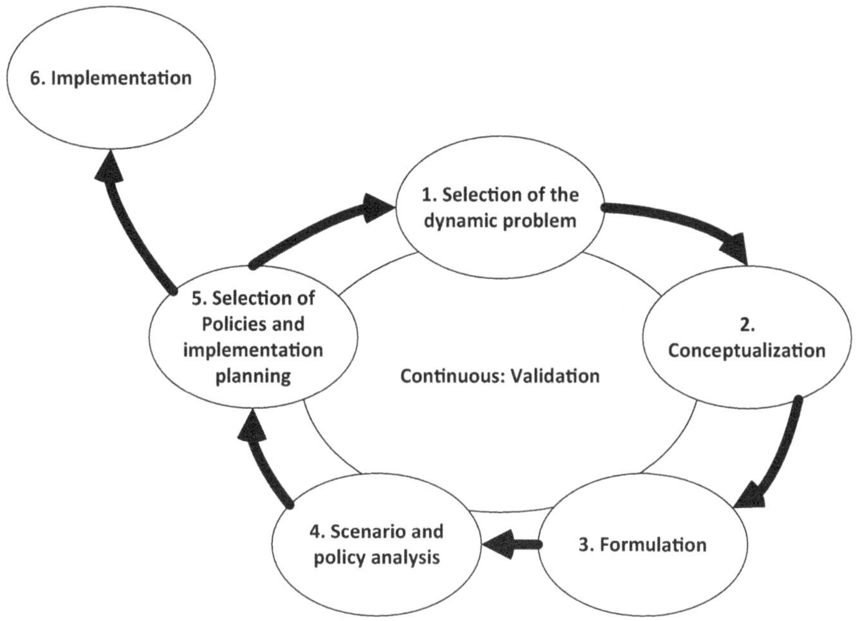


**Fig. 6** Process for developing system dynamics simulation models

"problem owners" and modellers to produce a high-quality model. Initially, the problem owners provide the essential information about the issue at hand and are then involved in every iterative modelling step. It is essential that the problem owners comprehend the basic functioning of the model and continuously validate the output of the model. After getting an initial feel for the environment of the model, the modeller formulates a dynamic hypothesis of the problem. This dynamic hypothesis is founded on the information provided by the owners as well any current theories which help to explain the problem.

### 4.2.2 Step 2: Conceptualization

After identifying and selecting the dynamic problem, the task is to decide upon a provisional list of variables and a suitable time horizon for the model, from which the necessary behaviour over time graphs (BOTs) can be generated. All this is done based on data or the expectations of the relevant stakeholders. This stage should not be considered as final since the modelling process is iterative and the modeller, together with the stakeholders and problem owner, will revise these decisions repeatedly until the model is completed. This iteration also includes repeated feedback from the stakeholders to gain a better understanding of the model.

### 4.2.3 Step 3: Formulation

Based on the available data resources (e.g., a previously generated Causal Context Model (CCM)) and the identified problem, the modeller now defines what kind of model is to be created. For some dynamic problems a qualitative model might suffice, meaning the model can start out as Causal Loop Diagram (CLD). If a quantified model is the goal, then a Stock- and Flow-Diagram (SFD) should be considered more suitable. In the case of a quantified model, after translating the variable list into a SFD, the modeller populates the variables with values to create a first iteration of the simulation model. Initially the values and functions added to the model can be guesses or estimates (or even guessimates!), as the modeller will revise them for every iterative step and continuously increase their precision. Also, continuously simulating the model will provide the modeller with insights for further model development. Step 3 also enables the modeller to continuously test their model BOTs by comparing it to the initially generated BOTs, by testing the robustness of the model and/or testing sensitivity.

### 4.2.4 Step 4: Scenario and Policy Analysis

Finally, when the modeller is satisfied that the model is of sufficient quality he or she can start analysing and evaluating policies and scenarios. Scenarios are analysed by changing exogenous variables to simulate different developments in the environment of the system. If for example the model depends on economic growth, the modeller can evaluate the impact and the sensitivity of the system to an economic slowdown or sudden increase in economic activity. The degree to which the system changes as a result of that external change reveals the model's sensitivity to that exogenous variable. This allows the practitioner to analyse the likelihood of any given situation to materialize under a certain set of external conditions. The model also allows the efficacy of different responses to external changes in the system to be tested. This gives the modeller the opportunity to select policies and responses to optimize the resilience of the system in the face of external shocks.

### 4.2.5 Step 5: Selection of Policies and Planning of Implementation

After agreeing on the most important scenario settings and most effective policies, the modeller applies these conditions to the model and discusses the results with the stakeholders. The stakeholders can then evaluate and define the most effective way to apply the policies in the system in question. With the insight gained from the discussion of the model, the stakeholders can then implement actions necessary to change the system in real life while already anticipating and validating whether the measures achieve the desired effect.

### 4.2.6 Step 6: Implementation

Implementing the planned changes and measures is in the responsibility of the problem owner. Often it is helpful, when the simulation model and its results are demonstrated to the people who are affected by the changes and measures. It is especially productive to hold demonstration workshops during which the participants can experiment with the simulation model for themselves. These sessions will often throw new light on the problem and provide fresh impetus to make any necessary changes.

## *4.3 Applying System Dynamics*

With regard to managing complexity, the following paragraphs describe five advantages of SD simulation methodology as well as explaining some of its disadvantages. First, any tool for decision-making has to satisfy several criteria to effectively deliver decision support. According to John D. C. Little (1970) these criteria are simplicity, robustness, ease of control, adaptiveness, completeness on important issues, and simplicity of communication. In close connection with the decision maker, a computational modelling process begins with a simple model structure and continuously improves in an evolutionary way using rapid prototyping. As a result, this process of elaboration and calibration creates a sufficient, robust and purpose-oriented model. Furthermore, the involved decision makers learn how to control the model during its execution. The unfolding model is permanently represented as a visual object to ensure transparent communication with the target audience (Black and Andersen 2012; Nistelrooij et al. 2015).

Second, the approach can improve a company's capabilities when analysing the interdependencies in their business models in the face of external changes in the environment. Since simulation approaches are capable of representing highly complex situations and handling them in a reasonably simple way, it becomes possible to address a higher degree of the dynamic complexity present in business reality (Groesser and Schwaninger 2012). As a direct consequence of structuring and linking knowledge about a business system, SD allows decision makers to take decisions which are based on integrative qualitative and quantitative analysis.

Third, risks can be identified through sensitivity analysis of the feedback dynamics in a simulation model. Risks are often identified in the following three areas: firstly, balancing feedback loops that limit a desired growth or decay; secondly, reinforcing feedback loops that lead to undesired growth or decay; and thirdly, external factors that exacerbate any of above two types of feedback loops. Analysis of feedback dynamics can make some systemic risks apparent, which otherwise might be too vague to attract notice. SD can be used to quantify risks which are attributed to be most relevant (Rodrigues and Bowers 1996).

Fourth, SD emphasizes a continuous perspective (Sterman 2000). This perspective strives to look beyond single events to see the dynamic patterns underlying them in the short-, as well as, long-term. Then, by identifying those patterns, simulations help to understand the causes of current issues and can support decision makers in tackling them. Moreover, applying computational modelling supports the validation of strategic initiatives and their effect on existing business models—just as engineers test new technologies or products extensively in a laboratory before their market launch. In particular, the ability to experiment with different scenarios and strategic initiatives in a computational environment has the potential to reduce erroneous management decisions and reveal overlooked factors and patterns that could become relevant in the future (Groesser 2015a, b, c).

And finally, by amalgamating computational methods with existing business modelling approaches SD provides an insightful, valid, relatively rapid, and inexpensive approach to business model analysis and design (Eden et al. 2000). Moreover, from a perspective of consistency, it is known that humans cannot deduce the behavioural consequences of a system with many interdependent elements (Miller 1956; Forrester 1961; Sterman et al. 2015). Computational modelling is one of the means, amongst others, of reducing the issue that qualitative models seem to be insufficient when systems are highly complex (Sterman 2000). Hence, it enables a deep and integrated understanding of a system through the quantitative exploration of systemic interdependencies.

Computational modelling of complex systems is a relatively innovative approach for top management decision makers. Some disadvantages of this method relate to the relative ease of linking variables together to quickly create large, highly complex models. Some users may, however, be overwhelmed by this complexity if they do not exercise a cautious approach to modelling (Groesser and Schwaninger 2012). The existence of user-friendly visual representations has, in some cases, been a disservice by offering the false impression that modelling is always simple and done quickly. In addition, inclusion of uncertain or only hypothesized feedback loops may create complex model behaviour that may be difficult to track, falsify, or validate. Moreover, the empirical evidence about the learning outcomes of computational modelling and its effectiveness is still inconclusive (Karakul and Qudrat-Ullah 2008; Sterman 2010; Qudrat-Ullah 2014). Consequently, it is not yet possible to state that businesses applying computational modelling systematically produce better results than those that do not use it and thus, the requirements of the strong market test are not yet met (Labro and Tuomela 2003). At the same time, this is a call for action to conduct more empirical research to prove (or disprove) the case for computational simulation methods.

## 5 Conclusion

This chapter introduced the reader to systemic methods which are highly beneficial in the analysis and management of complexity, especially in cases when managing high value assets. The chapter introduced two methods in more detail: the qualitative method, CCM, and the quantitative method, SD, methodology. The chapter explained both methods and provided the reasoning for their applications as well as discussing their potential benefits.

**Acknowledgements** I would like to thank Stefan Katz for his professional support during the development of cluster cases in the UIW-project. Also I want to thank Daniel Foord for his exceptional support with regard to the English in this chapter.

## References

Anderson, P. (1999). Complexity theory and organization science. *Organization Science, 10*(3), 216–232.

Anderson, P., & Meyer, A., et al. (1999). Introduction to the special issue: Applications of complexity theory to organization science. *Organization Science, 10*(3), 233–236.

Barlas, Y. (1996). Formal aspects of model validity and validation in system dynamics. *System Dynamics Review, 12*(3), 183–210.

Beer, S. (1979). *The heart of the enterprise*. Chichester: Wiley.

Beer, S. (1981). *Brain of the firm*. London: Penguin Press.

Beinhocker, E. D. (1997). Strategy at the edge of chaos. *McKiney Quarterly, 1*(24–39).

Black, L. J., & Andersen, D. F. (2012). Using visual representations as boundary objects to resolve conflict in collaborative model-building approaches. *Systems Research and Behavioral Science, 29*(2), 194–208.

Bleicher, K. (2004). Das Konzept Integriertes Management. Visionen - Missionen - Programme. Frankfurt, Campus.

Bonabeau, E., & Meyer, C. (2001). Swarm intelligence—A whole new way to think about business. *Harvard Business Review, 79*(5), 106–114.

Casti, J. L. (1994). *Complexification, explaining a paradoxial world through the science of surprise*. New York City: HarperCollins Publisher.

Checkland, P. (2001). Soft system methodology. In J. Rosenhead & J. Mingers (Eds.), *Rational analysis for a problematic world revisited: Problem structuring methods for complexity, uncertainty and conflict* (2nd ed.). Chichester, New York, Weinheim, Brisbane, Singapore, Toronto: Willey.

Denk, R., & Pfneissl, T. (2009). *Komplexitätsmanagement*. Wien: Linde.

Eberhart, R. C., & Shi, Y., et al. (2001). *Swarm intelligence*. Morgan Kaufmann.

Eden, C., Williams, T., et al. (2000). The role of feedback dynamics in disruption and delay on the nature of disruption and delay (D&D) in major projects. *The Journal of the Operational Research Society, 51*(3), 291–300.

Epstein, J. M., & Axtell, R. (1996). *Growing artificial societies: Social science from the bottom up*. Cambridge, Washington D.C.: Brookings Institution Press, The MIT Press.

Forrester, J. W. (1961). *Industrial dynamics*. Cambridge: Productivity Press.

Forrester, J. W., & Senge, P. M. (1980). Tests for building confidence in system dynamics models. In A. A. Legasto, J. W. Forrester, & J. M. Lyneis (Eds.), *System dynamics: TIMS studies in the management sciences* (Vol. 14). Amsterdam, North-Holland.

Gaddis, W. (1955). *The recognitions*. San Diego: Hartcourt Brace & Company.

Gell-Mann, M. (1995). *The quark and the jaguar: Adventures in the simple and the complex*. London: Abacus.

Granat, H. (2003). *Wisdom through the ages: Book two*. Bloomington: Trafford Publishing.

Groesser, S. N. (2014). Co-evolution of legal and voluntary standards: Development of energy efficiency in Swiss residential building codes. *Technological Forecasting and Social Change, 87*(1), 1–16.

Groesser, S. N. (2015). Lab or reality: Entwicklung und Anylse von Geschäftsmodellen durch das kybernetische Unternehmensmodell Blue Company. In *Exploring Cybernetics: Kybernetik im interdisziplinären Diskurs* (pp. 91–116). Berlin: Springer.

Groesser, S. N. (2015). *Stichwort: Dynamische Komplexität. Gabler Wirtschaftslexikon*. Heidelberg: Gabler.

Groesser, S. N. (2015). *Stichwort: System dynamics*. Gabler Wirtschaftslexikon.

Groesser, S. N. (2016). *Qualitative modellierung mit system dynamics*. North Charleston: CreateSpace Independent Publishing Platform.

Groesser, S. N., & Schaffernicht, M. (2012). Mental models of dynamic systems: Taking stock and looking ahead. *System Dynamics Review, 28*(1), 46–68.

Groesser, S. N., & Schwaninger, M. (2012). Contributions to model validation: Hierarchy, process, and cessation. *System Dynamics Review, 28*(2), 157–181.

Holbrook, M. B. (2003). Adventures in complexity. *Academy of Marketing Science Review, 6*(1–18).

Isanda, M. (2014). *Strategies for managing complexity*. University of Nairobi.

Karakul, M., & Qudrat-Ullah, H. (2008). *How to improve dynamic decision making? Practice and promise. Complex decision making* (pp. 3–24). Berlin: Springer.

Kastl, T., & Schmid, A. (2008). *Projektmanagement aus dem Blickwinkel von Komplexitäts- und Netzwerktheorie. Advanced Project Management. Herausforderungen - Praxiserfahrung - Perspektiven*. (pp. 213–232). Berlin: LIT.

Kersten, W., & Lammers, T., et al. (2012). *Schlussbericht zum Projekt "Komplexitätsanalyse von Distributionssystemen"*. Institut für Logistik und Unternehmensführung an der Technischen Universität Hamburg-Harburg.

Kirchhof, R. (2003). *Ganzheitliches Komplexitätsmanagement - Grundlagen und Methodik des Umgangs mit Komplexität im Unternehmen*. Wiesbaden: DUV.

Klabunde, S. (2003). *Wissensmanagement in der integrierten Produkt- und Prozessgestaltung: Best-Practice-Modelle zum Management von Meta-Wissen*. Wiesbaden: DUV.

Kupers, R. (2000). What organizational leaders should know about the new science of complexity. *Complexity, 6*(1), 14–19.

Labro, E., & Tuomela, T.-S. (2003). On bringing more action into management accounting research: Process considerations based on two constructive case studies. *European Accounting Review, 12*(3), 409–442.

Lane, D. C. (2008). The emergence and use of diagramming in system dynamics: A critical account. *Systems Research and Behavioral Science, 25*(1), 3–23.

Lane, D. C., & Oliva, R. (1998). The greater whole: Towards a synthesis of system dynamics and soft systems methodology. *European Journal of Operational Research, 107*(1), 214–235.

Levy, D. (1994). Chaos theory and strategy—Theory, application, and managerial implications. *Strategic Management Journal, 15*, 167–178.

Lewin, A. Y. (1999). Application of complexity theory to organization science. *Organization Science, 10*(3), 215.

Little, J. D. C. (1970). Models and managers: The concept of a decision calculus. *Management Science, 16*(8), 466–485.

Malik, F. (2008). *Strategie des Managements komplexer Systeme. Ein Beitrag zur Management-Kybernetik evolutionärer Systeme*. Bern: Haupt.

Miller, G. (1956). The magical number seven, plus or minus two: Some limits on our capacity for processing information. *The Psychological Review, 63*(1), 81–97.

Miller, J. H., & Page, S. (2007). *Complex adaptive systems: An introduction to computational models of social life*. In S. A. Levin & S. H. Strogatz (Eds.). Princeton Press.

Morecroft, J. D. W. (2007). *Strategic modelling and business dynamics: A feedback systems approach*. Chichester: Wiley.

Nistelrooij, L. P. J. V., & Rouwette, E. A. J. A., et al. (2015). The eye of the beholder: A case example of changing clients' perspectives through involvement in the model validation process. *Systems Research and Behavioral Science, 32*(4), 437–449.

Pascale, R. T. (1999). Surfing the edge of chaos. *MIT Sloan Management Review, 40*(3), 83–95.

Phelan, S. E. (2001). What is complexity science really? *Emergence, 3*(1), 120–136.
Qudrat-Ullah, H. (2014). Yes we can: Improving performance in dynamic tasks. *Decision Support Systems, 61*(2014), 22–33.
Rall, K., & Dallhöfer, J. (2004). Komplexität indirekter PRozesse bei der Erstellung variantenreicher Produkte. *Zum Wirtschaftlichen Fabrikbetrieb, 11*, 623–640.
Richardson, G. P., & Pugh, A. L., III. (1981). *Introduction to system dynamics modeling with DYNAMO*. Cambridge: MA, Productivity Press.
Rodrigues, A., & Bowers, J. (1996). The role of system dynamics in project management. *International Journal of Project Management, 14*(4), 213–220.
Rouwette, E. A. J. A., Korzilius, H., et al. (2011). Modeling as persuasion: The impact of group model building on attitudes and behavior. *System Dynamics Review (Wiley), 27*(1), 1–21.
Satell, G. (2013). *Management has to change in an increasingly complex world*. Business Insider.
Schaffernicht, M., & Groesser, S. (2014). The SEXTANT software: A tool for automating the comparative analysis of mental models of dynamic systems. *European Journal of Operational Research*.
Schaffernicht, M., & Groesser, S. N. (2011). A comprehensive method for comparing mental models of dynamic systems. *European Journal of Operational Research, 210*(1), 57–67.
Scherf, O. (2003). *Komplexität aus systemischer Sicht*. München: Difo-Druck.
Schoeneberg, K.-P. (2010). *Komplexität - Eine Einführung in die Komplexitätsforschung und Auswirkungen auf das Management komplexer Projekte. Marktorientierte Problemlösungen im Innovationsmarketing*. Wiesbaden: Gabler: 482 ff.
Schöneborn, F. (2003). *Strategisches controlling mit system dynamics*. Heidelberg: Physica-Verlag.
Schwaninger, M. (2009a). *Intelligent organizations: Powerful models for systemic management*. Berlin and Heidelberg: Springer Publishing.
Schwaninger, M. (2009b). System dynamics in the evolution of the systems approach. In R. Meyers (Ed.), *Encyclopedia of complexity and system science*. Berlin, London, Paris: Springer Publishing.
Schwaninger, M., & Groesser, S. N. (2008). Model-based theory-building with system dynamics. *Systems Research and Behavioral Science, 25*(4), 447–465.
Schwaninger, M., & Groesser, S. N. (2009). System dynamics modeling: Validation for quality assurance. In *Encyclopedia of complexity and system science*. London: Springer Publishing.
Schwaninger, M., & Ríos, J. P. (2008). System dynamics and cybernetics: A synergetic pair. *System Dynamics Review, 24*(2), 145–174.
Senge, P. M. (1990). *The fifth discipline: The art and practice of the learning organization*. New York: Currency & Doubleday.
Senge, P. M. (1996). *The fifth discipline and the infrastructures of a learning organization*. Pegasus Communications: Waltham, MA.
Simon, H. (1962). The architecture of complexity. *American Philosophical Society, 106*(6), 467–482.
Simon, H. A. (1997). *Administrative behavior: A study of decision-making processes in administrative organizations*. New York, London, Toronto, Sydney, Singapore: The Free Press.
Stacey, R. D. (1995). The science of complexity—An alternative perspective for strategic change processes. *Strategic Management Journal, 16*(6), 477–495.
Sterman, J. D. (1994). Learning in and about complex-systems. *System Dynamics Review, 10*(2–3), 291–330.
Sterman, J. D. (2000). *Business dynamics: Systems thinking and modeling for a complex world*. Boston: MA, McGraw-Hill.
Sterman, J. D. (2002). All models are wrong: Reflections on becoming a systems scientist. *System Dynamics Review, 18*(4), 501–531.
Sterman, J. D. (2010). Does formal system dynamics training improve people's understanding of accumulation? *System Dynamics Review, 26*(4), 316–334.

Sterman, J. D., Oliva, R., et al. (2015). System dynamics perspectives and modeling opportunities for research in operations management. *Journal of Operations Management, 39–40* (November), 1–5.

Straub, R. (2013). Why managers haven't embraced complexity. *Harvard Business Review, 56*(5).

Ulrich, H., & Probst, G. (1991). *Anleitung zum ganzheitlichen Denken: Ein Brevier für Führungskräfte*. Bern: Paul Haupt Verlag.

Ulrich, P., & Fluri, E. (1992). *Management*. Bern: Haupt.

Vennix, J. A. M. (1996). *Group model building: Facilitating team learning using system dynamics*. Chichester: Wiley.

Warren, K. (2008). Strategic management dynamics. Chichester, West Sussex, England: Wiley.

# Managing the Life Cycle to Reduce Environmental Impacts

**Tiina Pajula, Katri Behm, Saija Vatanen and Elina Saarivuori**

**Abstract** Driven by public awareness and international regulations and standards, sustainability and environmental impacts have become increasingly important distinguishing factors between competing products and services. Circular economy aims to increase economic growth by using natural resources and ecosystems in a more effective way with the aim of maintaining products, components and materials at their highest utility and value at all times. More effective use of materials enables the creation of more value both by cost savings and by developing new markets or by developing existing ones. Reduced acquisition of resources is a driver for innovation for sustainable use of materials, components and products as well as new business models. This chapter introduces methods and tools to assess and reduce environmental impacts, and improve resource efficiency and sustainability management. Life cycle thinking forms one of the basic principles of sustainable development, and Life Cycle Assessment (LCA) is the leading method for assessing the potential environmental impacts of a product, process or service throughout its life cycle (ISO 14040-44). Other methods based on life cycle thinking are also introduced. LCA focusing on the contribution of a product or service to global warming uses methods for Carbon Footprint measurement and facilitates the tracking of greenhouse gas (GHG) emissions (ISO 14067). Water footprint is a tool that assesses the magnitude of potential water-specific environmental impacts of water use associated with a product, process or organisation. It aims at describing the impact of water utilization on humans and ecosystems due to changes in water quality and quantity (ISO 14046 Environmental management—Water footprint—Principles, requirements and guidelines 2014). The concept of

T. Pajula (✉) · K. Behm · S. Vatanen · E. Saarivuori
VTT Technical Research Centre of Finland Ltd., Espoo, Finland
e-mail: tiina.pajula@vtt.fi

K. Behm
e-mail: katri.behm@vtt.fi

S. Vatanen
e-mail: saija.vatanen@vtt.fi

E. Saarivuori
e-mail: elina.saarivuori@vtt.fi



S.N. Grösser et al. (eds.), *Dynamics of Long-Life Assets*,
DOI 10.1007/978-3-319-45438-2_6

handprint has recently been introduced to measure and communicate the positive changes of actions and the beneficial impacts created within the life cycle of products, services, processes, companies, organizations or individuals. A handprint of a product can be created either by preventing or avoiding negative impacts (footprints), or by creating positive benefits. When adopting the circular economy way of thinking, companies need these tools and methods to ensure resource efficiency, cost cuts and improvements in their environmental performance which provide them with more earning opportunities. Fundamental changes throughout the value chain, from product design and production processes to new business models and consumption patterns, support this trend.

**Keywords** Life cycle assessment · Carbon footprint · Water footprint · Carbon handprint · Sustainability

## 1 Introduction

The interaction between industry and the natural environment is strong. The climate change and other environmental impacts related to industrial manufacturing have been discussed and agreed very widely during recent decades, which has increased pressure on industrial businesses (Lieder and Rashid 2016). Scientific understanding of the climate system and its sensitivity to greenhouse gas (GHG) emissions is nowadays more comprehensive than ever before. In December 2015, 195 countries and the European Union reached a global climate deal, agreeing to a long-term goal of limiting the increase in global average temperature to well below 2 °C, which means that countries need to scale up their efforts and actions to reduce emissions (European Commission 2016). This will bring great challenges for industries of different sectors, such as those considered in the Use-It-Wisely (UIW) project (turbines, machinery, space, trucks, shipping and furniture). The existence of environmental regulations has been a considerable influence on some of these companies.

In addition to the environmental considerations, the companies also face another challenge, since resources are becoming scarcer and the competition for their acquisition harder (Lieder and Rashid 2016). Earth Overshoot Day is the annual marker of when we begin living beyond our means in a given year (Global footprint network 2015, www.overshootday.org). Although only an approximate estimate of time and resource trends, Earth Overshoot Day is as close as science can get to measuring the gap between our demand for ecological resources and services, and how much the planet can provide. Our demand for renewable ecological resources and the services they provide is now equivalent to that of more than 1.5 Earths. The unsustainable use of resources brings challenges to resource supply and price, since the increasing requirements for resources cannot be met everywhere (Lieder and Rashid 2016). The changing markets require quick responses from the industry, requiring green growth and a resource-efficient economy.

Environmental topics have a direct effect on humans, but industry is also closely related to social aspects via employment and customer experiences related to the industrial products. Economic competence and growth bring new jobs to the market and thus create well-being, and satisfying customer experiences boosts the demand for products. Thus these three components—economic, environmental and social aspects of sustainability—create a positive circle supporting one another and can all be interlinked, managed and measured with a toolkit of various sustainability indicators.

The UIW-project aims to find solutions enabling rapid response to changing markets, business environments and customer needs. Sustainability methods and indicators presented in this article can help companies to achieve these goals by providing tools for managing and improving the sustainability performance of the manufacturing industry and its products. They can be used in finding new and improved business opportunities by e.g. increasing the efficiency of practices, and reducing waste streams both in the companies' own processes and elsewhere in the value chain. They can be applied in any industrial sector and for products as well as for services.

The methods presented in this chapter are based on life cycle thinking. It is a prerequisite to understand "the bigger picture", i.e. all the requirements and impacts that relate to the value chain of a product. Life cycle assessment (LCA) considers all materials and energy aspects during the entire supply chain, including raw material and fuel acquisition, different manufacturing and conversion processes, the use and consumption of the product and finally recycling or disposal. Together with life cycle thinking, circular economy emphasizes the sustainable use of resources by reducing, reusing and recycling materials and energy as much as possible (Yuan et al. 2006). Life cycle thinking and circular economy are presented in Sect. 2. These approaches ensure minimization of the overall environmental impacts and help avoid shifting the potential burden between different life cycle stages or individual production units or material and energy.

Section 3 introduces LCA, which is a method for assessing the environmental impacts created during the life cycle of a product. LCA can be used for identifying opportunities to improve the environmental performance of products; informing customers, stakeholders and other interest groups of environmental impacts from different stages of the life cycle; and marketing purposes in the forms of e.g. eco-labelling or environmental product declaration (EPD) (Tukker 2000). Section 4 describes other assessment methods that are based on life cycle thinking. The carbon footprint presented in Sect. 4.1 reflects the impact on climate change during the life cycle of a product. It typically describes the global warming potential within the next 100 years (BSI PAS2050:2011). Water footprint, presented in Sect. 4.2, is a measure of the magnitude of potential, water-specific environmental impacts of water use associated with a product, process or organisation, including both water quality and quantity aspects (ISO 14046 2014). Handprint, presented in Sect. 4.3, is a new concept that focuses on benefits rather than on negative impacts. The positive impacts can occur in the company's own actions or e.g. reduce the customer's footprint via improved product qualities (Shine 2015). Finally, the conclusions are presented in Sect. 5.

## 2 Life Cycle Thinking and Circular Economy

The basic understanding of life cycle methods is that all products and services have a value chain connected to them, that nothing in this world "stands alone", and that all our actions have consequences. Life cycle thinking considers all materials, fuels, energy and water consumed and the possible by-products, emissions and waste created when making, using and/or disposing a specific product. The life cycle begins from raw material extraction and conversion and continues via manufacturing and distribution to use and/or consumption. The life cycle ends with the so-called end-of life stage, including re-use, recycling of materials and energy recovery and/or disposal. In all these life cycle stages, the actions are connected to consequences, e.g. the materials used must be supplied from somewhere, with some energy demand and release of emissions. Resources are consumed and impacts to the environment are created within the life cycle of every product.

The core of life cycle thinking is to avoid shifting the environmental burden (European Commission 2010). This means that minimising impacts at one stage of the life cycle or in one environmental impact category should not cause increasing impacts elsewhere. Very often the value chains are international and the impacts e.g. on climate change have an effect on a global level. For example, saving energy during the use stage might increase the amount of material needed in manufacturing, or increase the energy needed in disposal of a product. Life cycle thinking aims to avoid these kinds of consequences.

The circular economy is based on sustainable use of resources. In a circular economy, the value of products and materials is maintained for as long as possible; waste and resource use are minimised, and resources are kept within the economy when a product has reached the end of its life, to be used again and again to create further value. The "3R" principles—reduce, reuse, and recycle materials and energy —describe different possibilities to practice circular economy (Yuan et al. 2006).

Traditional economic systems tend to be based on a linear "take-make-dispose" production model (Sitra 2015). Products and production are based only on the initial use of the product and recycling is segregated from production. For the circular economy, however, there is a difference between the consumption and use of materials. Consumed materials become waste, but the circular economy aims to reduce waste through the efficient use of materials and other resources. Waste is prevented if products and services were designed for reuse, remanufacture or recycling as secondary materials. The goal is to retain the maximum possible value, related to production and the used materials, within the circular economy (Sitra 2015).

The circulation of products and raw materials can be promoted in the following ways (Sitra 2015):

1. **Maintain**: Build products to last longer without repairs and offer maintenance services to prolong product life cycles, enabling longer use by the same owner.
2. **Reuse/redistribute**: Reuse the product for the same purpose on the resale markets.

3. **Remanufacture**: Plan the product life cycle as several life cycles and resell the product after thorough remanufacture.
4. **Recycle**: Recycle product materials for reuse and design products so that their materials are easy to sort. For biological materials, it would also be important to consider how to ensure the safe and sustainable return of nutrients to the nutrient cycle following their optimal use.
5. **Cascade**: Make use of a material or parts of it in another value chain, when it can no longer be used in the original sector.

The following conceptual diagram (Fig. 1) illustrates in a simplified way the main phases of a circular economy model. The phases are interlinked, as materials can be used in a cascading way, for example when industry exchanges by-products, products are refurbished or remanufactured, or consumers choose product-service systems. The aim is to minimise the resources escaping from the circle so that the system functions in an optimal way (European Commission 2014).

The circular economy seeks to make more efficient use of resources and materials, for the better recycling of their value and raw materials. Reuse and remanufacturing are good examples of the circular economy, since they save much of the energy used in the original production, such as in extraction of resources and further processing.

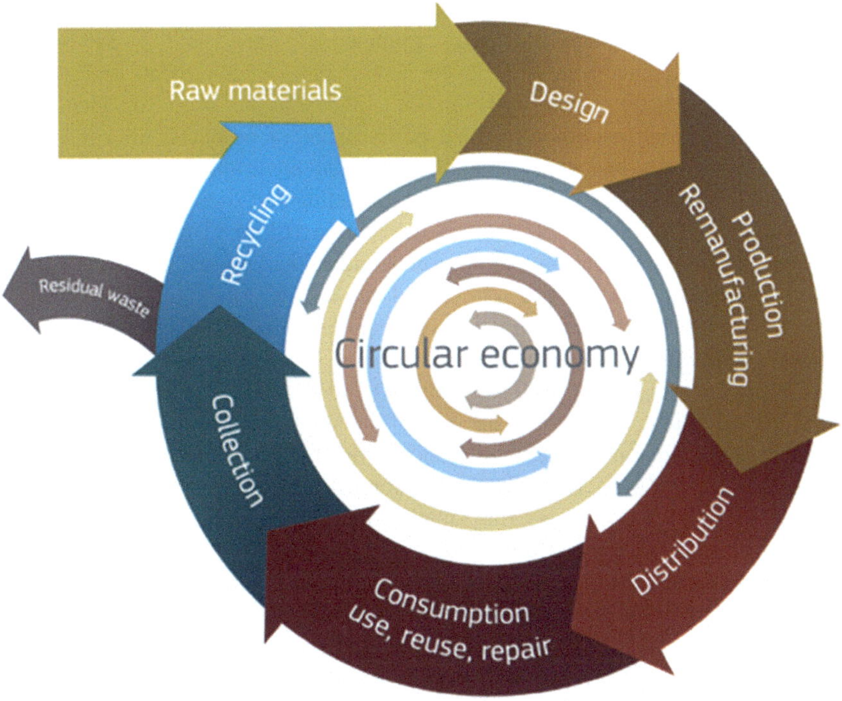


**Fig. 1** Circular economy and life cycle phases (European Commission 2014)

For companies, adopting the circular economy way of thinking would create opportunities to cut costs, grow their businesses and reposition themselves strategically (Sitra 2015). Resource and energy efficiency are precisely the areas where cost savings are most often achieved. Correspondingly, the circular economy provides companies with more earning opportunities for each manufactured product. However, this requires fundamental changes throughout the value chain, from product design and production processes to new business models and consumption patterns (EEA 2/2016). Whereas the order of magnitude of expected benefits of a transition to a circular economy is reasonably well known, the exact numbers in existing studies need to be treated with some caution, owing to methodological and data limitations. Furthermore, benefits will not be evenly distributed: some industrial sectors, businesses, regions and societal groups are likely to lose, while others will benefit. Chapter Sustainable Furniture that Grows with End-Users introduces how Gispen, a major office furniture producer in the Netherlands, has embraced circular economy principles to create new business, extend product life time and improve the adaptability of their products.

## 3 Life Cycle Assessment

The standards of LCA are ISO 14040:2006 "Environmental management—Life cycle assessment—Principles and framework" and ISO 14044:2006 "Environmental management—Life cycle assessment—Requirements and guidelines" (ISO 14040:2006; ISO 14044:2006). LCA can be used for identifying opportunities to improve environmental performance of products; informing customers, stakeholders and other interest groups of environmental impacts from different stages of a product's life cycle; and marketing purposes in the forms of e.g. eco-labelling or environmental product declaration (EPD) (Tukker 2000). LCA makes it possible to reveal mitigation points and critical phases along the supply chain of a product, process or a service and can also assist in strategic risk management, facilitate resource efficiency and optimization of environmental management as well as be a communication tool.

LCA has four stages (ISO 14040:2006; ISO 14044:2006). The first stage is Goal and scope definition. This defines the goal of the study, sets the system boundaries and lists the assumptions needed in the calculation. The second stage, called the life cycle inventory (LCI), includes data collection of input/output data and a balance calculation to all unit processes (the smallest element considered for which input and output data are quantified) in the life cycle. The results are presented as inputs and outputs of the entire system. The results from the inventory can be converted into impacts on the environment in the third stage, the life cycle impact assessment (LCIA). One example of this is the carbon footprint calculation; the emitted GHG from the inventory calculation are converted into global warming potentials in the impact assessment stage (ISO/TS 14067:2013). There are also several other impact categories, e.g. eutrophication, acidification and photochemical ozone formation.

The final stage of LCA is interpretation of the results, which is based on all three previous stages of the assessment and summarises and discusses the conclusions and possible recommendations in accordance with the goal and scope definition. In some cases, the goal of the study can be fulfilled with just the LCI calculation and the interpretation, and the LCIA phase can be omitted. These studies should be called LCI studies and not LCA studies (ISO 14040:2006; ISO 14044:2006). The stages of the LCA are presented in Fig. 2.

When calculating LCA, the life cycle is modelled from unit processes which are connected to each other with material or energy flows (ISO 14040:2006). Each process has inputs and outputs which are connected to previous and subsequent processes from the beginning until the end of the product life cycle.

LCA results are sensitive for the chosen system boundaries and assumptions. One of the most important issues is definition of the system boundaries, i.e. the determination of stages of the product's life cycle that are included in the assessment (Pajula 2014). Full LCA is calculated from "cradle to grave" or "cradle to cradle". In addition to the linear part of the life cycle (production of raw materials and energy, manufacturing of the product, all transportations, use phase, and any disposal of the product or other end-of-life treatment) a "cradle to cradle" study includes recycling, reuse or remanufacturing. "Cradle to cradle" coverage is necessary when evaluating the concept of circular economy. "Cradle to gate" and "cradle to customer" calculations are partial LCAs considering the life cycle until the production of the product only (cradle to gate) or until the product has been transported to the customer (cradle to customer), but excluding the use phase and end-of-life steps. They are mainly used for business to business communication and as a starting point for more comprehensive LCAs.

There are two types of LCA approaches, which have different perspectives and thus can be used for different types of needs (Finnveden et al. 2009).

- Attributional LCA can be seen as a "conventional" approach that focuses on describing the environmentally relevant flows and impacts related to a product or process. It includes the full life cycle as it is, uses allocation (partitioning of the input or output flows of a process between the product system under study and one or more other product systems) and typically uses average data.

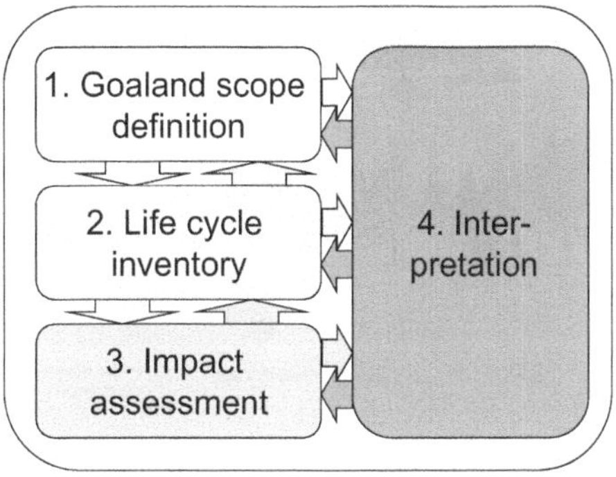


**Fig. 2** The four stages of life cycle assessment

- Consequential LCA studies the change in environmental impacts related to a change in the life cycle. The result describes the consequences of actions within the life cycle, allocation is avoided through system expansion, and marginal data is used in the calculations. The selection between attributional and consequential approach should be made in the goal and scope definition phase depending on the purpose of the study.

The unit processes within the life cycle can be grouped according to the life cycle steps (e.g. energy production, transportation) or other coding (raw material supply, own processes, end-of-life), and the results can be studied transparently (ISO 14040:2006; ISO 14044:2006). Figure 3 shows an example of a life cycle, presenting the life cycle steps of a fibre product and the types of input and output flows related to each life cycle step.

Life cycle inventory (stage 2) calculations require vast amounts of highly specific data. The procedures related to LCI are shown in Fig. 4. Data can be collected from the production sites within the value chain, or it may be obtained from other sources, e.g. public databases. The LCA standards set specific requirements for e.g. time-related coverage, geographical coverage, technology coverage, precision, completeness and representativeness of the data. In addition, uncertainty and sensitivity of assumptions can be demonstrated via sensitivity analyses. The results of LCA are represented per functional unit, which describes the need that is fulfilled with the product or service. Typical functional units are numbers of product (e.g. one car or a book) or amounts of product (e.g. 1000 kg paper or 1 l of diesel).

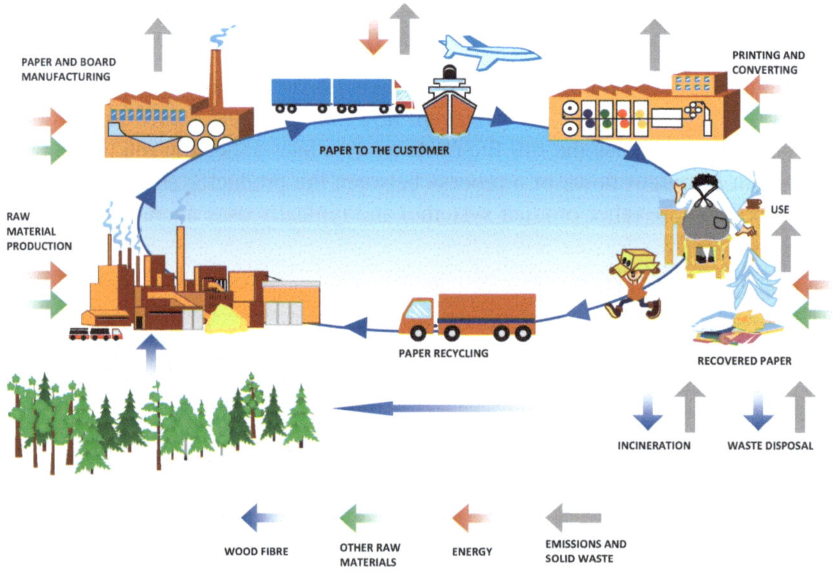


**Fig. 3** Life cycle example of a fibre product

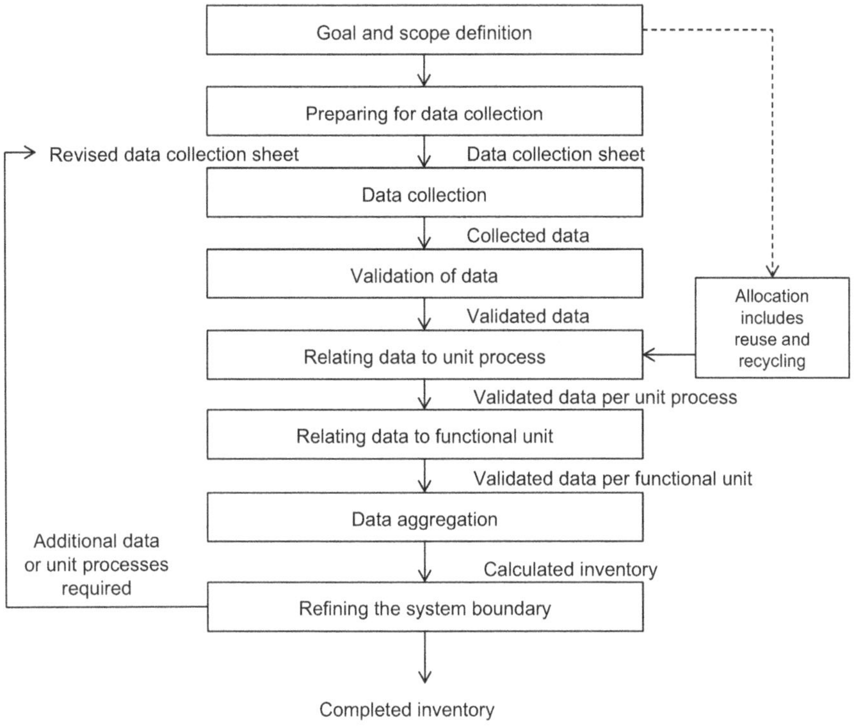


**Fig. 4** The simplified procedures of life cycle inventory (ISO 14044)

Life cycle impact assessment (stage 3) consists of the following steps (ISO 14044:2006):

- **Classification** assigns the LCI results to one or more impact categories, e.g. $CO_2$ influences global warming and $SO_2$ can impact human health and acidification.
- **Characterisation** converts the LCI results into common units and aggregates the results within the same impact category. For example, $CH_4$ and $N_2O$ are converted into $CO_2$ equivalents with emission-specific factors (a global warming potential of 1 kg $CH_4$ equals 25 kg $CO_2$ eq.) and reported as $CO_2$ equivalents.
- **Normalisation** calculates the magnitude of category indicator results relative to some reference information, which should be relevant considering the spatial and temporal scales of the study. The purpose is to better understand the relative magnitude for each indicator result of the product system studied. This step of impact assessment is optional, not mandatory.
- **Grouping** means that the impact categories are sorted and ranked. Grouping can be carried out either by sorting the impact categories on a nominal basis (e.g. by characteristics such as inputs and outputs) or by ranking the impact categories in

a given hierarchy (e.g. high, medium and low priority). Ranking is based on value-choices and the results may be different when calculated by different parties. This step of impact assessment is also optional, not mandatory.
- **Weighting** converts and possibly aggregates indicator results across impact categories using numerical factors based on value-choices. Sensitivity analysis can be used to assess the consequences of value-choices. This step of impact assessment is again optional, not mandatory.

The steps of impact assessment are presented in Fig. 5.

The LCA standards do not determine which impact assessment methods should be used in a study. Selection of the method should be made in the goal and scope definition phase (stage 1), considering the spatial and temporal aspects of the study. Some methods include only characterisation factors but not normalisation or weighting factors, and these methods are called "the midpoint methods". For example, the CML 2001 impact assessment method can be mentioned as a midpoint method (CML 2001), and the ReCiPe method includes both midpoint and endpoint-indicators (ReCiPe 2013). According to Goedkoop et al. (2008), the midpoint indicators without weighting can be seen as more robust and less subjective than the endpoint indicators, but they might be difficult to compare or interpret due to their abstract meaning.

Environmental Product Declaration (EPD) is an LCA-based tool to communicate the environmental performance of a product. It is a document that communicates information about the life cycle environmental impact of products in a transparent and comparable way (ISO 14025 2006). To control the calculations and data collection, detailed requirements for some product group are developed; these are called Product Category Rules (PCR). For example there is a PCR for the assessment of the environmental performance of office furniture (EPD 2012).

"Critical review" is a specifically determined process for LCA that aims to ensure consistency between a LCA study and the guidelines of the ISO standard. This has to be used if the results of the study are to be published and used for a comparative assertion. Critical review can be carried out by an internal or external

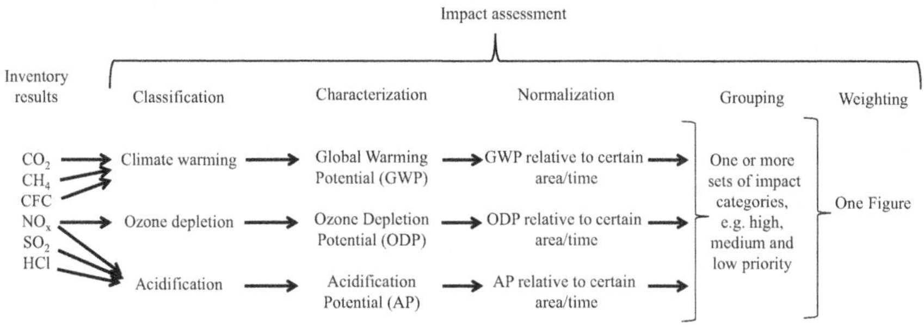


**Fig. 5** Steps of impact assessment

expert, who is independent of the LCA, or by a panel of interested parties. The review statement, comments of the expert and any responses to recommendations by the reviewer(s) must be included in the LCA report (ISO 14040:2006).

Since life cycle assessments are often rather extensive and the amounts of input/output data, flows and factors are very large, several calculation softwares have been developed to help the calculations. They often include generic databases and some impact assessment methodologies which are helpful in calculations. SimaPro, GaBi and SULCA can be mentioned as examples of LCA calculation tools (Loijos 2012; VTT 2014). Naturally, like every method, LCA has its limitations, for example, inclusion of biodiversity, littering, or animal well-being may be difficult in the calculations, due to lacking data and limitations in impact categories (Finkbeiner et al. 2014). Such challenges and limitations must be considered and recognized in the goal and scope definition phase when using the method.

## 4 Other Methods Based on Life Cycle Thinking

In addition to LCA, carbon and water footprint are currently the most commonly applied environmental assessment methods used by companies (Saurat et al. 2014). All three are based on life cycle thinking, but whereas LCA includes all environmental aspects, the others address specific environmental impacts such as climate change (carbon footprint) or water-specific environmental impacts (water footprint). As they were developed to study questions related to a certain specific environmental topic, it is important to be aware that carbon and water footprints cannot be used for an evaluation or communication of overall environmental superiority (ISO/TS 14067:2013; ISO 14046 2014). Extensive LCAs should be conducted first to identify the hotspots related to the production and value chains and to reveal the most critical environmental impacts. This then allows companies to focus later on the most important indicators, such as for example carbon footprint. This is possible especially for companies or sectors working with basically the same raw material, or mix of raw materials, from year to year, such as the aluminium or the forest industry (Saurat et al. 2014).

### *4.1 Carbon Footprint*

Climate change caused by human actions has created a need to measure and mitigate GHG emissions. Carbon footprint is a concept that describes the GHG emissions and removals over the life cycle of a product expressed as $CO_2$ equivalents (BSI PAS2050:2011). The quantification of a carbon footprint is based on the principles of LCA, focusing on the single impact category of climate change

(ISO/TS 14067:2013). Benefits of carbon footprint as an indicator are that it is easily understandable, globally interesting, broadly applicable and easy to implement for different strategies (Alvarez et al. 2016).

The carbon footprint of products standard (ISO/TS 14067:2013) provides principles, requirements and guidelines for the quantification and communication of the carbon footprint of products, including both goods and services. Calculations can also be made at an organisational level (ISO/TR 14069).

The $CO_2$ equivalent of a specific amount of a GHG is calculated as the mass of a given GHG multiplied by its global warming potential factor given by the Intergovernmental Panel on Climate Change (IPCC). The factors describe the global warming potential of emissions over the next 100 years. The $CO_2$ equivalents are then summed up and reported as carbon footprint. The factors for the most important GHG are reported in Table 1. The figures show that the impacts of different GHG on climate change vary so notably per physical unit that they cannot be directly compared and summed together at the inventory result level, but need to be converted into the impact assessment level instead (Fang and Heijungs 2015).

The typical sources of GHG emissions in carbon footprint calculations are energy production and consumption in the forms of electricity, heat or fuels, transportation and selection of raw materials. As in the LCA calculations, the results of footprint calculations can be divided into life cycle steps, and thus the most important emission sources are shown.

Carbon neutrality is a term that has been widely used in public discussion, although its meaning varies rather widely. It can be understood as zero fossil GHG emissions to the atmosphere, or as a situation in which the amount of released emissions is compensated by investing in projects that are mitigating GHG emissions elsewhere. Both perspectives have deficiencies, since the dynamics of biogenic carbon and land use change are very complex in the first approach, and the compensation does not remove the released emissions and their impacts from the atmosphere in the second approach. Thus the background and assumptions of carbon neutrality should always be reported in a high level of detail. The term "Offsetting" refers to compensating for all or for a part of the Carbon Footprint in a process outside the boundary of the product system through prevention, reduction or removal of GHG emissions, but it is not permitted in carbon footprint calculations (ISO/TS 14067 2013).

**Table 1** Conversion factors of the most important greenhouse gases to carbon dioxide equivalents by IPCC (2007)

| | Conversion factor by IPCC |
|---|---|
| Carbon dioxide, $CO_2$ | 1 |
| Methane, $CH_4$ | 25 |
| Dinitrogenmonoxide, $N_2O$ | 298 |

Scientific communities and international guidance agree that all GHG emissions arising from fossil sources shall be included in Carbon Footprint calculations, whereas the inclusion of biogenic carbon involves more complexity and there are different views on its inclusion (Pajula 2014). Carbon sequestration in forests and storage in end products create carbon stocks for years, decades or even centuries and make biogenic carbon time-dependent, whereas fossil emissions can be considered to be released "today" (ISO/TS 14067 2013). On the other hand, although a sustainably managed biomass system is usually carbon neutral or even accumulates carbon over time, the timing difference between the release and sequestration of forest biomass carbon leads to a situation in which part of the carbon remains in the atmosphere until it is fully sequestered back into the growing forest. This leads to the fact that carbon neutral does not equal to climate neutral. The timing difference between emission and sequestration results first in a warming effect, whereas over a long period the accumulation of carbon results in a stock (Pajula 2014). Therefore, the conclusions of a study strongly depend on the forest management system in use and the timeframe chosen for the assessment (see Fig. 6, cf. Helin et al. 2012). The suitability of the different approaches presented in the literature for biomass carbon accounting within LCA was discussed by Helin et al. (2012). As there is no scientifically correct timeframe, it is recommended that different timeframes should be considered. Moreover, the technical specification requires reporting of biogenic emissions separately from fossil-based emissions (ISO/TS 14067 2013).

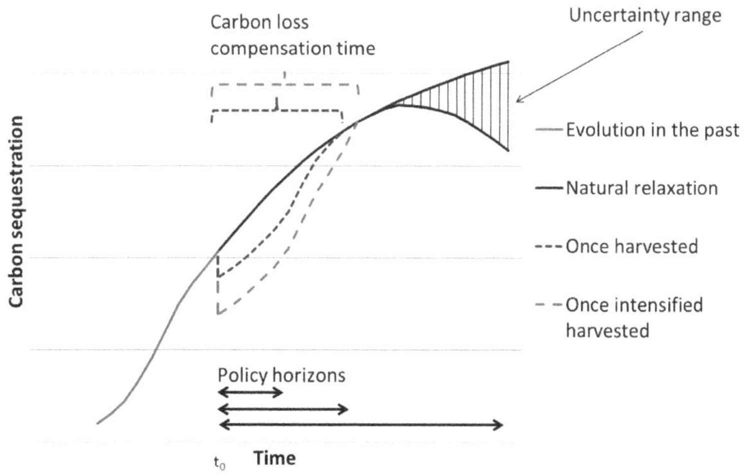


**Fig. 6** A policy horizon considering climate impacts (Helin et al. 2012)

## 4.2 Water Footprint

Water scarcity and the availability of fresh water is a global concern. Numerous industries have become vulnerable to water disruption. In recent years, there has been an increased interest to assess water-related impacts as a basis for improved water management at local, regional, national and global levels. At the company level, it is not only important to ensure a supply of water, control the emissions to water and maintain the local environment, but also to understand the indirect water and the risk factors that occur when operating in different regions. One of the methods developed for this purpose is water footprint.

Water footprint is a tool that assesses the magnitude of potential, water-specific environmental impacts of water use associated with a product, process or organisation. It aims at describing the impact of water use on humans and ecosystems due to changes in water quality and quantity, making it possible to reveal mitigation points along the supply chain. Compared to the product carbon footprint, which describes the global warming potential of a product with a global impact, the water footprint is a local indicator.

Various initiatives by different institutions and organisations have been launched in order to develop analytical tools to measure and assess freshwater use and water footprint (Hoekstra et al. 2011; Ridoutt and Pfister 2010). Due to a great variety of different methods, comparison of the results has been difficult. In order to harmonise the methodology and approach, the ISO Standard 14046 was launched in 2014. The standard provides principles, requirements and guidelines for water footprinting. A water footprint assessment conducted according to this standard is based on a LCA (ISO 14044 2006). An LCA-based water footprint is the fraction of impact assessment results which are related to water resources. Water footprint is a sum of the water footprint of different life cycle stages, identifies potential environmental impacts related to water, includes geographic and temporal dimensions, identifies quantity of water use and changes in water quality, and utilises hydrological knowledge. Because any change in water quality and in water quantity may have an impact on the availability or possible uses of water, it is important to consider both aspects in the impact assessment.

Although the standard sets principles for the water footprint assessment, specific methods or characterization factors that should be used for the assessment are not defined in the standard. Several methods have been developed proposing different inventory schemes and impact assessment models to account for the impacts associated with water consumption or water quality degradation. Different methods use different underlying assumptions, modelling choices, and conceptualisation of what actually constitutes an impact of water use (Boulay et al. 2015; Kounina et al. 2013). Impacts may include contributions to regional water scarcity, depriving other users of access to water, reducing the water flows required to maintain ecosystem functions, or degradation of water quality. No single method is available which comprehensively describes all potential impacts derived from fresh water use

(Kounina et al. 2013). Currently, the WULCA group (Water Use in LCA, UNEP-SETAC Life Cycle Initiative) is coordinating a consensus-building process and leading the scientific work towards achieving a harmonised method to assess water use in LCA (WULCA 2015).

Water footprint can be presented as the result of a stand-alone assessment (in which only potential environmental impacts related to water are assessed) or is a sub-set of results of a larger environmental assessment (e.g. LCA, in which consideration is given to all relevant potential environmental impacts). According to the ISO standard, a qualifier is used if a water footprint study is limited to only certain aspects. A "water scarcity footprint" or "water availability footprint" assesses impacts associated with water use only, and "water eutrophication footprint" assesses the impact related to eutrophication only. If all relevant water use impacts are included (e.g. water use, eutrophication, acidification, freshwater toxicity), the study can be called water footprint (with no qualifier).

Water footprint and environmental risk assessment can be connected to derive complementary data on product water sustainability (Saarivuori et al. 2015). This provides companies with a way to manage and foresee water use related impacts and risks and can be used as a basis for a broader water disclosure, providing a deeper understanding of water risks for the companies themselves, the investors and other stakeholders. In addition, water footprint provides a scientific basis and a framework to assess water efficiency.

## *4.3 Handprints*

The concept of handprint has been introduced rather recently (CEE 2007) to measure and communicate the positive changes of actions and the beneficial impacts, whereas the footprint measures the negative impacts in terms of emissions and resource consumption. Operating an organization always creates some kind of footprint, but it can also bring positive changes and benefits to the surrounding world. The estimate of those impacts of positive change is called a handprint (Norris 2015b).

The handprint concept can be applied to products, processes, companies, organizations or individuals, and it can consider the impacts on environment or society. Handprint evaluates the environmental impact of the object of study in two categories: the delivered benefit and the good the object of study does. Handprint builds on the concept of environmental footprint and the concept is characterized by unlimited potential and a self-reinforcing positive feedback loop (Biemer et al. 2013a, b). This means the handprint can sustain itself once it is established as companies tell others what they learned, and they in turn will tell others. The handprint and the footprint are not exclusive, but rather complementary ways of thinking.

According to Norris (2015a), a handprint of a product can be created either by preventing or avoiding negative impacts (footprints) that would otherwise have occurred, or by creating positive benefits that would not have occurred. The handprint of a company considers the footprint of the company itself, but also the positive changes the company may have on individuals or other companies. This includes changes in the supply chain and also takes into account the changes which are indirectly associated with the goods and services the company produces. Handprints can take place anywhere in the world and they can be composed of multiple small impact reductions.

Handprinting includes three steps (SHINE 2015):

1. Measure and reduce company footprint (e.g. reduce emissions, promote eco-efficiency in supply chains and dematerialize goods and services).
2. Support others to reduce their footprints (e.g. promote innovations in the supply chain which reduce the footprints of goods and services sold to other companies, improve use phase efficiency, educate downstream customers to use products more effectively or efficiently, share innovations with other businesses and increase demand for own products with better performance (smaller footprint) than that of displaced products).
3. Take actions which address the same kind of impact categories on which footprints are causing negative impacts.

Both consequential (change-oriented and focused on the consequences of possible future changes between alternative product systems) and attributional (impacts of a specific product system based on an account of the history of the product) LCA can be applied in these assessments (Norris 2013).

Generating handprints is about actions that increase sustainability and well-being and reduce harmful activities and impacts in terms of both humans and the planet (SHINE 2015). The idea is to create and communicate positive changes in the whole supply chain from factories to customers. Handprints complement the footprint and bring similar quantitative and life cycle based assessment methods to address a much wider scope of action (global focus and multiple impact categories for companies to strive towards being net positive). Handprinting also highlights the positive approach to impact assessment that can motivate and inspire company staffs and promote creativity and new ideas on how to create more positive company impacts. Handprint covers a growing set of sustainability dimensions such as climate change, human health, biodiversity and water consumption. There is also a growing set of social performance indicators. However, better assessment tools and further definition of the handprint calculation method are needed if companies want to communicate the benefits achieved and their high level of clean-tech knowhow.

## 5 Conclusion

The benefits of a transition towards a circular economy in Europe could be considerable, reducing environmental pressures in Europe and beyond and decreasing the continent's high and increasing dependence on imports (EEA 2/2016). Increasingly, this dependence could be a source of vulnerability. Growing global competition for natural resources has contributed to marked increases in price levels and volatility. Circular economy strategies could also result in considerable cost savings, increasing the competitiveness of Europe's industry while delivering net benefits in terms of job opportunities (EEA 2/2016).

Reduction of environmental impacts from industry can be obtained with effective life cycle management. Consideration of the full life cycle of products, i.e. life cycle thinking, is a prerequisite for full understanding of actions and their consequences, both in the industrial manufacturing phase and elsewhere in the life cycle. Sustainability indicators and tools can provide beneficial information for creating new business opportunities and innovation processes. They provide transparent information of resource and energy consumptions in different parts of the life cycle and also reveal the most important sources of emission and waste. Thus they can be of help in finding the most environmentally burdening processes and phases in the life cycle so that the correcting actions can be directed efficiently to those areas with the best improvement potentials. The life cycle management can also reduce the resource requirements and create more economic value by reducing, reusing and recycling of materials and energy while minimising the costs and the amount of waste created.

The methods listed in this article are focused on environmental impacts from the life cycles of products and services. Life cycle thinking, circular economy and LCA provide a starting point for companies to think, act and manage their production sustainably. Although still having some methodological challenges, such as the allocation of burden between products in recycling systems or inclusion of biogenic carbon, they are widely known and accepted approaches that have gained a permanent status as sustainability tools. They can be applied in all sectors, all products and all services in the world, globally and locally, and they can be used for existing processes or in the design and development phases of new products and processes. They provide information for internal use but also for communication and marketing purposes. The tools can bring benefits to the companies and industry sectors and increase the know-how of sustainability both at the producer and consumer level.

The carbon footprint and water footprint are nowadays standardized and accepted methods that are based on LCA. They focus on specific topics of climate change and water quality and scarcity, respectively. They can be useful when studying a specific product, industrial location or company, and they are rather easy to communicate and interpret. However, it is essential to keep in mind that environmental challenges are not limited to carbon or water, and optimizing a single indicator may cause trade-offs with other impacts.

The concept of handprints on the other hand is still being developed. Handprints aim at communicating the benefits of actions, the positive impacts rather than the negative impacts measured by the footprints. Companies should follow the development process of handprints and provide feedback to the concept developers in order to reach the full benefits that can be created. The positive impacts and their communication as handprints can generate competitive advantage for companies, improve the brand and reputation and increase demand for the company's products.

As new circular approaches emerge, frictions between the existing linear system and the new approaches are bound to arise. These may be perceived as threats by some stakeholders, but as opportunities by others. The UIW-project considers six clusters, namely turbines, machinery, space, trucks, shipping and office furniture. They can all apply the life cycle management options reported in this article to support sustainable design of product services and production processes. Life cycle thinking, efficient use and recycling of materials, environmental impact assessment and consideration of positive actions can enhance new business opportunities, improve competitiveness and extend the life cycles of industrial products/services. Good practical examples exist. For example, businesses are already employing or experimenting with new business models such as service- and function-based business models and collaborative consumption. Governments increasingly foster waste prevention, reuse and repair (EEA 2/2016). At the same time more information is needed to inform decision making and combine thinking about environmental, social and economic impacts. Better insight is needed into production structures and functions, consumption dynamics, finance and fiscal mechanisms, as well as triggers and pathways for technological and social innovations.

## References

Alvarez, S., Carballo-Penela, A., Mateo-Mantecón, I., & Rubio, A. (2016). Strengths-weaknesses-opportunities-threats analysis of carbon footprint indicator and derived recommendations. *Journal of Cleaner Production, 121*(2016), 238–247. http://www.sciencedirect.com/science/article/pii/S0959652616001736. Accessed May 09, 2016.

Biemer, J., Dixon, W., & Blackburn, N. (2013a). Our environmental handprint. The good we do. Institute of electrical and electronic engineers. Presented at the 2013 IEEE Conference on Technologies for Sustainability. http://handprint.in/Our_Envir_Handprint_IEEE_Paper_6-14-13wc.pdf. Accessed December 10, 2015.

Biemer, J., Dixon, W., & Blackburn, N. (2013b). Our environmental handprint. The good we do. In *SusTech 2013, Portland Oregon. Conference presentation*. http://sites.ieee.org/sustech/files/2013/12/QL1_BIEMER-Env_Handprint.pdf. Accessed December 10, 2015.

Boulay, A.-M., Motoshita, M., Pfister, S., Bulle, C., Muñoz, I., Franceschini, H., et al. (2015). Analysis of water use impact assessment methods (part A): Evaluation of modelling choices based on a quantitative comparison of scarcity and human health indicators. *International Journal of Life Cycle Assessment, 20*, 139–160. doi:10.1007/s11367-014-0814-2.

BSI PAS 2050:2011. (2011). *Specification for the assessment of the life cycle greenhouse gas emissions of goods and services* (Vol. 38). London, UK: British Standards Institution (BSI). ISBN 978 0 580 71382 8 http://shop.bsigroup.com/upload/shop/download/pas/pas2050.pdf. Accessed March 15, 2016.

CEE. (2007). *The 4th International Conference on Environment Education*. Ahmedabad, India: Centre for Environment Education (CEE). 24–28 November, 2007. http://www.ceeindia.org/tbilisiplus30/. Accessed March 02, 2016.

CML. (2001). *Impact assessment method.*

EEA Report No 2/2016. *Circular economy in Europe, developing the knowledge base.*

EPD. (2012). PCR 2012:19. In *Other furniture, of a kind used in offices and other furniture n.e.c. (Version 1.1).* http://www.environdec.com/en/PCR/Detail/?Pcr=8458&show_login=true&new_user=true. Accessed May 30, 2016.

European Commission. (2010). *Making sustainable consumption and production a reality. A guide for business and policy makers to life cycle thinking and assessment* (Vol. 32). Luxembourg: Publications Office of the European Union. http://ec.europa.eu/environment/pubs/pdf/sustainable.pdf. Accessed May 30, 2016.

European Commission. (2014). Communication from the commission to the European parliament, the council, the European economic and social committee and the committee of the regions. Towards a circular economy: A zero waste programme for Europe. In *COM (2014)* 398 final. 14.

European Commission. (2016). *Climate action. Paris agreement.* http://ec.europa.eu/clima/policies/international/negotiations/paris/index_en.htm. Accessed May 30, 2016.

Fang, K., & Heijungs, R. (2015). Investigating the inventory and characterization aspects of footprinting methods: Lessons for the classification and integration of footprints. *Journal of Cleaner Production, 108*(2015) part A, 1028–1036.

Finkbeiner, M., Ackermann, R., Bach, V., Berger, M., Brankatschk, G., Chang, Y.-J., et al. (2014). Challenges in life cycle assessment: An overview of current gaps and research needs. *Background and future prospects in life cycle assessment* (pp. 207–258). Berlin (DE): Springer.

Finnveden, G., Hauschild, M. Z., Ekvall, T., Guinée, J., Heijungs, R., Hellweg, S., et al. (2009). Recent developments in life cycle assessment. *Journal of Environmental Management, 91*(1), 1–21.

GeSI. (2012). GeSI SMARTer 2020: The role of ICT in driving a sustainable future. In *The Global e-Sustainability Initiative (GeSI).* http://gesi.org/assets/js/lib/tinymce/jscripts/tiny_mce/plugins/ajaxfilemanager/uploaded/SMARTer%202020%20-%20The%20Role%20of%20ICT%20in%20Driving%20a%20Sustainable%20Future%20-%20December%202012.pdf. Accessed March 6, 2016.

Goedkoop, M. J., Heijungs, R., Huijbregts, M., De Schryver. A., Struijs, J., & Van Zelm, R., ReCiPe. (2008). A life cycle impact assessment method which comprises harmonised category indicators at the midpoint and the endpoint level (1st ed.). In *Report I: Characterisation.* January 6, 2009. http://www.lcia-recipe.net. Accessed May 10, 2016.

Helin, T., Sokka, L., Soimakallio, S., Pingoud, K., & Pajula, T. (2012). Approaches for inclusion of forest carbon cycle in life cycle assessment—A review. *GCB Bioenergy, 5,* 475–486. doi:10.1111/gcbb.12016.

Hoekstra, A. Y., Chapagain, A. K., Aldaya, M. M., & Mekonnen, M. M. (2011). *The water footprint assessment manual: Setting the global standard.* London, UK: Earthscan.

ISO 14025. (2006). *Environmental labels and declarations—Type III environmental declarations—Principles and procedures.*

ISO 14040. (2006). *Environmental management, life cycle assessment, principles and framework.*

ISO 14044. (2006). *Environmental management, life cycle assessment, requirements and guidelines.*

ISO 14046. (2014). *Environmental management—Water footprint—Principles, requirements and guidelines.*

ISO/TS 14067. (2013). *Greenhouse gases. Carbon footprint of products. Requirements and guidelines for quantification and communication.*

IPCC. 2007: Climate Change (2007). *The Physical Science Basis*. In S. Solomon, D. Qin, M. Manning, Z. Chen, M. Marquis, K.B. Averyt, M. Tignor and H.L. Miller (Eds.), Contribution of Working Group I to the Fourth Assessment Report of the Intergovernmental Panel on Climate Change (996 pp)Cambridge, United Kingdom, New York, USA: Cambridge University Presshttp://www.ipcc.ch/pdf/assessment-report/ar4/wg1/ar4_wg1_full_report.pdf Accessed April 25, 2016.

Kounina, A., Margni, M., Bayart, J.-B., Boulay, A.-M., Berger, M., Bulle, C., et al. (2013). Review of methods addressing freshwater use in life cycle inventory and impact assessment. *International Journal of Life Cycle Assessment, 18*(3), 707–721.

Lieder, M., & Rashid, A. (2016). Towards circular economy implementation: A comprehensive review in context of manufacturing industry. *Journal of Cleaner Production, 115*(2016), 36–51.

Loijos, A. (2012). *Comparison of best life cycle assessment software*. http://www.linkcycle.com/comparison-of-best-life-cycle-assessment-software/ (online document). Accessed April 27, 2016.

Norris, G. (2013). The new requirement for social leadership: Healing. In S. Groschl (Ed.), *Uncertainty, diversity and the common good: Changing norms and new leadership paradigms*. London: Gower Publishing. http://www.chgeharvard.org/sites/default/files/resources/Introduction%20to%20Handprinting.pdf. Accessed November 24, 2015.

Norris, G. (2015a). *Handprint-based netpositive assessment*. Sustainability and Health Initiative for NetPositive Enterprise (SHINE), Center for Health and the Global Environment, Harvard T. H. Chan School of Public Health. http://www.chgeharvard.org/sites/default/files/resources/Handprint-Based%20NetPositive%20Assessment.pdf. Accessed January 4, 2016.

Norris, G. (2015b). *A one-page introduction to handprints*. Sustainability and Health Initiative for NetPositive Enterprise (SHINE), Center for Health and the Global Environment, Harvard T.H. Chan School of Public Health. Accessed December 2, 2015.

Outotec. (2015). *Maximizing our handprint—Outotec's sustainability report 2014*. http://www.outotec.com/ImageVaultFiles/id_1598/cf_2/27729-Outotec_Sustainability_aukeemittain.PDF. Accessed December 21, 2015.

Pajula, T. (2014). Life cycle assessment of biobased materials. In *Handbook of green materials* (Vol. 5, Chapter 17). World Scientific.

ReCiPe. (2013). *Methodology for life cycle impact assessment (LCIA)*.

Ridoutt, B. G., & Pfister, S. (2010). A revised approach to water footprinting to make transparent the impacts of consumption and production on global freshwater scarcity. *Global Environmental Change, 20,* 113–120.

Saarivuori, E., Molarius, R., Wessman-Jääskeläinen, H., & Poussa, L. (2015). Connecting water footprint and water risk assessment: Case packaging board. *Water Practice & Technology, 10* (1), 229–241.

Saurat, M., Ritthoff, M., Pihkola, H., Alonso, A., & Lopez, A. (2015). Description of current industry practice and definition of the evaluation criteria. In *EU SAMT, D2.1*.

Shine. (2015). *Shine summit 2015. Innovating for netpositive impact. Summary Report*. Sustainability and Health Initiative for NetPositive Enterprise (SHINE), Center for Health and the Global Environment, Harvard T.H. Chan School of Public Health. http://chgeharvard.org/sites/default/files/resources/Shine%20Paper%202015%20for%20web-update.pdf. Accessed December 2, 2015.

Sitra. (2015). The opportunities of a circular economy for Finland. In *Sitra studies 100* (72 pp). ISBN 978-951-563-938-7.

Tukker, A. (2000). Life cycle assessment as a tool in environmental impact assessment. *Environmental Impact Assessment Review, 20*(4), 435–456.

VTT. (2014). *SULCA—Sustainability tool for ecodesign, footprints & LCA*. SimulationStore, VTT Technical Research Centre of Finland LTD. https://www.simulationstore.com/sulca (online document). Accessed April 27, 2016.

WULCA. (2015). Consensual method development: Preliminary recommendation—AWaRe v1.1. In *Water use in LCA (WULCA) working group*. Accessible from: http://www.wulca-waterlca.org/. Accessed November 10, 2015.

Yuan, Z., Bi, J., & Moriguichi, Y. (2006). The circular economy: A new development strategy in China. *Journal of Industrial Ecology, 10*(1–2), 4–8.

# Virtual Reality and 3D Imaging to Support Collaborative Decision Making for Adaptation of Long-Life Assets

**Jonatan Berglund, Liang Gong, Hanna Sundström and Björn Johansson**

**Abstract** European companies of today are involved in many stages of the product life cycle. There is a trend towards the view of their business as a complex industrial product-service system (IPSS). This trend shifts the business focus from a traditional product oriented one to a function oriented one. With the function in focus, the seller shares the responsibility of for example maintenance of the product with the buyer. As such IPSS has been praised for supporting sustainable practices. This shift in focus also promotes longevity of products and promotes life extending work on the products such as adaptation and upgrades. Staying competitive requires continuous improvement of manufacturing and services to make them more flexible and adaptive to external changes. The adaptation itself needs to be performed efficiently without disrupting ongoing operations and needs to result in an acceptable after state. Virtual planning models are a key technology to enable planning and design of the future operations in parallel with ongoing operations. This chapter presents an approach to combine digitalization and virtual reality (VR) technologies to create the next generation of virtual planning environments. Through incorporating digitalization techniques such as 3D imaging, the models will reach a new level of fidelity and realism which in turn makes them accessible to a broader group of users and stakeholders. Increased accessibility facilitates a collaborative decision making process that invites and includes cross functional teams. Through such involvement, a broader range of experts, their skills, operational and tacit knowledge can be leveraged towards better planning of the upgrade process. This promises to shorten

J. Berglund (✉) · L. Gong · H. Sundström · B. Johansson
Product and Production Development, Chalmers University of Technology, Gothenburg, Sweden
e-mail: jonatan.berglund@chalmers.se

L. Gong
e-mail: liang.gong@chalmers.se

H. Sundström
e-mail: suhanna@student.chalmers.se

B. Johansson
e-mail: bjorn.johansson@chalmers.se



S.N. Grösser et al. (eds.), *Dynamics of Long-Life Assets*,
DOI 10.1007/978-3-319-45438-2_7

lead times and reduce risk in upgrade projects through better expert involvements and shorter iterations in the upgrade planning cycle.

**Keywords** 3D-imaging · Collaboration · Cross-functional teams · Manufacturing · Virtual reality · Simulation and modelling · Layout planning

## 1 Introduction

As stated by Reyes in Chapter "The Use-It-Wisely (UIW) Approach", European industries face significant challenges due to global off-shoring, rapid business environment change, shrinking investment budgets, and environmental pressures (Schuh et al. 2011). Companies that work with high investment assets need strategies and tools to enable prolonged service life and even upgrades of functionality and capability over time. A high investment asset is typically something that has an expected return on investment of several years or even decades. Their operation typically includes providing some sort of service to internal or external customers. There are plenty of examples, of which most can be modelled as product-service system (IPSS). These systems consist of Products, the physical objects that are being offered, and Services, the additional business proposals that are offered alongside the physical products (Mont 2002). Also included in this system view, and generally thought to add to the complexity are the different actors whom interact directly and indirectly with the system. A common denominator for the IPSS system discussed in this project are that their physical objects or entities exists to provide some service or function over a reasonably long time span. These systems tend to be complex in nature and are often operated on and interacted with by a large number of actors. The involved actors tend to each have their own individual needs and requirements to fulfil their tasks and purposes, making the alignment towards a common, holistically optimal, goal complex. There are many examples of the type of system mentioned here and the clusters in the Use-it-Wisely project represents a subset of them, for example a communications satellite put into orbit, a passenger vessel for shipping industry, or an automotive production facility.

This chapter explores the use of VR and 3D-imaging technologies to support such upgrades to extend the operational phase of the IPSS system's life cycle. Specific emphasis is put on how they can support maintenance, upgrade design, and implementation processes. VR technology provides immersive access to life sized models so that they can be experienced by end users in the design and upgrade stage. These users can be domain experts within the use-phase of the system that traditionally are not deeply involved in the development phase. When it comes to upgrades of existing systems, 3D-imaging provides generation of realistic, accurate, and up-to-date data which can be used as visualization models of the current system configuration. By merging these models with the upgrade design suggestions, realistic scenarios for the future system state can be created. Finally, by using VR technologies these future state models, can be reviewed by domain-experts early on in the design phase, giving them a tool to voice their needs and requirements in a concrete way. The involvement of cross functional actor teams is key in achieving a holistic approach to problem solving and ideation (Ahn et al. 2005; Song et al. 1998).

Section 2 gives an overview of the state of the art in the involved technologies. Section 3 presents the combined 3D-imaging and VR tool that was developed during the Use-it-Wisely project. Finally, Sect. 4 concludes the findings and lessons learned from this endeavour.

## 2 Generic Overview of Manufacturing Adaptation Processes and Related Technologies

The entry of computers to utilize digital tools and technologies in the design process has enabled an ever faster rate for developing products and services. It gives the ability for many engineers and other actors to work in parallel and share/replicate/combine their results across an infinite number of recipients with little added effort. Additions and changes to the design can be added without the need for any physical remake or rebuild of the objects. Thus, a development process can easily be shared between many actors and engineers in order to gain feedback and improvement suggestions. As the technology has been refined, more and more of the development and planning work can be conducted without the existence of any physical prototype. This reduces the need for multiple time consuming iterations of prototype building for verification and validation. This section serves as an introduction to VR, digital models, and 3D imaging in the upgrade design process.

### *2.1 Virtual Reality*

Most commonly known as virtual reality (VR), the technology is sometimes also referred to as telepresence (Steuer 1992). The use of *presence* in the wording alludes to the experience of being present in a virtual environment. In other words, the mind is perceiving another surrounding and setting than the actual physical environment that surrounds the body. Steuer phrases the following definition:

> A "virtual reality" is defined as a real or simulated environment in which a perceiver experiences telepresence
>
> VR Definition, Steuer (1992)

Steuer presents a framework of dimensions to appraise the quality of a given VR technology. These dimensions are Vividness and Interactivity. Vividness signifies the breadth of the VR medium, e.g. how many senses that are exposed to stimuli, it also encompasses the depth of the stimuli, meaning the level of detail. Interactivity denotes the user's possibility to navigate or affect the VR environment as well as how realistic that interaction is in terms of responsiveness and accuracy of movements (Steuer 1992).

> In general, the term virtual reality refers to an immersive, interactive experience generated by a computer.
>
> VR Definition, Pimentel and Texeira (1993)

Many authors have tried to characterize and measure VR-technologies in terms of quality of the experience. It is however an evasive quality and hard to measure in a quantifiable way. Gibson for example, who predates Steuer (1992) also talks of presence as the measure (Gibson 1979). In present terminology the word immersion is often used to describe the quality of the VR system. Immersion denotes the quality of the sensory stimuli that the system can produce. It is related, although not directly, to the subjective feeling of "presence" of the user. And logically the greater the quality of the stimuli the higher the probability of achieving a high level of presences. Though as many researchers in the field note, presence is highly dependent on the individual and some individuals have a greater capacity to experience presence. Presence can be interpreted as a measure of the extent the user forgets the medium to the benefit of the experience of "being" in the virtual environment (Loomis 1992).

Other examples are Loeffler and Anderson (1994) who defines VR as "a 3D virtual environment that is rendered in real time and controlled by the users". Similarly to Steuer (1992) framework, they include the concepts of vividness (rendering) and interactivity (control). Although it seems to be narrower in the sense that is only alludes to visual stimuli, rendering.

There have been attempts at quantifying both immersion and presence. Pausch attempted to quantify the level of immersion in VR (Pausch et al. 1997). Meehan et al. (2002) wrote about physiological measurements of the VR experience by invoking stress on the subjects to grasp the fleeing aspect of presence. The measurements extended to heart rate, skin conductance, and skin temperature to determine the reaction of the test subject and compare to the change in the same measures given a real situation. The logic being that if our reactions to a situation in the virtual environment mimics our reaction to the same situation in the real world, our mind and bodies are likely believing the experience. The topic is debated from a different standpoint by Bowman, who poses the question of how much immersion

**Table 1** Strengths and weaknesses of 3D visualisation (Teyseyre and Campo 2009)

| Strengths | Weaknesses |
|---|---|
| Greater information density | Intensive computation |
| Integration of local and global view | More complex implementation |
| Composition of multiples 2D views in a single 3D view | User adaptation of 3D metaphors and special devices |
| Facilitates perception of the human visual system | More difficult for users to understand 3D space and perform actions in it |
| Familiarity, realism and real world representations | Occlusion |

is enough (Bowman and McMahan 2007)? This is indeed an interesting aspect when the purpose is to facilitate work tasks in industry. Then the immersion lacks value in and off itself, as opposed to VR for entertainment purposes where elevated immersion is sought fiercely. Teyseyre and Campo (2009) represent one attempt at identifying the strengths and weaknesses of 3D visualisation in general. Their findings are shown in Table 1.

A general motivation to start using VR is the limitation of what information that can be presented by traditional 2D models (Smith and Heim 1999). The same authors argue that VR makes it possible to make accurate and rapid decisions through the added understanding an immersive virtual environment gives (Smith and Heim 1999). Another strong driver for using VR technology compared to traditional visualization of 3D models is the increased spatial understanding that is achieved in a VR environment. This helps experts in domains outside of 3D modelling and CAD to reach the same, or close to the same, understanding of the models as the model developer.

## 2.2 *Virtual Reality in the Adaptation Process*

Systems are designed to fulfil some function or need for its users. Inevitably, the needs or functions will be altered over time and to keep fulfilling these the system has to adapt accordingly. This adaptation can be achieved either by improving the system's current functions or by adding new functionality to the system. When designing and implementing adaptions to existing systems it is desirable to plan and foresee any problems that might arise. This is performed to ensure good quality and reduce the implementation time to minimize the downtime of the system during the adaptation process (Groover 2007).

Being able to access models through VR access to models through VR for better understanding. Access to models from various places. Many companies are operating on a global scale and need to be able to align and synchronize their efforts in a good and efficient way. This paper is concerned with upgrades and changes to long life assets. And specifically how to plan and optimize these upgrades in a collaborative way. Making use of the many various skills and expertise that exists in a company. In a sense, all the perceivable actors that interact with the IPSS should contribute their aspects and needs. This will support a holistic approach to the upgrade and reduces the risk of costly oversights of some critical functions and or aspects.

The idea of utilizing VR to support engineering work in general has been around for a long time. Deitz wrote in 1995 about the state of VR as a mechanical engineering tool. Concluding that it has the potential to "reduce the number of prototypes and engineering change orders", "simplify design reviews", and "make it easier for non-engineers to contribute to the design process" (Deitz 1995). High investment assets in nature tend to have many users and actors, many of them non-engineers, which interact with it over time. Often there are non-engineers that hold valuable tacit knowledge about the operational phase and maintenance of the asset. Enabling these individuals to be a part of the upgrade process can potentially bring about a more optimal end result that considers more aspects than a pure engineering solution would have.

This section goes into detail about VR, how it can be indexed and described and also gives an example of the various technological solutions that exist today. Further it introduces the field of 3D imaging as a technology to provide accurate digital 3D surface representations of the already existing assets. Discussing how these can be used in the ideation and design phase for an upgrade.

## 2.3 VR Technologies Related to Adaptation of Manufacturing Processes

For the purpose of the research presented in this project the focus has been on 3D environments for planning and evaluation of upcoming changes and updates of high investment assets. For this purpose, only a limited range of the field of VR have been considered and investigated. The aspects which have been included are visual stimuli, movements/locomotion in the environment and to some extent the ability to interact with modelled objects inside the virtual environment. For the extent of the implementation VR is defined as a 3D environment, rendered in real time over which the user has some ability to navigate around in *and interact with*. Apart from the addition in italics, this is much like the VR definition given by Loeffler and Anderson in 1994 (Loeffler and Anderson 1994).

When applying this scope to the field of VR there are a number of technologies to choose from. A number of them will be presented here. The selection is based on the purpose of using VR which is to give users a feeling of being inside the virtual environment, using some sort of display to visualise the 3D virtual environment (Korves and Loftus 1999).

Menck et al. lists general technologies used to create VR interfaces (Menck et al. 2012): computer display, head-mounted display (HMD), power wall, and cave automatic virtual environment (CAVE).

The above technologies are different on a number of factors, they present different inherent capabilities and their cost is also varying significantly, which can steer or limit the choice depending on application. From a capability perspective many aspects can be identified. For example; multi-user functionality, stereoscopic, real world blending or strictly virtual, passive or (inter-)active, and representing the user's (or users') body to name a few. These capabilities will have an effect on the level of immersion, or presence, that the users experience, as well as on their ability to conduct meaningful tasks in the virtual environment.

Computer displays are the most basic and least costly technology to interface the VE, movement is controlled using i.e. a 3D manipulator or even a regular computer mouse (Menck et al. 2012). Many users can be present at the same screen but all of them will share the same viewpoint and in that sense be passengers to the main user, who controls the navigation.

Head Mounted Displays (HMDs) have been available for a long time, but only recently have they developed to a level that can be said to trick the human sense well enough for an immersive experience. The HMD is worn over the head of the user and shuts out any external visual stimuli (Duarte Filho et al. 2010). Therefore the users is not inherently able to experience his or her body. There are ways of recording and rendering the users body and posture back into the virtual environment in real time, examples of this is using VR-gloves or 3D imaging sensors to map the user's movements (Korves and Loftus 2000; Mohler et al. 2010). If such a mapping is performed, this solution can support multi-user environments through rendering the mapped body and postures or an avatar representation of them back into the virtual environment (Beck et al. 2013; Mohler et al. 2010). Recent technological development has significantly decreased the cost of HMDs, compared to when the cited work was written. In Chapter "Sustainable Furniture That Grows with End-Users" of this publication, Berglund et al. state that the industrial partner views HMDs as a scalable solution based on the price point.

Power walls is an umbrella term for large scale back projected displays. Traditionally they are limited to one point of view in the same ways as a computer screen, although there are recent examples where this limitation is overcome through a combination of DLP projectors and shutter glasses (Kulik et al. 2011). The size of the power walls make them suitable for team collaboration, and allow for both active participants and passive spectators in a larger forum (Waurzyniak 2002).

CAVEs are room environments, encapsulated by screens on all (or at least three) sides. The user stands in-between the walls and the virtual environment is projected around him or her. Tracking equipment is used to manipulate the environment to constantly match the user's viewpoint (Duarte Filho et al. 2010).

With the many available solutions, choosing the appropriate one can be a challenging task. Mohler et al. (2010) stresses the importance of body representation in VR environments and shows that it significantly improves the users' ability to accurately judge scale and distance. Kulik et al. (2011) focus on the importance of multi-user support in VR, and even state that it isn't VR if it isn't multi-user. Figure 1 depicts an abstraction of the main components of a VR system, incorporating 3D imaging data.

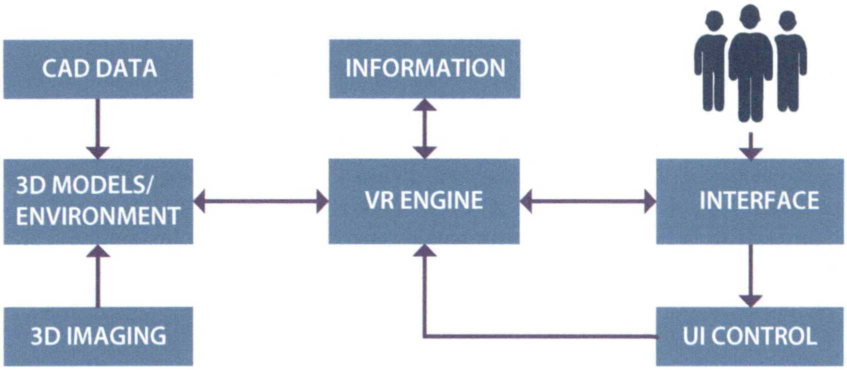


**Fig. 1** Schematic view of VR decision support tool

## 2.4 3D Imaging Introduction

Capturing spatial data can be done in a number of ways, utilizing a wide variety of technologies. These technologies are often categorised into tactile and non-tactile (Varady et al. 1997). The tactile technologies require physical contact with the measurand, while the non-tactile rely on some non-matter media for its interaction with the measurand. While tactile technologies are often characterized by high precision they also risk influencing the measured object during the measurement process. The inherent requirement of movement tends to result in comparably low data capture speeds and a limitation on the maximum measurement area. These drawbacks can create difficulties if the measurand has a soft or yielding surface, or is above a certain size (Varady et al. 1997). An industrially proven and frequently used type of tactile sensor is the Coordinate Measurement Machine, CMM. CMM machines rely on linear movement axes which provide three degrees of freedom coupled with a three degrees of freedom probe unit. The CMM machines are programmable and can be used as an integrated resource in a production facilities to conduct in-line automated measurement of products.

Non-tactile technologies exist in a number of forms, a common classification is active and passive non-contact sensors. Passive sensors make use of the existing background signals of the environment, such as light or noise. Active sensors emit some signal into the environment as uses the returned light to map the surroundings. 3D imaging describes the field of capturing spatial data from the real world and making it available in a digital form. It exists on a wide range of scales and for different purposes. The digital spatial data can be stored for future reference, or be processed in order to perform analysis for some specific purpose. The ASTM Subcommittee E57.01 on Terminology for 3D Imaging Systems defines 3D imaging systems as (ASTM 2011):

> A non-contact measurement instrument used to produce a 3D representation (e.g., point cloud) of an object or a site.

The term point cloud in the definition deserves a closer explanation. It comes from the descriptive of the contents of the data set which results from a 3D imaging procedure. The data is recorded as coordinates in space, points. The cloud word can be traced to the fact that these coordinate points are unstructured (however, it can be argued that their sampling pattern is directly a function of the operational parameters of the 3D imaging technology). The cloud can also be said to relate to the lack of any semantic information. The point cloud generated from a measurement holds no explicit concept of objects or relationships between points. These may of course be generated or extracted using various techniques in a post processing or analysis operation.

There exists a multitude of measurement instruments for 3D imaging. Several surveys of the field exists to classify and describe available technologies for 3D imaging (Besl 1988; Beraldin et al. 2007). Figure 2 presents one such classification.

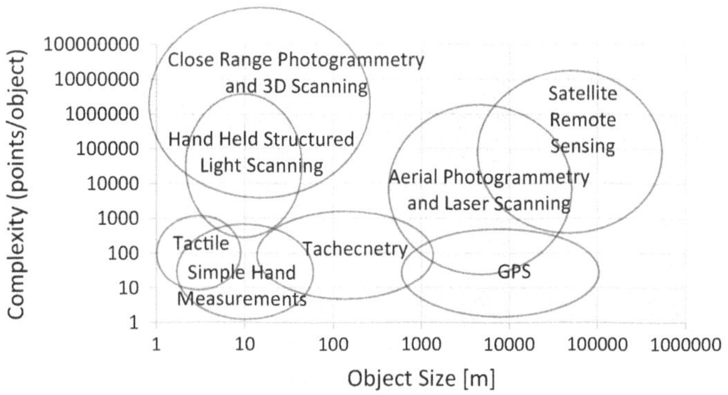


**Fig. 2** Spatial measurements and their suitability/application on scales of size and complexity (adopted from Boeheler 2005)

Since the publication of the work which Fig. 2 is based on the circles have widened considerably. An example is photogrammetry which now is capable of capturing the surface geometry of very complex and feature rich objects.

3D imaging is a technology used in many different fields. Some examples are given in Fig. 3a–d. The chosen technology is relate to both scale of the objects and data requirements connected to the intended use of the data.

- Figure 3a. Product scan: 3D imaging is used in product development to digitalize for example clay models of product designs. It is also used in production to validate process output, e.g. shape conformance of the physical product to the designed tolerances (Yao 2005; Druve 2016)
- Figure 3b. 3D Scanning of a building: Building Information Model (BIM) is an Area within facilities management that has adopted 3D imaging. For one, to map the existing facility more accurately, and for the other to improve visualization quality and real world likeness.
- Figure 3c. 3D imaging of Cultural heritage: For cultural heritage preservation and archaeology 3D imaging has made a significant impact in the last decade, by digitalizing artefacts in a museum or entire structures or archaeologic dig out sites they can be share among researchers or the public at a global scale. Archaeology students from anywhere in the world can access a digital version of the Cheops pyramid or the Incan temples of Machu Pichu (Pieraccini et al. 2001; Sansoni et al. 2009).
- Figure 3d. Pipe fitting to 3D imaging data: The use of reverse engineering of for example pipes is used frequently in process industry. Typically it provides current state in-data for installing new pipes and retrofitting old pipes (Olofsson et al. 2013).

Fig. 3 3D Imaging

### 2.4.1 3D Laser Scanning the Adaptation Process

3D Laser Scanning or Laser Detection and Ranging (LADAR) is a non-contact measurement technology for the capture of spatial data. The technology was developed within the field of surveying as a tool to map terrain as well as to control and monitor the status of construction jobs. Today it is used in a variety of fields, such as building and construction, tunnel and road surveying, robot cell verification, layout planning and Forensics (Slob and Hack 2004; Sansoni et al. 2009).

When capturing spatial data with a 3D scanner it is placed within the environment of interest; this could be an existing production system or a brown field factory floor. A laser pulse or beam is emitted around the environment and its reflection is logged as time of flight or phase shift. Today's scanners are able to map their entire field of view up to eighty meters away in a matter of minutes with a positional accuracy of a few millimetres (FARO 2012). The resulting data is often referred to as a point cloud, a set of coordinates in 3D space, typically numbering in the tens of millions. The latest 3D scanners are equipped with RGB sensors to add colour information to the coordinates to further improve visualization.

As this technology matures and the tools and methods to capture data become more readily available there is also a steadily growing range of software tools to support its usage (Bi and Wang 2010). These tools are either specialized to visualize and edit point cloud data sets or they are extensions of traditional CAD and simulation tools able to integrate point cloud data. The integration into existing tools enables hybrid modelling environments where CAD and point cloud data are used in parallel. Using hybrid models, CAD models of new machine equipment or products in design stage are put into existing scanned production facilities for planning verification.

Some challenges with this new technology are the size of the data and issues with interoperability between vendor-specific data formats. However, several research efforts strive to automate translation of point cloud data into CAD surfaces to reduce data size (Bosche and Haas 2008; Huang et al. 2009). And new optimized software for visualization of this data format is being developed (Rusu and Cousins 2011). Ongoing standards activities are developing neutral processing algorithms and data formats to ensure repeatability, traceability and interoperability when working with point cloud data (ASTM 2011).

Figure 4 gives an insight to the nature of 3D laser-scanning data by zooming further in on the model until the individual measurement points are distinguishable. The measurement points are singular positions plotted in a 3D space, thus the software visualising them gives them an arbitrary pixel size.

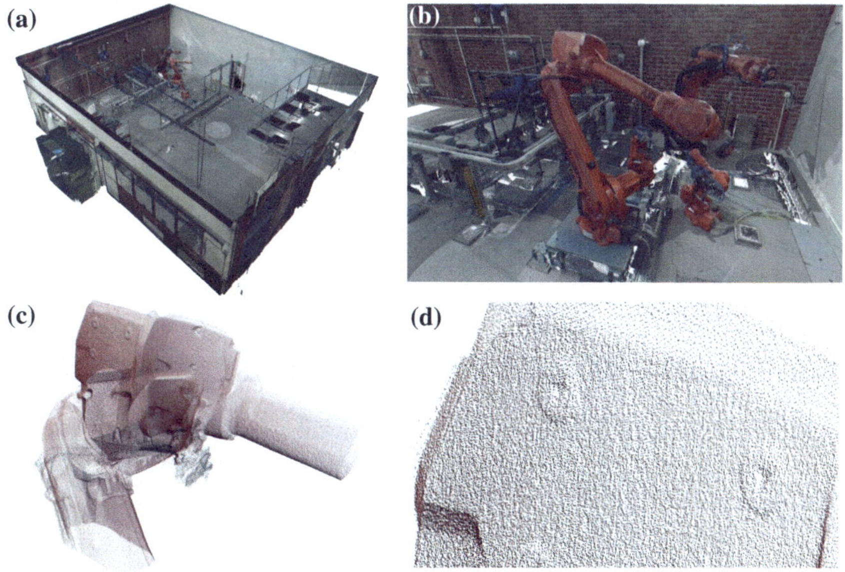


**Fig. 4** 3D laser-scanning

# 3 3D-Imaging and Virtual Reality Integration Tool

This section describes the tool for integration of 3D imaging and virtual reality which was developed during the UIW-project. The description includes how the tool should be applied, the expected result of such an application, along with the detected limitations.

## *3.1 Introduction*

The purpose of the tool is to understand reality through improved models and model exploration/visualization. 3D imaging provides a realistic and accurate model of current conditions. Virtual models can be accessed and viewed simultaneously by several actors regardless of physical location. The model also acts as a basis for modelling and designing additions and upgrades. Both for visualizing them and designing the physical properties of interfaces and connections to the existing system. Give users an experience that closely imitates physical presence and the possibilities associated with that. Shareable over time and space. Support collaborative work in cross functional, de-centralised project teams. Current status of the development can be found in Chapter "Sustainable Furniture That Grows with End-Users" *Adaptation of high variant automotive production system: A collaborative approach supported by 3D-imaging*.

## *3.2 The Application Process*

Following Fig. 5 from left to right including the feedback loop from the stakeholders/actors, the following steps can be identified:

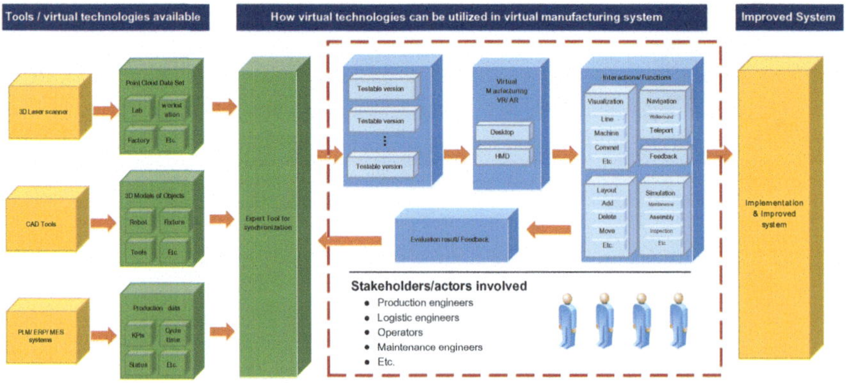


**Fig. 5** Planning process using virtual technologies for manufacturing process change

### 3.2.1 Tools/Virtual Technologies Available as Input Data for Expert Tool

Mapping the current state of the system with PLM/MRP/MES system as well as using existing 3D imaging technologies in combination with CAD. Choice of technologies and approach is determined by the objectives as well as the size and complexity of the related objects in the system.

### 3.2.2 Expert Tool

The currently available input data are then reengineered by bringing in design documents and files for solutions into the environment and combined to reach an upgraded system with new functionalities using the expert development tool/programming solutions. It usually involves process like post-processing of scanned data and make it compatible for the expert tool, preparation of CAD data that are needed and integration with PLM/MES system if necessary.

### 3.2.3 Preparation of Testable Solutions

Based on the requirements of proposed upgrade, testable solutions can be developed using the current state data that has been collected. Thus the potential solutions can be prepared by topic expert using the expert tool and ready for evaluation by all the actors that involved in the upgraded process.

### 3.2.4 Accessing Solutions via Different Interfaces

The prepared testable solutions can be accessed in different platforms such as desktop web browser, desktop projector as well as virtual reality HMD. Dependent on the purpose and context of the to-be-evaluated solutions, one can choose either platform or any combination of the available platforms to facilitate better understanding of the proposed solutions.

### 3.2.5 Interactions/Functionalities

Various interactions are available to support the evaluation of the proposed solutions, from the basic functions like visualization and navigation through walking around and teleporting, to the more advanced functions such as new layout planning and feedback.

#### 3.2.6 Evaluation Result/Feedback

All the involved actors give feedback based on their knowledge and experiences. The feedback is then gathered and reviewed to decide whether approve or disapprove proposed solutions. The synchronized feedback and improvements suggestions are sent upstream in the process to the designer who consolidates the information and if needed creates a new and improved set of solutions.

#### 3.2.7 Concept Refinement

Based on the feedback, an iteration could be appropriate where the expert tool synchronisation needs to have another round of improvements of functionality/visual aids/interfacing or similar. The improved design is then prepared for a new iteration with the involved actors to re-evaluate.

#### 3.2.8 Implementation

Once the concept and solution gives substantial benefits for the actors/stakeholders and they are satisfied with the tool, the next step will be to move towards implementation for structured use in real world cases incorporated in everyday work for the actors and stakeholders who has the most beneficial use out of the developed tool.

### *3.3 Expected Results from Application of the Tool*

The results expected from the application of this tool are many. In response to the challenge faced by modern day industries, this tool is expected to reduce the lead times for design iterations of projects. These iterations can otherwise be costly, but with the use of VR technology early on in the process it is also expected that problems with designs can be found earlier, thereby costing less. Being able to update designs quickly is also believed to reduce the risk of faulty input data into other processes, as there will be a lower occurrence of outdated models. As VR immerses people in an alternate reality (Ref) it is further expected that project members will be able to gain an improved understanding of the project and the design, thus to improve the overall quality of the system and products. Further, this could be used as a marketing tool, where designs can be communicated in an un-ambiguous manner. Last but not least, with the realistic virtual environment available, it not only widen the accessibility of the data to all the involved actors, but can also reduce the travel substantially, which used to be needed. Therefore, further reduction in cost and improvement in sustainability are expected.

## 3.4 *Limitations of the Tool*

The technologies involved are currently available as off the shelf products and can be purchased or rented as needed with little foreseeable issues. However, the usage and operation of these tools are not yet commonplace. There is a need for expert users both for collecting 3D imaging data and for processing and preparing the data into a testable model that can be evaluated by topic experts. The navigation and usage of VR tools is also requiring a fairly experienced user to reach its full efficiency potential. The medium should not take over and be the central part of the experience when viewing a model, or else the results from the actual study will be muddled and potentially biased.

### 3.4.1 3D Imaging Related Limitations

Furthermore, a 3D imaging data set is not the same as having a full-fledged CAD representation. The 3D imaging data, given present day conditions, does not include any semantic information and has to be interpreted by a human to make sense. This reduces the amount of automated analysis and optimisation that is possible. This extends into the scope of the data in the case of 3D imaging, there is often not any data captured from the internal structure of the objects. Unless two technologies are combined together the user will have to choose to capture either surface geometries or internal geometries thorough, e.g. X-ray or CT scanning.

It is also clear that despite the added realism that comes from integrating 3D imaging and VR, it is not equivalent of a physical model. The strength of 3D imaging comes from the possibility of capturing reality, what is actually there, rather than what was meant to be there, i.e. a design model. However, this does not eliminate the risk of having bad data, or outdated data. Perhaps it can even strengthen the risk in some cases through its high fidelity and accuracy. It is necessary to put processes in place that verify the relevance of the datasets. This could be related to i.e. date of capture, scope of capture etc.

While there is a lot of ongoing research into the reverse engineering process and its automation, there is currently no complete way of creating CAD data from the 3D imaging data sets. This means that the process of converting data into use in conventional design software could be costly. So perhaps organizations have to take a step and broaden their design software to incorporate 3D imaging data capabilities also. This is a business decision to take in concur-rent times, but might soon be unnecessary as more and more software developers are integrating 3D imaging data support into their existing software.

Another issue that might occur is the fact that some 3D imaging technologies require the object of capture to be completely at rest during the data capture procedure. In some cases, this is either infeasible, or associated with a large cost.

### 3.4.2 VR Related Limitations

The current technology for viewing and interacting with VR environments is perhaps not sufficiently powerful to smoothly handle large scale 3D imaging models. If the users experience lag tendencies or other graphical glitches it might take away from the immersion and involvement during design review sessions. For instance, some observers may experience motion sickness as a result of these limitations (Kennedy et al. 1993). Ergonomic related issues is another obstacle that needs more studies and improvements as current VR solutions are not suitable for prolong usage (Cobb et al. 1999). There is also currently a limitation on physical interaction between persons, while immersed in VR. At the moment, it is not possible for multi-user interaction, something that may prove crucial when evaluating models for feasibility or suitability.

## 4 Conclusion

Promising technological developments have recently been made in the field of 3D imaging and VR technologies. These developments facilitate both wide spread (all employees through web interfaces) as well as detailed modelling and analysis for interesting questions and decisions for several actors (maintenance, designers, operators etc.). UIW is one of the first applied science projects in direct collaboration with industry to actually make use of these new opportunities. Acceptance/diffusion if innovation in this field is not a fast process since the actual beneficiary initially does not even know that the technology exists, and yet is the methodologies and work tasks to be performed to be tailor-made and then standardised, which is some the work UIW provides to European industry. This project provides an insight into the use of these technologies in a wide range of industries and services.

## References

Ahn, H. J., Lee, H. J., Cho, K., & Park, S. J. (2005). Utilizing knowledge context in virtual collaborative work. *Decision Support Systems, 39*(4), 563–582.

ASTM E2544-11a. (2011). *Standard terminology for three-dimensional (3D) imaging systems*. West Conshohocken, PA: ASTM International. www.astm.org

ASTM Standard E2807. (2011). *Standard specification for 3D imaging data exchange, Version 1.0*. West Conshohocken, PA: ASTM International. www.astm.org

Beck, S., Kunert, A., Kulik, A., & Froehlich, B. (2013). Immersive group-to-group telepresence. *IEEE Transactions on Visualization and Computer Graphics, 19*(4), 616–625.

Beraldin, J. A., Blais, F., El-Hakim, S., Cournoyer, L., & Picard, M. (2007). Traceable 3D imaging metrology: Evaluation of 3D digitizing techniques in a dedicated metrology laboratory. In *Proceedings of the 8th Conference on Optical 3-D Measurement Techniques*.

Besl, P. J. (1988). Active, optical range imaging sensors. *Machine Vision and Applications, 1*(2), 127–152.

Bi, Z. M., & Wang, L. (2010). Advances in 3D data acquisition and processing for industrial applications. *Robotics and Computer-Integrated Manufacturing, 26*(5), 403–413.

Boeheler, W. (2005). Comparison of 3D laser scanning and other 3D measurement techniques. In *Recording, modeling and visualization of cultural heritage* (pp. 89–100). London: Taylor and Francis.

Bosche, F., & Haas, C. T. (2008). Automated retrieval of 3D CAD model objects in construction range images. *Automation in Construction, 17*(4), 499–512.

Bowman, Doug A., & McMahan, Ryan P. (2007). Virtual reality: how much immersion is enough? *Computer, 40*(7), 36–43.

Cobb, S. V., Nichols, S., Ramsey, A., & Wilson, J. R. (1999). Virtual reality-induced symptoms and effects (VRISE). *Presence, 8*(2), 169–186.

Deitz, D. (1995). Real engineering in a virtual world. *Mechanical Engineering, 117*(7), 78.

Druve, J. (2016). *Reverse engineering av 3D-skannad data*. Göteborg: Chalmers University of Technology.

Duarte Filho, N., Costa Botelho, S., Tyska Carvalho, J., Botelho Marcos, P., Queiroz Maffei, R., Remor Oliveira, R., et al. (2010). An immersive and collaborative visualization system for digital manufacturing. *The International Journal of Advanced Manufacturing Technology, 50*(9–12), 1253–1261.

FARO Technologies. (2012). FARO Technologies Inc.

Gibson, J. J. (1979). *The ecological approach to visual perception*. Boston: Houghton Mifflin.

Groover, M. P. (2007). *Automation, production systems, and computer-integrated manufacturing*. Prentice Hall Press.

Huang, H., Li, D., Zhang, H., Ascher, U., & Cohen-Or, D. (2009). Consolidation of unorganized point clouds for surface reconstruction. In *ACM Transactions on Graphics (TOG)* (Vol. 28, No. 5, p. 176). ACM.

Kennedy, R. S., Lane, N. E., Berbaum, K. S., & Lilienthal, M. G. (1993). Simulator sickness questionnaire: An enhanced method for quantifying simulator sickness. *The International Journal of Aviation Psychology, 3*(3), 203–220.

Korves, B., & Loftus, M. (1999). The application of immersive virtual reality for layout planning of manufacturing cells. *Proceedings of the Institution of Mechanical Engineers, Part B: Journal of Engineering Manufacture, 213*(1), 87–91.

Korves, B., & Loftus, M. (2000). Designing an immersive virtual reality interface for layout planning. *Journal of Materials Processing Technology, 107*(1), 425–430.

Kulik, A., Kunert, A., Beck, S., Reichel, R., Blach, R., Zink, A., et al. (2011). C1x6: A stereoscopic six-user display for co-located collaboration in shared virtual environments. *ACM Transactions on Graphics (TOG), 30*(6), 188.

Loeffler, C., & Anderson, T. (1994). *The virtual reality casebook*. Wiley.

Loomis, J. M. (1992). Distal attribution and presence. *Presence: Teleoperators and Virtual Environments, 1*, 113–119.

Meehan, M., Insko, B., Whitton, M., & Brooks Jr, F. P. (2002). Physiological measures of presence in stressful virtual environments. *ACM Transactions on Graphics (TOG), 21*(3), 645–652.

Menck, N., Yang, X., Weidig, C., Winkes, P., Lauer, C., Hagen, H., et al. (2012). Collaborative factory planning in virtual reality. In *45th CIRP Conference on Manufacturing Systems* (pp. 317–322).

Mohler, B. J., Creem-Regehr, S. H., Thompson, W. B., & Bülthoff, H. H. (2010). The effect of viewing a self-avatar on distance judgments in an HMD-based virtual environment. *Presence: Teleoperators and Virtual Environments, 19*(3), 230–242.

Mont, O. (2002). Clarifying the concept of product–service system. *Journal of Cleaner Production, 10*, 237–245. doi:10.1016/S0959-6526(01)00039-7

Neugebauer, R., Purzel, F., Schreiber, A., & Riedel, T. (2011). Virtual reality-aided planning for energy-autonomous factories. In *Proceedings of the 9th IEEE International Conference on Industrial Informatics (INDIN)* (pp. 250–254).

Olofsson, A., Sandgren, M., Stridsberg, L., & Westberg, R. (2013). *Användning av punktmolnsdata från laserskanning vid redigering, simulering och reverse engineering i en digital produktionsmiljö*. Göteborg: Chalmers University of Technology.

Pausch, R., Dennis, P., & Williams, G. (1997). Quantifying immersion in virtual reality. In *Proceedings of the 24th Annual Conference on Computer Graphics and Interactive Techniques* (pp. 13–18). ACM Press/Addison-Wesley Publishing Co.

Pieraccini, M., Guidi, G., & Atzeni, C. (2001). 3D digitizing of cultural heritage. *Journal of Cultural Heritage, 2*(1), 63–70.

Pimentel, K., & Texeira, K. (1993). *Virtual reality: Through the new looking-glass*. Intel/Windcrest McGraw Hill.

Rusu, R. B., & Cousins, S. (2011). 3d is here: Point cloud library (pcl). In *Proceedings of the IEEE International Conference on Robotics and Automation (ICRA)* (pp. 1–4). IEEE.

Sansoni, G., Trebeschi, M., & Docchio, F. (2009). State-of-the-art and applications of 3D imaging sensors in industry, cultural heritage, medicine, and criminal investigation. *Sensors, 9*(1), 568–601.

Schuh, G., Aghassi, S., Orilski, S., Schubert, J., Bambach, M., Freudenberg, R., et al. (2011). Technology roadmapping for the production in high-wage countries. *Production Engineering, 5*(4), 463–473.

Slob, S., & Hack, R. (2004). 3D terrestrial laser scanning as a new field measurement and monitoring technique. In *Engineering geology for infrastructure planning in Europe* (pp. 179–189). Berlin, Heidelberg: Springer.

Smith, R. P., & Heim, J. A. (1999). Virtual facility layout design: The value of an interactive three-dimensional representation. *International Journal of Production Research, 37*(17), 3941–3957.

Song, X. M., Thieme, R. J., & Xie, J. (1998). The impact of cross-functional joint involvement across product development stages: An exploratory study. *Journal of Product Innovation Management, 15*(4), 289–303.

Steuer, J. (1992). Defining virtual reality: Dimensions determining telepresence. *Journal of Communication, 42*(4), 73–93.

Teyseyre, A., & Campo, R. M. (2009). An overview of 3D software visualization. *IEEE TVCG, 15*(1), 87–105.

Varady, T., Martin, R. R., & Cox, J. (1997). Reverse engineering of geometric models—An introduction. *Computer Aided Design, 29*(4), 255–268.

Waurzyniak, P. (2002). Going virtual. *Manufacturing Engineering, 128*(5), 77–88.

Yao, A. W. L. (2005). Applications of 3D scanning and reverse engineering techniques for quality control of quick response products. *The International Journal of Advanced Manufacturing Technology, 26*(11–12), 1284–1288.

# Operator-Oriented Product and Production Process Design for Manufacturing, Maintenance and Upgrading

**Gu van Rhijn and Tim Bosch**

**Abstract** The nature of production in the manufacturing industry is changing, and companies face large challenges. Customers expect fast delivery times, proven sustainability, flexibility, and frequent product upgrades. To stay competitive and manage rapid technological demands, a parallel, iterative and interactive development approach for product and process design is required. Closed-loop systems will increase future customer demand for easy upgrading. This requires highly modular and operator-friendly product designs. Because the complexity, variety and unpredictability of products and production tasks will increase, information and support systems for operators are crucial elements. Human factor engineering methodologies are essential to take full advantage of new technologies that support operators in all stages of the product life cycle. Methods and tools that could support companies in improving product, process, and workstation design are presented, and directions for future research and tool development are discussed.

**Keywords** Production process design · Modular product design · Task allocation · Human factors · Operator support

## 1 Introduction

### *1.1 Industrial Challenges: Changing Market Demands*

The nature of production in the manufacturing industry is changing, and companies face large challenges (Fig. 1). Market demands are less predictable, and the time-to-market is shorter. Manufacturers of components, modules and products need to have flexible and efficient production processes to achieve fast delivery of

---

G. van Rhijn (✉) · T. Bosch
TNO, PO Box 3005 2301 DA, Leiden, The Netherlands
e-mail: Gu.vanrhijn@tno.nl

T. Bosch
e-mail: tim.bosch@tno.nl

 
S.N. Grösser et al. (eds.), *Dynamics of Long-Life Assets*,
DOI 10.1007/978-3-319-45438-2_8

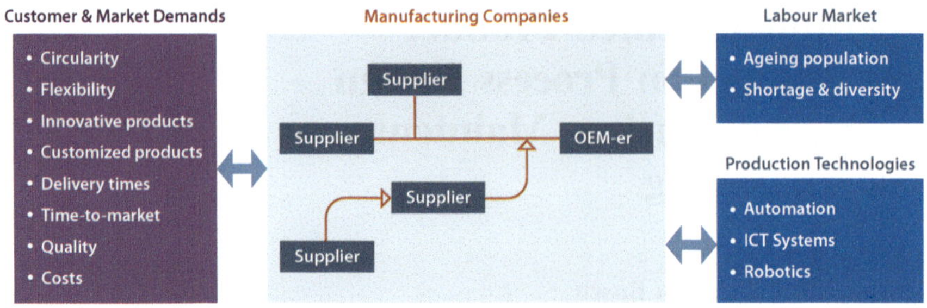


**Fig. 1** The nature of production in the manufacturing industry is changing

high quality products within the context of variation in volume demands, a large mix of customer-specific product types, and short product life cycles (Van Rhijn et al. 2005; Aberdeen Group 2014). Costs, efficiency, quality, and innovative designs are still important drivers of manufacturing companies. However, driven by market demands, short product development lead times, proven sustainability, flexibility, and frequent product upgrades will become crucial elements to guarantee competitiveness, especially for manufacturers of high-investment products.

Customers have become more environmentally conscious. The global market for environmentally friendly goods and services was estimated at €4.2 trillion in 2011 (Department for Business, Innovations and Skills 2012). Manufacturers of capital-intensive products must prove the circularity of product designs and manufacturing processes (e.g., end-of-life options, sources of materials, sustainability of suppliers). Currently, most products are designed, produced, and sold to the end-user. In case of malfunction, outdatedness, or the changing requirements of the end-user, a new product is designed, produced, and sold. The circular economy concept aims to keep products, components, and materials at their highest utility and value at all times (e.g., Ellen MacArthur Foundation 2013; McKinsey 2011). In contrast to a traditional linear economy, i.e., 'take-make-dispose', the circular economy emphasizes the reusability of products and raw materials as a starting point and minimizes waste in the entire industrial and ecological system. To take full advantage, it is important for manufacturers to consider that products and components can be given a second or longer life during the design process (e.g., by 'design for disassembly, for maintenance, for reuse or remanufacturing') (Bastein et al. 2013). These challenges are topics in the Use-it-Wisely (UIW) project and objectives: Design of adaptable and upgradable products and flexible (re)manufacturing processes are crucial aspects for realizing a circular economy-based business. Remanufacturing is commonly defined as "a series of manufacturing steps acting on an end-of-life part or product to return it to like-new or better performance, with warranty to match" (APPSRG 2014).

## *1.2 Industrial Challenges: Changing Production Technologies*

Simultaneously, production technology is developing quickly (Fig. 1). The trend of automation, including the use of robots and process control systems, has a large impact on manufacturing. Manufacturing companies (OEM = Original Equipment Manufacturers and their suppliers) face large challenges from the market, from a technology perspective and from the labour market. 'Full automation' however, is often not feasible in assembly work, specifically in the combination of low volumes, high product mix, and high product complexity. Therefore, hybrid production systems in which humans and robots or robot systems are intuitively collaborating are needed. A recent report on the current state of the Dutch manufacturing industry stated (Smart Industry, Dutch Industry fit for the future 2014): *"Humans are still the most flexible production factor. As smaller batches require higher investments and specialised production systems, especially in assembly, robots and robot systems will often mainly assist production personnel and remove some routine work"*. Finally, the labour market in itself is facing challenges; the proportion of older employees is rising due to the ageing population (Bloom et al. 2015). Skilled, flexible and motivated employees have become crucial 'assets' for companies to handle all those challenges.

The challenges and developments from the market (customers), technology breakthroughs and the labour market are summarized in Fig. 1. How can the manufacturing industry respond to the challenges of changing customer demands and technological developments?

In the UIW-project, tools and methods are developed and demonstrated to support companies in designing both adaptable and upgradable products and flexible (re)manufacturing processes. Closed-loop systems will necessitate the allowance of easy upgrading for future customer demands. This requires highly modular and operator-friendly product designs. To take full advantage of new technologies that support operators in all stages of the product life cycle, human factor engineering methodologies are essential. The starting point is a parallel, iterative and shared development approach for products and flexible (i.e., agile) production processes (Fig. 2). Part of this approach is two essential elements or 'building blocks':

1. **A highly modular and operator-friendly product design** that allows easy upgrading, remanufacturing and maintenance of new, refurbished and remanufactured products;
2. **Flexible, human-centred production processes** using new technologies, including workstations with correct levels of automation and assistive technology that support operators.

During the product and process development stage, manufacturing companies must pay attention to these two elements in an interconnected way because they are closely linked and thereby affect each other. Figure 2 shows an overview of the

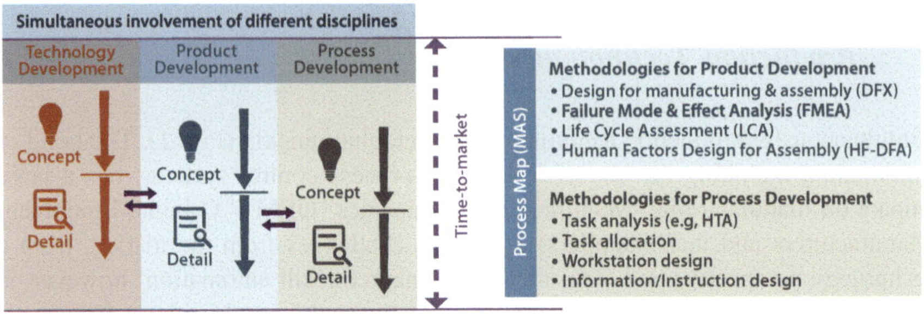


**Fig. 2** A parallel, iterative and interactive development approach for modular product and flexible human-centred production processes supported by different methodologies

methodologies available to support parallel and early-stage development of modular products and flexible, human-centred production processes within the scope of high-investment products in the manufacturing industry. In this chapter, we will describe solutions to manage the above-mentioned company challenges and provide more detail about specific methodologies. More specifically, Sect. 2 describes methodologies for parallel and early stage development of products and production processes. Section 3 describes methodologies for (dis)assembly, maintainability, upgrading and modular product design. Sect. 4 presents the application of assistive technologies to support operators in a proper manner.

## 2 Methodologies to Support Parallel Product and Process Design

To support companies in developing new products, (re)manufacturing and upgrading processes, which are sustainable throughout the complete life cycle, several engineering and human factor methodologies are described in the literature. These methodologies may be used during the development of new technologies, products and production processes (see Fig. 2).

Examples of methodologies used during the *product design phase* are:

- Design for manufacturing and assembly guidelines (DFA or HF-DFA) to create cost-effective and operator assembly-friendly products (e.g., Boothroyd et al. 2001; Village et al. 2014). These methods and guidelines are used in the application developed in "UIW: the Circular Economy Design Framework" (see Bosch, Chapter "Sustainable Furniture That Grows With End-Users" this book).
- Failure Mode and Effect Analysis (FMEA) to detect problems that might arise from malfunctions in a product (Ginn et al. 1998; Stamatis 2003).
- Sustainable design methodologies such as Life Cycle Assessment (LCA, Pajula, Chapter "Managing The Life Cycle to Reduce Environmental Impacts" this book).

*Process development* tools and upgrading methodologies include:

- The lean manufacturing philosophy in the pursuit of reducing wasteful activities and improving productivity and profits (Genaidy and Karwowski 2007).
- Lead time reduction by minimization of Manufacturing Critical-path Time in Quick Response Manufacturing (QRM, Suri 1998) and Demand Flow Factory (Pot and Van Rhijn 2012).
- Value Stream Mapping (VSM) or Business Process Modelling (BPM) tools to build a common perspective of a process workflow (e.g., Rother and Shook 2003).
- To allocate tasks at a process or workstation level, task or function allocation methodologies (e.g., Fasth and Stahre 2010; Challenger et al. 2013) are commonly used.

In practice, these methods are mostly used independently by different company disciplines (i.e., departments) for improving product or process design. Development of products and processes in parallel and with strong interaction between different disciplines: sales, product design, process engineering, and operations (operators from manufacturing, assembly, maintenance) is essential for manufacturing but even more for maintenance, upgrading, and remanufacturing processes. Furthermore, parallelizing technology, product and development (as shown in Fig. 2), shortens time-to-market (first time right) and can save a significant amount of money (Quan and Jianmin 2006). To involve different disciplines in the product and process design phase, a participatory approach can be used.

This participatory approach (e.g., Vink et al. 2008; Hirschheim 1989; Muller and Kuhn 1993) is a well-known and successful approach that could lead to quality improvements and a reduction in costs (European Foundation for the Improvement of Living and Working Conditions 1999). It is a design procedure in which the relevant company stakeholders (e.g., management) and the end-users, i.e., the operators in a production process, engineers developing new products or maintenance personnel out in the field, have the opportunity to influence the content of the design target (Bouckenooghe and Devos 2007; Lines 2004). If situations are complex, a stepwise and iterative approach could be adopted so that the anticipated effort and success could be reviewed. This interactive process, which is essential for gaining support and momentum to push innovation forward, improves communication, manages expectations and uses different perspectives and skills in the design process. The involvement of different disciplines and employees enables a potential resource for creativity and innovation (e.g., Shalley et al. 2004). Moreover, the involvement of employees from different disciplines is also essential because of the great deal of knowledge and experience they have about the products, production processes and problems that occur on a day-to-day basis. For instance, some or all of the workers who will work at a forthcoming plant could take part in a number of design sessions during different design stages (van Rhijn et al. 2014).

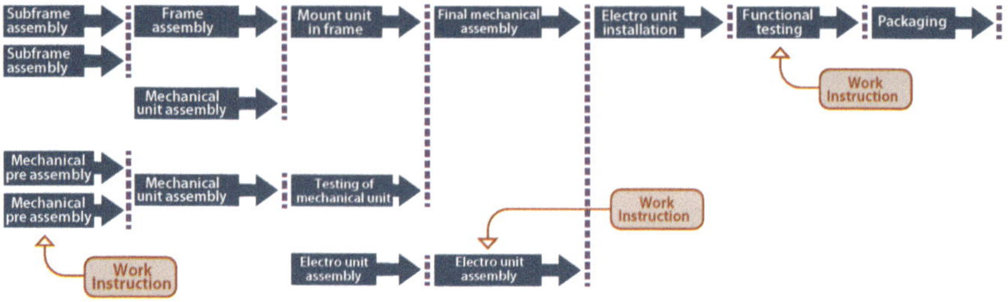


**Fig. 3** Schematic representation of the process steps of the (sub) assembly and testing stages with the MAS

A starting point in this (participatory and parallel product and process development) approach is creating a commonly shared process map using the 'MAS' methodology. MAS stands for '*Montage Afloop Schema'* (assembly process flow, Van Rhijn et al. 2014). MAS is a graphical representation of successive and parallel process stages, including timing estimates (Fig. 3). This assembly process map can be used to streamline product and process design. It can also be used to compare alternatives to the product structure and the structure of the assembly process in terms of their effects on lead times and productivity both at the concept level and during the detailed development stage.

This focus on process structuring during product design is crucial for delivering components and final products in small series in a short time, as well as for getting it right the first time.

In the product design phase, the MAS instrument is used in the following steps:

- Creating a working group of different disciplines: product designers, engineers, process engineers, and operators from assembly and service/installation. The concept or detailed product design is demonstrated to the working group using drawings, sketches or 3D models. The product structure will be clarified, and a distinction will be made between product modules and individual components.
- The successive and parallel assembly process steps that are needed to assemble the total product from beginning to end are drawn on paper. The starting point is the main process. Every arrow represents a process step, consisting of several (manual) actions/tasks. Just above the arrow, the main process step and the respective part/module is described. Next, to assembly of mounting steps, other essential steps such as handling, turning, rotating or testing the component or modules are described.
- After that, parallel processes in the workflow are listed, which can be assembly or test processes of subassemblies of product modules. These parallel processes are connected to the main process at the stages in which these subassemblies are needed.
- The graphical representation of assembly, testing, packaging activities is then be discussed and adapted by the working group. For instance, the sequence of process steps may be shifted.

- The time needed for every process step is estimated and added to the process scheme. Based on this, lead times and productivity can be evaluated. Other elements, if relevant, may be added as well. For instance, specific equipment and tools needed or special conditions (cleanroom levels).
- The next step is a review of the product design for modularity and operator-centred design (see Sect. 3), including modular product structure, exchangeability of modules and parts, reducing the number and variety of parts, simplicity of handling and positioning, and physical load during handling and mounting. Based on this analysis, both the product design and the assembly process scheme may be adapted and improved.

This process work flow method can be used to analyse assembly processes and other primary processes such as maintenance, service, and installation. The advantage of the MAS method is that product and process engineers are forced to think about possible scenarios for the assembly process. Which steps are needed to assemble the product and in which order? Moreover, the modular product structure becomes clear; which units or modules can be distinguished? Modularity results in opportunities for parallel structures that provide a means for shortening the lead time of the total process considerably. Modularity can also contribute to a higher level of service and upgrading, as service-sensitive parts can be exchanged quickly. Another advantage is the involvement of different disciplines in creating the assembly process scheme within the working group. Every company discipline and its specific knowledge is involved and used to improve the process and product design. At an early stage of design, everybody agrees on design decisions, which helps prevent costly modifications later. However, using MAS during the design phase requires the discipline and openness of product engineers. Furthermore, time is needed for all participants of the working group.

MAS can also be used as a starting point to develop a new production or assembly flow for a mix of products: the number of (sub)assembly workstations can be assessed. A clearer distinction between the flow and processing of standard and special orders can be made during the design phase. Closed-loop business processes lead to extra demands on the flexibility in and organization of (re)manufacturing processes. There can be very diverse flows of products and components using different routings on a shop floor. For instance, there could be single-piece products or small batches of products coming from customers that need to be disassembled on a disassembly line, components that need to be (re)manufactured, and (new) products that need to be assembled from new and used components and modules.

Finally, as MAS is a process scheme of all the assembly steps to be performed, it is frequently used as a starting point for development of work and test instructions for the operator at every workstation (see Sect. 4 and Fig. 3).

## 3 Product Development: Modular Product Architecture & Operator-Centred Product Design

Product design is crucial for the entire product life cycle, such as the production, assembly, use, upgrading and remanufacturing stages. Although the exact numbers are debatable (Ulrich and Pearson 1993), the design literature suggests that, in the average product design stage, 70–80% of the costs are already defined (e.g., Sheldon et al. 1990). Traditionally, durable goods manufacturing companies focused on designing and producing physical products for their customers and end-users. Today, many of these companies are shifting their focus towards producing value-adding services for their customers. To some extent, these services are independent of the physical products, but in most cases, these products are still at the core of the services as the companies extend their services from traditional spare part delivery and maintenance towards life-cycle services and extended products. The service activities typically focus on maintaining the performance of the physical product (spare parts, repair, preventive maintenance, online monitoring of equipment, IT-support diagnosis, remote support for maintenance) or on informing the user of how to use it (training, consultation, simulation, data services).

In UIW, there has been a focus on the changing role of the product development function in manufacturing companies. The main role of this function in a manufacturing company was to produce a design to fulfil the functional requirements of the products but, since the middle of the 20th century, the focus has moved towards the development of designs suitable for production. In the 1980s, there was a growing demand for easily assembled and manufactured designs. This changed the role of the product development function, which was required to review the designs from a growing number of viewpoints. This development has been called Design for X (Kuo al. 2001). After Design for Assembly and Design for Manufacturing there were, among others, Design for Maintenance, Design for Recycling (Gaustad et al. 2010), Design for Environment (Leonard 1991) and Design for Life-cycle (DFLC) (Ishii et al. 1994).

In the near future, designing products for the circular economy will once again set new requirements for the product development function. Products must be designed in a manner that easily allows upgrades (i.e., adapt to future use, reuse, or remanufacturing) in several closed loops between the customer and manufacturing companies. This requires new methods for identifying (future) user needs and values, module-based development teams instead of department-specific teams, early-stage testing and implementation of upgrades while the product is in use anywhere in the world. An essential part of circular economy-based design is the adaptability of products by introducing product modularity (Krikke et al. 2004) and operator-centred design. Product modularity, an approach based on the decomposition of the product into independent subassemblies (product modules, Ulrich 1995), has proven to have positive effects on multiple dimensions of competitive performance such as product quality, flexibility and lead times (e.g., Jacobs et al. 2007). Using product modularity in a traditional sense, a wide range of final products can be configured using flexible methods through intelligent configuration of the product range. Product modularity results in opportunities for parallelizing production processes and thereby considerable lead time reductions for the total manufacturing process can be achieved as long as there is sufficient manpower and space. Modularity also makes it possible to outsource entire sub-modules, such as sheet metal frames, power units, and control cabinets, to specialized suppliers. For circular economy-based design, modularity contributes to a higher level of service and installation, as service-sensitive parts can be exchanged quickly. Furthermore, product modularity supports upgrading the product at the customer site by exchanging modules or reusing used modules in other products within the same product family and thereby adheres to the main principles of the circular economy (i.e., maintain products at their highest utility and value at all times and avoid waste).

In addition to modularity, operator-centred design supports ease of (dis)assembly, maintenance and upgrading and thereby improves operational performance. The Human Factor Design for Assembly (HF-DFA) tool, based on the DFA methodology described by Boothroyd et al. (2001), can be used to evaluate the ease of assembly tasks from an operator perspective (Village et al. 2014) and improve product design. The face validity and simple scoring of the tool facilitates integration into the design process. To support operator-friendly fixture design, the Human Factors Design for Fixture (HF-DFF) guidelines can be applied in the design process (Village et al. 2012). Careful fixture design ensures both product quality and improved human factors. Another methodology that can be used to ensure human-centred product design is Design for Manufacturability (DfM) (Helander and Nagamachi 1992).

## 4 New Technologies in Flexible Production Processes: Levels of Automation and Assistive Operator Support

Once the production process is transparently and flexibly organized, a next step in further improving efficiency can be (partial) automation. Production technology is developing rapidly, and the trend of automation, including the use of robots, collaborative robots and process control systems, has a large impact on manufacturing and on its operators in particular. ‘Full automation’ however, is often not feasible in production work, specifically in the combination of low volumes, high product mix, and high product complexity. For years, product disassembly has been performed as a primarily manual activity. However, the high demand for manual work together with the labour cost generally make disassembly economically infeasible. To overcome this economic issue, replacing the human labour with full automation has been raised as a potential solution (Vongbunyong and Chen 2015). However, task automation requires a very advanced set of robotic technology and its practical implementation still represents a challenge in terms of robustness, accuracy and execution time. Humans are still the most flexible production factor. As smaller batches require higher investments and specialized production systems, especially in assembly, robots and robotic systems will often mainly assist production personnel and remove some routine work. In a semi-structured environment with hybrid production systems, intuitive user interfaces are needed, which could be programmed by operators themselves, to ensure that humans and robot systems are safely collaborating (Robotics 2020: Multi-Annual Roadmap for Robotics in Europe 2015).

In hybrid production systems, human failure is a source of potential error. This requires effective strategies to guarantee human reliability. A strategy to minimize human error is the implementation of automated systems that control the process to a large extent. These may reduce human errors but may also have a large impact on the operator and his or her task. While skilled workers may still be needed, the majority of tasks will become simple and less challenging. Decreased motivation and alertness, potentially jeopardizing human reliability and thereby counteracting potential error-reducing technological measures, are a serious concern. Companies experience these crucial labour issues in production-automation projects, but at the same time, they are 'hard to tackle'. The challenge is finding a good balance between the level of process control and the attractiveness of the work for the operator. Two steps in production automation projects are proven to be crucial (Fasth and Stahre 2010), which are presented in Fig. 4.

- Design of tasks: **Task Analysis** and **Allocation of Task** to humans and machines.
- **Design of operator support systems** in the case of manual activities.

A process map (e.g., MAS) can be used to create an overview of manufacturing process steps followed by a task analysis (e.g., HTA) to define the order of concrete tasks performed by operators and machines. Task allocation is used to allocate tasks to operators or machines. Finally, in the case of manual activities, the need for physical or cognitive support systems is determined.

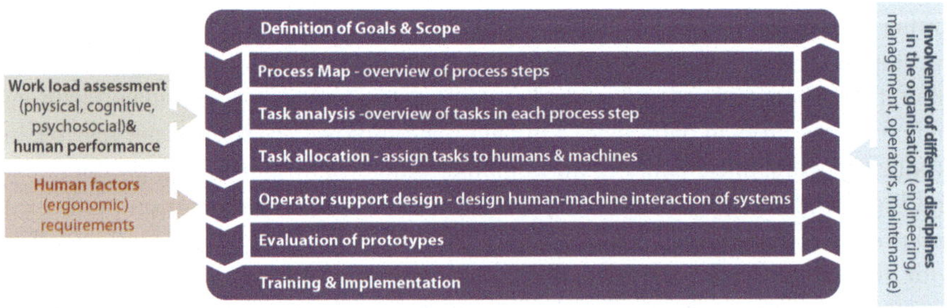


**Fig. 4** Schematic overview of the iterative participatory process design approach

## 4.1 Level of Automation

A first step is to create a well-balanced allocation of activities between humans and robots/machines based on a task analysis. The starting point for this task analysis is the production process analysis, which provides an overview of the process steps to complete an order from beginning to end. Each process step consists of one or more tasks performed by operators and machines. Task analyses can be action oriented approaches (e.g., handling, transportation, picking and placing, replacing tools) or focus on the mental processes as cognitive approaches (e.g., decision making, perception). A common methodology for task analysis is Hierarchical Task Analysis (HTA) described by Stanton (2006). It demonstrates the requirements that tasks necessitate from workers and machines and describes the order of tasks. Task analysis can be used for both current (existing) production processes and new (to be designed) processes.

The result of the task analysis is a starting point for the next step, task allocation between humans and machine. Since Fitts published a set of heuristics on the relative strengths and limitations of humans and machines in 1951 (MABA-MABA, 'men are better at' and 'machines are better at'; Fitts 1951), numerous methodologies have been developed to support task or function allocation between machines/robots and humans. An extensive body of literature describes task allocation models and approaches (e.g., Frohm et al. 2006; Fasth and Stahre 2010; Cummings 2014). In this context, the term Level of Automation (LoA) has been used to describe the relation between humans and technology in terms of task and/or function allocation (Frohm et al. 2006). LoA has been described as an indicator of the allocation of tasks in a manufacturing system and is expressed as an index of physical as well as cognitive tasks. These methodologies focus on balancing performance requirements (zero defects, productivity, costs) and human factors (physical, cognitive load, job satisfaction, motivation, alertness). All of these task allocation models should support the (optimal) division of tasks between robots and operators. The remaining human tasks should not exceed norms, recommendations and guidelines for physical, cognitive, psychosocial load and safety (e.g., ISO 11228-3 2007; ISO 9241 1997; Directive 2002/44/EC). Task allocation is often done once during the (re)design of a manufacturing process. In manufacturing and remanufacturing processes, products and its manufacturing tasks change during the day. There is a need for a more flexible/dynamic task allocation model in which the division between robots and humans can be considered continuously (on the fly), based on human-oriented parameters of workload (physical, cognitive, psychosocial load), safety, flexibility and performance criteria (quality, costs, productivity).

## 4.2 Operator Support Systems

Workmanship (i.e., craftsmanship) of the workforce, support from tools, support systems and work instructions are crucial ingredients for securing the quality of the manufacturing and assembly process. Especially in low-volume, high-variety and complex tasks, product-specific information and support for operators are required. If there is a (flexible or adaptive) level of automation, the remaining (inspection or manual) tasks of the operator require up to date information for the operator to perform his/her tasks properly. Here, quality refers to minimum failure costs, short lead times, ease of learning, and a high level of reproducibility of the process. In practice, work instructions are often too brief, bear too little relation to the operator's task at hand and are insufficiently systematically updated (Van Rhijn et al. 2014; Aehnelt and Bader 2015). These factors, as well as the unpredictable market, wide variety of products, flexible deployment of employees and diversity in operator characteristics (e.g., experience, backgrounds and languages), emphasize the importance of clear and updated operator assistance. For example, updated work instructions that fulfil the operator needs and feedback systems that provide a clear indication to the operator what went wrong. Especially in closed-loop systems and mixed-model assembly systems (e.g., Zeltzer et al. 2012), operator support and instructions are crucial for effective and efficient processes as the diversity of products coming back from customers is extreme. Aehnelt and Bader (2015) identify five aims of information assistance:

- *raising awareness*: increase operator awareness of relevant events within the work environment;
- *guiding*: feedforward and provide instructions;
- *monitoring*: collect relevant (sensor) data from the actual production setting;
- *documenting:* document quality issues directly in the system;
- *guarding*: monitor the actual operator status and prevent overloading.

In addition to these aims, Claeys et al. (2015) recently described a framework to support the development of industrial cognitive support systems. The authors differentiate:

- the information content: what to present. Operators need to have correct information on how to disassemble a product and how to diagnose the level of re-usability.
- the information carrier: how to present information (e.g., Google Glass, computer screens, projection, etc.). Recently, technologies such as Google Glass (Rauh et al. 2015) or gestural recognition software (Niedersteiner et al. 2015), have been used to support operators in assembly work. Augmented Reality technology has been used to assist assembly workers in the aerospace industry (e.g., Servan et al. 2012) and personnel in the field, supporting maintenance and facilitating the upgrade process (Re and Bordegoni 2014).
- in what kind of situation information should be presented: presenting information automatically or upon request depends on the operator needs and task demands.

Claeys et al. (2015) emphasize the importance of a personalized configuration, i.e., modifying instructions and feedback depending on the current state of the operator and the task at hand. Work instructions should be set out in a modular manner and applied in accordance with the degree of experience of the employees. In both manual and semi-automated or hybrid processes, operator guidance should be experienced as added value and should therefore not dictate either posture or work pace to avoid operator annoyance. The interaction should be natural and effortless. High system reliability is needed to avoid operator annoyance and mistakes (e.g., error messages should not occur if a correct action has been performed by the operator). Operator support guidelines for transferring information using text, images or signals must be used so that the information is more appropriately tailored to the operator and task at hand.

## 5 Conclusions

In the near future, short product development lead times, proven sustainability, flexibility, and upgrades will become crucial elements to guarantee competitive business in the manufacturing industry. Upgrading high-investment products driven by rapidly changing customer demands requires highly modular product design, flexible production processes (for new, refurbished and remanufactured products) including (semi) automated and manual workstations and a flexible, motivated and skilled workforce. To face these challenges, several methods and tools for both product, process and task design are described in scientific and grey literature. Several of these methods are described in this chapter. However, many manufacturing companies, especially small- and medium-sized enterprises, do not use these tools and methods. Possible reasons for this are that the methods are not well known or that there is a lack of experience using the tools in a correct manner. Furthermore, the practical application of scientific methodologies is difficult for engineers, as the methodologies do not use the language of their users (e.g., engineers) or are not part of their standardized working procedures, for instance, see Village et al. (2012) regarding ergonomics.

In addition to barriers for efficient tool use in companies, further development of methodologies should be closely connected to future company needs. For instance, most of the current methods are suitable and developed for designing products and processes based on the more traditional linear economy. The circular economy emphasizes the reusability of products and raw materials as a starting point and minimizing waste in the entire industrial and ecological system. Designing adaptable and upgradable products and flexible (re)manufacturing processes are crucial aspects in realizing a circular economy-based business. These aspects should be considered and integrated in the next generation of methods for product and process design.

Finally, communities of practice (see Houghton, Chapter "Fostering a Community of Practice for Industrial Processes" this book) could serve as a dedicated platform to share state-of-the-art methodologies, tools and checklists and documentation of company best practices so that practical cases and tools could be made available to SME companies.

**Acknowledgements** The authors would like to thank Michiel de Looze and Karin Verploegen for their useful comments on earlier versions of this chapter.

## References

Aberdeen Group (2014). Bridging the gap between product development and operations. http://www.aberdeen.com/research/9340/rr-manufacturing-product-development/content.aspx#sthash.K8rq0kXI.dpf

Aehnelt, M., & Bader, S. (2015). Information assistance for smart assembly stations. In Proceedings of the 7th International Conference on Agents and Artificial Intelligence (pp. 143–150).

APPSRG (2014). Remanufacturing: Towards a resource efficient economy. All Party Parliamentary Sustainable Resource Group.

Bastein, T., Roelofs, E., Rietveld, E., & Hoogendoorn, A. (2013). *Kansen voor de circulaire economie in Nederland*. Delft, The Netherlands: TNO.

Bloom, D. E., Canning, D., & Lubet, A. (2015). Global population aging: Facts, challenges, solutions & perspectives. *Daedalus, 144*(2), 80–92.

Boothroyd, G., Dewhurst, P., & Knight, W. A. (2001). What is design for manufacture and assembly? *Product design for manufacture and assembly* (pp. 1–44). Boca Raton, FL: CRC Press, Taylor and Francis.

Bouckenooghe, D., & Devos, G. (2007). The role of process, context and individual characteristics in explaining readiness to change: A multilevel analyses. Vlerick Leuven Gent Working Paper Series 2007/12.

Challenger, R., Clegg, C. W., & Shepherd, C. (2013). Function allocation in complex systems: Reframing an old problem. *Ergonomics, 56*(7), 1051–1069.

Claeys, A., Hoedt, S., Soete, N., Van Landeghem, H., & Cottyn, J. (2015). Framework for evaluating cognitive support in mixed model assembly systems. *IFAC-PapersOnLine, 48*(3), 924–929.

Cummings, M. M. (2014). Man versus machine or man + machine? *IEEE Intelligent Systems, 29* (5), 62–69.

DIRECTIVE 2002/44/EC of 25 June 2002 on the minimum health and safety requirements regarding the exposure of workers to the risks arising from physical agents (vibration) (sixteenth individual Directive within the meaning of Article 16(1) of Directive 89/391/EEC).

Department for Business, Innovations and Skills (2012). Low carbon environmental goods and services.

Ellen MacArthur Foundation (2013). Towards the circular economy. In: Economic and Business Rationale for an Accelerated Transition, Vol. 1. Ellen MacArthur Foundation available from: www.ellenmacarthurfoundation.org

European Foundation for the Improvement of Living and Working Conditions (1999). Communique, July/August, Vol. 2. EFILWC, Dublin.

Fasth, A., & Stahre, J. (2010). Concept model towards optimising Levels of Automation (LoA) in assembly systems. In Proceedings of the 3rd CIRP Conference on Assembly Technologies and Systems, Trondheim, Norway.

Fitts, P. M. (1951). Human engineering for an effective air navigation and traffic control system. Tech. Report, Nat'l Research Council.

Frohm, J., Granell, V., Winroth, M., & Stahre, J. (2006). The industry's view on automation in manufacturing. In F. Mayer, & J. Stahre (Eds.), Proceedings of the 9th Symposium IFAC on Automated Systems Based on Human Skills and Knowledge.

Gaustad, G., Olivetti, E., & Kirchain, R. (2010). Design for recycling. *Journal of Industrial Ecology, 14*(2), 286–308.

Genaidy, A., & Karwowski, W. (2007). A roadmap for a methodology to assess, improve and sustain intra- and inter-enterprise system performance with respect to technology-product life cycle in small and medium manufacturers. *Human Factors and Ergonomics in Manufacturing, 18*(1), 70–84.

Ginn, D. M., Jones, D. V., Rahnejat, H., & Zairi, M. (1998). The "qfd/fmea interface". *European Journal of Innovation Management, 1*(1), 7–20.

Helander, M., & Nagamachi, M. (1992). Design for manufacturability: A systems approach to concurrent engineering and ergonomics Taylor & Francis.

Hirschheim, R. (1989). User participation in practice: Experiences with participative system design. In K. Knight (Ed.), *Participation in Systems Development* (pp. 194–204). Columbia GP Publishing.

Ishii, K., Eubanks, C. F., & Di Marco, P. (1994). Design for product retirement and material life-cycle. *Materials and Design, 15*(4), 225–233.

International Standard Organisation ISO 11228-3. Ergonomics—manual handling: Part 3: Handling of low loads at high frequency, 2007.

EN ISO 9241-1:1997 "Ergonomic requirements for office work with visual display terminals (VDTs)—Part 1: General introduction (ISO 9241-1:1997/Amd. 1:2001)" and its amendment A1:2001.

Jacobs, M., Vickery, S. K., & Droge, C. (2007). The effects of product modularity on competitive performance: Do integration strategies mediate the relationship? *International Journal of Operations & Production Management, 27*(10), 1046–1068.

Krikke, H., le Blanc, I., & van de Velde, S. (2004). Product modularity and the design of closed-loop supply chains. *California Management Review, 46*(2), 23–39.

Kuo, T. C., Huang, S. H., & Zhang, H. C. (2001). Design for manufacture and design for 'X': Concepts, applications, and perspectives. *Computers & Industrial Engineering, 41*(3), 241–260.

Leonard, L. (1991). Design for environment. In Plastics Design Forum: 25–32.

Lines, R. (2004). Influence of participation in strategic change: Resistance, organizational commitment and change goal achievement. *Journal of Change Management, 4*(3), 193–215.

McKinsey (2011). Resource revolution: Meeting the world's energy, materials, food, and water needs. McKinsey Global Institute; McKinsey and Company Sustainability, Resource Productivity Practice. Available from: http://www.mckinsey.com/mgi

Muller, M. J., & Kuhn, S. (1993). Participatory design. *Communications of the ACM, 36,* 24–28.

Niedersteiner, S., Pohlt, C., & Schlegl, T. (2015). Smart workbench: A multimodal and bidirectional assistance system for industrial application. In Industrial Electronics Society (pp. 2938–2943).

Quan, W., & Jianmin, H. (2006). A study on collaborative mechanism for product design in distributed concurrent engineering. IEEE 7th International Conference on Digital Object Identifier (pp. 1–5).

Rauh, S., Zsebedits, D., Tamplon, E., Bolch, S., & Meixner, G. (2015). Using Google Glass for mobile maintenance and calibration tasks in the AUDI A8 production line. In Emerging Technologies & Factory Automation (pp. 1–4).
Re, G. M., & Bordegoni, M. (2014). An augmented reality framework for supporting and monitoring operators during maintenance tasks. In R. Shumaker & S. Lackey (Eds.), *Virtual, augmented and mixed reality applications of virtual and augmented reality* (pp. 443–454). Berlin: Springer.
van Rhijn, J. W., de Looze, M. P., Tuinzaad, G. H., Groenesteijn, L., de Groot, M. P., & Vink, P. (2005). Changing from batch to flow assembly in the production of emergency lighting devices. *International Journal of Production Research, 43,* 3687–3701.
Rhijn van, J.W., Tuinzaad, B., Bosch, T., & Vos, F. (2014). Increasing productivity and flexibility in manufacturing. TNO Hoofddorp.
Robotics 2020: Multi-annual roadmap for Robotics in Europe (2015). http://sparc-robotics.eu/wp-content/uploads/2014/05/H2020-Robotics-Multi-Annual-Roadmap-ICT-2016.pdf
Rother, M., & Shook, J. (2003). Learning to see: Value stream mapping to add value and eliminate muda. Lean Enterprise Institute.
Pot, F., & Rhijn van, J.W. (2012). Slimmer Werken in het MKB van de maakindustrie. http://www.industriebeleid.nl/documenten/Slimmer%20werken%20in%20het%20MKB%20van%20de%20maakindustrie.pdf
Servan, J., Mas, F., & Menendez, J.L. et al (2012). Using augmented reality in AIRBUS A400M shop floor assembly work instructions. In The 4th Manufacturing Engineering Society International Conference, Cadiz (pp.,633–640).
Shalley, C. E., Zhou, J., & Oldham, G. R. (2004). The effects of personal and contextual characteristics on creativity. *Journal of Management, 30,* 933–958.
Sheldon, D. F., Perks, R., Jackson, M., Miles, B. L., & Holland, J. (1990). Designing for whole life costs at the concept stage. *Journal of Engineering Design, 1,* 131–145.
Smart industry, Dutch industry fit for the future (2014). http://www.smartindustry.nl/wp-content/uploads/2014/07/Opmaak-Smart-Industry.pdf
Stamatis, D.H. (2003). Failure mode and effect analysis: FMEA from theory to execution. ASQ Quality Press.
Stanton, N. A. (2006). Hierarchical task analysis: Developments, applications, and extensions. *Applied Ergonomics, 37*(1), 55–79.
Suri, R. (1998). Quick response manufacturing: A companywide approach to reducing lead times. Productivity Press.
Ulrich, K. T. (1995). The role of product architecture in the manufacturing firm. *Research Policy, 24*(3), 419–440.
Ulrich, K.T., & Pearson, S.A. (1993). Does product design really determine 80% of manufacturing cost? Working paper. Massachusetts: Sloan School of Management Cambridge.
Village, J., Greig, M., Zolfaghari, S., Salustri, F., & Neumann, W. P. (2014). Adapting engineering design tools to include human factors. *IIE Transactions on Occupational Ergonomics and Human Factors, 2*(1), 1–14.
Village, J., Annett, T., Greig, M., & Neumann, W.P. (2012). Ergonomic design-for-fixture guidelines and process of implementation. A case study. In Association of Canadian Ergonomists Annual Conference, Halifax, Nova Scotia. http://digitalcommons.ryerson.ca/ie/27/
Vink, P., Imada, A. S., & Zink, K. J. (2008). Defining stakeholder involvement in participatory design processes. *Applied Ergonomics, 39*(4), 519–526.

Vongbunyong, S., & Chen, W.H. (2015). Disassembly automation: Automated systems with cognitive abilities. Springer.

Zeltzer, L., Limere, V., Aghezzaf, E.H., & Van Landeghem, H. (2012). Measuring the objective complexity of assembly workstations. In ICCGI 2012, The Seventh International Multi-Conference on Computing in the Global Information Technology (pp. 341–346).

# Fostering a Community of Practice for Industrial Processes

**Alyson Langley, Harshada Patel and Robert J. Houghton**

**Abstract** A Community of Practice (CoP) is a framework for the facilitation of knowledge management and involves groups of individuals who engage in the process of collective learning around a specific topic. Recent advances in computer technology and Web 2.0 applications now allow for virtual communities to be established which permit interaction and collaboration between individuals across organisational boundaries and geographical locations. The Use-it-Wisely (UIW) project aims to design and develop a cross-industrial virtual community to support the operating environment of manufacturing organisations. Successful implementation of a virtual community has the potential to strengthen the competitive advantage of the industries involved, securing domestic employment and providing products and services that are capable of adapting to the organisational goals. This chapter provides a general overview of the literature on CoPs and virtual communities. It discusses the development of the concept of CoPs, and considers how this relates to knowledge management lifecycle and learning theories. This is followed by a discussion on the use of CoPs and virtual communities as a knowledge management strategy for the manufacturing industry, including multinational companies and Small and Medium-sized Enterprises (SMEs). The chapter finishes by discussing the essential elements for creating and maintaining a self-sustainable virtual community to enable information sharing and decision support across and between the organisations. This includes the factors required to foster a successful virtual community concerning the purpose, content, context, conversations, connections and technology, and the risks and challenges that could lead to the failure of a CoP to be sustained.

**Keywords** Knowledge management · Community of practice · Virtual community · Industrial manufacturing

---

A. Langley (✉) · H. Patel · R.J. Houghton
Human Factors Research Group, University of Nottingham, Nottingham, UK
e-mail: alyson.langley@nottingham.ac.uk

H. Patel
e-mail: harshada.patel@nottingham.ac.uk

R.J. Houghton
e-mail: robert.houghton@nottingham.ac.uk



S.N. Grösser et al. (eds.), *Dynamics of Long-Life Assets*,
DOI 10.1007/978-3-319-45438-2_9

# 1 Introduction

Knowledge management has emerged as a major factor for sustainability in the increasingly evolving and competitive marketplace of today's modern manufacturing industry (Pan and Leidner 2003; Patel et al. 2012). Numerous knowledge management principles have been proposed over the years (Davenport 1996; Allee 1997; Studer et al. 1998; Luen and Al-Hawamdeh 2001), including research that has linked the concept of communities of practice (CoP) with organisational knowledge management (Lave and Wenger 1991; Brown and Duguid 1991; Wenger 1998; Wenger and Snyder 2000; Storck and Hill 2000; Wenger et al. 2002; Ardichvili et al. 2003; Dubé et al. 2006; Eckert 2006; Du Plessis 2008; Scarso and Bolisani 2008).

Wenger et al. (2002) defined CoPs as, "*a group of people who share a concern, a set of problems, or a passion about a topic, and who deepen their knowledge and expertise in this area by interacting on an ongoing basis*". It is through the process of regular interaction that members gain knowledge (Du Plessis 2007), for example, engineers working on a problem, university students studying together or managers sharing organisational information (Wenger 2009). This shared involvement over time, allows members of the community to develop opinions, ideas and ways of performing that deepens their knowledge and expertise on a particular subject or process, as they participate in practices and develop a common history (Gunawardena et al. 2009).

In the past, the size and scope of a CoP has been determined by geographical boundaries. However, recent advances in computer technology and Web 2.0 applications now allow for virtual communities to be established. Virtual communities are a specific type of CoP that uses a web-based platform to provide an environment where geographically distributed members can interact, and share information, knowledge and expertise (Rothaermel and Sugiyama 2001). This allows them to overcome the geographical limitations of traditional CoPs and although, members of a virtual community may participate in telephone conferences and face-to-face meetings, most interaction will involve the posting or viewing of information through web-based technology (Andrews 2002).

The ability of virtual communities to enable collaborations over time and across organisational boundaries provides the flexibility required for the strategic management of knowledge within industrial manufacturing. Interaction between the members includes distribution of news through events, announcements, and publications; problem solving opportunities from question and answer postings and best practice forums; and communication mediums such as discussion groups (Koh et al. 2007). Virtual communities have the potential to access information from different devices, and through interaction with other members, data or virtual objects (Hibbert and Rich 2006). The management of knowledge using the concept of virtual communities has the potential to increase the overall productivity and innovation of the organisation (Chiu et al. 2006).

One of the objectives of the UIW-project is to design and develop a knowledge management strategy to support the operating environment across industrial manufacturing organisations. The development of a cross-industrial virtual community, to support complex industrial activities in response to new products or the upgrading of existing products, has the potential to strengthen the industrial position of the organisations involved, securing domestic employment and providing products and services that are capable of adapting to the organisational strategy.

# 2 General Overview of Communities of Practice

This section aims to provide a general overview of CoPs and virtual communities by examining the literature relating to learning theories, knowledge management and its relevance to manufacturing industries. The section starts with a summary of the development of the concept of CoPs and how this supports the management of knowledge. This is followed by a discussion of the relevance of virtual communities for the manufacturing industry, including multinational companies and Small and Medium-sized Enterprises (SMEs).

## *2.1 The Development of the Concept of Communities of Practice*

Individuals have engaged in the process of collective learning through sharing of experiences and knowledge for many years (Hoadley 2012). However, it was Jean Lave and Etienne Wenger who first used the phrase "*community of practice*" (Cox 2005) and introduced CoPs as a new approach to workplace learning for novice apprentices (Lave and Wenger 1991). Their studies focused on informal interaction and investigated how new workers are socialised into working practices and learn their job through legitimate peripheral participation. Legitimate peripheral participation is explained by Lave and Wenger as *legitimate* because all individuals accept the position of the novice apprentice as a potential community member, *peripheral* because the novices are initially on the edge of the community until trust is established and *participation* because it is through participating in the practice that they acquire knowledge (Cox 2005).

Lave and Wenger's findings showed that novice apprentices learnt the required knowledge mainly from informal social interaction, practice and participation. The authors concluded that learning was a continuous and active engagement, situated in context and social interaction (Lave and Wenger 1991). This was in contrast to the cognitive learning theory, which involved knowledge being conveyed by experts to learners through formally planned methods and was the dominant theory of that time (Cox 2005). This new approach suggested that learning is more than the acquisition of knowledge, and includes peripheral participation and active involvement in the practice (Lave and Wenger 1991). However, this approach only considered the transfer of existing knowledge and did not consider CoPs as a platform for innovation, problem solving or as a potential driver of change (Østerlund and Carlile 2003).

In the same year as Lave and Wenger proposed their new approach, Brown and Duguid (1991) also used the phrase "*community of practice*". This work was based on data from Julian Orr's earlier studies of Xerox photocopier repairmen and aimed to show how informal groups generate solutions to work-related problems (Brown and Duguid 1991) although, Orr did not use the phrase "*community of practice*", preferring to use the term "*occupational community*" (Cox 2007). The study observed how knowledge was better created and transferred through the sharing of experiences and collective problem solving activities, compared to the more traditional learning processes of expert instruction and manuals. Brown and Duguid suggested that knowledge and learning, were embedded in social practices and extended the concept of CoPs to include them as a tool for resolving work-based problems (Brown and Duguid 1991), as opposed to Lave and Wenger's concept that focused only on the reproduction of existing knowledge (Cox 2004).

Although the term "*community of practice*" was used by both Lave and Wenger (1991) and Brown and Duguid (1991), a rigorous formal definition was not offered. This was mainly due to the different interests and viewpoints of the studies and those involved (Cox 2005). However, Wenger (1998) finally defines CoPs as, "*a group that coheres through sustained mutual engagement' on an 'indigenous' (or appropriated) enterprise, and creating a common repertoire*". Wenger expanded on the initial concept of CoPs (Lave and Wenger 1991), from a theory of learning to a knowledge management strategy and discards the concept of legitimate peripheral participation in favour of social identity and trajectories of participation (Wenger 1998). The study focused on the formation and management of CoPs across organisational boundaries to enhance performance, and states that it is through the common understandings of an activity involving large amounts of interaction and problem solving, that relationships are built and CoPs are established (Wenger 1998).

Over time, the interpretation of a CoP moved from a descriptive concept (Lave and Wenger 1991) to a more prescriptive application provided by Wenger et al. (2002), who redefined CoPs as, "*groups of people who share a concern, a set of problems, or a passion about a topic, and who deepen their knowledge and expertise in this area by interacting on an ongoing basis*". Wenger provided a guide for the formation and management of CoPs to enhance performance and drew together ideas put forward in previous works while focussing on the value of the CoP as a knowledge management tool for innovation and problem solving, where the purpose is to learn and share knowledge and not specifically with accomplishing a common task (Cox 2005).

## 2.2 *Communities of Practice and the Management of Knowledge*

Complex knowledge, that is critical to the ability of an organisation to adapt in a fast-paced globalised marketplace, is becoming increasingly specialised and tacit in nature (Hinton 2003). Tacit knowledge is considered to be a valuable source of context-based information, but is stored and composed in the minds of individuals, so is difficult to obtain and develop (Hildreth and Kimble 2002). Duguid (2005) explains the difference between explicit knowledge and tacit knowledge, as *knowing what* and *knowing how*, respectively. Optimal performance within an organisation requires the transfer of knowledge between tacit and explicit knowledge. Novice workers need to be able to convert explicit knowledge (theory) into tacit knowledge (practice) and experienced workers need to convert their tacit knowledge (information within their head) into explicit knowledge for training and learning purposes (Duguid 2005). The process for the successful transfer between tacit knowledge and explicit knowledge is not fully understood, but is a critical resource for organisational innovation (Stephenson 1998).

CoPs have the potential to support the knowledge management process by creating a link between learning and performance (Wenger et al. 2002). This can make a significant organisational impact, by allowing managers to connect tacit knowledge to organisational processes and strategically steer innovation towards industrial growth (Du Plessis 2008). Studies have shown that workers are five times more likely to turn to a co-worker and obtain tacit knowledge about an activity, compared to obtaining knowledge from an explicit source such as a manual (Davenport and Prusak 2000). In addition, members of a CoP have reported an increase in communication, less dependence on physical proximity, and accessibility to new knowledge, which can result in open discussions and brainstorming activities, leading to new capabilities (Ardichvili et al. 2003). This sharing of tacit knowledge for manufacturing processes has the potential to increase learning trajectories and reduce workplace errors, resulting in overall organisational benefits.

A central theory for the ability of CoPs to exploit tacit knowledge is the theory of situated learning (Hoadley 2012). Situated learning describes a method of knowledge acquisition that is '*situated*' in context and interactions between individuals, professions, or pursuits (Lave and Wenger 1991). Brown and Duguid (1991) provided an example of learning by photocopy repairmen, which was situated in the context of problem solving and showed knowledge as being co-constructed, through the sharing of experiences, allowing individuals to better understand their job (Cox 2005). A number of studies have suggested that tacit knowledge, can best be transferred in the context of situated learning processes and social practices (Brown and Duguid 1991; Lave and Wenger 1991; Cox 2005; Hoadley 2012), with a number of theories suggesting that knowledge can only exist in social context and interactions, and is not in the possession of a single individual (Hoadley 2012). This implies that CoPs provide a natural environment for the existence of knowledge.

## 2.3 Communities of Practice and Industry

Knowledge lifecycle refers to the creation, distribution and collection of knowledge and the influence that it has on the working environment (Du Plessis 2008). Effective and efficient industrial knowledge management throughout this lifecycle facilitates collaborative work and innovation for large multinational companies and SMEs either locally or across organisational boundaries (Patel et al. 2012). However, the structure of modern multinational organisations, which can consist of many dispersed teams that span across organisational boundaries, can often impede the effective recovery, transfer and reuse of knowledge, especially when the company operates at a global level, across geographical distances and with distinct cultural and language differences (Scarso and Bolisani 2008).

The recognition that knowledge is a critical element that needs to be managed strategically, has led to the intentional formation of virtual communities to manage knowledge between different teams, departments and locations and involve groups of co-workers that exchange information to overcome complex work-related challenges (Ardichvili et al. 2003; Dubé et al. 2006; Du Plessis 2008; Scarso and Bolisani 2008; Wenger 2009). Each member of the CoP has the potential to bring a unique skill set and contribute to a greater body of knowledge that is available indefinitely and can be called upon even when they leave the community (Wenger et al. 2002). This provides the organisation with significant knowledge input for creative innovation and development of strategic capabilities, while keeping up with current progress in such areas as state-of-the-art technology, customer demands and market changes (Du Plessis 2008). In addition, knowledge transfer and learning activities associated with CoPs offer these organisations a complementary alternative to more traditional training methods (Wenger 2009).

One of the first industrial CoPs to be developed was applied to Xerox photocopy repairmen when the organisation saw the value of the informal exchange of information concerning working activities (Brown and Duguid 2001). In response to their observations, the company created a virtual community that allowed these interactions to be shared across their global network, saving the organisation time and money (Cox 2005). Following this, Shell Oil Company formed a virtual community to facilitate knowledge sharing among different teams, while Daimler-Chrysler Automobile Company designed a virtual community for problem sharing activities (Cox 2005). Since then, the concept of virtual communities have been employed by a number of multinational organizations (Eckert 2006) such as Hewlett Packard, British Petroleum, Chevron, Ford, Boeing and IBM to support workflow processes and the dissemination of case-histories through the use of meetings, forums, document repositories and libraries (Scarso and Bolisani 2008). This results in an environment where knowledge that is created, shared and collected, can influence the development of innovations, increase market responsiveness, improve performance and provide a flow of information linked to the organisational strategy (Du Plessis 2008).

Adapting to the rapid change in processes, systems and economies is also essential for SMEs within the manufacturing industry, as their product will often be more specialised and their profit margins smaller, compared to multinational organisations (Desouza and Awazu 2006). Virtual communities are a good method for introducing knowledge management processes and principles into SME organisations, which may often find it difficult to structure a knowledge management infrastructure (Du Plessis 2008). SMEs can utilise CoPs for controlling the knowledge management lifecycle, ensuring that knowledge generates value through which innovation can take place and also as a communication tool especially if their communication strategies are inadequate (Desouza and Awazu 2006). Virtual communities can support SMEs in the prediction of work activities and provide them with current information on market trends and technological advancements (Du Plessis 2008).

There are unique challenges for SMEs in the development of virtual communities. SMEs deal with information that can be very specialised and they do not manage knowledge in the same way as larger organizations therefore, scaling down knowledge management in practices found in multinational organisations to suit SMEs, is not appropriate because of financial and resource constraints. This requires that SMEs be more creative in working around these limitations in order to manage knowledge (Desouza and Awazu 2006). A significant number of SMEs do not have the network infrastructure, technological tools, ability or economics to establish a virtual community. In addition, their computer-based systems may be more basic with limited functionalities or slower speeds for data retrieval when compared to larger organisations (Du Plessis 2008). The impact is that staff must keep up with changes in the rapidly changing industrial manufacturing markets, without the assistance of the necessary tools and equipment (Du Plessis 2008). However, one solution to the financial and resource constraints of an SME is to participate in a cross-industrial CoP where a number of industries can contribute to the development of the site, the resources and the content of knowledge.

## *2.4 Communities of Practice and Cross-Industrial Knowledge Flow*

Cross-industrial virtual communities have the potential to traverse structural boundaries and promote knowledge flow between different organisations or from different areas of industry. Cross-industrial knowledge flow can highlight current principles and processes that can be transferred between industries such as novel approaches, techniques, tools and methodologies (Du Plessis 2008) and promotes the development of a common body of industrial knowledge between different industries by the sharing of information without the members necessarily needing to work together (Wenger et al. 2002; Hinton 2003).

The benefit of cross-industrial virtual communities include

- sharing of network technology and tools
- division of economic commitments
- working with others to improve processes and innovation
- collaboration with others that may have the relevant skills needed
- development of experts and expertise through collaboration (Du Plessis 2008).

However, industrial organisations are currently only doing this to a limited extent in certain areas, such as technical exchanges, joint ventures, and research and development partnerships. (Du Plessis 2008). The rarity of cross-industrial virtual communities is due to industries' knowledge being part of the asset that sets them apart from other organisations when competing for contracts. Industries protect their knowledge and are not disposed to share it, unless there is some kind of reward or incentive in place. In addition, cross-industrial virtual communities also face additional barriers such as cultures, customs, language and time constraints that inhibit individuals from engaging in knowledge exchange (Wasko and Faraj 2000).

Ultimately, it is the strength of relationships between co-workers that determines the operational potential of an organisation, with innovation, productivity and staff satisfaction, relying on the strength of these relationships. (Du Plessis 2008). CoPs have the ability to assist in the building of social networks including the strengthening of relationships, and the establishment of values and norms providing a platform for knowledge life-cycle management (Du Plessis 2008).

## 3 Form and Function for a Successful Virtual Community

This section aims to provide a broad guideline for creating and maintaining a self-sustainable collaborative virtual community. It discusses the requirements that need to be considered for an initial framework that enables information sharing and decision support across and between organisations. The section starts with a summary of the structure of all CoPs (including virtual communities) and how this supports the management of knowledge, followed by a discussion on the challenges for a successful virtual communities are explained including guidelines concerning the purpose, content, context, conversations, connections and technology that should be employed for the general development of the UIW-virtual community.

UIW's cross-industrial virtual community aims to support a framework for cross-industrial knowledge management. It not only faces the same limitations of any other CoP, but also specific challenges that facilitate knowledge exchange across different industries. Developers of the community not only have to deal with communication, motivation and leadership issues but also take into consideration the different interests and expectations of the community and the interoperability of the communication technology, that each industry employs (Koh et al. 2007).

## *3.1 Structural Characteristics of a Community of Practice*

While CoPs including virtual communities, come in many forms, three structural characteristics have been identified as being central to the framework of all CoPs. These are a domain, a community and a practice (Wenger et al. 2002). Within this structural framework, major factors for a successful community include a clear and focused purpose, high quality content, correct context, meaningful conversation, relationship-building connections and high performing technological tools (Wenger 2009). The structural characteristics of a CoP are discussed first, followed by a review of the major factors.

The first structural characteristic is the domain. The domain represents the shared interest that unites the members of the community (Wenger 2009). Relevant domains of knowledge where experiences of the individual members can be communicated include particular hobbies or interests or work-related activities such as research projects, business activities, technological advancement, training and educational methodologies (Wenger et al. 2002). The domain can be local or global, with some communities meeting face-to-face, while others mostly interact online. It is not a community grouped by geographical location such as a neighbourhood or workplace, but is defined by membership and commitment to the domain and to the development of a shared understanding, resulting in the creation of personal meaning and strategic knowledge (Gunawardena et al. 2009).

The community defines all the members that interact and learn from each other. As the members of a community interact, they build relationships through dialogue and conversation, resulting in an environment of trust, from which they can learn from each other (Wenger 2009). It is not a community grouped by shared characteristics such as age, gender, ethnicity or religion but is a system of knowledge, beliefs, behaviours, and customs, which serve as the basis for further interaction (Gunawardena et al. 2009). The community can be small or large, often with a central group and many peripheral members and may contain individuals from the same organization or from different institutions (Wenger 2009).

The practice is a result of sustained mutual engagement in the community over time, with members being jointly responsible for the development of knowledge and learning (Wenger 2009). The time spent building relationships and collaborating is vital in the development of a practice and also allows for the repetition of circumstances, situations, and events, resulting in a commitment to the engagement for shared knowledge. This provides the conditions for setting down new cultural norms and conventions within the practice and the development of a common history (Eckert 2006).

The multi-industrial element of the Use-it-Wisely virtual community requires the consideration of these structural characteristics. The domain has to be general enough to encompass the different industries and their external stakeholder partners while being specific enough to encourage a commitment to the community, allowing personal meaning and strategic knowledge to be formed. The community needs to develop trust and confidence within and between the industries, so that relationships can be built and members can learn from each other. Finally, the practice needs to be flexible enough to cover all the industries and provide an environment that develops new cultural norms, conventions and a common history.

## *3.2 Major Factors for a Successful Virtual Community*

Although the number of virtual communities has increased, there appears to be a limited consensus within the literature on the factors which underlie a successful practice. However most of the research agrees that the success of a virtual community relies on its members having both the opportunity and the motivation to participate and contribute knowledge (Rothaermel and Sugiyama 2001; Ardichvili et al. 2003; Koh et al. 2007; Wenger 2009). The factors for any successful CoP, including the UIW-virtual community are dictated by the community itself and usually evolve over time. However, major factors for consideration in the initial design stage of a virtual community include the purpose, content, context, conversation, connections and technology.

### 3.2.1 Purpose

All the shared ideas, interests and common goals of the members of a virtual community constitute its purpose. A shared purpose is essential for a successful collaborative environment because it unifies everything that occurs within the virtual community. Furthermore, clarity of purpose is also important because it creates energy and interaction, generating trust and connections between the members (Hoadley and Kilner 2005). However, it can be difficult to reach a consensus that clearly defines the shared purpose, especially when members come from different professions or industries (Koh et al. 2007). Establishing and developing good community leaders and leadership roles that can identify and act upon the needs of the members, is important for the generation and clarity of a shared practice (Koh et al. 2007). Nevertheless, even when a shared purpose is clearly defined, the actual purpose will evolve through the content, conversations, and connections, of its members, with every contribution either reinforcing or disrupting the stated purpose (Hoadley and Kilner 2005).

For the UIW-virtual community a clear, focused and shared purpose will increase interaction and collaboration. However, the different requirements from the industry partners may hinder the chances of establishing a specific shared purpose. Initially, a more general purpose may be more appropriate, which over time, may be defined more clearly by its members as they form connections, establish trust and share knowledge.

### 3.2.2 Content and Context

The content of the virtual community refers to the contributions the members make in relation to their experiences, understanding and development (Eckert 2006), while context refers to the known information about the origin of the knowledge posted and how it has been previously applied (Hoadley and Kilner 2005). Both are vital for a sustainable virtual community.

The continuous delivery of good quality content is important because it supplies a basis for conversation and attracts new members by communicating a clear purpose (Hoadley and Kilner 2005). Generating quality content is a major challenge when establishing a virtual community, but the reasons why members contribute content is not clear, although a number of processes have been proposed that can assist in its generation (Ardichvili et al. 2003). Requesting specific contributions from members will stimulate content as individuals are more inclined to contribute when they are asked (Hoadley and Kilner 2005). Reviving conversations that have been posted about a particular topic into, for example, a new format or from a new point of view can stimulate new objectives and ideas and generate fresh content (Hoadley and Kilner 2005), and introducing an evaluation system that filters out redundant or obsolete postings based on periodic examination, ensures that high value content is maintained (Koh et al. 2007).

Posting is central to the quality of the content but viewing is just as important. Koh et al. (2007) reported that there was an increase in viewings when the content of a virtual community were perceived to be valuable or useful. Therefore collecting and displaying good quality content, which is updated regularly, is important for promoting the viewing activity of community members (Hoadley and Kilner 2005). Posting and viewing are so important for the development of a sustainable virtual community that they must always be taken into consideration when any changes are made (Koh et al. 2007). A key finding in the study by Koh et al. (2007) was that postings were influenced by offline events while viewing was influenced by the quality of the technological infrastructure and the usefulness of the community. The size of a community can be an important element in the sustainability of a community because the amount of a community's posting and viewing is related to the number of members (Koh et al. 2007). Therefore, it is essential at the formation of a virtual community to actively recruit and include community members. However, there are limitations to the amount of time people can devote to a community and as the commitment and energy of members decreases, so does the quality of the content (Koh et al. 2007).

Providing the right information context to enable members to learn more effectively is also an important factor for a productive virtual community. Context helps a community member know the source of a piece of knowledge and how it has been applied in the past and might consist of information about the author and their situation, including details, cross-references, and stories (Patel et al. 2012). Knowing the context of a piece of information contributes to the applicability and understanding of the members of a community in the communication (Hoadley and Kilner 2005). When conversations reinforce a community's purpose in their content, the result is a clearer context for everyone involved. In addition, when members are connected through a relationship, they gain access to context about contributions to the community. However, the challenge for virtual communities is to situate the knowledge context through conversation and connections among members who are geographically distributed (Hoadley and Kilner 2005).

Posting and viewing are major factors in the sustainability of any virtual community and the UIW-virtual community needs to establish good quality content presented in the right context at an early stage of development. This will provide a basis for each of the industries to connect and converse, to build trust and learn from each other.

### 3.2.3 Conversation and Connections

Conversation and connections are the fundamental elements for establishing confidence and trust among the members of a virtual community. Conversation in a virtual community, relates to any communication including electronic interaction such as video conferencing, text messaging and emails that relay knowledge. Connections relate to the relationships made within a virtual community that enable members to build relationships and share knowledge (Hoadley and Kilner 2005). Both the conversation and the stability of the connections made are primary factors for a productive virtual community.

The transfer of knowledge is most easily generated through conversation. Conversation offers a personal connection to members of a community and supplies the content for the domain and the context for the information. Without efficient forms of conversation, community members from differing geographical locations will not benefit from the knowledge transfer processes (Jin et al. 2010). The challenge within a virtual community is to generate dialogue that elicits meaningful conversation, which is focused and relevant to the community's purpose (Hoadley and Kilner 2005). Effective conversation can be stimulated by social presence, however within virtual communities the dominant communication channel is the exchange of text messaging, which is low in social presence (Fulk et al. 1990). To overcome this challenge it is important to support community members with relevant graphical and video interfaces such as video-conferencing and avatar chatting and to integrate ways to strengthen social identity by linking offline meetings to online activities (Koh et al. 2007).

Making connections within a virtual community involves forming relationships between members to facilitate the transfer of knowledge (Jin et al. 2010). Stable relationships contribute to a culture of trust in which members feel safe to contribute knowledge content, challenge assumptions and propose unconventional ideas (Hoadley and Kilner 2005). In a virtual community, the lack of social connections can often result in an evolution of the site into either an online document repository or a chat room. Having a clear purpose so that members are aware that they all share a common interest, quality content and conversation that facilitates dialogue, all reduce barriers so that connections can be made. In addition, linking member profiles with their knowledge contributions facilitates connections, as other members contribute to the conversation (Hoadley and Kilner 2005).

Providing an environment that allows connections and conversations between the members of the UIW-virtual community is a fundamental element that can facilitate interaction and collaboration. Interactions between the members from different areas of industry can promote diverse relationships and comprehensive processes that can lead to innovative practices. However, there are many barriers to generating conversation and establishing connections over geographical distances and between differing industries including language, culture, background and organisational principles.

### 3.2.4 Technology

The advancement of web-based technology has facilitated the integration of knowledge and networks of individuals, to such an extent that they have transformed the concept of CoPs, allowing them to effectively become virtual. New web-based applications break down the geographical barriers of traditional CoPs, with virtual communities extending over a variety of contexts and geographical areas (Wenger et al. 2009). The ability of virtual communities to transverse geographical distances allows for communication and interaction between members of differing cultures, disciplines and backgrounds, who can work from anywhere with mobile or internet coverage (Wenger et al. 2009).

Web 2.0 is the term that describes the second generation of development for the World Wide Web (Hossain and Aydin 2011). It refers to the transition from static HTML Web pages to more dynamic user-generated tools, resulting in increased collaboration and communication speeds. By utilizing the different tools made available by Web 2.0 technologies, knowledge sharing and communication capabilities of virtual communities is enhanced (Hossain and Aydin 2011).

The rise of Web 2.0 technologies has provided the tools to shape the scale and scope of the UIW-virtual community, providing new sources of knowledge on real world activities. This allows the members to situate themselves within the context of the knowledge and link it to the practices performed in everyday life. However, technological advances can only be effective if the correct applications for the right situation are applied in a structured and systematic way (Boulos et al. 2006).

Every virtual community encounters technological challenges and a wide range of user requirements that cannot be met, which can restrict community activity. In addition the diversity of technological skills among members creates further challenges (Koh et al. 2007). A rapid system response time is a necessary requirement in any virtual community, along with user-friendly interfaces and system reliability, all of which facilitate the relationships within the community and the level of activity (Koh et al. 2007).

### *3.3 Current Collaborative Tools*

The rapid increase in the use of Web 2.0 applications includes a number of on-line platforms that have characteristics that align with the concept of virtual communities. These include Social Network sites such as Facebook, Twitter, Flickr and Google+, Apps, Wikis, and blogs. Their ease of use and speed at which they can distribute information, makes them powerful tools for obtaining knowledge (Boulos et al. 2006).

By definition all virtual communities are Social Networks, in that they involve making connections and establishing relationships between the members of the community. The members of Social Network sites form social relationships despite geographical distances and can obtain, interact, contribute and reshape knowledge in a way that is consistent with the norms and standards of their social group (Office of Educational Access and Success 2012) although, virtual communities are distinguished by having a domain as a source of identification, which is not a requirement of a Social Network (Jin et al. 2010). However, social networks can provide a valid and appealing tool that could be incorporated into a virtual community either directly or indirectly as a link, to form connections and stimulate conversation.

Web Apps are mobile applications that use HTML-based software to provide interactivity through portable devices such as smartphones and tablets (Godwin-Jones 2011) and support the idea of '*anytime, anyplace*' learning (Corbeil and Valdes-Corbeil 2007). Recently developed Apps, such as Instagram (www.instagram.com) and WhatsApp (www.whatsapp.com), support photo and video sharing and mobile communication networks (Gachago and Ivala 2015). These apps make connections between broad ranges of motivated individuals and have the potential to establish a collection of knowledge. They are affordable and easy to use and the speed at which they can circulate knowledge, due to their mobile nature (Newman et al. 2012), makes them ideal tools for virtual communities.

A Wiki is a web-based platform whose members can contribute to articles and share dialogue using simple editing tools while contributing to the development of a collection of knowledge (Boulos et al. 2006). The best example of a Wiki is Wikipedia, an online encyclopaedia that can be used a source for obtaining knowledge, allowing members to obtain expert knowledge and engage in learning, although they do not provide the opportunity to establish relationships as social network sites and specific Apps (Office of Educational Access and Success 2012). The ability of Wikis to facilitate the development and transfer of knowledge makes them a potentially valuable inclusion into a virtual community (Office of Educational Access and Success 2012).

A Blog is a contraction of the term '*Web Log*', and is an on-line journal that offers an information-sharing environment using multimedia technology. Blogs feature posting tools, archives of previous posts presented in reverse chronological order, and standalone Web pages with their own unique URL address, to provide an information-sharing tool for deliberation and discussion around a specific topic.

A single user can write them or they can be written by a group of individuals, with entries usually containing dialogue, images and links to other Web sites (Boulos et al. 2006). While the specificity of the topics often results in a limited number of contributors the ease at which Blogs facilitate the linking of knowledge to a potentially global audience through the World Wide Web (Boulos et al. 2006), makes them ideal features to include within a virtual community.

Social networks, apps, wikis, and blogs have the potential to be effective tools for the UIW-virtual community. They are all simple to implement and use, and many are Open source or free of charge, which may be one reason for their popularity (Boulos et al. 2006). Although, none of these tools constitute a virtual community, the context to which they are applied has the potential to facilitate the transfer of knowledge, providing opportunities for virtual collaboration from a wide range of members, who have different needs and preferences of communication. The integration of these applications as part of a framework for learning within the UIW-virtual community has the potential to improve the knowledge sharing experience by facilitating interaction and collaboration (Boulos et al. 2006).

## 4 Conclusion

The development of the UIW cross industrial virtual community stems from the requirement to engage a wide range of potential members. These include designers, engineers, trainers, managers, directors, support staff, affiliated organisations and customers, that need support in different areas such as community development, communication, collaboration, and sharing of practices. This chapter has identified and described six elements that need to be considered when developing the UIW-virtual community: a clear purpose, quality content, situated context, meaningful conversation, stable connections, along with a stable, high-speed IT infrastructure and web-based tools that promote discussion. Intertwined within these elements are a number of factors that also need attention, including good community leadership and member roles, viewing and posting activity, size, technological tools and applications and offline interaction to strengthen connections. In addition, it is also important that the platform is secure, easily maintained, and easy to use. Nonetheless, virtual communities are only sustainable when they provide benefits that surpass the costs of membership in relation to time. It is important for all members to be proactive at the beginning of a development to establish communication and interest. This may be time consuming especially when recruiting and instructing new members.

This chapter has taken into consideration the requirements of the UIW-project and suggested a potential guide to facilitate the first step towards understanding the basics factors for a successful virtual community platform. However, virtual communities evolve in a natural way over time and cannot be forced into an organisational structure. Changes will take place as the individuals, goals and objectives change within the community. In addition, a change in industrial culture, economic climate or organisational strategy, will also contribute to the evolution of the virtual community (Du Plessis 2008).

## References


Allee, V. (1997). 12 principles of knowledge management. *Training & Development*.

Andrews, D. C. (2002). Audience-specific online community design. *Communications of the ACM, 45*(4), 64–68.

Ardichvili, A., Page, V., & Wentling, T. (2003). Motivation and barriers to participation in virtual knowledge-sharing communities of practice. *Journal of Knowledge Management, 7*(1), 64–77.

Boulos, M. N., Maramba, I., & Wheeler, S. (2006). Wikis, blogs and podcasts: A new generation of Web-based tools for virtual collaborative clinical practice and education. *BMC Medical Education, 6*(1), 41.

Brown, J. S., & Duguid, P. (1991). Organizational learning and communities-of-practice: Toward a unified view of working, learning, and innovation. *Organization Science, 2*(1), 40–57.

Brown, J. S., & Duguid, P. (2001). Knowledge and organization: A social-practice perspective. *Organization Science, 12*(2), 198–213.

Chiu, C. M., Hsu, M. H., & Wang, E. T. (2006). Understanding knowledge sharing in virtual communities: An integration of social capital and social cognitive theories. *Decision Support Systems, 42*(3), 1872–1888.

Corbeil, J. R., & Valdes-Corbeil, M. E. (2007). Are you ready for mobile learning? *Educause Quarterly, 30*(2), 51.

Cox, A. (2004). What are communities of practice? A critical review of four seminal works. In *Fifth European Conference on Organizational Knowledge, Learning, and Capabilities*.

Cox, A. (2005). What are communities of practice? A comparative review of four seminal works. *Journal of Information Science, 31*(6), 527–540.

Cox, A. (2007). Reproducing knowledge: Xerox and the story of knowledge management. *Knowledge Management Research & Practice, 5*(1), 3–12.

Davenport, T. H. (1996). Some principles of knowledge management. *Strategy & Business, 1*(2), 34–40.

Davenport, T. H., & Prusak, L. (2000). *Working knowledge: How organizations know what they know*. Boston, MA: Harvard Business School Press.

Desouza, K. C., & Awazu, Y. (2006). Knowledge management at SMEs: Five peculiarities. *Journal of Knowledge Management, 10*(1), 32–43.

Du Plessis, M. (2007). The role of knowledge management in innovation. *Journal of Knowledge Management, 11*(4), 20–29.

Du Plessis, M. (2008). The strategic drivers and objectives of communities of practice as vehicles for knowledge management in small and medium enterprises. *International Journal of Information Management, 28*(1), 61–67.

Dubé, L., Bourhis, A., & Jacob, R. (2006). Towards a typology of virtual communities of practice. *Interdisciplinary Journal of Information, Knowledge, and Management, 1*(1), 69–93.

Duguid, P. (2005). "The art of knowing": Social and tacit dimensions of knowledge and the limits of the community of practice. *The Information Society, 21*(2), 109–118.

Eckert, P. (2006). Communities of practice. *Encyclopedia of Language and Linguistics, 2*(2006), 683–685.

Fulk, J., Schmitz, J., & Steinfield, C. W. (1990). A social influence model of technology use. *Organizations and Communication Technology, 117,* 140.

Gachago, D., & Ivala, E. (2015). Web 2.0 and social media: Essential tools for contemporary teaching and learning. In *Moving beyond the hype: A contextualised view of learning with technology in higher education* (p. 19).

Godwin-Jones, R. (2011). Emerging technologies: Mobile apps for language learning. *Language Learning & Technology, 15*(2), 2–11.
Gunawardena, C. N., Hermans, M. B., Sanchez, D., Richmond, C., Bohley, M., & Tuttle, R. (2009). A theoretical framework for building online communities of practice with social networking tools. *Educational Media International, 46*(1), 3–16.
Hibbert, K., & Rich, S. (2006). Virtual communities of practice. In *The international handbook of virtual learning environments* (pp. 563–579).
Hildreth, P. M., & Kimble, C. (2002). The duality of knowledge. *Information Research, 8*(1).
Hinton, B. (2003). Knowledge management and communities of practice: An experience from Rabobank Australia and New Zealand. *International Food and Agribusiness Management Review, 5*(3).
Hoadley, C. (2012). 12 What is a community of practice and how can we support it?. In *Theoretical foundations of learning environments* (p. 286).
Hoadley, C. M., & Kilner, P. G. (2005). Using technology to transform communities of practice into knowledge-building communities. *ACM SIGGROUP Bulletin, 25*(1), 31–40.
Hossain, M., & Aydin, H. (2011). A Web 2.0-based collaborative model for multicultural education. *Multicultural Education & Technology Journal, 5*(2), 116–128.
Jin, L., Wen, Z., & Gough, N. (2010). Social virtual worlds for technology-enhanced learning on an augmented learning platform. *Learning, Media and Technology, 35*(2), 139–153.
Koh, J., Kim, Y. G., Butler, B., & Bock, G. W. (2007). Encouraging participation in virtual communities. *Communications of the ACM, 50*(2), 68–73.
Lave, J., & Wenger, E. (1991). *Situated learning: Legitimate peripheral participation*. Cambridge University Press.
Luen, T. W., & Al-Hawamdeh, S. (2001). Knowledge management in the public sector: Principles and practices in police work. *Journal of Information Science, 27*(5), 311–318.
Newman, G., Wiggins, A., Crall, A., Graham, E., Newman, S., & Crowston, K. (2012). The future of citizen science: Emerging technologies and shifting paradigms. *Frontiers in Ecology and the Environment, 10*(6), 298–304.
Office of Educational Access and Success. (2012). Development of virtual communities of practice to support programmatic efforts within university systems. Some considerations and recommendations. University System of Georgia in collaboration with Georgia Institute of Technology. OEAS Working Paper Series #12-01, Atlanta, Georgia.
Østerlund, C., & Carlile, P. (2003). How practice matters: A relational view of knowledge sharing. In *Communities and technologies* (pp. 1–22). Springer Netherlands.
Pan, S. L., & Leidner, D. E. (2003). Bridging communities of practice with information technology in pursuit of global knowledge sharing. *The Journal of Strategic Information Systems, 12*(1), 71–88.
Patel, H., Pettitt, M., & Wilson, J. R. (2012). Factors of collaborative working: A framework for a collaboration model. *Applied Ergonomics, 43*(1), 1–26.
Rothaermel, F., & Sugiyama, S. (2001). Virtual Internet communities and commercial success: Individual and community-level theory grounded in the atypical case of TimeZone.com. *Journal of Management, 27*(3), 297–312.
Scarso, E., & Bolisani, E. (2008). Communities of practice as structures for managing knowledge in networked corporations. *Journal of Manufacturing Technology Management, 19*(3), 374–390.
Stephenson, K. (1998). What knowledge tears apart, networks make whole. *Internal Communication Focus, 36,* 1–6.
Storck, J., & Hill, P., (2000). Knowledge diffusion through strategic communities. Sloan Management Review, 63–74.
Studer, R., Benjamins, V. R., & Fensel, D. (1998). Knowledge engineering: Principles and methods. *Data & Knowledge Engineering, 25*(1), 161–197.
Wasko, M. M., & Faraj, S. (2000). "It is what one does": Why people participate and help others in electronic communities of practice. *The Journal of Strategic Information Systems, 9*(2), 155–173.
Wenger, E. (1998). Communities of practice: Learning as a social system. *Systems Thinker, 9*(5), 2–3.

Wenger, E. (2009). Communities of practice. *Communities, 22,* 57.
Wenger, E., White, N., & Smith, J. D. (2009). *Digital habitats: Stewarding technology for communities*. CPsquare.
Wenger, E., McDermott, R. A., & Snyder, W. (2002). *Cultivating communities of practice: A guide to managing knowledge*. Harvard Business Press.
Wenger, E. C., & Snyder, W. M. (2000). Communities of practice: The organizational frontier. *Harvard Business Review*, *78*(1), 139–146.

# Extending the System Model

**Mauro Pasquinelli, Luis Molina-Tanco, Arcadio Reyes-Lecuona and Michele Cencetti**

**Abstract** This chapter briefly reviews the state of the art in existing system modelling practice in support of project activities that span a product's lifecycle in different industry types (e.g., large series, small series, one-of-a-kind). Issues of collaboration, gaps in supporting the entire lifecycle and the advantages of defining (and sharing) semantics are discussed. The benefits achieved through the use of models to maintain control of system consistency are described, along with examples of the requirements for using this approach in practice and the potential impacts on company workflow. The maturity and expected advantages of known solutions and proposed extensions to current practices are also described.

**Keywords** Model-based systems engineering · Product life-cycle · Realizations modelling · Model-driven engineering modelling · Analysis and simulation

## 1 Introduction

Modelling can be defined as the definition of systems, processes and/or associated methods. Modelling requires dedicated processes, controls and resources. The modelling approach is not necessarily efficient; the associated effort may be lower

M. Pasquinelli (✉)
Domain Exploration and Science Italy, Engineering,
Thales Alenia Space, Turin, Italy
e-mail: mauro.pasquinelli@thalesaleniaspace.com

L. Molina-Tanco · A. Reyes-Lecuona
DIANA Research Group, Dpt. Tecnología Electrónica,
ETSI Telecomunicación, University of Málaga, Málaga, Spain
e-mail: lmtanco@uma.es

A. Reyes-Lecuona
e-mail: areyes@uma.es

M. Cencetti
Mission Operations and Training, ALTEC, Turin, Italy
e-mail: michele.cencetti@altecspace.it



S.N. Grösser et al. (eds.), *Dynamics of Long-Life Assets*,
DOI 10.1007/978-3-319-45438-2_10

or higher than the related savings or earnings due to improvement in quality, reduction of data exchange effort, reduction of programmatic and technical risks, prototype cost savings, easier feedback from stakeholders and provision of additional services regarding the physical or digital good produced.

The main objective of Use-it-Wisely (UIW) is to enable innovative continuous upgrades of high-investment product-services (see Granholm and Groesser in Chapter "The Use-It-Wisely (UIW) Approach" of this book), which requires:

(1) Customer involvement, including providing the required information, receiving and capturing their feedback and anticipating their needs (one of the seven challenges identified in Chapter "The Challenge").
(2) Understanding the customers' needs and transforming them into valuable innovative solutions through an adequate ideation and creativity process (see Chapter "Complexity Management and System Dynamics Thinking" for details).
(3) An industrial strategic approach to analyse, plan, simulate and anticipate the impacts of the upgrade at the company, market and environmental levels (see Chapters "Complexity Management and System Dynamics Thinking", "Managing the Life Cycle to Reduce Environmental Impacts" and "Collaborative Management of Inspection Results in Power Plant Turbines" for details).
(4) Efficient and effective improvement of technical work to rapidly analyse updates and product innovation from as-required status to realized status through design, verification and post-delivery activities, to provide adequate engineering services for the customer and enter the design, verification or operations loop (the main purpose of this Chapter is to provide the means to respond to this need through a system-level neutral layer for all stakeholders).
(5) Collaborative work between the project teams, customers and project stakeholders, supported by adequate approaches (see Chapter "Virtual Reality and 3D Imaging to Support Collaborative Decision Making for Adaptation of Long-Life Assets" for a potential solution for this need).

The complexity of these elements can be managed through modelling. This Chapter analyses modelling methodologies in the context of innovative upgrading of complex technical systems (e.g., space, airborne, heavy machinery, naval or energy systems).

How can issues related to the technical management of complex systems be handled efficiently? This question has already been answered: Through systems engineering and model-based approaches. Systems engineering is defined by the International Council on Systems Engineering (INCOSE) (Wiley and others 2015) as "an interdisciplinary approach and means to enable the realization of successful systems. It focuses on defining customer needs and required functionality early in the development cycle, documenting requirements, then proceeding with design synthesis and system validation while considering the complete problem […]. Systems Engineering integrates all the disciplines and specialty groups into a team effort forming a structured development process that proceeds from concept to production to operation. Systems Engineering considers both the business and the technical needs of all customers with the goal of providing a quality product that meets the user needs."

Systems engineering is not a self-standing activity; it is based on continuous consultation and collaboration with the other technical disciplines and with the program/project-level management. In parallel with this, system engineer activities rely on support from other SE activities for projects in different lifecycle phases.

Hence, an effective system approach relies primarily on the knowledge of those working on the team, a well-defined process, the collaboration, and the availability of required information.

Application of the systems engineering approach has led to the definition of various standards and methods to support all the perspectives that characterize a project. Different standards have matured to support systems engineering activities and reduce errors related to information exchange between different environments.

The model-based approach is a consolidated method to involve all the technical disciplines and relies on modelling to manage complexity and improve the effectiveness of the conception, definition, verification or operational activities using appropriate tools to improve efficiency.

Model-based approaches at the system level that replace or sustain the traditional document-based approach are applied or planned in many fields, such as military, space, transport, healthcare, robotics and telecommunications. This is revealed by the wide variety of universities, agencies and companies that are interested in the field and participate in projects and conferences worldwide (e.g., IEEE Systems of Systems Engineering Conference, INCOSE International Workshop and IEEE Systems Conference).

There are benefits to application of a model-based approach despite the limits to its current scope. The development of a transversal application that profits from modelling as much as possible throughout the entire project or product lifecycle and that unifies different disciplines and those beyond the company boundaries is still an open field of innovation.

This Chapter analyses some of the fundamental aspects of reaching such a vision. Section 2 provides a brief overview of the main types of modelling. Section 3 provides an analysis of the practical implementation of some models, proposes extensions and changes to available models and describes visions for the future before summarizing the conclusions in Sect. 4.

## 2 State of the Art in System Modelling for Systems Engineering and Technical Simulation

Systems engineering is currently gaining an increasing role in the design process for complex products. System modelling is a multidisciplinary approach that addresses the development of balanced solutions for different stakeholder's needs. This balance involves both management and technical processes, with the main aim of reducing the possible risks affecting the success of a project. Management activities mainly address monitoring development costs, schedules and technical performance, ensuring that the project objectives are met. These processes are related to risk management and decision making activities. Some of the most important activities performed at different levels of system development are:

- Elicit and analyse stakeholder needs
- Specify the system
- Synthesize alternative system solutions
- Perform trade-off analysis
- Maintain traceability

Two of the most interesting and challenging phases are synthesizing alternative solutions and performing trade-off analyses. A clear understanding of stakeholders' needs is crucial because the decisions made during this early definition process can affect the effectiveness of the final product. It is extremely important to understand how the external systems, users and physical environments interface with the system to clearly define the boundary of the system and the associated interfaces. This process is often characterized by the definition of the functions and related non-functional requirements that must comply with the customer requirements (functional analysis), specifying their sequence and ordering. After the functional analysis is performed, development proceeds with the design and testing of components, providing feedback to the specification process. In this manner, the design evolves iteratively towards the definition of the final system solution.

During this process, it is important to clearly define the information flow from the stakeholder needs to the component requirements. The system representation often includes broad stakeholder perspectives and involves the participation of many engineering and non-engineering disciplines. A typical systems engineering team should include viewpoints from each of these perspectives. Teams from different domain-specific fields must work together in a complex environment in which all the disciplines are deeply integrated.

The complexity of the systems drives the definition of a system of systems (SoS) structure in which an individual element is part of another system with a higher level of definition. The appropriate management of system complexity has led to the definition of various systems engineering standards to support different perspectives on the same project. Reduction of as many data exchange errors as possible is one goal of the standards. An overview of some of the most relevant systems engineering standards is available from (Friedenthal et al. 2014).

System modelling aims to define the processes and components that characterize a product through the entire lifecycle and across different domains. The main objective of the modelling standards is the identification of a common language for describing physical system architecture, behavioural models and functional flow.

Model and data exchange are among the most challenging and critical activities during development, especially when different domain-specific tools must interact for data sharing. Different modelling approaches and protocols are currently available in the context of systems engineering. The XML Metadata Interchange

(XMI) specification is an example of such a standard for facilitating model data exchange. In the same manner, the model-driven architecture (MDA) paradigm addresses the definition of standards, ideally enabling the transformation between models and different modelling languages. These efforts address improvement of tool interoperability, modular modelling processes and re-use of system design products, reducing the time and costs of implementing defined components.

Interdisciplinary communication is essential in establishing stakeholder needs. The integration of system modelling environments and frameworks for technical simulation is often affected by the communication between domain-specific disciplines. Communication among those with different backgrounds is challenging but critical for the effectiveness of the developed system. The use of different tools, procedures and formats to model and analyse the same product must be properly coordinated. A common conceptual infrastructure can improve the effective exploitation of simulation environments to support system modelling, ensuring a seamless exchange of data across disciplines.

## *2.1 Model-Based Systems Engineering*

The model-based systems engineering (MBSE) methodology is one of the most interesting approaches in the system modelling domain and shows promising capabilities for management of the phases that characterize a project. The application of the MBSE methodology to support the design of complex systems has been assessed through different research initiatives such as in Space Engineering, a domain characterized by a high level of complexity in which the number of products, people, disciplines and processes leads to an environment that is difficult to manage and control.

The increasing number of variables and stakeholders, often from different backgrounds, make the task of properly managing a complex product very difficult. MBSE provides the basis for a rational organization of work with respect to traditional approaches. MBSE has been defined as (Technical Operations International Council on Systems Engineering (INCOSE) 2007):

> Model-based systems engineering (MBSE) is the formalized application of modeling to support system requirements, design, analysis, verification and validation activities beginning in the conceptual design phase and continuing through-out development and later life-cycle phases.

One of the key concepts in the MBSE approach is Architecting, which is strictly related to the process that drives the identification of design solutions starting from system objectives. This process is characterized by the analysis and technical simulation necessary to evaluate system performances. During this phase, systems engineering work is also affected by policies, principles, procedures, budgets, reviews and other activities. Under these conditions, the system design process can be potentially characterized by omissions, misinterpretations and inconsistencies that can be the source of issues in subsequent development phases. The main aim of MBSE methodology is the reduction of such problems because they can affect the system performance or delay the expected time to market.

In industry, lifecycle management generally includes product lifecycle management (PLM) and the related concepts that must be considered. PLM can be defined as the process of managing the entire lifecycle of a product, from the initial idea to the subsequent phases of design, manufacturing, operative service and final disposal. PLM integrates people, data, processes and business infrastructures, building the product information backbone for industrial companies to fulfil their mission. The lifecycle management processes of different products are characterized by slightly different phases with different temporal extents and conventions though they are all conceived to organize the work from the preliminary steps to the more detailed ones. Figure 1 depicts the activities and related relationships that generally characterize the overall process, from customer needs to the final system solution.

In the last decade, large-scale system projects have been created using different lifecycle development models. There are no constraints on the development models used by organizations, academia or industry. They often use their own lifecycle patterns, but the most common lifecycle models are Royce's Waterfall model (Royce 1970), Boehm's spiral model (Boehm 1988), and Forsberg and Mooz's "Vee" model (Forsberg and Mooz 1992). Each defines the lifecycle differently, as shown in their conceptual representations in Figs. 2, 3 and 4. Such lifecycle representations are partially derived from patterns used to implement software products and the same approaches can be applied and extended to the development of one-of-a-kind complex systems involving hardware and software.

The definition of development processes through V-shaped diagrams allows for a graphical description of the overall process of system design and development. This representation can be used to model the same conceptual process at different levels of detail because the same structure can be adopted to define the whole system and single subsystems or components.

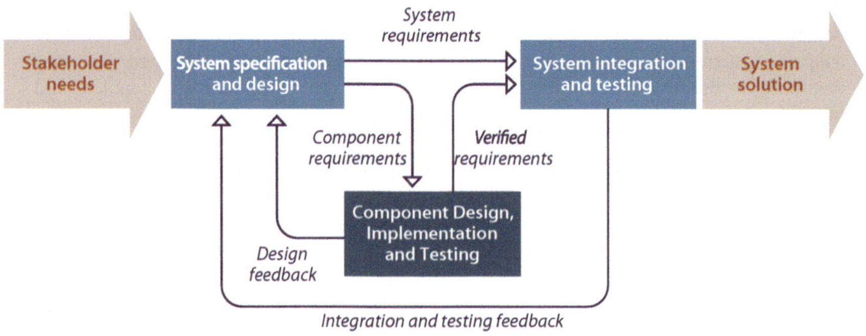


**Fig. 1** Development process from customer needs to system solution

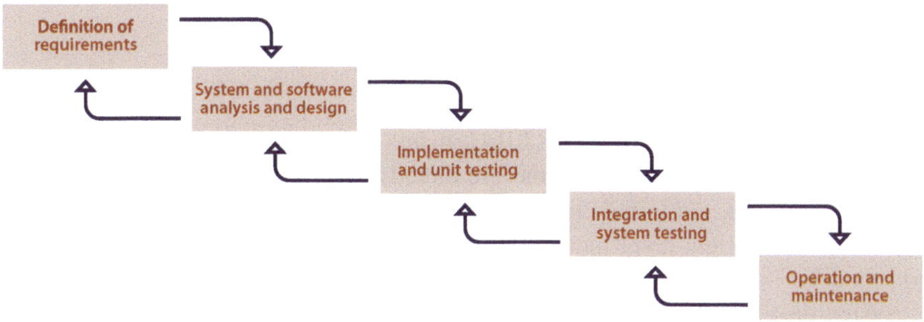


**Fig. 2** Royce's Waterfall model (1970)

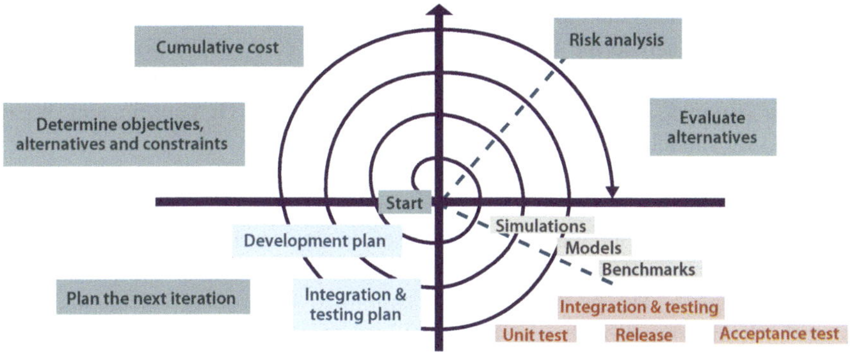


**Fig. 3** Boehm's spiral model (1988)

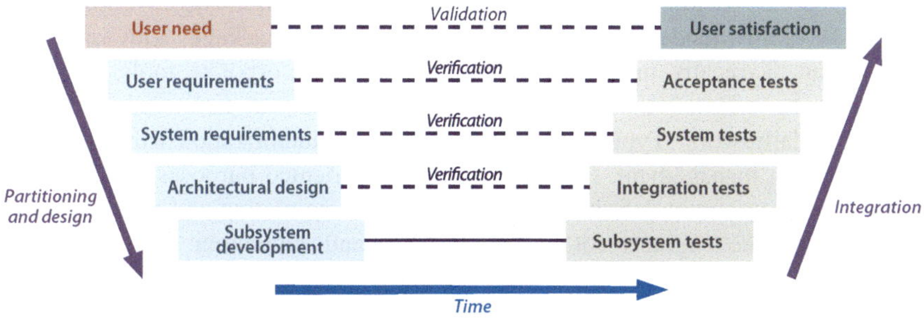


**Fig. 4** Forsberg and Moog's "Vee" model (1992)

## 2.2 Technical Analysis and Simulation: Languages, Methods and Tools

As described in Pasquinelli et al. (2014), many types of models can be used in a model-based environment, and some are already widely used, especially in engineering disciplines. An initial classification limited to engineering activities may be organized into system-level models, engineering discipline models and collaboration models.

System-level models formally describe system-level views of system data (e.g., functional, architectural, behavioural, requirements). The Object Management Group standardized UML (Object Management Group 2015) (mainly for software) and SysML (Object Management Group 2013) (for systems). The xAF architectural framework (Rouhani et al. 2015) describes high-level (e.g., enterprise) architecture. Other examples include the ESA OCDT (de Koning et al. 2014) (for preliminary design) or VSEE (Rey 2013) (intended for entire lifecycle), the Thales ARCADIA approach (Roques 2016) and the TAS DEVICE model (Di Giorgio and Wiart 2012). CAD models define and maintain physical configurations, item arrangements, related interfaces and harness routing and are currently supported by many commercial tools.

Discipline-specific models are widely used in engineering for simulation and analysis. They represent a simplification of the real system from the perspective of a specific discipline. The geometry can be simplified for specific calculations and control. Continuous models can be discretized to solve problems using partial differential or differential algebraic equations. Software and logic models represent specific behaviours for implementation in system software or simulation of external operational entities.

Project collaboration models are also extensively used to manage workflow and change. Workflow models help define team tasks or work packages with associated input/output. Typically managed using PDM/PLM or corporate tools, they can sometimes be oriented to the formalization of contractual tasks rather than in support of daily work. Typically, such tools include authorization workflows and documentation management. For more technically oriented purposes, such models include the input/output definition from analysis and simulation and give control to a system architect/engineer for system analysis and simulation while gathering discipline-specific models. Change management models typically analyse relationships between existing models and can help provide an impact analysis in the case of a change.

Finally, optimization models typically connect different parametric models and enable finding the optimal solution according to objectives (Cencetti 2014).

As shown in Fig. 5, a centralized unique system model cannot exist because many models rely on its data and should be kept consistent. The system-level model could be a federation of models such as a SysML model or a Capella (Roques 2016) model for functional aspects (or an evolution based on semantics such as the

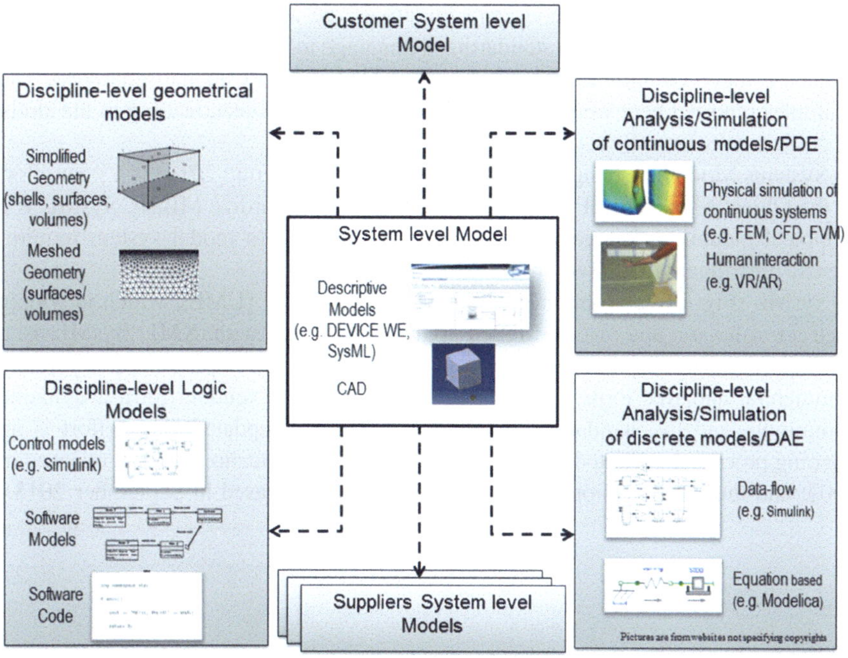


**Fig. 5** Discipline-specific models rely on data and should be kept consistent

TAS DEVICE model) connected with the geometrical baseline (typical a CAD model).

The system-level information is mostly generated by discipline-level activities, providing analysis of requirements and evolution of the design in lower-level detail. Typically, discipline-level activities require a subset of the system model data and provide another subset of the system model data that is needed by other disciplines.

However, discipline-level models are not a subset of the system model. For instance, the geometry of a thermal model can be simplified with respect to a CAD model, excepting some items and including fictional items related to the simplification of the model for calculation purposes (especially in early phases and for some specific analyses). A mechanical FEM model includes more items than the CAD model meshes and has many properties that do not need to be shared. A software model could be mapped to system functions but it is not useful to share and maintain software-specific items (classes, protocols, etc.) in a central repository.

One typically overlooked aspect is the collaboration with different industrial tiers (i.e., customers and suppliers). In the case of model-based environments in industrial teams, a connection between models (with precise workflow and rule management) is essential for the highest profit from consistency control, clear flow of data between partners and control of impacts in the case of changes.

System/Architectural methods and initiatives are approached differently, from the SysML effort to provide a standardized language to other initiatives at company, project, or open communities levels (e.g., the DEVICE or Capella initiatives). The examples reported here were analysed during the UIW-project, leading to the study of custom solutions.

Systems Modelling Language (Object Management Group 2013) is a joint effort of the Object Management Group and INCOSE to standardize MBSE. SysML is a graphical modelling language with nine diagram types to model system requirements, functionality, behaviour and structure.

SysML (Fig. 6) has roots in Unified Model Language (UML), which is widely used in software and was designed to be exchanged with XMI. SysML is a methodology-agnostic and tool-agnostic open standard, implemented by many commercial and free tools. The OMG SysML and tool vendors form a dynamic community and the standard and tools are frequently updated. This effort is an ongoing process that started in 2001; OMG SysML specification 1.0 was released in 2007, and the latest version 1.4 of the standard was released in September 2015.

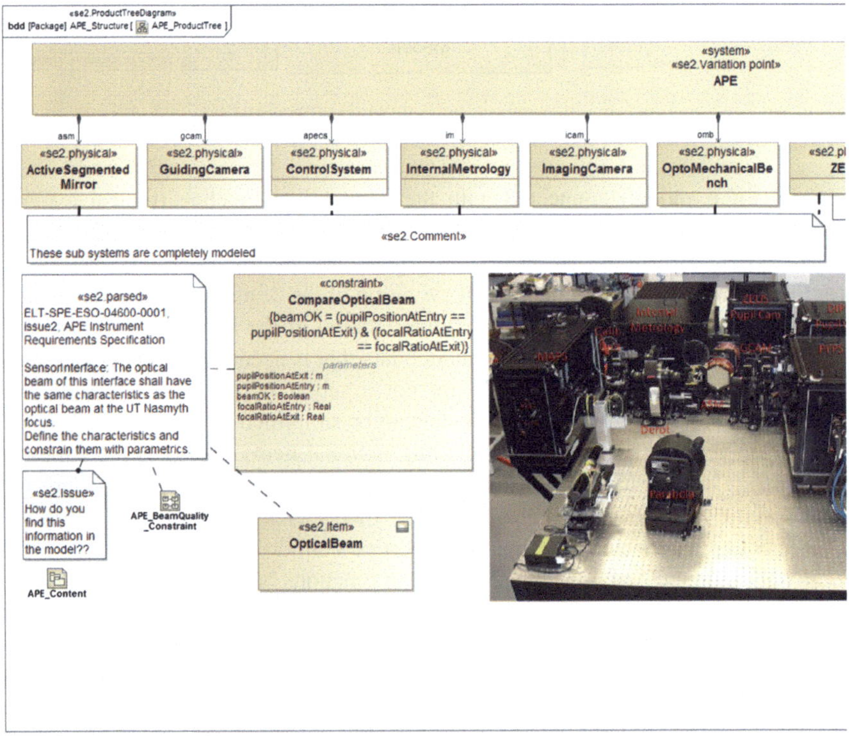


**Fig. 6** A fragment of a structural SysML diagram (Karban et al. 2011)

Recent commercial tool vendor efforts have situated SysML at the centre of the MBSE approach (Fig. 7). Syndeia software for lifecycle management (Intercax 2016) claims to use the language to interconnect models between discipline-specific tools such as CAD, project management, requirement management, simulation, PLM and relational databases.

DEVICE (Distributed Environment for Virtual Integrated Collaborative Engineering) is a collector of Thales Alenia Space Italia internal research devoted to study, development, validation and proposal of new methodologies/tools to improve systems engineering and multidisciplinary collaboration since 2007 (Di Giorgio and Wiart 2012). This research was recently realigned with the Thales engineering environment deployed across all Thales business units and also partially deployed (for model-based system architecture tooling) since 2015 as the Capella open-source initiative under the Polarsys project (Blondelle et al. 2015).

The modelling portion of the DEVICE infrastructure is currently a customized conceptual meta-model that was conceived to be compatible with European standardization, e.g., ECSS-E-TM-10-23 and ECSS-E-TM-10-23 data models, which are not current standards but are meant to change significantly in the future. The end product is incrementally defined in terms of structure and behaviour with regards to

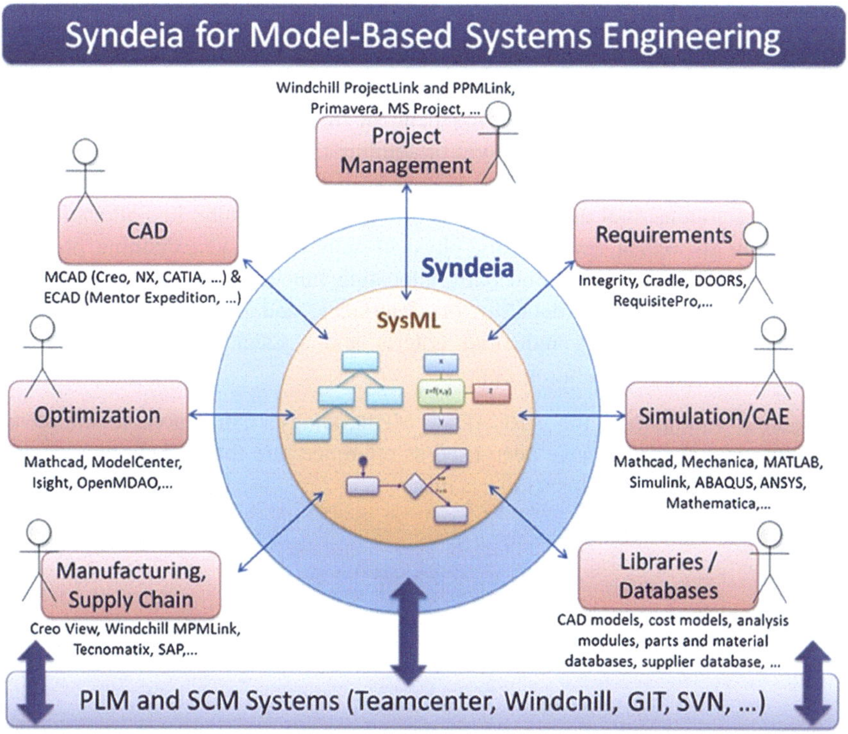


**Fig. 7** SysML is in the centre of a tool-interconnection effort (Intercax 2016)

the lifecycle phase. Different design methods are allowed for logical and physical architectures, with relationships that allow precise semantics but do not create many different items. The defined semantics allow the product model to be used as a virtual model for simulation, allowing linkage with design tools, analysis models, test equipment and operational data.

The end product definition and verification are driven by requirements and reference scenarios, the requirements that are defined using models and are related to design items for automatic consistency checks. The scenarios consist of the definition of activities that will be performed in the in-flight utilization phase and during the production, integration, on-ground testing and logistics.

The UIW-project provided a cross-linked environment between the DEVICE research, typically validated in space activities and other domains and lifecycle activities that can enrich the existing models and approaches and inspire novel usage of standard tools such as SysML-based commercial tools or open source platforms such as Capella. The following section describes some of these results.

ARCADIA (Roques 2016) is a model-based engineering method for systems, hardware and software architectural design. It was developed by Thales between 2005 and 2010 through an iterative process involving operational architects from all Thales business domains. ARCADIA is the systems engineering methodology supported by the Capella tool (Roques 2016). This methodology was developed internally by the Thales Group and has been made open source. This methodology relies on several interconnected modelling levels:

- Needs understanding in operational analysis, i.e., an understanding of the operational environment that is independent from the existence of the system, and system analysis with objectives of defining the boundary of the system with respect to external actors and the system-level functions.
- Solution architectural design in terms of logical architecture, i.e., allocating the functions to logical components, physical architecture, i.e., defining how the system will be developed and built, allocating functions to hardware and software components, and detailing the interfaces, and end-product breakdown structure for managing industrial criteria and associating requirements and interfaces with configuration items

Figure 8 summarizes the ARCADIA Methodology. Other notable initiatives from the space field that have been used as references are the OCDT (https://ocdt.esa.int) and the VSEE (https://vsd.esa.int).

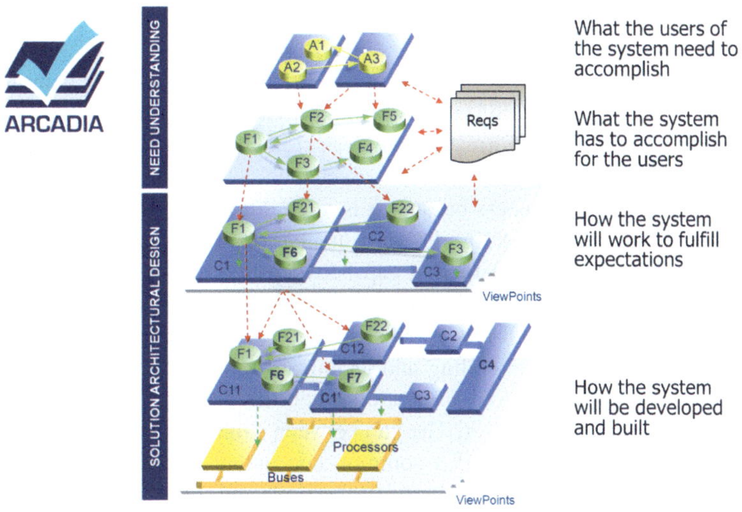


**Fig. 8** The ARCADIA methodology (Roques 2016)

## 3 Extending the System Model to Cover the Entire Lifecycle

Three main gaps were identified in the ideal integrated methodology shown in Fig. 5: (1) integration of system modelling with simulation, (2) use of system modelling across the entire lifecycle and between different activities, and (3) tool limitations: security, data exchange, collaboration and user culture. A quick overview of such gaps is provided below.

Different issues can arise when system modelling methodologies are integrated in simulation environments. Development of the proper interfaces is strongly affected by the manner in which the integration is implemented within the overall design and analysis process. A clear understanding of the overall process and the related infrastructure can reduce issues that arise as development proceeds. A clear conceptual framework is fundamental to support modelling activities because it paves the way for effective exploitation of available resources.

Each of the existing methodologies is based on a specific data structure developed for specific applications, reducing the possibility of re-using the related environments within other contexts or domains.

The integration of simulation environments and system modelling frameworks can be approached in different manners depending on the final objectives and on the specific workflow that characterizes the company. Technical simulations can be used to investigate the product performance based on available data; the management of this information affects the integration architecture. The potential solutions can change based on the tools and required capabilities. Multidisciplinary analyses can be supported using dedicated platforms to manage the results generated by simulation tools.

The exploitation of technical simulations is strictly related to the capabilities of external analysis platforms. System modelling environments can be used to store the representative project information whereas simulation platforms use such data to set up and execute analyses. The data exchange across different environments represents a challenging process because it is often difficult to integrate information from different sources in a straightforward manner. Currently, different tools support system modelling, but there is a gap between the available information and analysis capabilities (sensitivity analysis, optimization, uncertainty quantification, and parameter estimation). Object-oriented solutions can enhance the advantages of a unique environment for modelling and technical simulations and can reduce the efforts required for consistency verification when the data are exchanged directly with an external process manager. The gap between simulation tools and modelling environments can be mitigated if a common conceptual infrastructure is defined. Such integration can be realized only if the platforms and related methodologies are clear and well-posed.

The improvements related to a successful MBSE method on a system engineer/architect level can be jeopardized by an ineffective connection with discipline-level work, especially for data exchanged between different disciplines and managed for consistency at a system level.

SysML, ARCADIA, UML, xAF and other frameworks rely on a data model that was created for specific purposes and was not intended to serve for the entire lifecycle or for all engineering activities. Moreover, such methods (and related tools) were initially developed to support SE activities and not for an asynchronous collaboration between different team members using different tools. Recent advancements in such model-based methods and tools have attempted to overcome this limitation. However, the lack of semantics (for simulation use) is still an issue in many methods and it often necessitates ad hoc solutions, e.g., with a specific profile for the SysML. In such cases, the standardization is often replaced by vendor-level, company-level or project-level profiling.

Many different companies and institutions already rely on MBSE solutions, SysML-based (Spangelo et al. 2012) or custom (Di Giorgio and Wiart 2012), and almost all large enterprises rely on legacy systems that include relevant data for past and current projects.

Currently, the system modelling–simulation connection is an open area in which many improvements can be made, especially with the objective of an improved rapid response to the customer.

**System modelling across the lifecycle**

Systems engineering is often regarded as an approach to provide system solutions but after deployment other disciplines such as project management are more prevalent. MBSE has followed this view and focuses on the initial concept and development stages, i.e., on the as-designed system rather than on the as-built system.

SysML, the main example of ongoing MBSE standardization, has a similar bias, lacking clear semantics to differentiate views of the system at different life-cycle stages. This limits the adoption of MBSE for the management of stages beyond concept and development. It also limits the mapping and interchange of information between tools across the life-cycle. One example is the configuration management of as-designed system components that can model design evolution versus configuration management of the as-built system components that can model system part maintenance and replacement. The link between the as-designed and the as-built statuses of a system is often at the frontier between tools and is often not explicitly managed in any of them.

Moreover, a typical Vee cycle should be supported by different types of tooling and methods for the relevant activities performed at each stage. In the space field, concept and feasibility studies conducted at the beginning of the typical life-cycle often rely on parametric models for early sizing and analysis to understand the system-level feasibility of the proposed solution.

In later phases of system and product definition (phases A/B in the European space standardization), a more complex industrial team is formed and more complex analysis is required. Moving towards the detailed definition and production phases, the overall consistency should be managed at different levels and the management of changes and requirements becomes more formal and controlled to assure the highest product quality and reduce risks. In serial production, the product and component variants and the ever-growing trend of customization increase the complexity. Modelling of product features, options and variants is not directly addressed in this chapter but their application is essential to any type of production, including one-of-a-kind, because they allow re-use of components that generates savings. The operational and disposal phases are typically supported by models to support the users, operators, maintenance and anomaly investigation teams (Fig. 9).

The analysis of the potential system- and product-level model-based activities is performed from a project lifecycle point of view and could be called "vertical", viewed as a sequence diagram, with time progressing from the top to the bottom. There is also a horizontal perspective that should be considered as each activity runs in parallel to activities in other projects or even in other companies involved in the project. This issue has two main associated topics to consider:

1. Collaboration: in model-based systems engineering, the capability of IT tools to exchange models and synchronize them with limited effort by the user is essential for effectiveness and efficiency. Security issues should also be considered to avoid spreading sensitive company knowledge outside of authorized boundaries. Moreover, the use of common rules, object libraries and conventions is essential to assure an effective collaboration and reduce related risks.
2. Return of experience: experience gained in other projects or activities should be appropriately incorporated into the current activity. The MBSE approach can

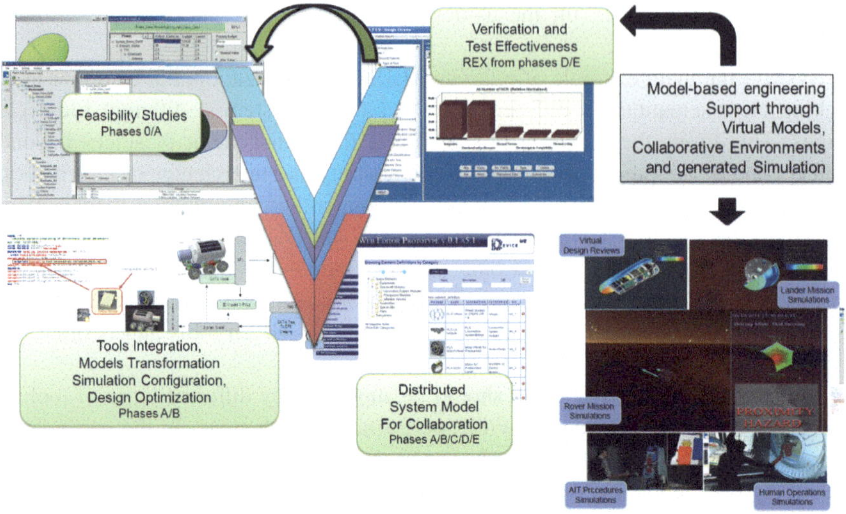


**Fig. 9** Model-based usage across the lifecycle (Pasquinelli et al. 2014)

generate a large amount of data that, in contrast to the classic document-based approach, can be processed in a more effective manner.

**Tool limitations: security, data exchange, collaboration and user culture**

In many cases, the limitations are not in the methodology or languages but in the tools, toolchains and complexity of the information system networking in a multifaceted industrial scenario. There are three main factors that limit the seamless adoption of a tool by an end-user:

- Overwhelming complexity: if managing the data in the tool or understanding the user interface requires more time and mental effort than usual, the end-user may be reluctant to adopt new approaches. This is often the case with MBSE methodologies and tools. Simplified user interfaces, complexity management through different levels of detail, and easy navigation and immediate visualization are key aspects to consider.
- Annoying constraints: each company must take preventive action to avoid unwanted flow of sensitive data, propagation of human errors or negative impacts on company performance and security. This is typically translated into necessary constraints that are considered annoying limits by the end user. Tools that allow more fine-grained control of the flow of information may ease the constraints and improve overall security.
- Demanding collaboration and different cultures: collaboration among different users and stakeholders is typically a source of misunderstanding and requires well established processes and procedures. Even when consolidated in practice

due to past experience, any change brings new risk and should be disseminated correctly. When using different tools, this also translates into interface and compatibility issues (between both tools and people).

## 4 Proposed Extensions

Three main extensions to the current modelling solutions can fill these gaps:

(1) Extending the current data models with knowledge-oriented and simulation-oriented concepts, leading to the definition of an executable virtual product.
(2) Extending the current data models to include all statuses of a product (in PLM, from as-required to as-designed, as-analysed, as-built, and as-maintained), closing the gap between early engineering studies, detailed engineering tasks, production, testing, operations and maintenance.
(3) Extending the data models, related tooling and current processes to derive the system definition as a set of engineering services and related connections to project and company management.

### *4.1 Knowledge- and Simulation-Oriented Concepts*

There are two main needs in the modelling and simulation field: (1) a modelling methodology that is generic enough to not constrain the solution definition, and (2) a modelling methodology that is specific enough to allow data to be univocally interpreted.

For example, SysML responds to the first need but is lacking in the second need, so a typical user specializes and customizes the language to meet their needs. The current trends (e.g., use of ontologies, the semantic web, and more detailed data models) respond to the second need but their definition and interpretation is often limited to IT experts. A potential solution is to decouple the two needs so that (1) generic concepts (such as the fact that a product is composed of other products and may be interfaced with other products) could be defined in a generic modelling methodology, adopted across different industrial domains and types of expertise, and (2) specific concepts are standardized at a community level (a community may be related to a specific industrial domain, a specific scientific field, or to a specific project or team).

This approach can also replace the current standardization in document-based approaches. The end purpose is to produce models with items whose semantics can be understood by any target user and can be interpreted univocally by a machine (e.g., a simulation software code). This would allow a transition between a view of the MBSE as a model-based description of a system and related systems engineering data to a view of MBSE as the definition of a virtual product that can be interpreted and executed throughout the life-cycle, with capabilities related to a specific definition level of detail, input between users and the different product variants.

### 4.2 From Definitions to Realizations

Current data model support in MBSE tools– and the prevalent standardization effort of SysML-lacks explicit support for including the status of a product, from as-required to as-designed, as-analysed, as-built and as-maintained. This can be an obstacle for data interchange among tools employed throughout the product life-cycle (such as PLM tools). Using the example of the mass of a system component, a component may have an as-required mass, an as-designed mass and an as-measured mass. All three must be stored and tracked throughout the system life-cycle.

A first step is differentiating between component definitions and component realizations. Each component definition can be realized many times and each component realization corresponds to only one component definition. This difference is made explicit by recent MBSE efforts (Rey 2013) promising but still focused on a specific industrial sector, biased by the specificities of one-of-a-kind-products.

For example, the design of a product can be modelled by a component definition. The product can be realized (manufactured) many times. Examples of component realizations and definitions are the manufactured units and their designs. The component definitions can have an associated as-designed mass and component realizations can have an associated as-measured mass. Design upgrades can be modelled as component definition versions and product upgrades due to maintenance can be modelled by component realization versions.

### 4.3 Service-Based Engineering

The conceptual infrastructure that defines the data structure of a system model has a key role in the management of the available information. A clear representation of all possible data sources and their relations is fundamental for designing an effective system. The development of modelling processes in which the customer is increasingly involved within the design activity shows promising capabilities for the near future. Customer-in-the-loop strategies highlight interesting benefits regarding the expected system performance and a better exploitation of available resources. A clear and deeper involvement of the customer in the decision-making process can help generate a product that is better aligned with market expectations.

This aspect is common to different markets and the same approach can be used, with minor changes, across different domains.

These considerations highlight how a conceptual infrastructure for service modelling can help include additional scenarios in the context of system definition. The development of the objects and the relationships that characterize a service can enhance the communication between customers and system designers. This vision of the customer-in-the-loop strategy can be pursued through application of a model-based philosophy, providing all the features and benefits that aid in the definition of a system project. The related data structure can be used to drive information exchange between stakeholders and track of the current baseline and changes in a consistent manner.

## 5 Conclusion

The experiments conducted in UIW, especially those in the space and ship building domains, show interesting results for the extension of system models. Extensions include web-based collaboration, the connection with simulation and virtual reality, and the use of services and probes. However, the experience with causal context models, the circular economy model and other strategic/company level models should be linked with technical choices, collaboration aspects, project management and company strategy. Models that relate economic and strategic domains are often difficult to formalize, but a clear integration of the related concepts with the current system model can greatly enhance the lifecycle process.

Extending the model to include maintenance activities yielded interesting and promising results. Additional details are presented in Chapter "Collaborative Management of Inspection Results in Power plant Turbines" in the context of maintenance of power plant turbines. Efforts for harmonizing the product structure from the assembly point of view with alternate methods of structuring information derived from the maintenance processes have shown improvements in communication and information sharing among the different actors involved. However, extending the system model to cover both the product and the service views would require changes to the companies' information systems. However, such a step and the adoption of an MBSE approach, which is not the case for some traditional industries, are required to ensure the convergence of the actual practice towards a more effective data management solution.

The UIW-experience allowed determination of the common issues among different design processes. Such problems can be faced with a more effective design approach, and a model-based philosophy can provide useful tools to mitigate the current situation. Additional features can be integrated within the system model to cover common areas among different companies. For example, a well-formalized system model can pave the way for tools and techniques that can support the decision-making process. Currently, system solutions and design choices are strictly dependent on the context and seldom can all the knowledge elaborated during these processes be re-used in other projects. It is often difficult to track the rationales that drive a design choice because it is difficult to formalize how such information can be defined. An extension of the system model to include such aspects can improve the design process across different industry domains, especially with respect to company strategies and objectives. The system data can be exploited in a more effective manner if defined properly following the pattern of a formalized system model. In this manner, the information collected in a project can be re-used in another one with less effort than the traditional approaches. Company expertise can also be managed in a more consistent manner to help correlate all available information for product design.

For example, the decision-making process can take advantage of a model-based approach because optimizations, trade-offs or sensitivity analyses can be performed consistently with the available system data. Another interesting advantage is that all the related information for optimization, trade-off or sensitivity analyses is not only helpful for the current design but can be re-used in the future because it follows the structured data representation of a common system model. However, such an extension of the system model requires a clear understanding of the current optimization or sensitivity analyses practices so that the largest number of design scenarios is covered. The variety of optimization or sensitivity analyses scenarios is generally broad due to the characteristics of the computational models, inputs and outputs.

## References

Blondelle, G., Bordeleau, F., & Exertier, D. (2015). Polarsys: A new collaborative ecosystem for open source solutions for systems engineering driven by major industry players. *INSIGHT, 18* (2), 35–38.

Boehm, B. W. (1988). A spiral model of software development and enhancement. *Computer, 21* (5), 61–72.

Cencetti, M. (2014). *Evolution of model-based system engineering methodologies for the design of space systems in the advanced stages of the project (Phases BC)*. Politecnico di Torino. Retrieved from http://porto.polito.it/2572760

de Koning, H. P., Gerené, S., Ferreira, I., Pickering, A., Beyer, F., & Vennekens, J. (2014). Open concurrent design tool—ESA community open source ready to go! In *Presented at the 6th International Conference on Systems and Concurrent Engineering for Space Applications, Stuttgart*. Retrieved from http://congrexprojects.com/2014-events/14c08/

Di Giorgio, F., & Wiart, B. (2012). Applying collaborative system engineering in Thales: Lessons learned and best practices. In *Presented at the 5th International Workshop on Systems & Concurrent Engineering for Space Applications (SECESA 2012), Lisbon*. Retrieved from http://www.congrexprojects.com/12c12/

Forsberg, K., & Mooz, H. (1992). The relationship of systems engineering to the project cycle. *Engineering Management Journal, 4*(3), 36–43.

Friedenthal, S., Moore, A., & Steiner, R. (2014). *A Practical guide to SysML, third edition: The systems modeling language* (3 ed.). Morgan Kaufmann.

Intercax. (2016). *Syndeia (formerly SLIM for Systems Lifecycle Management)*. Retrieved from intercax.com

Karban, R., Weilkiens, T., Hauber, R., Zamparelli, M., Diekmann, R., & Hein, A. (2011). *CookBook for MBSE with SysML*. SE2 Challenge Team. Retrieved from http://mbse.gfse.de/

Object Management Group. (2013). *Systems modelling language (OMG SysML) V1.4*. Retrieved from http://www.omg.org/spec/SysML/1.4/

Object Management Group. (2015, June). *Unified modeling language (UML) V2.5*. Retrieved from http://www.omg.org/spec/UML/2.5/

Pasquinelli, M., Basso, V., Mazzini, S., Baracchi, L., Puri, S., Gerbaz, D., … Viitaniemi, J. (2014). Model-based approach for the verification enhancement across the lifecycle of a space system. In *6th International Conference on Systems and Concurrent Engineering for Space Applications*. Stuttgart. Retrieved from http://ceur-ws.org/Vol-1300/ID11.pdf

Rey, J. (2013). *Modeling with VSEE: Definition of guidelines and exploitation of the models* (p. 48). European Space Agency. Retrieved from http://www.vsd-project.org/download/documents/YGT%20final%20report%20Rey%20V2.pdf

Roques, P. (2016). MBSE with the ARCADIA method and the Capella tool. In *8th European Congress on Embedded Real Time Software and Systems (ERTS 2016), Toulouse, France*. Retrieved from https://hal.archives-ouvertes.fr/hal-01258014

Rouhani, B. D., Mahrin, M. N., Nikpay, F., Ahmad, R. B., & Nikfard, P. (2015). A systematic literature review on enterprise architecture implementation methodologies. *Information and Software Technology*, *62*, 1–20. https://doi.org/10.1016/j.infsof.2015.01.012

Royce, W. W. (1970). Managing the development of large software systems. In *proceedings of IEEE WESCON* (Vol. 26, pp. 1–9). Los Angeles. Retrieved from http://leadinganswers.typepad.com/leading_answers/files/original_waterfall_paper_winston_royce.pdf

Spangelo, S. C., Kaslow, D., Delp, C., Cole, B., Anderson, L., Fosse, E., … Cutler, J. (2012). Applying model based systems engineering (MBSE) to a standard CubeSat. In *Aerospace Conference, 2012 IEEE* (pp. 1–20). IEEE. Retrieved from http://ieeexplore.ieee.org/xpls/abs_all.jsp?arnumber=6187339

Technical Operations International Council on Systems Engineering (INCOSE). (2007). *INCOSE systems engineering vision 2020* (No. INCOS E-TP-2004-004-02). International Council on Systems Engineering. Retrieved from http://oldsite.incose.org/ProductsPubs/pdf/SEVision2020_20071003_v2_03.pdf

Wiley, & Others. (2015). *INCOSE systems engineering handbook: A guide for system life cycle processes and activities*. Wiley. Retrieved from https://books.google.es/books?hl=es&lr=&id=8-cbBgAAQBAJ&oi=fnd&pg=PA145&dq=Systems+Engineering+Handbook+INCOSE&ots=wjK2AWl7Nj&sig=auPtFAItomJSjQ0axlwqK4IHm58

# Part III
# From Theory to Practice

# Collaborative Management of Inspection Results in Power Plant Turbines

**Daniel Gonzalez-Toledo, Maria Cuevas-Rodriguez and Susana Flores-Holgado**

**Abstract** This chapter presents an industrial case study that investigates a collaborative tool for use in the fossil and nuclear power plant industries. The tool makes the results of technical inspections on fossil and nuclear power plants available to all stakeholders and assists in the post-inspection decision-making process by highlighting decisions that minimise the outage duration and prolong the turbine's service life. Before development commenced, an actor-product-service (APS) model was employed to establish the problem, the process of which is presented in this chapter. This model describes the relationships between the elements that the system must store and manage. In this particular industrial case, the APS model defines the product as the power plant turbine and the service as technical inspections. Henceforth, this model describes the relation between the inspection tasks and results and the turbine parts that are inspected. In addition, the APS model allows the application to work jointly with the product and the service, representing the information in a way closer to the mental model of each user profile, which should result in an improvement in productivity.

**Keywords** Collaborative tools · 3D interaction · 3D viewer · Web-based application · Inspection services · Turbine maintenance

D. Gonzalez-Toledo (✉) · M. Cuevas-Rodriguez
DIANA Research Group, Departamento de Tecnología Electrónica,
ETSI Telecomunicación, Universidad de Málaga, Malaga, Spain
e-mail: dgonzalezt@uma.es

M. Cuevas-Rodriguez
e-mail: mariacuevas@uma.es

S. Flores-Holgado
Materials and Life Management, Tecnatom, San Sebastián de los Reyes, Spain
e-mail: sflores@tecnatom.es



S.N. Grösser et al. (eds.), *Dynamics of Long-Life Assets*,
DOI 10.1007/978-3-319-45438-2_11

# 1 Introduction

Tecnatom is an engineering company that provides services to a number of markets, including the nuclear energy, combined cycle and thermal, aircraft and aerospace, transport, and petrochemical markets. The company's main activity is performing inspection services and training operation personnel by means of full-scope simulators to support plant operations.

As part of the evaluation of the structural integrity of nuclear power plants' components and industrial facilities in general, Tecnatom performs inspections and tests based on applicable standards. Once an inspection has been carried out, the results are recorded, transmitted and evaluated. When defects are detected, the flow of information becomes crucial because there are many actors involved, including the companies that design, supervise and manufacture the turbines; the companies that perform the inspections; engineering companies; the power plant managers; and maintenance and repair companies. It is essential that those involved understand the problem, share information, analyse the results and propose a solution in the shortest amount of time possible.

Within the UIW-context, this industrial case is centred on the power plant steam turbine (Fig. 1). Turbines are long-lasting, high-investment components whose operation directly affects power generation and hence productivity. A collaborative tool that manages the inspections carried out on turbine components and the results has the potential to contribute to improving company services.

## *1.1 Company Necessities*

During the last 15 years, Tecnatom has developed and successfully established a software tool to manage inspections and testing plans and the results of such inspections in several Spanish power plants. The system also stores all the

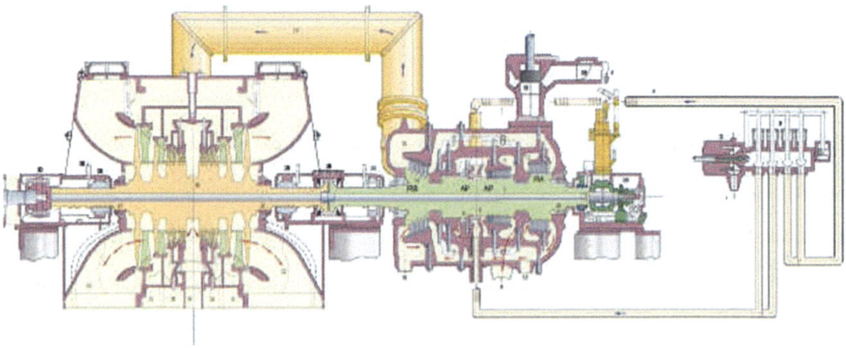

**Fig. 1** Typical turbine-generator set scheme

information required by technicians to fulfil inspection tasks, including inspection and maintenance procedures; information regarding inspection areas, techniques, and frequencies for each component; and 2D drawings of systems and components. Figure 2 shows a schematic diagram of the information flow managed by the system.

Although the system has had prolonged success, some users have suggested that improvements are needed to obtain a more reliable tool and provide added-value services in a collaborative environment by supporting the decision-making process throughout the life cycle of power plants components. This updated application would allow designers and engineers to analyse the problem, propose a definitive solution and even modify the design to avoid similar problems in future versions of the product.

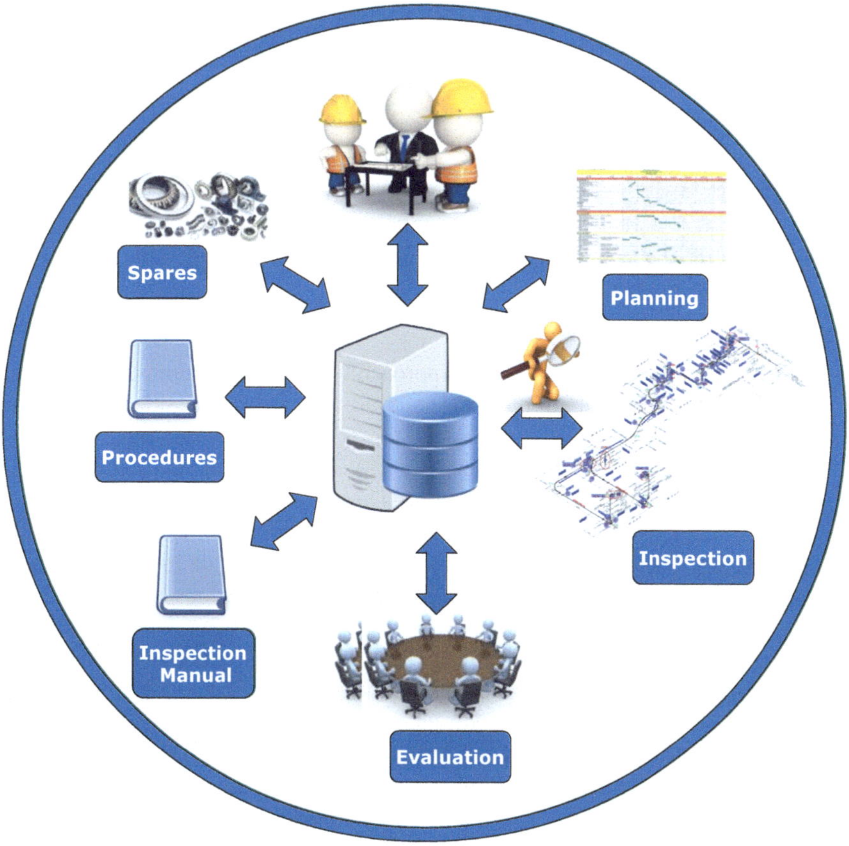


**Fig. 2** Flow of information and working team

In relation to the Tecnatom industrial case, added-value services would be the 3D visualisation of the whole turbine and 3D interaction with turbine components (Bowman et al. 2004), along with relevant information about the turbine, linked to the 3D model (Elmqvist and Tsigas 2008). These services would allow the user to more quickly assess the situation when a problem arises, resulting in the optimal solution in a short period of time. In addition, the system could create an environment that allows decisions to be made among all the stakeholders in a collaborative way while registering and storing the comments and the agreed solution for future use. This would allow comparisons to be made when issues arise with similar components by taking into account lessons learned or previously stored operating experiences.

In summary, the main goal of this industrial case is to investigate the different possibilities and technologies for the development of an innovative collaborative prototype system that will work as a decision support tool for the life-cycle management of power plant steam turbines. Taking into account the company requirements, the aim of this industrial case study is to provide (1) interactive 3D models of the turbines, (2) visualisation of augmented information in the 3D models to understand the structure and issues, (3) information linked to the 3D model regarding the inspection results and (4) a discussion management tool to share information and comments related to inspection results.

## *1.2 Industrial Case Approach in the Use-It-Wisely Project Context*

In Chapter "The Use-It-Wisely (UIW) Approach" of this book, common challenges of industrial cases were identified and organised within a framework (see Chapter "The Use-It-Wisely (UIW) Approach", Fig. 7) that contains three different domains: (1) market and data analysis, (2) collaboration management and (3) actor-product-service (APS) modelling. These three domains cover the challenges that manufacturing industries such as Tecnatom experience in providing services for high value, long-life products related to the upgrade initiating process.

Considering the company needs presented in the previous subsection, the challenges to be addressed can be allocated into two framework domains: APS modelling and collaboration management. The APS modelling domain organises all the information related to the turbine (the product), the inspections tasks and results (the service), whereas the collaboration management domain includes a discussion management tool to assist in optimal decision-making and a 3D application that depicts the inspection process, allowing for the visualisation and management of a turbine's technical information in a 3D interactive environment.

## 2 Modelling the Problem, from Theory Towards Implementation

To improve the management of inspection results in power plant turbines using the collaborative tool, the industrial case problem must be modelled. Therefore, this section aims to describe the specifications related to the industrial case problems, including a brief summary of the system use cases and requirements in the first sub-section, the APS model in the second sub-section, and the proposed implementation approach and system architecture in the third subsection. A conceptual prototype of the tool and a description of the industrial case can also be found in Reyes-Lecuona et al. (2014).

### 2.1 *Requirements and Use Cases*

This section describes an industrial use-case model of the system that can solve the problem of information flow among actors involved in the overall management of turbine inspections. In this industrial case, these actors are an inspection team (in charge of planning and performing inspections and informing on the results), an engineering team (in charge of analysing results and inputting them into the model), a plant team (representing different technicians and workers from the power plant) and administrators (technicians who are in charge of managing the model to create, edit, complete and adjust instantiations of each turbine with the Tecnatom databases).

A wide list of requirements has been defined to specify the system in a technical way. These include requirements related to how the system represents the inspection results and links them to the 3D model of the turbine, as well as the requirement for visualisation and discussion management tools. These requirements are associated with a set of system use cases, which are listed below.

- *Activity login.* The system identifies every actor before giving the actor access to the system to control which information and functionalities are available.
- *Inspection result input.* The Tecnatom inspection team inputs the results of an inspection into the system. If needed, the actor opens and prepares a discussion related to these results.
- *Visualising information.* The actors navigate through the turbine model, obtaining information about the different parts of the turbine, specific inspection data (defects/flaws, repairs performed, etc.) or information related to the corrective maintenance of a specific part. The actors visualise this information supported by the 3D geometry of the turbine.
- *Input location and size of defects.* When flaws are discovered during an inspection, their position and size can be registered into the model. Inspectors are able to graphically sketch the location of the defects using the system.

- *Management of discussions*. The actors can collaborate in a discussion related to a registered inspection point. The actors may add proposals to the discussion and relate it to other discussions until it is closed by an authorised actor.

## 2.2 Actor Product Service Model

From a high-level perspective, the APS model aims to describe the different business elements of the company and the relationships between them. These elements refer to both human and non-human factors. In other words, the APS model aims to detail the relationships between the workers and/or departments of the company and third-party customer companies and to model the information needed to manage the work and information flows among the relevant stakeholders.

In this industrial case, the APS model design was built based on the model-based systems engineering methodology defined within the context of the project Virtual Spacecraft Design (Rey 2013), which is described in Chapter "Extending the System Model". The model focuses on identifying the structure of any relevant information that the system has to store and manage to provide the needed functionalities. It was produced through a functional analysis based on the requirements and use cases shown in the previous subsection. After several revisions, the model shown in Fig. 3 was reached.

The model consists of two elements: the product, which involves the power plant turbine, and the service, which involves the inspection of the turbine for maintenance purposes. Actors can also be classified into two categories: (1) those who approach the problem from the point of view of the product and (2) those who approach the problem from the point of view of the service. The first category of

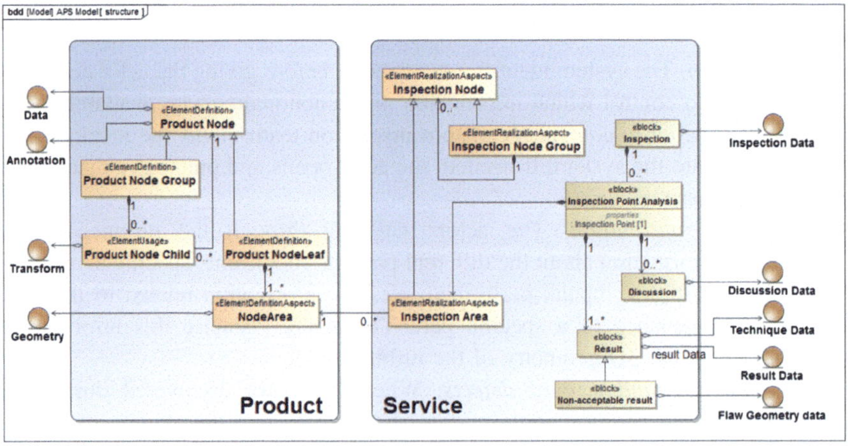


Fig. 3 Actor-product-service model diagram

actors consists of technicians and workers from the power plant who are interested in the product and its operation as a whole. The second category consists of technicians from the maintenance company who are interested in the planning, execution and analysis of the inspection results and who will be entering these data into the model.

The APS diagram presented in Fig. 3, based on SysML modelling languages (Friedenthal et al. 2014), represents both the product and service. These two models are organised in hierarchical trees and are connected to each other by their leaf nodes. After several attempts, this structure arose as the best way to organise the information.

In the product model, each node represents a component of the turbine in such a way that every component consists of the assembly of its children. The product model represents how the whole product is formed or assembled by the sub-systems, which in turn are formed by more basic sub-systems and so on, until the basic components are reached. The leaves of the product model tree are formed by the basic parts of the product, which does not mean they are small or simple; rather, they are simply pieces that are not formed by others. These blocks are shown in Fig. 3 as *NodeLeafs*.

Hanging from the leaves are areas that are not part of the product itself but are areas of interest within the *NodeLeaf* components. These areas are an important concept because different areas of a component have different physical requirements and are not subject to the same conditions. Therefore, the model specifies each of these areas (called *NodeArea* in Fig. 3).

The service model is formed by the inspection tree and the results. Whereas the product tree was intended to show the hierarchical structure of the product, the service tree has been created to express the way in which inspections are performed. Thus, the nodes of this tree represent not the physical parts of the product but parts or layers of the inspection. In this way, the model represents the structure and organisation of the whole turbine inspection. Just as the product structure is stable, so too is the service model structure throughout the turbine life-cycle.

The leaf nodes of the inspection tree are the *Inspection Areas*, which are the points that are going to be inspected. The service model represents turbine sections that are inspected at the same time (inspection areas), regardless of whether they are part of the same physical component of the product. It is important to keep together parts that are physically close or under the same operation/environmental conditions. As shown in Fig. 3, the two models are related by the areas formed by one or more products.

The model presents a block called *Inspection Point Analysis* that is associated with each inspection area. This is where new results and the associated data are stored after every inspection. In addition, the model allows for discussions related to each inspection point. This feature allows the technicians to analyse the results in a collaborative way. In addition, by keeping the entire history of decisions over the product stored together with its model, the risk of information fragmentation is avoided. In the service model, the discussion block hangs from either the Inspection

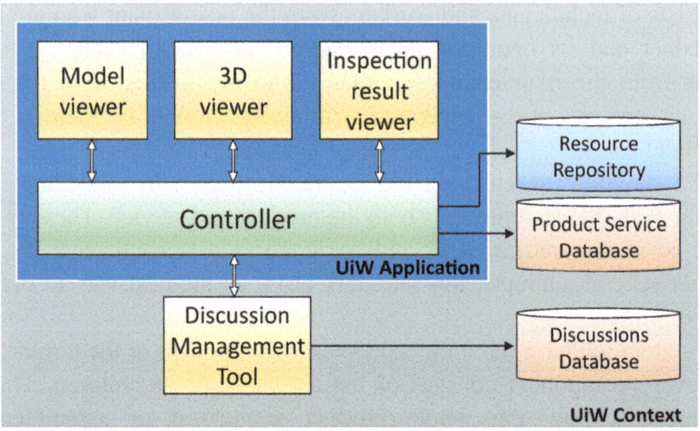


**Fig. 4** Block architecture of the system

Point Analysis or from each result. However, discussions for decision-making are often based on several results, which is why this discussion block is associated with the Inspection Point Analysis block.

All the hierarchical information regarding products and services is stored in a database called *Product Service database* (Fig. 4). This database also contains all the data regarding the service (inspections, techniques, results and flaw geometry) and the product (technical specifications, annotations and geometrical transformations). However, the 3D models files, inspections result pictures, technical documents and other additional information are stored in a repository called *Resources repository*. All the information regarding discussion management is stored in its own database.

## 2.3 *Implementation Approach*

To meet the industrial case requirements, a system architecture composed of four main modules was designed (described in more detail in Sect. 3):

- *Model viewer*. This module is an interactive viewer in which the user can navigate the different elements of the product and service models using a hierarchical tree (presented in the previous subsection).
- *3D viewer*. This module consists of an interactive viewer that shows the three-dimensional geometry model of the product (the power plant turbine) and presents information about the service (inspection results) linked to the 3D product model.
- *Interactive Inspection result viewer*. This third module is a viewer that shows the inspection tasks and results stored in the database (*Product Service database*) and in the repository (*Resources repository*).

- *Discussion management tool*. This module is an external application that allows users to discuss the inspection results, make proposals, make comparisons with other results, etc. The purpose of these discussions is to achieve a final decision about how to proceed after carrying out inspections. This module is a customisation of an existing opensource tool called Redmine (Redmine 2006).

Figure 4 shows a simplified representation of the system architecture, in which the four modules are connected and managed by a controller that is also in charge of the communication with the Product Service database and the Resource repository. The database contains information regarding the product and service models, following the structure of the APS model. Currently, the company database contains only some of the product information and is organised following a model based solely on the service. One of the contributions of this industrial case is to extend the company database to the APS model so that it is organised according to a model that takes into account both products and services.

The repository stores different resources, such as the 3D model files, inspection result pictures, technical documents and additional information. The discussion management tool does not use the controller to access the discussion database but rather has direct access.

The physical architecture of the system is shown in Fig. 5. This architecture also presents the decisions adopted regarding the platforms and tools used to develop the system. The implemented system has been designed as a web-based client-server distributed architecture that allows the user to access the system through a web browser. The 3D viewer runs on Web Graphics Library (WebGL 2001).

The 3D viewer module has been developed using the Unity (Unity 2005) platform and integrated in the ASP project using WebGL. Originally, the 3D viewer module was built and integrated using the Unity plugin for web navigators (Unity 2015), whose operation was based on the Netscape Plug-in API (NPAPI). However, the majority of web browsers have now disabled support from this API (Google Chrome did so in its version 42, April 2015) because, according to web browser companies, it has become a leading cause of hangs, crashes, security incidents, and code complexity (Chromium Blog 2013).

The modules *inspection result viewer and model viewer* were implemented using ASP.NET (ASP 2002). The server side also contains a set of databases and repositories that form the Product Service database and Resources repository. These repositories store all the information and data that the application needs. Finally, the discussion management module is based on an existing tool named Redmine, an opensource project management web application written using Ruby on Rails (Ruby 2005). This module has its own database.

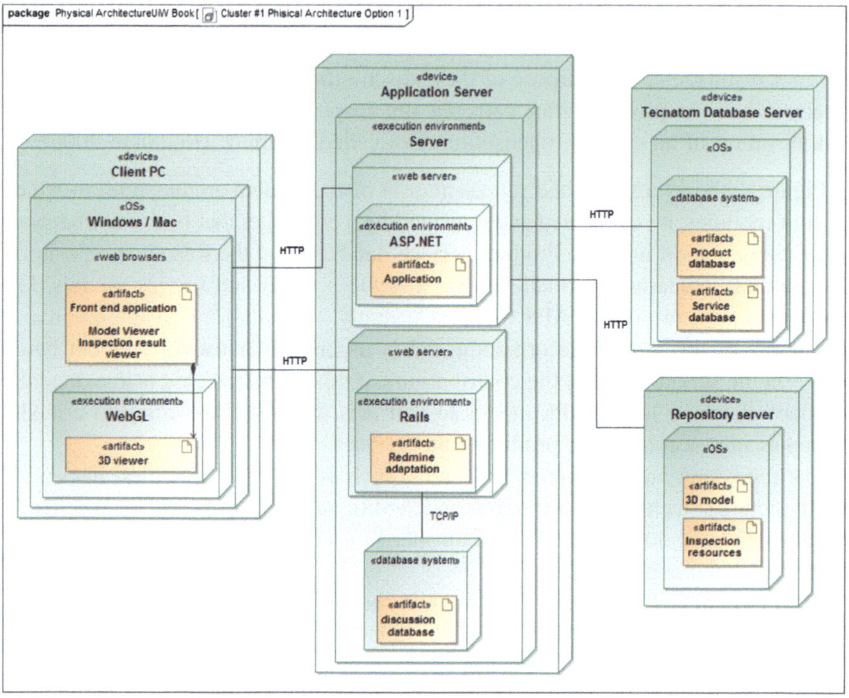


**Fig. 5** Physical system architecture diagram

## 3 Contributions and Implementation, Virtual Reality in a Web Context

A layout of the implemented application, which is divided into four modules presented in the architecture (*model viewer, 3D viewer, interactive inspection result viewer and discussion management*), is shown in Figs. 6 and 7. Figure 6 presents the interactive views and Fig. 7 presents the discussion management tools, which will be describe hereafter. The implementation was carried out taking into account the company needs, the system requirements and the use cases. More details about the system can be found in Gonzalez-Toledo et al. (2015).

### *3.1 Model Viewer Module*

In this industrial case, the product consists of a power plant turbine, whereas the service consists of the instructions for planning the inspections and the inspections carried out in the turbine. The model viewer allows actors to gain access to all the information stored in the system in an efficient and collaborative way.

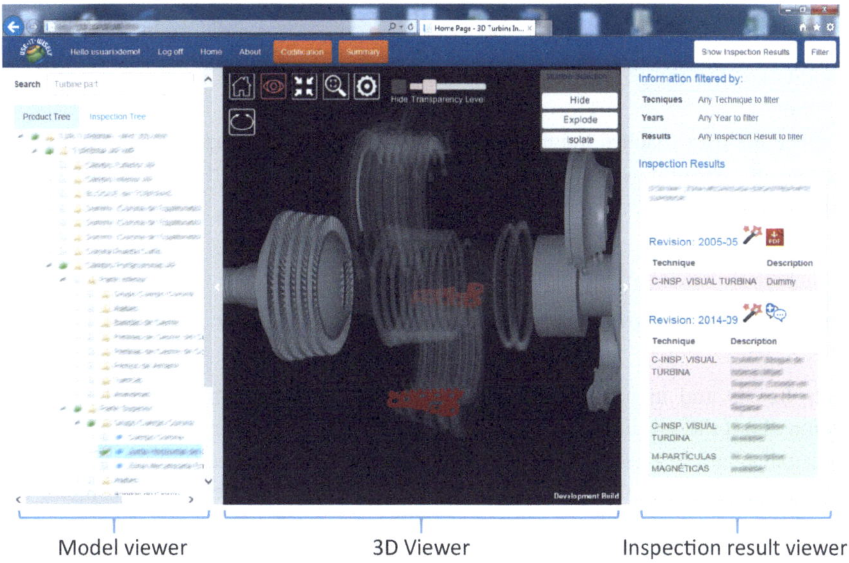


**Fig. 6** Application user interface. *From left to right* model viewer, 3D viewer and inspection result viewer

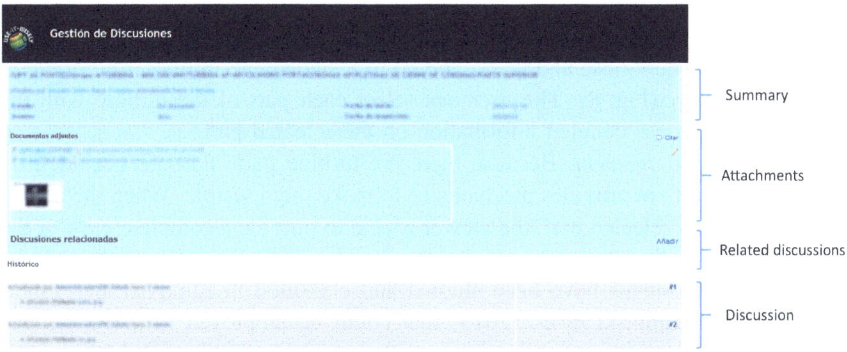


**Fig. 7** Discussion management tool

The system has two types of potential users: the staff of the inspection and maintenance company and the staff of the power plant owner company. The first group might be more interested in navigating through the inspection tree model to conduct the inspection, whereas the latter might be more interested in navigating through the information from the point of view of the product.

When using the model viewer, users can choose which of the two navigation trees they want to use and can easily change between them by clicking on the corresponding tab. This allows the users to navigate through the product or inspection model interchangeably. The system is in charge of keeping the displayed information consistent and allows different users to use the application and collaborate so that they can analyse the product (turbine) state and make decisions together.

Once the user reaches the node of interest and selects the appropriate options in the tree, the system will show the requested information with the support of the other viewers.

## 3.2 3D and Inspection Result Interactive Viewer Modules

Both the 3D and inspection result viewers (Fig. 6) work together to show information about the product and the service. The 3D model of the turbine allows users to visualise and interact with the product model and understand information about the service, whereas the inspection result viewer allows users to investigate the inspection results in depth.

The module 3D viewer graphically represents the 3D geometry of the turbine model. In addition, the application allows users to interact with the product by navigating around the turbine 3D model. To help the user with the visualisation of hidden parts, mechanisms have been implemented, such as an advanced navigation system, identification and selection of different parts and occlusion management:

- *Navigation around the 3D model.* The user can navigate around the turbine model using the mouse and the keyboard to visualise the turbine from different points of view (Fig. 8). The user can select each part of the turbine with the mouse and access detailed information on the selected part.
- *Occlusion Management.* Because there are turbine parts that are occluded by others, the system provides mechanisms to make them visible. When the user is interested in a selected part, the viewer is able to provide a complete view of the part without losing its spatial relationship between the other parts of the turbine. Several mechanisms have been studied and classified in Elmqvist and Tsigas (2008) and Tominski et al. (2014) that could be employed to allow for this function, such as the cutaway views (Burns et al. 2008), 3D Magic Lens (Ropinski et al. 2004), transparency techniques (Burns 2011) and exploded views (Li et al. 2008). The last two techniques are both implemented within this system.

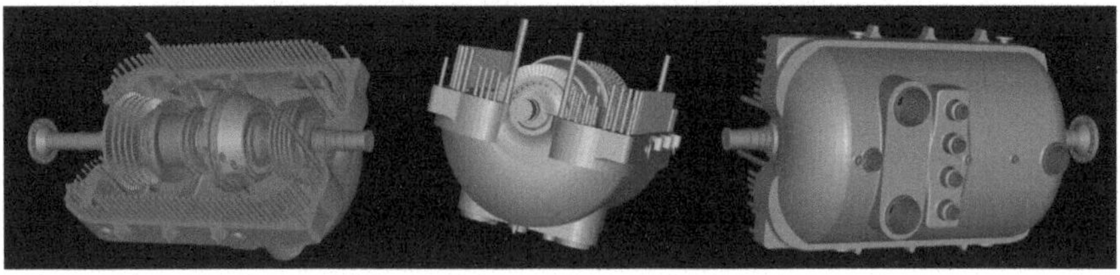

**Fig. 8** The user navigates around the turbine, obtaining different points of view

The *adaptive transparency* mechanism makes each part that occludes the selected part transparent. In addition, when the user navigates around the turbine, the transparent objects change according to the user's point of view, as shown in Fig. 9.

The exploded view allows the user to discover and access the internal parts of the turbine (Fig. 10). The explosion refers to the simultaneous separation of parts in an explosive way and takes into account the assembly information stored in the product model.

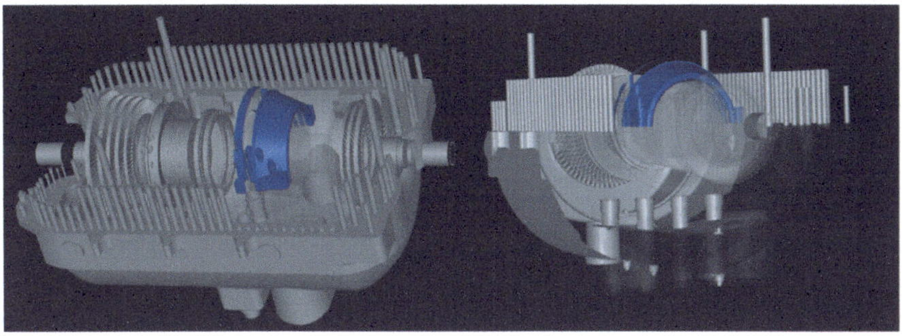

**Fig. 9** Adaptive transparency view

**Fig. 10** Exploded view

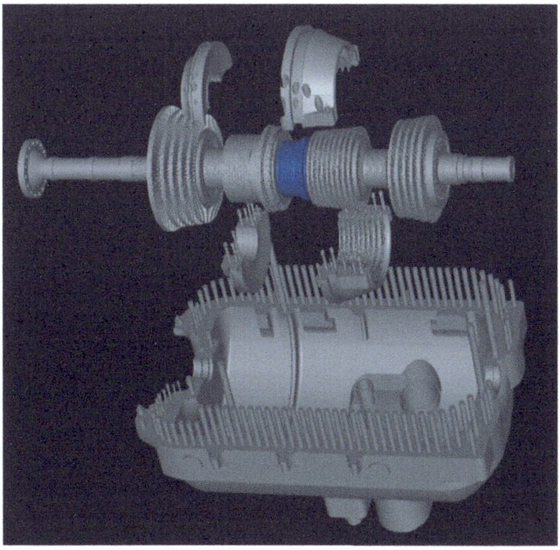

Regarding to the module inspection result viewer module, the inspection data can be shown in two ways:

- Together with the 3D model. Different mechanisms have been implemented to present the inspection result information in the 3D viewer. One of the mechanisms consists of overlaying the turbine graphical model with symbols and colours and relevant information regarding inspections, flaws and repairs. To achieve this, the application uses different symbols and colours that correspond to specific information, for example, whether the inspection result is acceptable (the turbine part does not need to be repaired) or not (the turbine part must be repaired). Another mechanism consists of pointing and tagging inspections results in a specific location of the turbine (over the 3D turbine geometry).
- Within the *Inspection Result Information panel*. The inspection results can also be presented in the Inspection Result Information Panel. This panel shows a summary of the inspection results carried out on a specific turbine part, for example, the technique used in the inspection, the sum of all flaws found at a selected part or their description. The shown information can be selected and filtered by the user. This panel also provides a set of links through the discussion management tool that connects the inspection results with the associated discussion.

## *3.3 Discussion Management Tool*

The discussion management tool allows for analyse of the inspection results in a collaborative way by allowing the different users (power plant operators, inspection service engineers, power plants manager, etc.) to be involved in the final decision-making process, such as re-scheduling future inspections or scheduling maintenance activities to repair or replace an affected turbine part. This tool increases the amount of communication among actors, makes documentation easily accessible and enables the sharing of past experiences. Discussions that are associated to specific inspection results are accessible from the *Inspection Result Information panel*. Once the user has selected a discussion, the tool is opened (Fig. 7).

The discussion can be at two different states: open and close. If the discussion is open, the tool provides a set of controls for registering new contributions (text or attached files) and setting connections between different discussions. Different users will have access to different topics of discussion depending on their role. Once the users have a make a decision and conclude their discussion, it is closed and the system provides a report of the discussion and the decision.

## 4 Conclusions

The main aim of this chapter was to report on the development of a UIW-collaborative tool that assists in the collaborative management of inspection results. By decreasing the decision-making time and the amount of time taken for repair and maintenance procedures, the tool optimises the activities and increases the productivity of the power plants.

The UIW-methodology has made it possible to identify challenges that must be addressed in an effective way. The problem was modelled by use cases, requirements and a system architecture. In addition, an APS model was used to identify the structure of the relevant information that the system stores and manages to provide the needed functionalities.

As result of the work developed and the experience accumulated in this industrial case, it seems appropriate that the information systems of a company that has a problem such as the two hierarchical trees should be consistent with the APS presented. The APS model has been presented as an important output of this project; using a system that follows this structure would yield important benefits for the company.

Finally, this chapter demonstrates the implementation of a tool that offers a web-based application for the visualisation of the product and the data regarding inspection results, such as inspection data, techniques used and information about flaws found in a specific part of the turbine. This information is shown in two ways: (1) through a classic web app, that is, with hypertext, using plain text, tables, lists, photographs, 2D planes, etc. and (2) through a 3D module. The latter allows users to see information in a three-dimensional model of the turbine geometry and to navigate through the different parts of the turbine. The tool also includes a collaborative decision-making application to manage all stakeholders' proposals, annotations and discussions to assist in the decision-making process.

## References


ASP. (2002). Microsoft ASP.NET. http://www.asp.net/. Accessed March 11, 2016

Bowman, D. A., Kruijff, E., LaViola Jr, J. J., & Poupyrev, I. (2004). *3D user interfaces: Theory and practice*. USA: Addison-Wesley.

Burns, M. S. (2011). *Efficient and comprehensible visualization of complex 3-D scenes* (Ph.D. thesis). Princeton University.

Burns, M., & Finkelstein, A. (2008). Adaptive cutaways for comprehensible rendering of polygonal scenes. *ACM Transactions on Graphics, 27*(5), 1.

Chromium Blog. (2013). *Saying goodbye to our old friend NPAPI*. http://blog.chromium.org/2013/09/saying-goodbye-to-our-old-friend-npapi.html. Accessed March 16, 2016

Elmqvist, N., & Tsigas, P. (2008). A taxonomy of 3d occlusion management for visualization. *IEEE Transactions on Visualization and Computer Graphics, 14*(5), 1095–1109.

Friedenthal, S., Moore, A., & Steine, R. (2014). *A practical guide to SysML, the System modeling language*. Burlington: Morgan Kaufmann.

Gonzalez-Toledo, D., Cuevas-Rodriguez, M., Garre, C., Molina-Tanco, L., & Reyes-Lecuona, A. (2015). A tool for collaborative decision making on service information linked to 3D geometry of complex hierarchical products. In *Presented at EuroVR2015 Conference, Campus Politecnico Milano, Lecco (Italy)*, October 15–16, 2015.

Li, W., Agrawala, M., Curless, B., & Salesin, D. (2008). Automated generation of interactive 3D exploded view diagrams. In *ACM Transactions on Graphics (TOG)* (vol. 27, No. 3, p. 101). ACM.

Redmine. (2006). *Redmine*. http://www.redmine.org/. Accessed March 11, 2016

Rey, J. (2013). *Modeling with VSEE: Definition of guidelines and exploitation of the models*. YGT Final Report. Available via http://www.vsd-project.org/download/documents/YGT%20final%20report%20Rey%20V2.pdf. Accessed March 16, 2016.

Reyes-Lecuona, A., Molina-Tanco, L., González-Toledo, D., Flores, S., Frutos, E., Patel, H., et al. (2014). *Design, maintenance and refurbishment of turbines in a collaborative environment*. Presented at AHFE 2014, Kraków, Poland, July 19–23, 2014.

Ropinski, T., & Hinrichs, K. (2004). Real-time rendering of 3D magic lenses having arbitrary convex shapes.

Ruby. (2005). *Ruby on rails*. http://rubyonrails.org/. Accessed March 11, 2016.

Tominski, C., Gladisch, S., Kister, U., Dachselt, R., & Schumann, H. (2014). *A survey on interactive lenses in visualization*. EuroVis State-of-the-Art Reports (pp. 43–62).

Unity. (2005). *Unity technologies*. https://unity3d.com/. Accessed March 11, 2016.

Unity. (2015). *Web publishing following chrome NPAPI deprecation*. http://blogs.unity3d.com/2015/05/28/web-publishing-following-chrome-npapi-deprecation/. Accessed 16 March 2016.

WebGL. (2001). *Web graphics library*. https://www.khronos.org/webgl/. Accessed March 11, 2016.

# Rock Crusher Upgrade Business from a PLM Perspective

**Simo-Pekka Leino, Susanna Aromaa and Kaj Helin**

**Abstract** Global trends of ecology and sustainable development, safety awareness, changing legislation, and urbanization, together with the economic situation, force industry to find solutions for extending product lifecycles, while maintaining and improving machine system performance and other properties during the lifecycles. Together with these societal issues, firms are struggling with competitiveness. This chapter introduces the new Use-it-Wisely (UIW) approach to upgrading rock crushers at customer sites. The higher level problem needing to be solved concerned making upgrade delivery projects profitable and more desirable for customers, manufacturing OEMs and suppliers. The main recognized and treated bottlenecks were related to knowing the actual status of the upgrade target, communication and collaboration with stakeholders, verification and validation of upgrade specifications and an efficient information flow between the stakeholders. Augmented reality (AR), Virtual environments (VE), camera based 3D scanning, and cloud based solutions are the selected pieces of technology for solving the bottlenecks. They enable better communication, collaboration and involvement of all stakeholders, including customers, internal stakeholders, suppliers and partners. They also better enable the planning and discussing of service quality activities. Product life-cycle management (PLM) is the framework for developing and managing product related information, processes and collaboration expanding towards product middle-of-life, end-of-life, and service lifecycle management. This study is a proof-of-concept that demonstrates the potential of contributions to business model innovations and game changes for upgrading business.

S.-P. Leino (✉) · S. Aromaa · K. Helin
VTT Technical Research Centre of Finland Ltd., Espoo, Finland
e-mail: simo-pekka.leino@vtt.fi

S. Aromaa
e-mail: susanna.aromaa@vtt.fi

K. Helin
e-mail: kaj.helin@vtt.fi



S.N. Grösser et al. (eds.), *Dynamics of Long-Life Assets*,
DOI 10.1007/978-3-319-45438-2_12

**Keywords** Technological support of collaboration · Upgrading of assets · Business model innovation · Product life cycle management · Mining and construction

# 1 Introduction

This chapter introduces how novel digital technology may enable an innovative new business model for upgrading old machines, in the mining and construction industry. Global trends of ecology and sustainable development, safety awareness, changing legislation, and urbanization, together with the economic situation, are forcing development of solutions for extending product lifecycles, while maintaining and improving machine system performance and other properties during the lifecycles. Together with these societal issues, firms are struggling with competitiveness. Often, they optimize short-term financial performance, while missing the most important customer needs and ignoring the broader influences that determine their long-term success (Porter and Kramer 2011). A true understanding of customer and user needs, and the needs of society, in general, is often missing. Simultaneously, core competences and key assets, such as knowledge and skills of employees and partners are underrated.

However, the most enlightened manufacturing firms are seeking new business and revenues from services and maintenance, such as the upgrading of older machine individuals. However, service design raises new challenges, compared to traditional product design engineering. Compared to physical products, services are generally under-designed and inefficiently developed (Cavalieri and Pezzotta 2012). This problem is the focus of Product-Service System (PSS) research. On the other hand, Product Lifecycle Management (PLM) is a strategic approach, where business is seen from a product perspective covering product related information, processes and collaboration. Thus, PLM should be a framework, where PSS and service products are developed and managed. However, conventional views of PLM tend to stress the design, engineering and production phases, while the use and end of life phases are, typically, not very well covered (Wuest 2015). This is the challenge of the case company, as well. It faces the problems of maximizing customer value and societal satisfaction, while increasing their own profitability. The principle of "shared value" (Porter and Kramer 2011) is proposed as a solution for creating economic value in a way that also creates value for society, by addressing its needs and challenges.

## *1.1 The Industrial Case*

The industrial case relates to equipment manufacturing and services for the mining and construction sectors. Two companies, an original equipment manufacturer

(OEM) and a research and development (R&D) partner in upgrade services, were involved in the case study. The OEM case company, a manufacturer of rock crushers wants to serve their customers by providing machine upgrade solutions that support machine utilization and the customers' capability for crushing rocks, for instance, near urban areas, by decreasing the noise and dust levels of the machines. This is challenging, because every partially configurable machine individual is different when it leaves the factory and it is often modified by the customer or a third party during its lifecycle. The lifecycle may exceed ten years and, during that time, machine deformations typically occur, due to harsh conditions. Therefore, it is difficult to know the status of the machines at the customer sites, around the world. Thus, machine upgrade projects are, generally, not very attractive or profitable. The major high level business questions are:

- How to make upgrade business profitable
- How to establish a successful business model for rock crushing machine upgrades
- How to effectively manage upgrade service projects?

## 1.2 Product Life Perspective and Product Life-Cycle Approach

Having a long tradition (Wuest 2015) in both engineering and management science, Product Life-cycle Management (PLM) proposes to help with the challenges of maintaining the performance of existing products and developing new competitive products for changing and turbulent business environments. Fast reactions to these changing markets and customer requirements, as well as the involvement of stakeholders, requires a sound information basis, which, in manufacturing, could be provided by PLM (Wiesner et al. 2015). Besides product and process related data, PLM also takes into account the interdependencies of information and communication between all of the stakeholders involved in the product lifecycle (Wuest 2015).

PLM originates from Product Data Management (PDM) with its original focus on design engineering data for Computer Aided Design and Computer Aided Engineering (CAD/CAE) (Wiesner et al. 2015); however, PLM increasingly focuses on the whole product lifecycle (both the product types and product individuals) and promises to manage all involved data and information (Wuest 2015). While the initial objectives of PDM were to improve product quality and reduce costs, additional objectives also became important (Wiesner et al. 2015): time reduction, streamlining of processes, increased value for the customer and innovation. Thus, newer PLM approaches are aligned to changes in market conditions and technical opportunities (Wiesner et al. 2015).

In PLM, life phases of products can roughly be divided (Wiesner et al. 2015) into the Beginning of Life (BoL), the Middle of Life (MoL), and the End of Life (EoL). This view is different from marketing, where a product life is divided into five phases: introduction, growth, maturity, saturation and degeneration (Wuest 2015). To elaborate, the three phases of product life in PLM are (Wiesner et al. 2015):

- **BoL**: The product is imagined as an idea in the minds of the designers, which are then converted into a detailed product specification, in the definition stage. During the realization phase, the product is manufactured and delivered to the customer.
- **MoL**: The product is in the possession of the customer, who uses it for their applications. The product is also supported by the manufacturer, in order to maintain its functionalities.
- **EoL**: The product loses its usefulness for its intended purpose. It is retired or upgraded by the manufacturer or disposed of by the customer for eventual reuse or recycling.

By definition, PLM takes a holistic view to product life, taking into account both the lifecycles of product types and families, as well as product individuals. However, as previously stated, the focus of PLM has been more on the beginning of life than on the middle or end of life phases. Newer proposed approaches such as "*Closed-loop PLM*" (Jun et al. 2007), take an even greater holistic view upon of the entire product lifecycle, which, ideally, also includes the end of one lifecycle merging into the beginning of the next (Wuest 2015). The concept of a closed loop PLM provides the opportunity to maximize the benefits of the lifecycle operations. This raises the importance of knowing what the whole product lifecycle activities consist of, how its information is created, used, and modified during the product lifecycle, and which lifecycle information affects the product lifecycle operation (Jun et al. 2007). The aim of a closed-loop PLM is to close the information gaps between the different phases and processes of the product lifecycle of individual products, both backwards and forwards (Wuest 2015). Recent PLM approaches also consider product related service in the lifecycle of products (Wiesner et al. 2015). However, closed-loop PLM and service requires dealing with products as item-level individuals, which is still a common challenge (Wuest 2015). In other words, manufacturing companies that want to develop and offer service products, e.g. product upgrades, often do not know the exact status of product individuals at their customer sites. The common question is how product individual level upgrades and service products can be supported in PLM?

### *1.3 Tool Selection*

The main industrial problem treated in this chapter concerns making upgrade services profitable and establishing a business model to support that goal. This chapter covers the biggest bottlenecks. These are:

- Knowing the actual status of the upgrade target, thus getting initial data and information for an upgrade delivery project
- Global communication with customers in the field, to form a true understanding of their needs and possible limitations
- Validation of customer requirements, to ensure that the needs are understood and correctly specified
- Management of upgrade service products and offerings
- Support of engineering design of upgrades, taking into account the limitations
- Collaboration and communication between the upgrade stakeholders
- Validation of the proposed upgrade solution with the customer
- Efficient information flow during delivery of the upgrade project.

As previously stated, PLM, for the case company, is the framework of developing and managing product related information, processes and collaboration. On the other hand, PLM as a theoretical concept as well as from an industrial implementation viewpoint, is just expanding to cover a product's middle-of-life, end-of-life, and service lifecycle management. The above listed bottlenecks are, at the same time, common PLM research targets and problems related to the case companies' upgrade service business. PLM is about creating, using, modifying, and managing product and service related information, for all stakeholders. In this case, information related problems are more specifically related to issues in Table 1.

The preliminary and principle selection of the proposed tools and solutions for the above described bottlenecks and the PLM information related problems are partly based on previous experiences with certain tools and techniques, and partly on a collaboration with other Clusters and partners, in the Use-it-Wisely (UIW) EU-project. The proposed main solutions to the problems and expected advantages are listed in Table 1.

**Table 1** PLM related challenges of rock crusher upgrading and proposed solutions

| PLM related challenge | Proposed solution | Expected advantage |
|---|---|---|
| Creating digital data and information about the target machine, including 3D geometry | 3D scanning (3D data capture) | Fast and cost-efficient way to get the actual status and geometry |
| Visualization of upgrade service offerings and proposed solutions for customers | Augmented Reality (AR)<br>Virtual Environments (VE) | Mobile and cheap solution for operations in field<br>Possibility to test non-existing solutions and environments |
| Visualization of the target machine status and boundary conditions for engineering designers | Virtual Environments (VE) | Possibility to test non-existing solutions and environments<br>Effective way to share information and knowledge |
| Keeping digital data and information up-to-date and sharing it in an appropriate format, for all required stakeholders | Cloud-based PLM module | Possibility to automate information management and dynamically involve different stakeholders |

Two major principles in proposing and selecting tools and solutions for the described problems are: (1) To utilize "COTS" Commercial Off-The-Shelf solutions and (2) the possibility to integrate them into company processes and information management systems, so that they benefit business. Different versions of the selected technologies are tested and developed from the perspective of functionality, user acceptance and business process benefit.

Finally, data processing and information flow between the applications that support the upgrade sales-delivery process is established, based on cloud technology and a product lifecycle management system. Modular and configurable upgrade solutions enable information re-use and an effective engineering design phase of the project.

Utilization of techniques and methodologies, such as VE and AR in this case context, can be put under the umbrella of "virtual prototyping", which is defined by (Wang, 2002) as follows: "*Virtual prototype, or digital mock-up, is a computer simulation of a physical product that can be presented, analyzed, and tested from concerned product life-cycle aspects such as design/engineering, manufacturing, service, and recycling as if on a real physical model. The construction and testing of a virtual prototype is called virtual prototyping (VP)*". When virtual prototyping is considered from an engineering design and product development viewpoint, taking into account product information management and the whole product lifecycle, it should be connected with PLM development. In (Leino 2015) the theory and practice of virtual environments, based on virtual prototyping in product development and product lifecycle management, is discussed. Furthermore, (Ovtcharova 2010) provides a practical outline of the process definition and IT-system environment of "virtual engineering", and (Bordegoni et al. 2009) introduces a mixed prototyping approach and framework for product assessment. They see it as a practice for effective and rapid design reviews and validation of new products from an ergonomic and usability perspective. Engineering design reviews (see e.g. Huet et al. 2007) are one of the most important application areas of virtual prototyping. However, the majority of the published virtual prototyping examples are related to new product development, which is not really the case, in this research. The important question is: how to mix the virtual and physical worlds of existing and to-be-defined objects?

## 1.4 State-of-the-Art of the Proposed Technical Solutions

**Augmented (Mixed) Reality (AR)** was proposed as a means of improving the customer interface, including visualization of upgrade offerings, as well as validation of upgrade solutions. It was also intended to assist service and maintenance workers in the field, for instance, in assembling the upgrade solution on top of an old machine. Augmented (Mixed) Reality involves the superposition of computer graphics over real objects or scenes (Shen et al. 2010). Compared with VR, AR is a semi-immersive design environment in which the users can see the real world, while performing feature modelling, on a virtual product. Recent industrial applications of AR include, for instance, collaborative product design and development (Shen et al. 2010), design reviews (Verlinden et al. 2009), development and planning of complex production processes and systems (Dangelmaier et al. 2005) and architectural and Construction Site Visualization (Woodward and Hakkarainen 2011). AR helps the understanding of project documentation (Meža et al. 2015) and enables graphical highlighting of an interesting phenomenon already in the design phase, thus, determining problems and risks, sooner (Tuma et al. 2014).

**Virtual Environments (VE)** were recognized as a medium for collaborative engineering design and as a communication medium between the upgrade service stakeholders, including the customers and partners in the supply network. Virtual Environments can be defined as "*interactive, virtual image displays enhanced by special processing and by nonvisual display modalities, such as auditory and haptic, to convince users that they are immersed in a synthetic space.*" (Ellis 1994). However, VE have presented challenges to human-computer interaction (Wilson and D'Cruz 2006). Research with VE started in the 1960s, with NASA being one of the pioneer institutes. However, after several decades, the technical and methodological development of VE is now becoming mature enough for real and serious utilization in industry. VE is currently reliving a renaissance.

VE for virtual prototyping of assembly and maintenance verifications has already been introduced by Gomes de Sá and Zachmann (1998). They saw it as a very promising technology, but they also state that it would not become a wide-spread tool before being integrated with IT infrastructure. One of the recent studies related to the design review of complex industrial assemblies was introduced by Di Gironimo et al. (2014). They have already solved many of the product information management challenges specifically related to VE and PDM interfaces. Other manual assembly and maintenance related VE research were reported, for example, by Chryssolouris et al. (2000) and Gomes de Sá and Zachmann (1999).

**3D scanning** was proposed as a piece of technology that enables efficient initial data gathering (i.e. 3D geometry) at the customer site. 3D scanning is a technology that analyses real-world objects and environments in order to gather data on shape and appearance. From the data, three dimensional models of reality can be constructed. In principle, there exist two commercially available methods on the market: (1) active (e.g. laser, sonar) and (2) passive (e.g. photogrammetric scanning using mobile digital cameras). There are many recent examples of the use of different 3D scanning technologies in industry and civil engineering. The approach of Erdos et al. (2014) on retrofitting complex engineering objects, such as factories and utilization computer aided design, is similar to ours; however, their paper is more focused on the technical development of 3D scanning devices. Bosche and Haas (2008) report technical 3D scanning advancements in the architectural and construction sectors as do (Bi and Wang 2010) in manufacturing. Many of the recent technical developments are related to 3D scanning with portable devices, such as smartphones, tablets and PDAs. Examples of such research are reported, e.g. by Ancona et al. (2015), Kolev et al. (2014), Tanskanen et al. (2013).

3D laser scanning and point cloud based applications are used, for instance, in the renewal of electrical substations, when the original CAD models are outdated (Gonzalez-Aguilera et al. 2012), which is also similar to our approach. Kumar et al. (2012) have utilized point clouds in reverse-engineering and they introduced a detailed methodology of scanning and applications. Berglund et al. (2014) have reported how 3D laser scanning enables the capturing of spatial digitized data, quickly, in order to support discrete event simulations of production systems. This integration of point cloud data, with simulations, is supposed to enable better decision-making (Berglund et al. 2013). It is also based on the created realistic visualization and better common understanding of the redesigned production systems (Lindskog et al. 2014). Based on the experiences of (Weidlich et al. 2009), 3D laser scanning can enhance the creation of virtual test scenarios related to optimization and extension of existing environments.

### *1.5 Outline of This Chapter*

The rest of this chapter is organized as follows: The next section introduces more detail on how the technical solutions were applied, what they are, and how they were tested and evaluated. Furthermore, the next section describes the conceptual definition of the new product upgrade service model. First, the as-is situation and requirements analysis are explained.

After that, in the Discussion section, the benefits and limitations of selected and developed technical solutions are reported and discussed compared to the requirements and situation before the projects, as well as compared to other published research. Also discussed are what implications can be drawn from this research for PLM development and implementation. Finally, concluding remarks are made on benefits and further challenges.

## 2 Tool Applications and Solution to the Company Challenges

The major business problems are:

- How to make upgrade business profitable
- How to establish a successful business model for rock crushing machine upgrades
- How to manage upgrade service projects efficiently.

These questions were approached by modelling the as-is situation in the case companies, discussing it with the product stakeholders and recognizing the most remarkable bottlenecks of the machine upgrade projects. These included communication channels on the customer interface, validation of the problem definition with the customer, getting the initial data for the project, effectively designing an upgrade solution, verification of the solution and validation with the customer and end user. The business cases were created with the requirement of cheap and easy to use technology that can be integrated with business solutions.

Figure 1 illustrates the complex network of internal and external product upgrade stakeholders, and their concerns. The rich picture shows how society and authorities put into place regulations and ethical demands for the end-customers of the OEM manufacturing company concerning, for instance, noise and dust levels near urban areas. These demands originate with the end-customer and end-users and go to the OEM. For example, if end-users need to decrease the noise levels of their rock crushing machines, they may ask the OEM to upgrade the machine to fulfil the noise level requirements of the authorities. The OEM wants to serve the end-customer as well as possible, while simultaneously trying to keep their business profitable. They need to effectively manage the end-customer interface as well as their internal and external upgrade delivery processes. Previously, these processes have not been optimal, causing productivity challenges.

As was described in the Introduction section, AR, VE and 3D scanning were proposed as technical tools in order to meet the business goals of upgrading old rock crushing machines at customer sites. Cloud solutions and PLM system configurations were adopted to support the required information management processes. The following section introduces evaluation of the proposed technical applications.

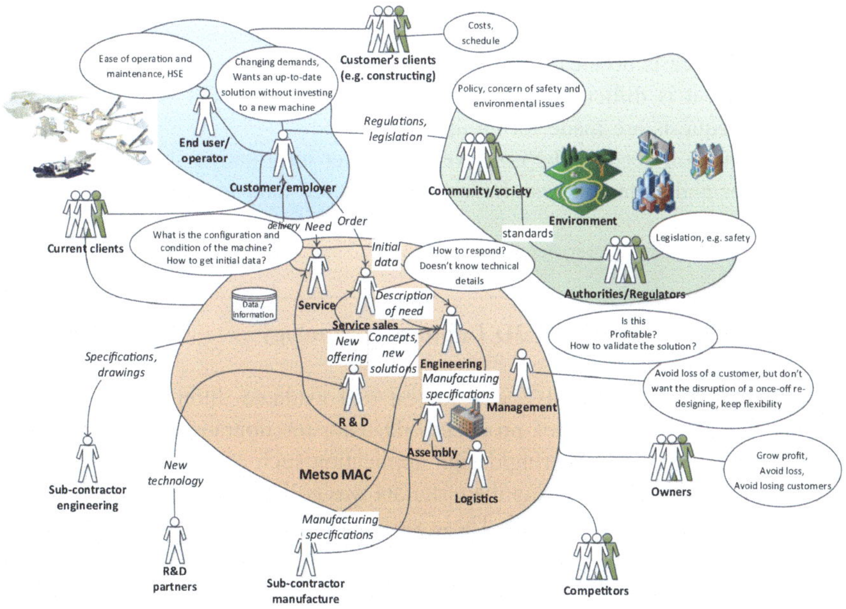


**Fig. 1** Rich Picture model describing the complexity of an as-is situation between stakeholders

## 2.1 Trials and Demonstrations

The tools and solutions to enable an innovative new business model for upgrading old machines were tested and developed during three trials and a demonstration period. This section introduces a summary of the goals, methods and results of the trials and demonstrations.

### 2.1.1 Trial 1: Evaluation of the Proposed Business Model

*Goal*: The objective in Trial 1 was to discuss and evaluate a new proposed business model and preliminary ideas concerning new upgrade delivery processes and tools. The new business model should provide the possibility to design, configure and customize upgrades for the customers, machines, based on a catalogue of upgrades, with the support of advanced tools and solutions, which would help to reduce cost and delivery time. The aim was to improve profitability and systematize work.

*Material and method:* A process diagram ("Swim-Lane") was made from the proposed business model. It described a hypothetical sales-delivery process within the new business model in which organizational functions and/or networked companies are involved. The process diagram was evaluated by using a walk-through method in a focus group session.

*Results*: The new proposed business model received common acceptance from the focus group. However, the main discussion continued to be on current business challenges. Therefore, the summarized main challenges in the current upgrade process, were as follows:

1. Presently there is no clear upgrade process
2. Sometimes it is difficult to prepare a reliable and fast offer for a client after specific requests are made for an upgrade
3. Documentation needs to be improved for better information sharing
4. An easier and faster process for collecting initial data for upgrade projects is needed.

### 2.1.2 Trial 2: Evaluation of 3D Capture Technology

*Goal*: The objective in Trial 2 was to test and evaluate different 3D scanning systems and the usefulness of produced 3D data, for upgrade design in Virtual Environments and in engineering/design application such as CAD/CAE.

*Materials and method*: During the test, data was collected and three different 3D scanning systems were compared. These systems included one laser scanning and two different systems for 3D reconstruction from multiple camera images. There were three different cases:

1. A mobile rock crushing unit of the OEM
2. A commercial component—gear box
3. Production line—jaw crusher assembly line.

Two different 3D scanning techniques were tested: (1) laser (active) and (2) photogrammetric (passive) mobile digital camera (still and video) based. Figures 2 and 3 are from the first tests of camera based scanning.

*Results*: 3D scanning seemed to be a very useful technology. However, based on these tests, the data pipeline from the scanned raw data to CAD/CAE or VE software was only working properly in the photogrammetrically generated 3D models. This scanning accuracy is not always suitable for detailed design, but can be applied to concept design and discussing the boundary conditions for the design. The accuracy of laser scanning is probably also suitable for detailed design, however, the data import to the CAD and VR software did not yet work properly, with the given pieces of technology. Table 2 explains the evaluated advantages and disadvantages of the two 3D scanning methods.

For instance, (Golparvar-Fard et al. 2011) have also compared two 3D scanning methods, camera based and 3D laser scanning, in modelling the as-built status of a construction site. They concluded that camera based methods are less accurate, but that both methods are capable of producing 3D representations for visualizing the environment, from different viewpoints.

**Fig. 2** In the Trial 2 Camera based photogrammetric 3D capture was applied in scanning a gear box at the OEM factory

**Fig. 3** Laser scanning and generated point cloud representation

### 2.1.3 Trial 3: Evaluation of Digital Visualization Technology

*Goal*: The goal of Trial 3 was to evaluate two different 3D visualization systems, during an upgrade design. AR and VE systems were tested to support design reviews.

*Materials and methods*: The design object, reviewed in the test, was a machine maintenance platform attached to a mobile rock crushing machine. This was an upgrade module for an existing machine. The purpose of the maintenance platform was to provide a safe, ergonomic and efficient workspace for maintenance workers. In the AR test, the system included a virtual model of the upgrade module (the maintenance platform), the real rock crushing machine, a virtual frame and a cover, a real environment, three different postures of a digital human model (DHM) and a human participant. In the VE test system, the model included a virtual model of the product (the maintenance platform), a virtual model of the rock crushing machine, a virtual environment, three different postures of a DHM, a human participant and 3D models of hands and shoes. Nine people from the OEM company participated in the AR test and ten people from the company participated in the VE test. Questionnaires and interviews were used as data collection methods. Figure 4

**Table 2** Advantages and disadvantages of 3D laser scanning and camera based 3D capture

| Method | Advantages | Disadvantages |
|---|---|---|
| 3D laser scanning | Accuracy<br>Speed | Not portable<br>Requires special training<br>Limited and/or laborious possibility to generate 3D models for VE and CAD/CAE |
| Camera based | Can be used with a normal smartphone<br>Easy-to-use<br>Relatively inexpensive | Limited accuracy<br>Model quality depends on user skills<br>Sensitive to light conditions |

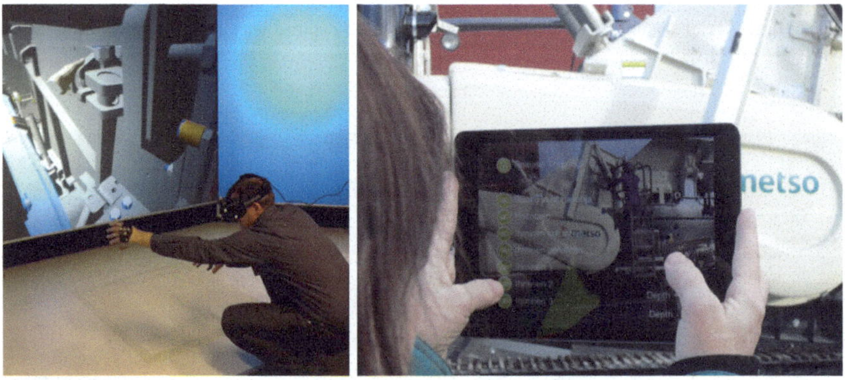

**Fig. 4** Upgrade design review in a VE (*left*) and upgrade validation with an AR application (*right*)

shows the testing of the VE with the upgrade design engineer (left), and the testing of the upgrade visualization AR application, with an end user.

*Results* indicate that both of the AR and VE prototypes were suitable for assessment of certain human factor/ergonomic (HFE) related issues (Aromaa and Väänänen 2016). AR-systems could be particularly valuable for illustrating upgrade solutions to the upgrade stakeholders (marketing, customers and assembly workers) in the field. The VE prototype was more comprehensive and immersive for the designers, when reviewing the HFE issues of the upgrade machine.

In addition, data sharing was tested. Data sharing was tested by means of the RD Cloud™ platform. It allowed the 3D scanned data (point clouds, polygon models and design models related to photos and video) to be stored in the cloud, as well as the data collected from the AR-system. The users were able to understand and appreciate the potential of the tool, but it needs greater customization, according to the users' needs (i.e. show photos preview, allow CAD data conversion in other formats, enhance the uploading feature, etc.).

**The demonstration** phase was aimed at proving the technical maturity, usability and usefulness from the viewpoints of end users, customers and other stakeholders, as well as to demonstrate the big picture (capability from upgrade delivery process and data management viewpoints) and business impact potential. The three demonstration cases, and their evaluation criteria, are listed in Table 3.

Figure 5 shows how the new pieces of technology should contribute to the upgrade delivery projects. Previously, there were no process or method definitions

**Table 3** Demonstration cases and their evaluation criteria

| # | Demonstration case | Evaluation criteria |
|---|---|---|
| **1** | Smartphone, video based, 3D-scanning and automatic 3D model creation. Data collection for upgrades with collaboration with engineering service provider | Anyone should be able to use a smartphone for scanning (no restrictive requirements on how to record the video)<br>The quality of the pictures, the transfer speed and the quality of the created 3D model<br>Also the usability and the overall workload and time of this scanning method |
| **2** | Noise encapsulation demonstration for a customer (or sales personnel) with AR and VR. Review a large scale machine upgrade with a customer, verify key customer requirements, such as maintainability, transportability etc. | User experience, interviews and monitoring (end-customer, serviceman, designer) |
| **3** | Dust suppression or safety upgrade installation (combination of Cases #1 and #2). Review a minor/mid-size machine upgrade with engineering and customer | Get initial data from existing products (3D scanning with video)<br>Check the upgrade installation in 3D CAD, with a scanned model<br>Also check with a virtual model and AR<br>Data pipeline<br>Interview test users (assembly workers, designers, servicemen, sales, customer) |

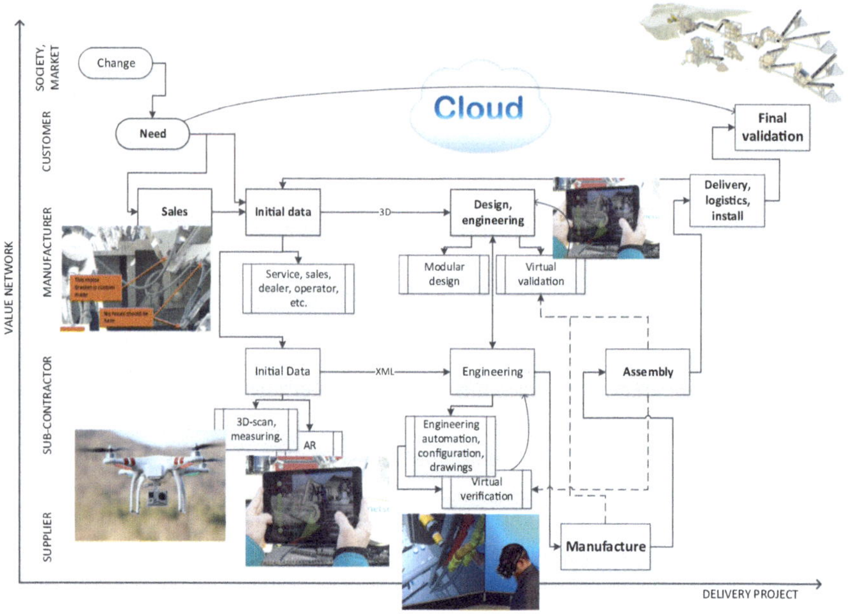


**Fig. 5** The new innovative rock crusher upgrade delivery process that exploits 3D capture, AR/VE and Cloud

for old machine upgrade projects. It has been more of an ad hoc activity, as described in Fig. 1. Product processes of the OEM company have been optimized for configuring and producing new machine variants, and the upgrade projects have been disturbing this day-to-day business. Moreover, it has had a narrow perspective without taking into consideration the roles of partners, suppliers and customers. Firstly, the UIW-approach made these processes and roles explicit, taking into account the whole chain, from customer needs to upgrade deliveries. Secondly, in the UIW-approach, the aforementioned pieces of technology enable the retrieval of information on the initial situation at a customer site, collaborative design and verification and validation of the upgrade solutions (Fig. 5). Cloud solutions enable information flow and processing.

## 3 Discussion

The main high level industrial problems touched in this chapter was about making upgrade services profitable and establishing a business model to support that goal. However, this chapter does not describe a business model; neither does it show quantitative evidence about increased profitability. Nevertheless, this chapter does discuss how future novel pieces of technology may change upgrade project processes and remove current major process bottlenecks that hinder profitability. There is no quantitative data supporting the claimed productivity increase. Instead, productivity is claimed to be increased by better effectivity, more value adding work and less waste in the upgrade processes. This was preliminary assessed by using as-is and to-be process models and simulation games. The main bottlenecks of upgrade service profitability are related to knowing the actual status of the upgrade target, communication and collaboration with stakeholders such as customers, engineers, service personnel and supply networks, as well as effective tool, method and information management, during an upgrade delivery project. Thus, optimal support for the design process requires integrated 3D digitalization and a multidisciplinary approach in order to solve the complex problems (Weidlich et al. 2009).

The new approach is based on clever engineering design solutions for the upgrade products, as well as on the digitalization of information flows of the upgrade projects. Clever engineering design solutions mean modularized upgrade products and services that can be configured, at least partially, for a specific customer need. Thus, less engineering work from scratch is needed. Digitalization of information flows means, of course, that information is in digital format, but also that it flows through an upgrade service project smoothly. It means that the data and information are correct, up-to-date and available for all stakeholders, when needed. This is the task of PLM. PLM should support (Jun et al. 2007): Management of lifecycle objects, collaboration between customers, partners and suppliers, and the firm's ability to analyse challenges and make decisions on them. In most cases, it is necessary to share product information with several suppliers and partners.

Digitalization saves a lot of calendar time and unproductive work, but it also makes information content richer. When, for instance, a realistic digital 3D model of the upgrade target is instantly available to designers, they can begin the definition upgrade solution immediately, with more reliable initial data. Furthermore, additional information about the upgrade target status can be attached to the model. This means making information content rich, which is also the task of PLM. Productivity increases by decreasing unproductive work during an upgrade delivery project. When information is correct and available, there is less need for searching and rework due to wrong status information and corrections. The status information can be discussed among all stakeholders and decisions can be made based on better quality information. For instance, 3D laser scanned models can increase understanding and bridge the gap between different areas of expertise (Lindskog et al. 2013).

Requirement specifications of the upgrade can be validated with the customer and the proposed upgrade solutions can be verified against the requirements and validated with the customer, based on virtual models. Virtual design reviews allow multiple designers and other stakeholder to highlight possible design flaws and make choices in real time (Di Gironimo et al. 2014). When design flaws are recognized earlier, with a virtual prototype model, and engineering changes are made based on them, there is a potential for decreasing changes with manufactured physical products.

Furthermore, AR- and VE-based visualization enables better understanding of information, and thus, better communication and involvement of the stakeholders. People with different backgrounds and prior knowledge can create similar mental models, which enables better discussion and decision making (Lindskog et al. 2013; Leino 2015). Virtual models enable stakeholders that are unexperienced with CAD to work with virtual prototypes (Gomes de Sá and Zachmann 1999). Additionally, the stakeholders can virtually test and train the use of the products, before they exist, which can lead to improved usability and ergonomics (Ottosson 2002).

Therefore, more knowledge is involved in the process, which decreases uncertainty and improves the quality of decision making. The changing market situation and customer needs can be responded to with better knowledge management, leading to new product-service innovations. VE based virtual prototyping does have the potential to improve overall product quality, especially for those business processes where humans play an important role (Gomes de Sá and Zachmann 1999). Therefore, the potential business impact of VE is also manifested though a more holistic view of the PSS, rather than just a component or product centric view (Ovtcharova 2010).

## *3.1 Product Lifecycle Management Perspective*

There is an industrial need to have easy access to product use phase (MoL) information, in order to better provide a value adding combination of products and services for customers (Lejon and Jeppsson 2015). On the other hand, manufacturing companies still have a traditional engineering approach to the tangible part of engineering and leave the intangible service element to intuitive processes and methods (Cavalieri and Pezzotta 2012). The shift from traditional product centric product development to PSS development is an opportunity to create radical innovations (McAloone and Andreasen 2004), but it requires an increased awareness of complex lifecycle issues, including variance of stakeholders and societal issues. Cavalieri and Pezzotta have discussed using virtual environments for interaction between service providers and clients and visualizing new service concepts. A similar approach is part of our UIW-concept, as well. Virtual environments and virtual prototyping enables extending the virtual phase of the product lifecycle towards service planning and management, thus integrating traditional PLM and SLM (Service Lifecycle Management).

However, from a PLM perspective, a sound methodology to combine product lifecycle and service lifecycle does not exist. Therefore, challenges remain for closing feedback loops from, for example, the service delivery to the BoL phase of products (Wiesner et al. 2015). The closed-loop PLM approach intends to close these loops and emerging new technologies enable the gathering and analysing of product lifecycle information and decision making, without spatial and temporal constraints (Jun et al. 2007). In recent papers, e.g. (Lejon and Jeppsson 2015) feedback loops are closed using advanced sensor technology that records the events and status of the technical product, itself. Thus, our UIW-approach contributes to the closed-loop PLM and service lifecycle management by providing an approach that utilizes AR, VE and 3D scanning for gathering and analysing product lifecycle information.

The main phases of product life are the beginning of life (BoL), the middle of life (MoL), and the end of life (EoL). In the closed-loop PLM, designers and production engineers receive feedback information from distributors, maintenance/ service, customers, re-manufacturers, etc. This information, from the MoL and the EoL, can also be indirectly used for the design and production of the next generation products (Jun et al. 2007). Traditionally, this kind of product individual status information is lacking in product design and development, but the closed-loop PLM aims to enable it in successful business operations. Thus, our UIW-approach contributes to closing two information loops in product life:

1. Upgrading a product individual at a customer site
2. Bringing the product MoL and EoL knowledge to a new product and service design and development.

The Closed-loop PLM can have direct and indirect loops of information flows over an extended product lifecycle, meaning that a lot of product lifecycle information can be accumulated and used, not only in the current lifecycle, but also with the next (Jun et al. 2007). Our UIW-approach enables the gathering of the digital status data and information, such as a 3D model of an item-level product individual and information about its use and circumstances, at the customer site. This approach can contribute to the concept of Product Avatars (Wiesner et al. 2015), where the idea is to create virtual, item-level, product individual models, where product lifecycle information is linked. It encompasses philosophical ideas similar to that of the German "Industry4.0" concept (see e.g. Brettel et al. 2014), where production systems and product individuals should have virtual twins. Our 3D approach enables both the effective design and development of an upgrade delivery PSS through the virtualization of the product and the related work tasks. Furthermore, it enables the taking of product MoL and EoL information into account, when designing and developing new generation products and services (Fig. 6).

## *3.2 Tool Use Limitations*

Relatively new pieces of technology have been developed and tested as part of the UIW-product-service upgrade approach. They have not really been implemented into business processes; this study has been more of a proof-of-concept. The technology maturity, usability and benefits have been evaluated against business cases in order to assess the realistic potential in creating new value and innovative upgrade business. Here, it is important to understand that value cannot be purely measured quantitatively in money, but rather that value is created in more fluent

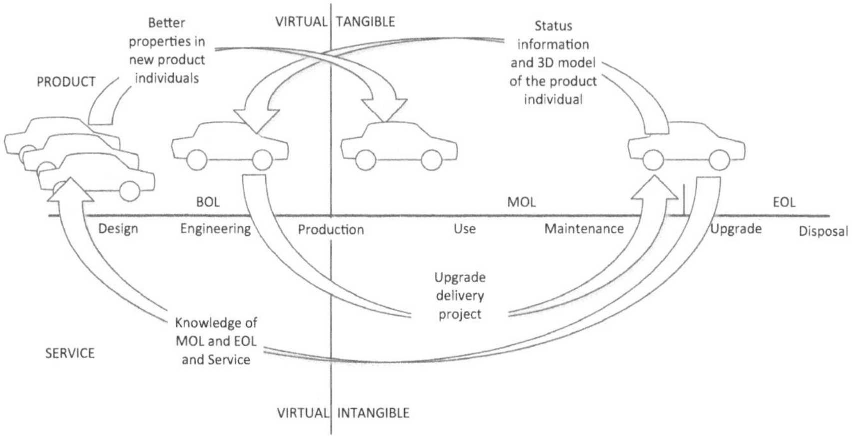


**Fig. 6** Closing knowledge loops of product lifecycle by virtualisation product representations

processes, such as customer satisfaction and quality. On the other hand, if we consider the impacts on productivity (Tangen 2005), we need to distinguish between efficiency (doing things right), effectivity (doing the right things) and usability. Previously, it was claimed, that our UIW-approach increases productivity by decreasing the amount of waste, such as searching for information and unnecessary rework. This can only be evaluated by looking at the impact at the business success level. The difference between evaluating the usability and efficiency of a certain tool, such as an AR device, and the effectivity on a business process level, can be described with the distal/proximal evaluation model (Blessing and Chakrabarti 2009). What clearly increases productivity, where the total upgrade process is concerned, is the use of digital models created in VE as instruction material in AR (Damgrave et al. 2014).

The limitations of the present VE system result in an inability to test all aspects of design, which often leads to only emphasizing the testable aspects (Damgrave et al. 2014). Virtual prototyping, which is also VE and AR based, has been commonly claimed to shorten product development lead times and increase flexibility. However, the above mentioned problem, of the possibility to simulate all aspects of design, may lead to a situation of "*pseudoflexibility*" (Damgrave et al. 2014).

So far, in the UIW-project, it has not been possible to see the actual distal impacts, i.e. business benefits. However, the tested tools and methodology seem very promising. Considering the rapid technological progress, it is safe to say that it may be a potential game changer in upgrading business.

However, there is a "*Virtual prototyping paradox*" (Leino 2015) involving the difference between the claimed benefits and the expectations related to VE and virtual prototyping, and the actual industrial implementations and evidence for business advantages. On the one hand, this may be caused by the ambiguous definition of virtual prototyping. It seems to be useful for practically everything, but this broad applicability can also be a source of difficulty (Ellis 1994). Thus, the barriers of implementing VE and other such technology are not only caused by costs of equipment, but also by the knowledge of how to work with it (Ottosson 2002). Without seamless integration with a firm's processes, information management and way of working, this technology will not create the potential value. In all likelihood, both the new tool and existing processes, as well as the fundamental way of thinking, will require adjustment in order to create the maximum value (Damgrave et al. 2014). Without making clear connections with the input and output of other process and project phases, there is a risk that VE will just be handled as a tool, separate from the product processes.

From the technology perspective, the described UIW-approach includes AR, VE, camera based 3D scanning, as well as cloud and PLM solutions. They were tested and proven to have great potential for making product-service upgrade business more profitable. Affordable technology, such as mobile phones can already be used for 3D scanning and AR-applications. Some researchers (Meža et al. 2015) also see the potential of, such things as AR applications, but they are sceptical as to the possibility of replacing the conventional product information presentation techniques. Concerning virtual assembly simulations, (Chryssolouris et al. 2000) state that despite the time technical level and realism of VE, its feasibility and usefulness was demonstrated, especially when taking into account human involvement, in the process.

However, there are still some limitations (Table 4) related to technical maturity and user friendliness of AR/VE and 3D-scanning. The human factors of these technologies are also critical and they are dealt with, e.g., in the paper of (Wilson and D'Cruz 2006). Most of the current VE applications still require a high level of craftsmanship to achieve the potential advantages, and the applications are often built for a dedicated process or project (Damgrave et al. 2014). According to

**Table 4** Limitations and anticipated near future improvements of the used technology

| Piece of technology | Current limitations | Near future improvements |
|---|---|---|
| Augmented Reality (AR) | Data pipeline<br>Integration with PLM<br>Often requires tailoring<br>Technical problems, such as stability of images | Standardization of data formats and information models<br>Growing market will foster SW and HW development of COTS |
| Virtual Environments (VE) | Needs an expert operator<br>Integration with PLM | VE will be integrated with PLM and CAE<br>Standardization of data formats and information models |
| 3D scanning | Accuracy<br>Usability | Growing market will foster SW and HW development of mobile devices |
| Product Lifecycle Management (PLM) and Cloud | Integration<br>Information models | New PLM models including MoL, EoL and service<br>Standardization of data formats and information models |

Damgrave et al., one reason for this is a lack of standardization, but so is the ignorance of technology developers in regard to available possibilities and real user needs. However, technology is progressing fast and this is the right time for establishing prerequisites for digitalization of machine upgrade processes.

# 4 Conclusion

This chapter has introduced the UIW-approach to upgrading rock crushers at customer sites. The high level business problem to be solved concerned making upgrade delivery projects profitable and more desirable for customers, manufacturing OEMs and suppliers. The main recognized and treated bottlenecks were related to knowing the actual status of the upgrade target, communication and collaboration with stakeholders, verification and validation of upgrade specifications, and an efficient information flow between the stakeholders.

AR, VE, camera based 3D scanning, and cloud based solutions were selected in order to solve the bottlenecks. One principle in the selection was to use commercial off-the-shelf (COTS) tools, as much as possible. Laser based 3D scanning (active) was also tested and compared with camera based photogrammetric scanning (passive). The accuracy of laser scanning was better, but camera based was chosen because of its mobility and ease of use. Nowadays, almost everyone carries a smartphone, which makes camera-based 3D scanning attractive. 3D scanning enables fast and cost efficient acquisition of the actual 3D model of the product individuals, at customer sites. VE is a means to visualize scan based 3D models, as well as CAD based 3D models, so that all stakeholders can better understand them. This enables better communication, collaboration and involvement of all stakeholders, including customers, internal stakeholders, suppliers and partners. With the use of VE and AR, it is possible to illustrate upgrade offerings for customers and to test proposed solutions, virtually. They also enable the planning and discussing of service activities. The proposed solutions can be verified and validated, before building physical products. VE/AR and PLM based solutions enable more fluent information flows and sharing, which improves overall productivity. Cloud based PLM enables automation of data operations and flows dynamically between the stakeholders.

Technology maturity, usability and usefulness were evaluated from a business benefit viewpoint. It can be concluded that maturity and usability are not yet quite good enough, but taking into account the current speed of development of such devices, they probably will be good enough, in the near future. However, this study was more of a proof-of-concept, which demonstrated the potential of contributing to business model innovation and game change, in an upgrade business. The tools and methods were not actually integrated with business processes and information management systems in production. Questions still remain as to what level of integration is needed between the tools and the IT systems for cost efficiency, and what kind of PLM information model development is needed. However, these aspects were kept in mind and carefully considered. In principle, there are no major technical obstacles for implementation and integration of the whole architecture. However, in addition to the technical issues, new processes and work methods may require an even greater effort.

This study has practical implications in industry and implications in PLM and engineering design research. This paper shows how novel technology can be utilized in industry and how it might enable business model innovations related to individual product upgrade services. However, this also requires a holistic and humanistic approach, taking into account processes, organizations, networks, leadership and ways of working. This paper contributes to research by discussing the closed-loop PLM concept, involving virtualization of PSS development and upgrading product individuals in MoL and EoL lifecycle phases. Connection to Product Avatars and the Industry4.0 concept was also discussed, from the perspective of the virtualization of product individuals and the enrichment of the digital 3D model, with knowledge from the middle and end of life phases. How VE and AR contribute to PLM was also discussed, in this context.

In a more philosophical way, the value of the UIW-approach can be explained with the notion of "*Bounded Rationality*" (Simon 1995). It means that human rationality is bounded by the very narrow focus of human attention. Because design is a process of searching, discovering the right goals, and finding information about constraints and available alternatives, it is highly valuable if we can extend the focus of designers and help then to see the right goals and choose the right alternatives. In the PLM and product development context, it must be understood that all stakeholders are also designers who not only contribute to the technical solution, but also to each other's success and well-being. This can also be understood with the shared value approach (Porter and Kramer 2011), which emphasizes a firm's opportunity to better utilize skills, resources, and management capabilities in order to better understand customers and mechanisms that influence productivity and success, both from economic growth and social progress perspectives.

**Acknowledgements** The research leading to these results has received funding from the European Community's Seventh Framework Programme under grant agreement No. 609027 (Project UIW). We want to express our gratitude to all colleagues and partners in UIW, especially for people of VTT, Metso Minerals, and RDVelho.

## References

Ancona, M., Clini, P., Dellacasa, A., Falzone, P., La Camera, A., & Quattrini, R. (2015). Extending a mobile device with low-cost 3d modeling and building-scale mapping capabilities, for application in architecture and archaeology. In *The International Archives of the Photogrammetry, Remote Sensing and Spatial Information Sciences* (Vol. XL, pp. 25–27).

Aromaa, S., & Väänänen, K. (2016). Suitability of virtual prototypes to support human factors/ergonomics evaluation during the design. *Applied Ergonomics, 56,* 11–18.

Berglund, J., Lindskog, E., Johansson, B., Stahre, J., & Vallhagen, J. (2013). Integration of 3D laser scanning into traditional DES project methodology. In *Proceedings of the 2013 Winter Simulation Conference* (pp. 4014–4015).

Berglund, J., Lindskog, E., Johansson, B., & Vallhagen, J. (2014). Using 3D laser scanning to support discrete event simulation of production systems: Lessons learned. In *Proceedings of the 2014 Winter Simulation Conference* (pp. 2990–2999).

Bi, Z. M., & Wang, L. (2010). Advances in 3D data acquisition and processing for industrial applications. *Robotics and Computer Integrated Manufacturing, 26*(5), 403–413.

Blessing, L. T. M., & Chakrabarti, A. (2009). *DRM, a design research methodology*. London: Springer.

Bordegoni, M., Cugini, U., Caruso, G., & Polistina, S. (2009). Mixed prototyping for product assessment: A reference framework. *International Journal on Interactive Design and Manufacturing (IJIDeM), 3*(3), 177–187.

Bosche, F., & Haas, C. T. (2008). Automated retrieval of 3D CAD model objects in construction range images. *Automation in Construction, 17,* 499–512.

Brettel, M., Friederichsen, N., Keller, M., & Rosenberg, M. (2014). How virtualization, decentralization and network building change the manufacturing landscape: An industry 4.0 perspective. *International Journal of Mechanical, Aerospace, Industrial and Mechatronics Engineering, 8*(1), 37–44.

Cavalieri, S., & Pezzotta, G. (2012). Product—Service systems engineering: State of the art and research challenges. *Computers in Industry, 63*(4), 278–288.

Chryssolouris, G., Mavrikios, D., Fragos, D., & Karabatsou, V. (2000). A virtual reality-based experimentation environment for the verification of human-related factors in assembly processes. *Robotics and Computer Integrated Manufacturing, 16,* 267–276.

Damgrave, R. G. J., Lutters, E., & Drukker, J. W. (2014). Rationalizing virtual reality based on manufacturing paradigms. *Procedia CIRP, 21,* 264–269.

Dangelmaier, W., Fischer, M., Gausemeier, J., Grafe, M., Matysczok, C., & Mueck, B. (2005). Virtual and augmented reality support for discrete manufacturing system simulation. *Computers in Industry, 56,* 371–383.

Di Gironimo, G., Lanzotti, A., & Tarallo, A. (2014). A virtual reality framework for the design review of complex industrial assemblies: Case study on the interiors of superjet 100 aircraft. In I. Horváth & Z. Rusak (Eds.), *Proceedings of TMCE 2014*, May 19–23, 2014, Budapest, Hungary (pp. 1553–1560).

Ellis, S. R. (1994). What are virtual environments? *IEEE Computer Graphics and Applications, 14*(1), 17–22.

Erdos, G., Nakano, T., & Vancza, J. (2014). Adapting CAD models of complex engineering objects to measured point cloud data. *CIRP Annals—Manufacturing Technology, 63,* 157–160. doi:10.1016/j.cirp.2014.03.090.

Golparvar-Fard, M., Bohn, J., Teizer, J., Savarese, S., & Peña-Mora, F. (2011). Evaluation of image-based modeling and laser scanning accuracy for emerging automated performance monitoring techniques. *Automation in Construction, 20*(8), 1143–1155.

Gomes de Sá, A., & Zachmann, G. (1998). Integrating virtual reality for virtual prototyping. In *Proceedings of DETC'98 1998 ASME Design Engineering Technical Conferences* September 13–16, 1998, Atlanta, Georgia, USA.

Gomes de Sá, A., & Zachmann, G. (1999). Virtual reality as a tool for verification of assembly and maintenance processes. *Computers and Graphics, 23,* 389–403.

Gonzalez-Aguilera, D., Pozo, S. Del, Lopez, G., & Rodriguez-Gonzalvez, P. (2012). From point cloud to CAD models: Laser and optics geotechnology for the design of electrical substations. *Optics & Laser Technology, 44*(5), 1384–1392.

Huet, G., Culley, S., McMahon, C., & Fortin, C. (2007). Making sense of engineering design review activities. *Artificial Intelligence for Engineering Design, Analysis and Manufacturing, 21,* 243–265.

Jun, H., Kiritsis, D., & Xirouchakis, P. (2007). Research issues on closed-loop PLM. *Computers in Industry, 58,* 855–868.

Kolev, K., Tanskanen, P., Speciale, P., & Pollefeys, M. (2014). Turning mobile phones into 3D scanners. In *2014 IEEE Conference on Computer Vision and Pattern Recognition* (pp. 3946–3953).

Kumar, A., Jain, P. K., & Pathak, P. M. (2012). Industrial application of point cloud/STL data for reverse engineering. In *DAAAM International Scientific Book* (pp. 445–462).

Leino, S.-P. (2015). Reframing the value of virtual prototyping Intermediary virtual prototyping—The evolving approach of virtual environments based virtual prototyping in the context of new product development and low volume production. Tampere University of Technology.

Lejon, E., & Jeppsson, P. (2015). Integrating use phase information and virtual product representation to support Functional Products. *Procedia CIRP, 38,* 204–209.

Lindskog, E., Berglund, J., Vallhagen, J., & Johansson, B. (2013). Visualization support for virtual redesign of manufacturing systems. *Procedia CIRP, 7,* 419–424.

Lindskog, E., Berglund, J., Vallhagen, J., & Johansson, B. (2014). Lean based problem solving using 3D laser scanned visualizations of production systems. *International Journal of Engineering Science and Innovative Technology, 3*(3), 556–565.

McAloone, T. C., & Andreasen, M. M. (2004). Design for utility, sustainability and societal virtues: Developing product service systems. In *International Design Conference—Design 2004* (pp. 1–8).

Meža, S., Turk, Ž., & Dolenc, M. (2015). Measuring the potential of augmented reality in civil engineering. *Advances in Engineering Software, 90,* 1–10.

Ottosson, S. (2002). Virtual reality in the product development process. *Journal of Engineering Design, 13*(January), 159–172.

Ovtcharova, J. G. (2010). Virtual engineering: Principles, methods and applications. In *International Design Conference—DESIGN 2010* (pp. 1267–1274).

Porter, M. E., & Kramer, M. R. (2011). The big idea: Creating shared value. *Harvard Business Review, 89*(1), 0001.

Shen, Y., Ong, S. K., & Nee, A. Y. C. (2010). Augmented reality for collaborative product design and development. *Design Studies, 31*(2), 118–145. doi:10.1016/j.destud.2009.11.001.

Simon, H. A. (1995). Problem forming, problem finding, and problem solving in design. In Collen & Gasparski (Eds.), *Design and systems: General applications of methodology* (Vol. 3, pp. 245–257). New Brunswick: Transaction Publishers.

Tangen, S. (2005). Demystifying productivity and performance. *International Journal of Productivity and Performance Management, 54.*

Tanskanen, P., Kolev, K., Meier, L., Camposeco, F., Saurer, O., & Pollefeys, M. (2013). Live metric 3d reconstruction on mobile phones. In *Proceedings of the IEEE International Conference on Computer Vision* (pp. 65–72).

Tuma, Z., Knoflicek, R., Tuma, J., Bradac, F., & Blecha, P. (2014). The process simulation using by virtual reality. *Procedia Engineering, 69,* 1015–1020.

Verlinden, J., Horváth, I., & Nam, T.-J. (2009). Recording augmented reality experiences to capture design reviews. *International Journal on Interactive Design and Manufacturing (IJIDeM), 3*(3), 189–200.

Wang, G. G. (2002). Definition and review of virtual prototyping. *Journal of Computing and Information Science in Engineering, 2*(3), 232.

Weidlich, D., Zickner, H., Riedel, T., Processes, P., & Chemnitz, F. T. (2009). Real 3D geometry and motion data as a basis for virtual design and testing. In *Proceedings of the 19th CIRP Design Conference* (pp. 30–31).

Wiesner, S., Freitag, M., Westphal, I., & Thoben, K. (2015). Interactions between service and product lifecycle management. *Procedia CIRP, 30,* 36–41.

Wilson, J. R., & D'Cruz, M. (2006). Virtual and interactive environments for work of the future. *International Journal of Human-Computer Studies, 64*(3), 158–169.

Woodward, C., & Hakkarainen, M. (2011). *Mobile mixed reality system for architectural and construction site visualization*. INTECH Open Access Publisher.
Wuest, T. (2015). Current approaches with a focus on holistic information management in manufacturing. In *Identifying Product and Process State Drivers in Manufacturing Systems Using Supervised Machine Learning* (pp. 51–67).

# Space Systems Development

**Mauro Pasquinelli, Valter Basso, Stefano T. Chiadò, Carlo Vizzi and Michele Cencetti**

**Abstract** This chapter describes the Space cluster use case using the innovative Space Tug project as an example. It provides an overview of the objectives (customer in the loop, quicker technical response) and related methods to support foreseen improvements through a dedicated toolchain. The IT infrastructure used for the demonstration is used as an enabling and demonstrative system with a focus on modelling and collaboration aspects, as outlined in Chapter "Extending the System Model", on the flow of information, and on tool infrastructure and project costs. Descriptions of the developed tools are as follows:

- A web-based toolchain that includes functional analysis, discipline analysis, 3D modelling and virtual reality for project team collaboration.
- A workflow manager for collaboration between different companies.
- Small devices called 'probes' to ensure security and data protection in inter-company collaboration.
- A configurable customer front-end to ensure that the customer remains informed.

M. Pasquinelli (✉) · V. Basso
Domain Exploration and Science Italy—Engineering,
Thales Alenia Space, Turin, Italy
e-mail: mauro.pasquinelli@thalesaleniaspace.com

V. Basso
e-mail: valter.basso@thalesaleniaspace.com

S.T. Chiadò
Vastalla, Turin, Italy
e-mail: stefano.chiado@vastalla.com

C. Vizzi
Technology Research Advanced Projects & Studies, ALTEC, Turin, Italy
e-mail: carlo.vizzi@altecspace.it

M. Cencetti
Mission Operations and Training, ALTEC, Turin, Italy
e-mail: michele.cencetti@altecspace.it



S.N. Grösser et al. (eds.), *Dynamics of Long-Life Assets*,
DOI 10.1007/978-3-319-45438-2_13

**Keywords** Spacecraft · Collaborative engineering · Virtual reality · Model based engineering · Modelling and simulation · Model based collaboration · Workflow manager · Process management · Customer front-end · Interdisciplinary engineering

# 1 Introduction

## *1.1 Competition and Challenges in the Space Industry*

The space era started during the Cold War, and tight competition between USA and USSR accelerated technological achievements, enabling the launch of an artificial satellite in 1957, the survival of a human orbiting the Earth in 1961 and landing on the Moon in 1969. This challenge led to a dramatic change, bringing a legacy of technologies that are evident to any person using a map, navigating using a GPS or using one of the many technologies that emerged from space research.

Currently, there are more than one thousand active artificial satellites, most of which are telecommunication and Earth observation satellites that monitor the environment, support disaster management, provide data to the scientific community, and support civil protection and military operations. There is also an outpost with a permanent crew of six people orbiting the Earth. There are also spacecraft exploring our solar system; observing or landing on planets, comets and asteroids; and telescopes observing the farthest zones of our universe.

Sixty years after the first artificial satellite, new challenges that are very different from those of the 20th century have arisen and may lead to improvements and progress for humanity. Examples of current challenges can be found in the roadmaps of the International Space Exploration Coordination Group (ISECG 2016), regarding a return to the Moon, paving the way for a human landing on Mars, and the current attempts to enhance satellite coverage to enable high-speed internet access using satellites.

What has changed in recent years? The current trends highlighted in the OECD (Organisation for Economic Co-operation and Development) report (OECD 2014) on the space economy reveal that:

- *Competition is increasing.* "Major challenges lie ahead both for the incumbents and for the new entrants into the space economy. In a globalised world, few sectors are sheltered from competition as the rapidly evolving global value chains in the space sector demonstrate. In addition, a new industrial revolution is looming on the horizon which holds out the prospect of deep-seated change in the traditional space industry" (OECD 2014).
- *Industrial complexity is increasing.* "private industry supply chains are getting more complex, influenced by the multinational nature of major space companies" (OECD 2014).

- *Exploration Missions are becoming more complex* and require international collaboration (ISECG 2016).
- *An additional commercial market is growing.* "The key drivers for more globalisation will include sustained institutional support from new sources worldwide, double sourcing guaranteed on the market offering new commercial opportunities, and a wider global addressable market size for all actors" (OECD 2014).
- *National space budgets are not increasing.* The space budget as a share of the GDP in European countries varies from 0.05 to 0.10% (OECD 2014).

Economy-driven and economy-driving challenges are expected in the future. The space industry is experienced and has technological capabilities. New improvements are needed to manage the prospective constraints that future scenarios involve. Among the many possible improvements (e.g., in product policies or technological R&D), this section analyses and proposes a solution for preparation of complex solutions by complex technical teams with continuous customer involvement.

## 1.2 Speeding up the Interdisciplinary Approach for a Quicker Response to the Customer

Adaptation to customer demand, continuous upgrades of provided services and products, and a quicker response to the customer are needed to manage the future space economy. These objectives of the Use-it-Wisely (UIW) project were analysed by the space cluster regarding the improvement of capabilities and efficiency of technical work.

The space industry handles complex products in a complex industrial organization that typically includes the customer; the customer participates in the design, verification and operations loops with engineering, scientific and high-tech capabilities. Customers may make decisions based on many key factors, such as political constraints (e.g., geographical return for member states in the case of the European Space Agency), the soundness of the solution, costs, schedule, and risks. For a commercial customer, the ability to quickly respond with an appropriate solution with the highest possible confidence that it meets the related needs is essential. The more complex the proposed solution is, the more of the following issues may appear:

- Understanding of real needs and constraints: the expressed needs and constraints may be incomplete or provided without a clear rationale (for instance, providing costly constraints that can be drastically reduced using alternative concepts).
- Feedback capture: customer feedback is essential to providing an alternative solution or to improving future products/services quickly.

- Traceability: the customer and user needs should be traced to the technical solution, changes should be clearly identified and their impact traced in the technical solution and retained for future evolution of the product.

The needs that arise from a customer-supplier relationship can be further broken down into technical team-level requirements:

- Responding to customer (or potential customer) requests or changes quickly, while managing complex technical issues in a distributed team, managing a large amount of technical data in a distributed team, and maintaining the required levels of quality and risks.
- Clearly presenting the technical solution to a potential customer, showing the advantages with regards to competitors by providing information at different levels of detail, clearly supporting any proposal for change by describing the advantages to the customer, and using clear, complete and visual means to show the solution and related operations (e.g., using simulation and 3D graphics).

## 1.3 The Proposed Solution

The proposed solution is based on analysis of an operational scenario, simplified but without loss of generality, comprising the following entities:

- The (potential) customer technical team: in charge of providing the needs and technically evaluating the solution or proposed changes.
- The solution provider technical team: manages the solution for the entire industrial team and acting as the main interface with the customer.
- The supplier technical team: a supplier of the solution provider, maintained in the loop to elaborate the solution.

As described in Chapter "Extending the System Model", modelling methodologies are expected to provide advantages for technical (and project) data management. Moreover, the current trends in industry show extensive usage of MBSE (model-based systems engineering) methodologies, the quality and benefits of which should grow in the upcoming decades.

The solution is a federated environment in which each of the actors from the aforementioned operational entities can work in a distributed model-based environment that fits their organization and their needs. Such a federated environment is based on the following assumptions:

- **Each environment is web-based,** meaning that the models can be accessed through dedicated services available on the company network (with security restrictions). This is already the case for some commercial or custom tools and the current trend is to move towards web-based solutions.

- **Any technical discipline can profit from such a system-level environment** to retrieve required information from the other disciplines and to provide the system-level information required to the other entities.
- The web-based environment shall be **semantically unique**, i.e., the data can be retrieved, inserted and processed univocally by a human operator or an automated routine programmed by an operator independent of the data originator/owner. This is explained in detail in Chapter "Extending the System Model". ECSS-E-TM-10-23A technical memorandum (ECSS 2016) describes the current effort in the European space domain to proceed towards an interoperable space systems data repository.

Based on the experience we have gained with model-based environments in recent years, difficulties arise in handling the interoperability of environments and security requirement compliance. These include four main issues, with related solutions:

- Data compatibility: solved using data semantics and well-defined and generic interfaces.
- Workflow realization: solved using the concept of services-based exchange between different entities and dedicated task definition and realization managers.
- Data security: solved using semantics and dedicated processes that allow a filtered exchange of information, clearly identifying what data exit the company network perimeter.
- Cost and maintainability of the IT infrastructure: solved using integration between tools that is based not on tool versions or custom formats but on mapping to common semantic data models or custom data structures defined at the user level (not at the tool vendor level).

The evaluation of a solution that follows such assumptions and constraints is performed for a demonstrative case. It is based on the future provision of an unconventional space-to-space re-utilizable product: a type of taxi service in space to move spacecraft from one position (orbit) to another that provides other servicing options. This concept is typically called Space Tug[1] and is assumed to be proposed as service to a commercial customer who decides to use this service or not based on their requirements.

This case was used because it includes a high level of complexity and can be briefly described and divided by entity:

[1]This case is freely derived from a national Italian project to have a clear idea of the consistency of the approach with a real study involving Thales Alenia Space and ALTEC (and other partners) but with no direct connection to the project. The data and ideas described in this chapter are not connected to the project and the data and concepts proposed are demonstrative.

- *Customer:*
  - Commercial customer: not constrained by political decisions or national budget allocation, intense worldwide competition.
  - Needs are (1) to determine if the proposed solution is effective, valid and advantageous, (2) to be supported during its design phase to eventually de-risk the interface with the Space Tug system, and (3) to be supported during operations.
- *Solution Provider:*
  - Provides the Space Tug, which will provide In-space Services: the Tug interfaces with the customer system or a dedicated interface, and related operations are coordinated.
  - Services provided are (1) engineering/project services provided to a potential customer during the preliminary design phase: to decide if the in-space service is suitable for its needs. (2) Engineering/Project Services provided to a customer during the design phase: to support any evaluation or potential changes and upgrades. (3) Engineering/Project Services provided to a customer during the operations: to support the operations and potential anomaly investigations or upgrade requested services.
- *Supplier:*
  - Provides the Ground Segment and the Ground Operations teams and manages operations.
  - Services provided are (1) engineering/Project Services provided to the solution provider to complement the space segment solution with ground-related operations, and (2) engineering/Project Services provided to the customer to support operations.

The following chapters show how the space cluster of the UIW project analysed a potential solution to support such actors and process. The space cluster is composed of Thales Alenia Space, ALTEC and Vastalla.

Thales Alenia Space has designed, integrated, tested, operated and delivered innovative space systems for 40 years. The UIW-project relied on the experience of the Collaborative System Engineering (COSE) Centre (at the TAS Turin site) on virtual reality, model-based interdisciplinary data exchange and systems engineering, and the design of exploration and science spacecraft.

The Aerospace Logistics Technology Engineering Company (ALTEC) is an Italian centre of excellence for the provision of engineering and logistics services to support International Space Station operations and utilization and the development and implementation of planetary exploration missions. The experience related to engineering and operations and competence in virtual reality and model-based design possessed by ALTEC were used in the project.

Vastalla is an IT company that offers consulting services, software development and IT system activities with an emphasis on IT security. Its experience was used for the collaboration portion of the overall solution and for the customer front-end.

### *1.4 Chapter Outline*

Section 2 provides an overview of the application of the proposed solution. Section 3 provides a description of the demonstration and its outcomes. Section 4 provides conclusions and describes possible future applications.

## 2 Detailed Application of the Solution to Overcome the Challenges

### *2.1 The Users-Tools Functional Chain*

The issues and considerations in Sect. 1 are translated into a modelling and collaboration methodology, a reference logical architecture and a tool chain to provide a demonstrative case to validate the approach.

Figure 1 shows the functional architecture of this tool chain, with the related tools or responsibilities implemented in the UIW-demonstration. The architecture is defined using a model-based approach with the ARCADIA methodology and Capella tool notation (Polarsys 2016)

For simplicity, the MBSE interdisciplinary and distributed environment is depicted only for the solution provider side and includes:

- *System Models, Simulation Models and Services Process manager:* this functional block is needed to support the interdisciplinary work between people and discipline-specific tools through dedicated adapters. This functional block also includes the definition of Engineering or Project Services to be provided to a customer.
- *System Simulation and Visualization:* this functional block is needed to support the visualization of the product, activities and simulation results.
- *Simulation Execution:* this functional block is needed to provide system level simulation, integrate discipline-level simulations, or provide early system-level simulation.
- *Extranet Interface:* this functional block is the gatekeeper that assures a safe flow of data.

On the customer side, we need to be able to respond to requests based on the services provided. Moreover, some services must be provided globally (e.g., workflow management) and could be allocated to a third-party such as an IT services provider, namely:

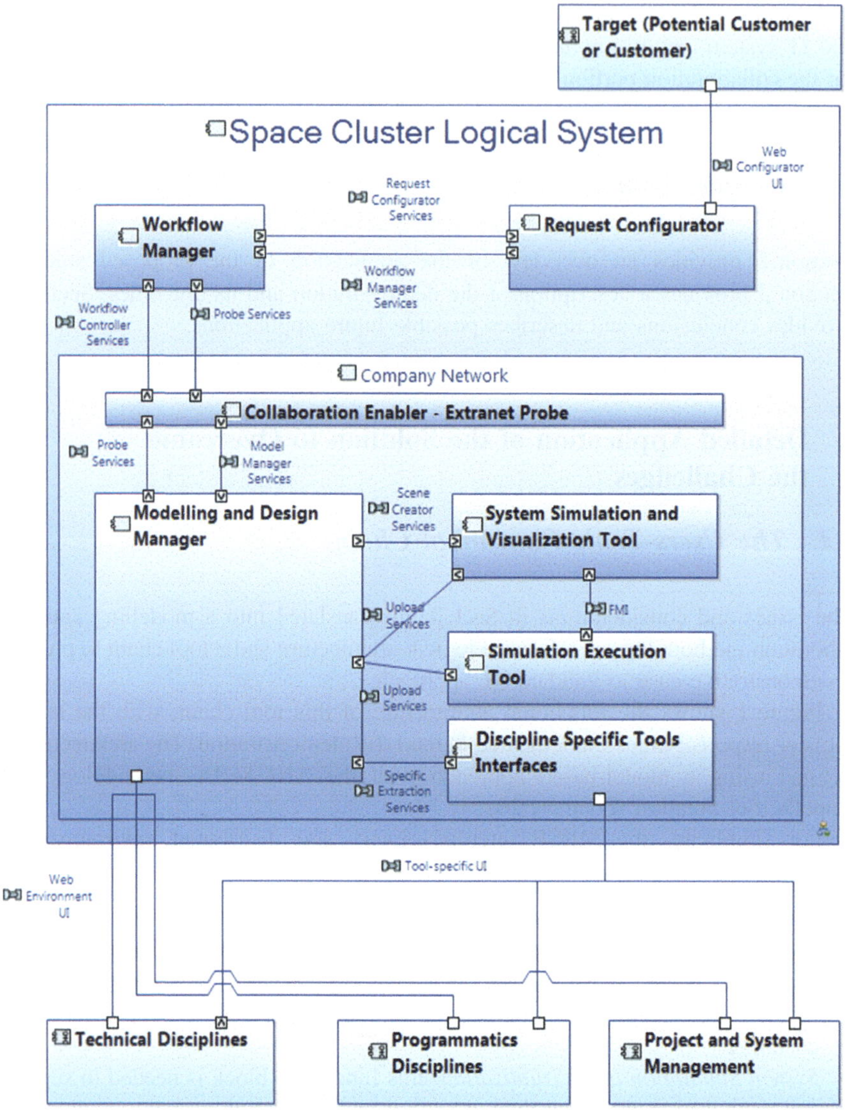


**Fig. 1** Logical architecture of the solution

- *Workflow Control:* this functional block orchestrates the flow of information between actors.
- *Communication Tools:* this functional block allows for controlled communications that are external to the typical communication means.
- *Repository:* this functional block allows for a controlled repository of shared data.

On the supplier side, the MBSE environment is not explicit and is called Mission Control, based on the related function in the demonstration.

This functional architecture is then translated into a physical architecture, i.e., actual tools and applications, used in the UIW-project to provide an answer to the project challenges addressed in the first chapters of this book.

Maintaining customer involvement from the beginning is very important to guarantee the success of complex projects that manage extensive structured data, many companies working together, and many actors in the supply chain. In these business cases, supplier-generated feasibility and cost estimates take several days, so it is of paramount importance to keep the customer in the loop from the first day. Tools that maintain an appropriate flow of information to the customer can be easily deployed.

Customers can access a web application that acts as a bridge between them and the suppliers. This web application is called the **Request Configurator**, developed by Vastalla. Using this web application, customers can login, request new quotations for an array of commercial Space services, review past requests, or order a commercial Space service.

This web application is closely connected to other software modules that form the backbone of the IT infrastructure and allow for a smooth relationship with the customers.

Customers are in the loop. This mean that they are informed in real time about the current state of their requests. Furthermore, they can exchange relevant information that allows the suppliers to correctly quote the requested service.

All requests, past and present, are managed by the **Workflow Manager** developed by Vastalla. This software component traces the status of requests along workflows. These workflows differ one from another depending on the commercial Space service being requested. The Workflow manager is an API-based software that is automatically configured (on-the-fly dynamic configuration) by the Web Environment. The Workflow Manager is designed as an open software that easily integrates with other software components through pre-defined APIs.

The Web Environment is the software component that generates the commercial Space services workflows. The dialogue between the Workflow Manager and the Web Environment is mediated by the **probes**, small devices that act as gatekeepers of the communication flow between the Intranet portion of the global infrastructure architecture and the common Workflow Manager.

The probes are very small devices (approximately the size of a cigarette pack) that use Raspberry Pi technology (Rapsberry 2016) and have the capability to filter the IP traffic going through them to allow only legitimate traffic to pass to the Workflow Manager. The probes act as gatekeepers and can be implemented as separate devices depending on company decisions. For demonstrative purposes, Raspberry PI® devices have been deployed (Fig. 2).

The Web Environment is part of the TAS DEVICE (Distributed Environment for Virtual Integrated Collaborative Engineering) Architecture (Pasquinelli et al. 2014), which also comprises the **Virtual Environment** (VERITAS) and the adapter to the discipline-specific tools. For this demonstration, a CAD adapter called RAP

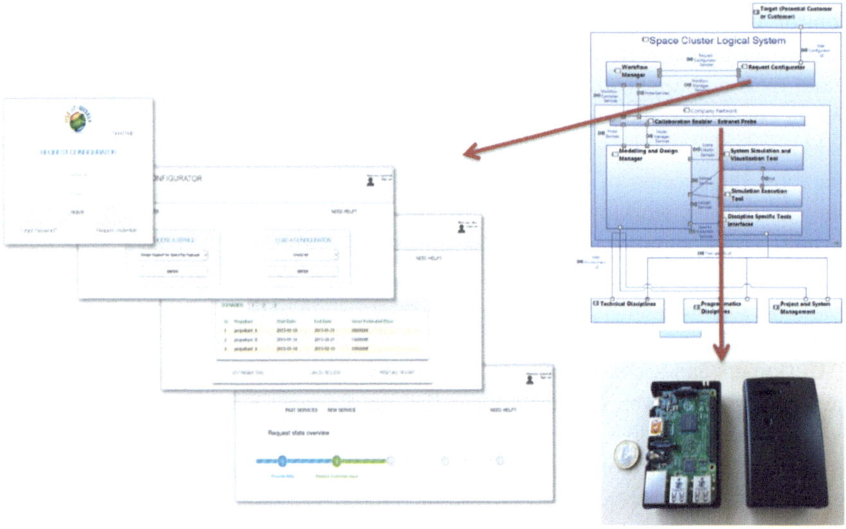


**Fig. 2** Request configurator user interface and physical implementation of a probe (Raspberry Pi®)

(Retrieve cAd Parameters, internal TAS development) is used. **Modelica** (Modelica Association 2016) is used as the language for the low-fidelity system-level simulation using OpenModelica (OpenModelica 2016) or Dymola (Dassault Systemes 2016) to execute the code.

The **Web Environment** is a model-based and web-based operational prototype developed by TAS that is inspired by the current European space domain efforts (e.g., ECSS-E-TM-10-23A (ESA 2016) and ECSS-E-TM-10-25A (ECSS 2016) technical memoranda), OMG efforts (OMG 2016) and THALES corporate-level (see Capella (Polarsys 2016)) initiatives but with a clear objective of enabling a social-technical network of people and tools to collaborate on technical solutions.

It is worth noting that the solution described in this section is a demonstrative research case to demonstrate and validate the architecture and methodology and that these prototype tools have not been deployed in the TAS or ALTEC networks.

The application of MBSE methodology is helpful not only during the design phases but also during the operational scenario of a Space system (Cencetti 2014). A model-based approach allows for better organization of the information that characterizes the execution of a space mission. The definition of a structured data pattern can help manage the information and ensure a more straightforward connection with the product baseline.

Elaboration of the information that emerges from a complex system is often not easy to manage during an operational scenario. For example, manned spacecraft and other classes of space systems are often characterized by a broad set of parameters, subsystems and data that must be properly understood and monitored to avoid incorrect interpretation of actual scenarios. Troubleshooting activities often require the retrieval and analysis of system documentation, which are generally difficult to perform when the information is not collected in a structured manner. These issues also arise during the design phases of a complex system when different domains are involved and many people with different backgrounds and skills collaborate on the same project. All the information generated during the design process is generally used during the operational phase in management of the space system. Space Operations are currently investigating and developing innovative solutions for exploiting system data. The increasing complexity of aerospace products leads to increasingly difficult management of available resources and telemetry data. From the literature, it is possible to see how different research initiatives address the definition and assessment of more effective approaches than the traditional ones. For example, web-based frameworks and MBSE methodologies are some of the research topics that are starting to spread across different phases of the spacecraft lifecycle, from design activities to dismissal processes. In the last few years, the development of MBSE design and analysis methodologies has gained increasing interest in the industry. The implementation of design solutions that ensure more effective management of system information allows for significant time and cost reductions.

Examples in academic literature show how the application of MBSE starting from the preliminary design phases can ensure more straightforward information management during operational activities.

A model-based approach can generally be used to support two main aspects of the product lifecycle: operational design process and space mission execution.

The main objective of the operational design process is to focus on organization of all the activities that will characterize the actual space mission. This process mainly addresses the design of the features of the operational phase. The same concepts can also be used during the execution of the real mission, ensuring a better connection between the data generated during the design process and the available information, e.g., telemetry. Examples of elements that characterize the design and organization of the operational phases are:

- Launcher constraints
- Ground station characteristics
- Spacecraft constraints
- Mission-specific constraints
- Payload constraints
- Launch window prediction
- Spacecraft and launch vehicle separation sequence
- Positioning and manoeuvring strategy
- Tracking schedule
- Scheduling operational events
- Ground station coverage
- Impact of the space environment on operations
- Payload operations strategy
- Data circulation scheme

- Feasibility of the mission
- Operational feasibility of the mission
- Mission operations concepts
- Ground segment internal and external interfaces
- Format and method of data exchange
- Data processing tools
- Mission operations team organization (preparation and execution phases)
- Testing strategies, methods and scenarios

These functions and processes represent some of the key elements that characterize the ground system and operations domain (ECSS 2008).

The information collected during design activities can be used to support preliminary analyses of a space mission with dedicated simulators of system performance. These data allow for more effective generation of simulation scenarios than in traditional approaches. A model-based philosophy ensures a seamless connection and consistency with the available baseline data. Analyses such as mission feasibility or ground station coverage can be performed within the same environment.

The design parameters of a system or equipment can be mapped with data such as telemetry to allow a direct connection with the product baseline. Thus, it is potentially easier to recover information for troubleshooting or anomaly characterization. The monitoring of a specific variable can be better supported if the operational range and other information are linked to reduce issues that can arise, as in the error-prone process of data retrieval from documentation.

The use of a model-based approach from the preliminary design activities to production can also benefit the operational phases. The information collected in a common system model can be used to properly support operational scenarios because the data can be navigated and tracked more consistently.

## 2.2 Development Innovation

When new methodologies are introduced in a company, there is some natural resistance due to the cost of the introduction and maintenance of a prospective new or updated tool chain, as well as the need for users to adapt their comfort zones. This has been experienced by the authors of this chapter in many fields.

Currently, the actual evolution of a concept into improved ways of working should be evaluated from a technical innovation perspective and also from business innovation and IT perspectives. The latter two are not trivial, especially the IT perspective. Many medium-large companies rely on complex software infrastructure, and even if their processes are acceptable and independent from the IT tools, daily work and related infrastructure costs are highly impacted. Therefore, the Space cluster scenario considered two main issues: (1) Tool interoperability and the maintenance cost of the interfaces, and (2) security and collaboration between different networks.

The first issue is easy to identify in any tool chain. Any tool has input/output capabilities and typically has custom interfaces or standard interfaces (e.g., using reference formats common for that type of application). For models, the model data interchange format is quite difficult to exchange because even if it is based on standard languages or semantics, the user typically enhances it for their own purposes to create a new "dialect" of the language or can base their interfaces on custom object libraries.

Moreover, format updates, tool updates and even technological updates can add to the high maintenance cost of the original tool interfaces.

The second issue is very critical, considering that company network security is a very sensitive topic, especially in companies that handle confidential data (e.g., working on protected innovation or with governments or military entities). Security is a continuous issue that limits the effectiveness of the daily work of those collaborating with an entity external to its network. The solutions studied by the space cluster in the UIW-project were:

(1) Use of semantic models to define the product, activities, services, actors, requirements and needs.
(2) Use of probes as interfaces between networks, profiting from the semantics of the I/O data.
(3) Simplification of interfaces and user-oriented management of the models and related formats.

There are many initiatives related to the enhancement of semantics in data generation, management and exchange. In our case, we used a simplified approach based on:

- Class diagrams to represent semantic classes, attributes and relationships; these class diagrams can be transformed into classes in an object-oriented language or simply mapped or transformed to data exchange formats using specific rules.
- Libraries of objects, specific to the domain or the project, to provide an additional level of semantics for the technical toolchain or to enhance the user experience.

Figure 3 shows an example of how the use of such class diagrams improved tool interoperability. The definition of services, as in the Web Environment, is read by the Request Configurator and used to create the customer form. The two tools were developed by two different people using different languages. To adapt the interfaces, a meeting on the semantics and a meeting on the integration tests were sufficient to produce a working prototype.

The Web Environment tool is based on a complex data model with more than one hundred classes (and related relationships) but the most important level of semantics is the possibility for the user to generate libraries of categories, properties and other types of knowledge based on their experience and specific expertise.

The Probes are compact devices that, from a hardware point of view, are Raspberry Pi devices: they have enough computational power and overall features

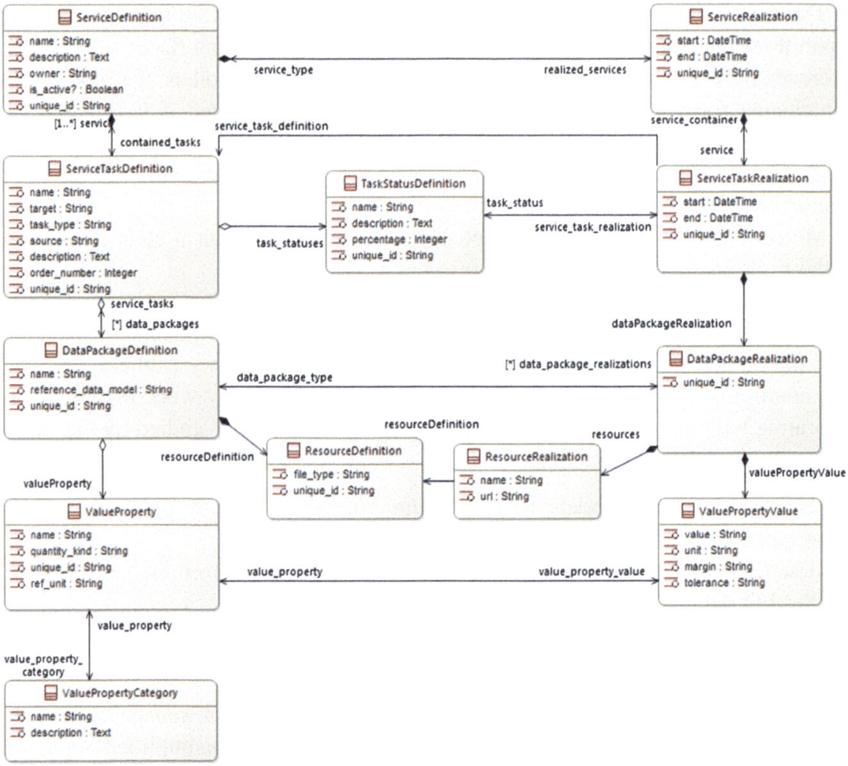


**Fig. 3** Example class diagram representing the data model of a service (partial view)

to perform their task in the architecture. The Probes host business logic together with the necessary tools for managing the traffic and requests that goes through them. Disclosure properties are tagged within the data so the Probes can communicate to the Workflow Manager how to treat different data flows depending on the tag.

The software on the Probes consists of an open source framework (nodejs 2016) that is based on a Linux distribution tailored for Raspberry Pi devices [Raspbian (Rapsberry 2016)]. The Probes primarily exchange JSON files with the upper and lower parts of the architecture.

The innovative standpoint is that some tasks that were once delegated to complex and expensive ad hoc-designed appliances can now be largely replaced by very simple devices that have enough computing power and features to filter TCP/IP traffic efficiently and offer programmers a flexible platform to easily develop programs.

The Request Configurator and the Workflow Manager are software components that can be programmed dynamically using an API-based paradigm.

In our case, the Request Configurator and the Workflow Manager are programmed in real time from the Web Environment. This means these systems are not rigid or static from a design point of view.

Thus, the Web Environment can leverage these capabilities, and engineers who work on the Web Environment can change workflows on their side and these changes are automatically mirrored in other parts of the architecture without the need to reprogram the source code.

This is a clear advantage because it summarizes the advantages of decoupling systems and seamless integration using publicly available APIs.

Information tagging helps to preserve data privacy. Some data needs to be disclosed to the customer whereas other data might not. Some data needs to be disclosed to other parts of the supply chain/toolchain and so the Probes handle this part along with the Workflow Manager.

## *2.3 Results*

Space Cluster's objective was to build a Model-Based Collaborative Environment for collaboration through the entire lifecycle and technical activities that involves potential customers and the industrial consortium.

The approach used by the Cluster to achieve this objective is described in the architecture below (Fig. 4).

The components of this architecture show the processes and tools developed by the Space Cluster within the UIW-project. They have been upgraded and improved during each iteration until obtaining tool interoperability at the end of Trial 3. The main achievements of these upgrade process are summarized below:

- It was possible to show how the logical architecture was implemented in the physical architecture and interoperability of the tools.
- The web-based Engineering Environment can define and expose services.
- The service requested by the user can be composed of several tasks defined in the Web Environment. A task is used to manage the flow of information or provide the customer feedback on the current status because it is possible to associate data and potential statuses with each task.
- Tasks can be visualized in a tree map to manage and understand the service more easily.
- The connection between the Request Web Configurator (RC) and the probe was successfully defined and tested and the Workflow Manager enabled management of the flow of data and information between the probe and the RC.
- All the actors involved in the process were successfully involved. ALTEC Mission Control was implemented and defined in the Web Environment.
- The tools that are part of the prototype were rapidly integrated.

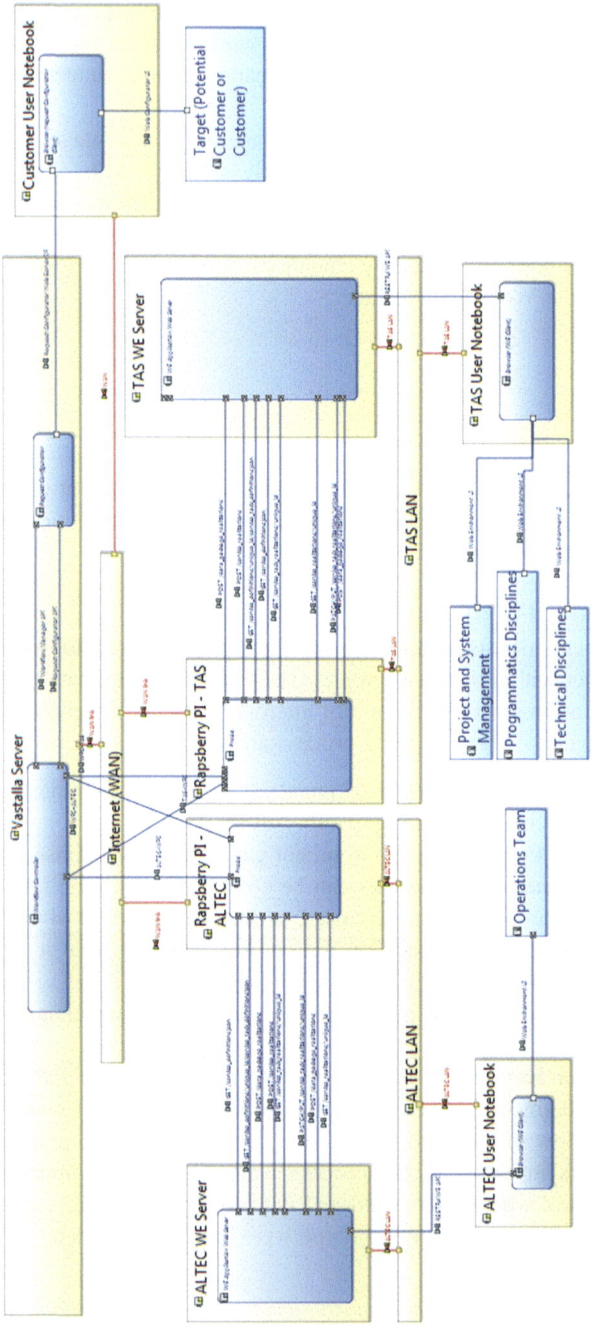


**Fig. 4** Physical architecture of the overall demonstrative environment

The purpose of the demonstration phase is to create an end-to-end process to validate the tools and the related methodologies and acquire feedback from end users and process stakeholders.

# 3 Outcomes from the Application

## *3.1 Benefits of the Methodology and Related Tools*

There are three main aspects in which benefits were demonstrated: (1) Support software development and maintenance, (2) user experience, and (3) potential impacts on the project. Regarding software aspects, the methodology chosen for the Request Configurator, Workflow Manager and Probes allows for easy integration of different components using APIs. Furthermore, maintenance of the software components is easier, leveraging on existing and widespread programming frameworks (Fig. 5).

Using APIs enables easily extending the features of the software components, provided they are designed with APIs in mind.

The methodology used to develop the Engineering distributed architecture, i.e., web-based tools for collaboration, visual supports (VR and in-browser 3D/2D visualization), web APIs for model-to-tools interfaces and use of data models and libraries for semantics, enabled the development, modification and integration of a complex environment using a rapid prototyping approach and rapid evaluation of outcomes (Fig. 6).

Regarding user experience, at first glance, the user is typically afraid of new tools and methodologies. The feedback gained from a preliminary dry run of the demonstration (a complete demonstration is planned a month after the conclusion of this chapter) showed interest from the participants, the user interface and process felt comfortable and were seen as potentially improving efficiency in daily work. The main aspects that were appreciated were:

- The availability of all the information in an easily accessible format, saving time searching for data or verifying that the data is the latest. In late phases of the project, this is typically well established with current processes that strictly control the baselines and changes but these processes are typically too expensive in early phases and for quick upgrades. A methodology similar to the one presented is expected to bring a new perspective in this sense.
- The presentation of information for any type of user (visual 3D/2D data and tables available in the browser) allows for a clear understanding by the entire team at a glance.
- The possibility for more controlled communication with external entities is considered a great improvement that has become particularly critical recently (due to security limitations).

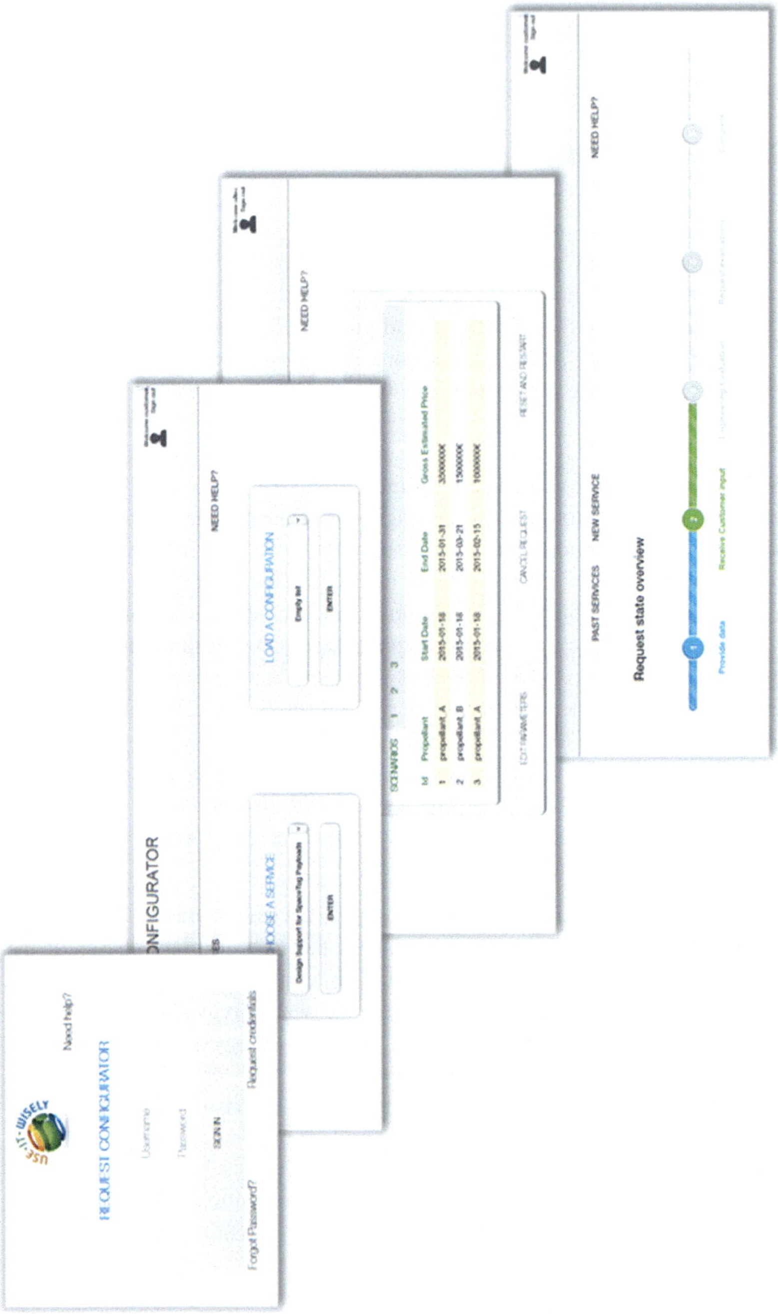


**Fig. 5** Sample images from the request configurator

**Fig. 6** Web modelling environment and virtual reality data accessible using simple but effective technologies

- The possibility of a direct and controlled link with many customers is considered as potentially improving the relationships during the upgrade or order process and to store experience and retain customer feedback for future reference.

Visualization capabilities can also be used to support data exploitation and graphical elements can be generated based on data available from the system model. Thus, information can be exchanged in a more straightforward manner. An example of an orbital representation is provided in Fig. 7. Both the analytical solution (conics) and the numerical solution can be represented using the same interface.

Regarding potential programme improvements, the use of an MBSE methodology within the context of operational scenarios leads to several advantages over traditional approaches. The definition of a structured system model that includes all the elements pertaining to the actual space mission positively affects the management of a space system. This approach reduces the time and resources needed during the design phase because data are managed in a structured manner. For example, the documentation can be generated in a straightforward manner to reduce the time spent on version control, consistency verification and updates. In the same manner, a model-based approach can also be used to support the management activities for a space system during a mission. Possible data that can be supported in

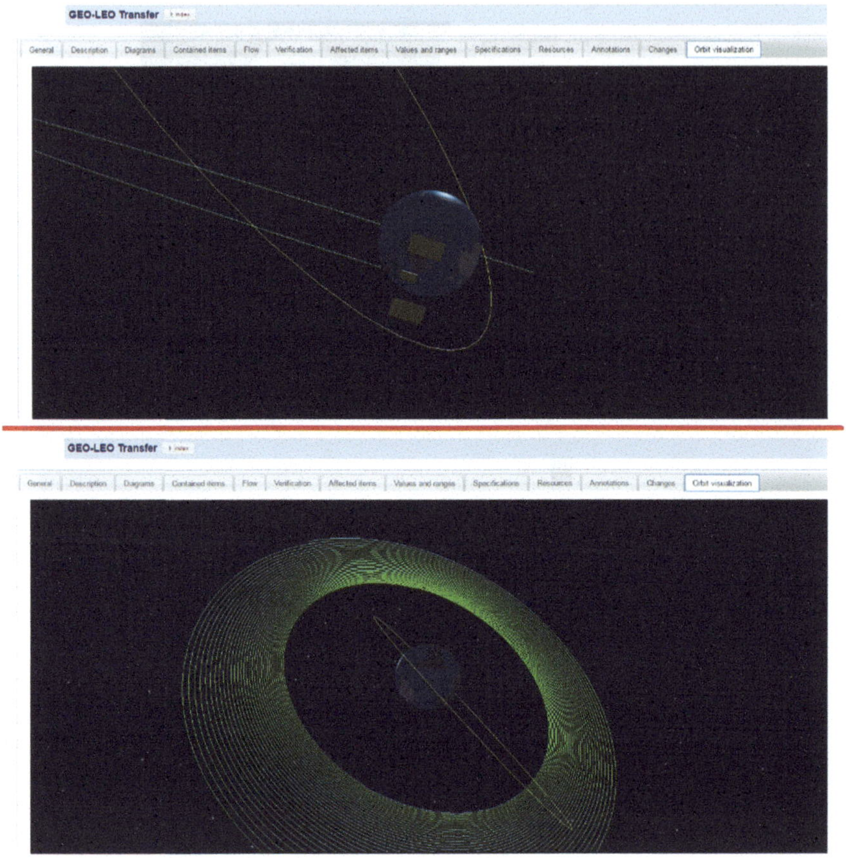


**Fig. 7** Orbit visualization capabilities

this manner include: anomaly reports, stowage notes, mission action requests, electronic flight notes, international procedures, and generic ground-rules, requirements and constraints.

These products can be collected and mapped in a more effective manner and linked to the system baseline. This connection improves the capability to manage issues and non-conformances that can arise during the mission.

The planning of operational activities can be widely enhanced through a model-based methodology. Activities such as procedure scheduling can be performed in a more straightforward manner, reducing the time spent on activities such as document versioning or updates. For example, procedure generation can be performed using the information collected within the system model. In this manner, the changes to the current baseline of the operational activities can be tracked with fewer problems.

The operational scenarios can be designed during system development using the same model-based approach that characterizes all the other engineering domains. The use of a model-based methodology also ensures better exploitation of the data available from the system design. The information generated during the design phase can be exploited during the actual operational scenario, reducing the gaps that often occur during real missions. This information can be used to properly manage troubleshooting activities, telemetry elaboration and historical data retrieval. A formal data structure can reduce the time spent on data inconsistencies or baseline updates. This is also reflected in the data exchange process that can be performed with less effort than the traditional approach.

## 4 Conclusions and Future Work

The technologies that we use have proven to be very promising and show potential to address many more issues and challenges that we experience in our everyday working life.

The Request Configurator, Workflow Manager and Probes will be improved further to add additional features and expand their capabilities.

The Web Environment and its connection with Visualization, Simulation and Discipline tools demonstrated good maturity, and their use is currently planned in parallel with a project, to continue the validation approach in a more complex environment. The outcome of the UIW-project provided the team with very good feedback regarding potential benefits and areas for improvement of identified limitations. Such feedback will be used internally to the companies and with the relevant partners in order to improve the way we are transitioning to model-based engineering environments.

## References

Cencetti, M. (2014). *Evolution of Model-Based System Engineering Methodologies for the Design of Space Systems in the Advanced Stages of the Project.* Torino: Politecnico di Torino, (Ph.D. Thesis). Dassault Systemes, 2016. *CATIA System Engineering—Dymola.* Available at: http://www.3ds.com/products-services/catia/products/dymola/ (Online). Accessed July 2016.

ECSS. (2008). *Space engineering—ground systems and operations.* s.l.: ECSS Secretariat.

ECSS. (2016). *ECSS-E-TM-10-25 Annex A accessible using registration in the OCDT portal.* Available at: https://ocdt.esa.int (Online). Accessed July 2016.

ESA. (2016). *ECSS-E-TM-10-23A Metamodel* (Online).

ISECG. (2016). *International Space Exploration Coordination Group.* Available at: http://www.globalspaceexploration.org/ (Online). Accessed July 2016.

Modelica Association. (2016). *Modelica and the Modelica Association.* Available at: https://www.modelica.org/ (Online). Accessed July 2016.

nodejs. (2016). *Node.js Foundation, Node.js.* Available at: https://nodejs.org/en/ (Online). Accessed July 2016.

OECD. (2014). *The space economy at a glance 2014*. s.l.: OECD Publishing.

OMG. (2016). *OMG SysML specification*. Available at: http://www.omg.org/spec/SysML/1.4/ (Online). Accessed July 2016.

OpenModelica. (2016). *Open Modelica*. Available at: https://www.openmodelica.org/ (Online). Accessed July 2016.

Pasquinelli, M., et al. (2014). Collaborative model-based methodology applied to a complex conceptual study. In *Stuttgard, 6th International Conference on Systems and Concurrent Engineering for Space Applications, SECESA 2014*.

Polarsys. (2016). *Capella website* Available at: http://polarsys.org/capella/ (Online). Accessed July 2016.

Rapsberry. (2016). *Rapsberry Pi and Rapsberry Pi Foundation* (Online). Accessed July 2016.

# Adaptation of High-Variant Automotive Production System Using a Collaborative Approach

**Jonatan Berglund, Liang Gong, Hanna Sundström and Björn Johansson**

**Abstract** Automotive manufacturing systems are high investment assets in need of continuous upgrades and changes to remain relevant and effective. The complexity of such a system is reflected in the difficulty of making holistically informed decisions regarding the upgrades and changes. To reach holistic and sound decisions it is important to collaborate between departments, experts, and operational actors during the planning and development of upgrades and changes. Such collaboration should be supported by tools, models, and methods that facilitate understanding and enable the users to express their input and feedback in a clear and understandable manner. This chapter describes the development and evaluation of one set of tools. The developed tools combine 3D imaging and virtual reality technologies to facilitate the creation of decision support models that are accurate, realistic, and intuitive to understand. The developed tools are evaluated by industrial engineers in the area of manufacturing R&D.

**Keywords** 3D-imaging · Collaboration · Cross-functional teams · Manufacturing · Virtual reality · Simulation and modelling · Layout planning

## 1 Introduction

This chapter describes the Use-it-Wisely (UIW) approach being implemented in the industrial production of automotive products in the heavy and medium sized truck segment. The high investment product-service referred to in this part of the project is

J. Berglund (✉) · L. Gong · H. Sundström · B. Johansson
Product and Production Development, Chalmers University of Technology, Gothenburg, Sweden
e-mail: jonatan.berglund@chalmers.se

L. Gong
e-mail: liang.gong@chalmers.se

H. Sundström
e-mail: suhanna@student.chalmers.se

B. Johansson
e-mail: bjorn.johansson@chalmers.se



S.N. Grösser et al. (eds.), *Dynamics of Long-Life Assets*,
DOI 10.1007/978-3-319-45438-2_14

thus the production system put in place to physically realise the trucks developed and sold by Volvo Group. The act of establishing a production system, the truck factory, is indeed related to a high investment and a long term commitment. The truck manufacturing industry is characterised by high product variability (Johansson et al. 2016). This means that customers are able to customise their purchases by selecting various features to a high degree. While this is a competitive advantage in the market place, it can be both costly and technically challenging to realise on the manufacturing side. In short, for a production line to reach optimal efficiency it needs to be perfectly balanced, meaning that the work carried out in each step takes an equal amount of time to perform. It is theoretically possible to design such a production line, given that each product is identical, from an assembly process perspective, to the previous/next one. In the case of products as component rich and complex as trucks this is never the case, and instead, manufacturing companies resort to managing the variation in their products. In the end, it comes to a trade-off between flexibility and cost.

A manufacturing system is a complex entity consisting of several subsystems such as building infrastructure, material handling, equipment, electrical wiring, maintenance and support, and so forth. These subsystems are different in nature. For example, the building infrastructure is physical and rather stationary; walls can be torn down or put up and the roof can be lifted but for the most part the building exists as it is. The material handling subsystem is necessary for the operation of the plant. It consists of, for example, physical assets like storage structures, forklifts that move products and components, software that handles the manufacturing execution information, and the personnel in the logistics department. All these subsystems share the same physical space where they need to co-exist and, ideally, function in harmony to achieve the overall goal of the manufacturing system.

As the product, the truck, develops and changes over time, to follow market trends, regulations, and technical innovations, so must the factory that produces it. This again emphasis the continuous need for upgrades and improvements on the existing manufacturing system over time. However, the upgrade and improvement process of a factory is a complex task, as indicated by the many subsystems and actors that exist in it. The actors, or functions if you will that are responsible for doing so are often not directly involved with the operational activities and day to day workings of the factory itself. As a result, there is a largely underutilised body of tacit knowledge and experience represented in the operational part of the organisation. If this knowledge and experience can be utilized in upgrade and improvement projects, the information input of these projects would be expanded. It is important to capture the viewpoint and perspective of all involved actors in order to make informed and holistically beneficial decisions. The work behind this chapter has put a lot of focus on reaching and harnessing this knowledge and experience in areas where it was previously overlooked. The hypothesis is that by involving relevant actors and stakeholders in the upgrade process there is a reduction of the risk of errors and a higher frequency of first time right in the process of upgrading the manufacturing system.

This chapter presents the development and evaluation of methods and tools that support the production engineering organisation to carry out the planning and design of upgrades of the production system. The approach combines 3D-imaging technology and the latest in virtual reality to make the design and planning process more inclusive and to draw upon the tacit and empirical knowledge of the operative actors in the production organisation.

This chapter is structured as follows: Sect. 2 provides an introduction to the automotive production system at hand. Then, Sect. 3 presents the application of the collaborative tool, previously described in Chapter "Operator-Oriented Product and Production Process Design for Manufacturing, Maintenance and Upgrading", in the production system context. Finally, Sect. 4 gives a summary of the findings based on surveys and interviews with pilot users of the developed tools.

## 2 The Industrial Case

This section provides an overview of the production system at Volvo Trucks, which has been the specific subject of this work. The purpose is for the reader to get a feeling for the environment and context which has shaped the development of tools and which is the basis for evaluation of the implementation of the tool.

### *2.1 Describing the Problem*

The Volvo Trucks manufacturing organization is represented on every continent, totalling over 20 factories worldwide taking part in producing the various models and brands of Volvo Groups Truck Operations (Volvo Group Financial Report 2014). As a manufacturer of automotive products Volvo is bound by regulations and strict rules for conformance to these regulations. This means that a much of the product is subject to testing with regards to function, safety, and quality. But how does such a large company ensure that their products are produced in the same way and with the same result in all of their various locations? Often times, work conditions and workplace safety regulations differ between countries, not to mention between continents. And the manufacturing equipment and machinery which is available for purchase in Kaluga, Russia, may not be available to the plants in the US or Brazilian markets. Transporting equipment across borders is costly and would result in dependency on a supplier that is situated half a planet away.

To combat this, and related issues, Volvo uses something called Master Processes. These are guidelines that govern any business process within the company, including manufacturing. It sets the basic requirements of the process, and gives guidelines to how it should be designed. Take for example the assembly of the firewall component. The firewall is a barrier situated in front of the driver in the cab, it separates the driver environment from the engine. If the assembly of the firewall is performed according to the same specification in the various plants there is a greater probability that the resulting trucks are equal. Another benefit with this

**Table 1** Targeted impacts and means of attacking them for the collaborative approach of managing upgrades

| Targeted impact area | Means of impact | Variable name |
|---|---|---|
| Production and delivery of personalised final products | Rapid reconfiguration of production system based on point-cloud scanned facility models | Market agility and flexibility |
| Cost and time in product/process development | Proactive system testing and pre-validated performance | Ramp-up time |
| Time reduction for new processes and plant designs | Virtual assessment of manufacturability based on hybrid digital models (3D scan + CAD). Proactive development and operator training efforts | Production set up time |
| Environmental footprint and the resources consumption during the production and use phase | Reduction of error rates, scrap and waste generated by the production system | Environmental footprint |

strategy is that improvements to the processes that are found in one location of the globe are possible to implement in all other locations. This strategy can found in other sectors, for example in heavily standardised fast-food restaurant chains. These tend to be constructed in a very similar way regardless of their location, especially the production system, e.g. kitchen and ordering section. Thereby allowing companies to collect data from several locations and aggregate them to draw more robust conclusions in a limited amount of time. Furthermore, it makes it possible to implement operational improvements invented and validated in one location across the entire organization.

As can be inferred by the above section, there are many challenges facing a production company in this sector. At the outset of the UIW-project, a number of areas were targeted to bring improvement to the change and upgrade processes, see Table 1.

## 2.2 Actors and Their Tasks in the Production Organisation

The production system is a cyber physical system in the sense that it consists of technical equipment and machinery that is, to a large extent, operated by humans following a set of rules and methods. Therefore, to make any attempt to change and impact the operations of the production system it is important to understand its users, from here on out referred to as actors, and their relation to each other and the technical system. To understand who the actors in the production organization are and what work tasks they perform, a mapping effort was carried out. The mapping was supported by data from three sources within the company:

- **Available documentation**: All work positions are described in documentation in the Human Relations (HR) department. The information is used for hiring new personnel and the content is the responsibility of the technical manager of the relevant area. These documents provide a technical and objective view of the different actors involved.
- **Discussions with researchers**: Through open dialogue with researchers that participate in the UIW-project a rich picture was created. The rich picture maps both internal and external actors on a more abstract level, to model their needs and motivations and how they relate to each other.
- **Structured interviews with managers in the production organisation**: There were three departments in the production organisation responsible for change work. Managers from each department were interviewed about the practical implementation of the change process. Some of the practices differ from the documentation, and in some instances the output from these interviews helped clarify and interpret the formal information.

The following actors along with their work tasks were identified during the process:

- **Line Builders**: This actor represents the external suppliers of machines, tools and equipment for installation and integration into the Volvo production system.

  *Responsibilities*:

  - Delivery and installation of equipment.
  - Service of equipment according to service level agreements.
  - Support in training of maintenance personnel.
  - Support in improvement, re-furbishing and new investment of equipment.

- **Managers**: This actor represents the management of Volvo production facilities.

  *Responsibilities*:

  - Lead and control the operations.
  - Manage personnel, follow legal instructions on work environment.
  - Development of processes and personnel.
  - Take decisions on improvements and investments.
  - Implement changes in the production system when needed.
  - Follow-up on operative KPIs.
  - Drive strategy work.

- **Maintenance planner**: This actor represents the role of maintenance planning in the factory.

  *Responsibilities*:

  - Planning and preparation of work-orders and planned maintenance by ordering the needed material and services.
  - Provide work-instructions when needed.

- Daily/weekly planning, weekly reports.
- Analysis and follow-up of work-orders with the maintenance personnel.
- Ordering of spare parts, materials and services.
- Work cross-functional and participate in needed forums.
- Educate personnel in maintenance planning system.
- Track and follow-up on maintenance KPI's.
- Contacts with suppliers of equipment and machines (service, purchasing, ordering).
- Equipment and machine management and handling of unit exchanges.

– **Manufacturing Engineers**: This actor represents technicians of Volvo in charge of the design and implement of any update or change into the production system.

  *Responsibilities*:

  - Follow-up, analyse and improve the process within the delegated area of work regarding quality, OEE and productivity.
  - Propose and implement improvements.
  - Perform studies on methods and update description on methods within the delegated area of work.
  - Preparation and planning of manning, operations, work instructions.
  - Participate in work environment meetings.

– **Simulation and layout technicians/engineers**:

  *Responsibilities*:

  - Performs simulation assignments on product and process, off-line simulations.
  - Strategies on off-line robots for production, introduction of new solutions.
  - Understanding of visualization, simulation, off-line programming in production.
  - Investigations on process and product regarding flows, stations and fixtures.
  - Ensure that changes are implemented according to strategies and VPS directives.
  - Develop and present suggestions for improvements.
  - Coordinate changes in process layouts (2D and 3D).
  - Participation in Volvo Virtual Manufacturing network.

– **Operators**: This actor represents shop floor operators of Volvo that performs the daily work in assembling the product.

  *Responsibilities*:

  - Follow work instructions.
  - Perform assembly and material handling.
  - Quality assurance of product assembly.
  - Report issues on product or process/methods to manufacturing engineers.

- **Material Handlers/logistics engineers**: This actor represents technicians of Volvo working with internal material handling and logistics.

  *Responsibilities*:

  - Support internal Material Handling organisation with Logistics.
  - Engineering work (manning/balancing, material façade, routing etc.) in selected areas.
  - Support Global Sourcing logistics representatives in the sourcing process.
  - Prepare selected new parts and suppliers for being taken care of, and implemented in a quality assured way.
  - Parameter settings needed in local material systems for selected parts and suppliers.
  - Continuously monitoring of, and act on, compliance to or any need of changes in-present logistics set up due to changes in e.g. volumes.
  - Follow up globally agreed, or other relevant, (K)PIs.
  - Participate in the continuous improvement work in the daily work.
  - Participate in local/regional a/o global networks to contribute to the process development.

- **Introduction Engineers**: This actor represents Engineers of Volvo working with introduction of product changes into the production systems.

  *Responsibilities*:

  - Keeping the global master processes updated and compatible with the new products.
  - Work on a local, regional and global level to adjust and align manufacturing processes.
  - Coordinate the testing and verification of new products into the production system.
  - Assess and abridge consequences and product- and production requirements between construction and product development departments.
  - Coordinate the introduction of new product change orders.
  - Assess and abridge product- and production requirements between manufacturing engineering/product development and local site technicians.
  - Coordinate product and process issues with local site technicians.

A holistic system understanding is of great importance when working with complex systems (Checkland 2000). To place the identified actors and their work tasks in context, a rich picture (or context map) was created during a workshop. The picture links the actors and their motivations and needs with each other and the core entities of the company, Fig. 1.

The rich picture takes on the perspective of the manufacturing organisation and centres on a factory. At the core are things that the manufacturing organization can control to some extent. Such as the production line, the work instructions and the maintenance. Further out from the centre are entities that exist in the environment

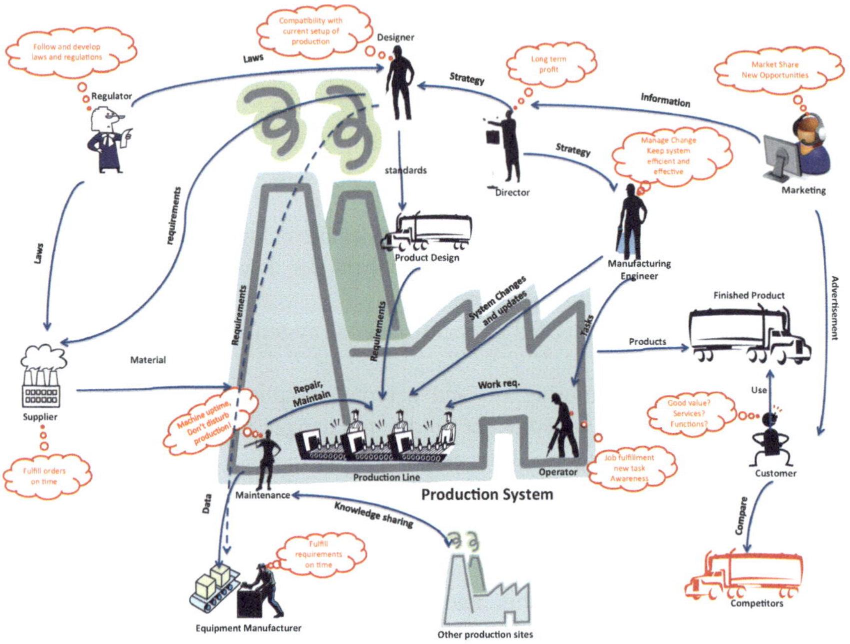


**Fig. 1** Rich picture illustration of the different actors, their motivations and relationships to the manufacturing system

around the factory. These can be internal to the overall organisation, such as product designers, marketing department, and other production sites. They can also be external to the overall organisation, such as the customers, legislators, and suppliers. Together this network of actors creates a very complex canvas on which the manufacturing of trucks must exist and perform over time.

## 2.3 *Adaptation of Production Systems: Changes and Upgrades*

As stated in the introduction to this chapter, the truck manufacturing industry is a high variant product sector, and as such it is prone to changes (Johansson et al. 2016). Changes in the production systems of Volvo are driven by needs coming from either the product or the production process itself. Product driven change occurs when the product changes, or when new products are introduced. Process driven changes are motivated by cost savings, technology upgrades, or quality issues. Also business related motives such as moving parts of production in-between production sites can be said to belong in the process driven change category. Through interviews with company employees at management level and

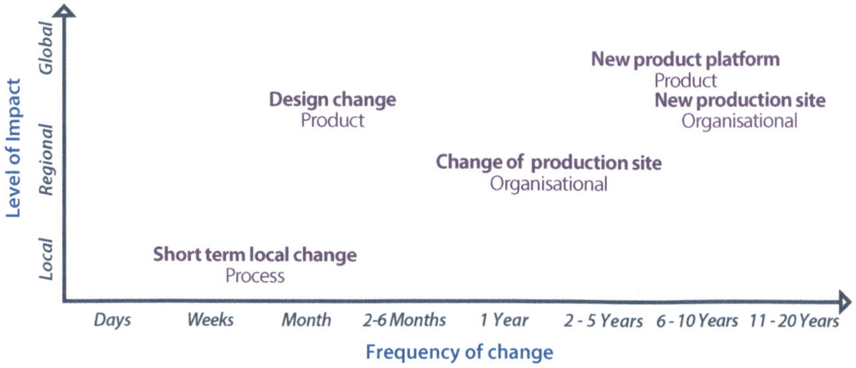


**Fig. 2** On production system change at Volvo Trucks; their frequency and level of impact on the organisation

documentation in production project process guidelines, a number of change types were identified. These types along with their frequency and level of impact are visualised in Fig. 2.

As mentioned earlier, there are guidelines and steering documents that govern the change and upgrade process. Depending on the impact and size of the change process, different sets of guidelines and steering documents are applicable. To gather these guidelines and support engineers that work with changes, Volvo has developed a project steering model. It covers all project stages chronologically starting from the investigation stage, which covers the needs and drivers for change, through to the ramping up of production in the new system and a follow-up on the results. While this project steering model is used by the engineer managing the change process, many of the actors described earlier are involved through their stated work descriptions.

Anytime a change or upgrade is to be implemented in the factory, it has to be planned for and modelled in advance as to not disturb the ongoing operations more than necessary. This is due to the fact that a production system is a high cost investment that relies on continuous use, e.g. the manufacturing of products, to bear its investment cost. For these models to be valuable and valid as decision support they need to accurately reflect the current conditions of the system (Berglund et al. 2016). Figure 3 shows an example of a model from the robotic laboratory at Chalmers, incorporating the 3D imaging technologies described in Chapter "Operator-Oriented Product and Production Process Design for Manufacturing, Maintenance and Upgrading.

There are oftentimes CAD models of the production system available that were created during the installation of the system, or at the latest change or upgrade to it. However due to the natural entropy of such complex systems, such models are seldom up to date with the current conditions. Using out of date models can lead to unforeseen issues such as new equipment not fitting into the allotted space, or that developed solutions are not feasible in reality. By using a modelling tool which can

**Fig. 3** A hybrid point-cloud and CAD planning environment to position a conveyor in the existing factory layout

include spatially captured properties of the existing environment, e.g. 3D-imaging data, companies can reduce the risk of bad decision due to outdated or incorrect information, while saving time and money in the planning phase of new development projects (Lindskog 2014).

As previously mentioned, a holistic approach and view of the system is necessary to avoid sub-optimization and to leverage resources in an effective way. One way of achieving this is cross functional actor involvement, and letting the end users of the system have a say in the planning process. In the case discussed here, end users are represented by e.g. assembly operators, material handlers, or maintenance engineers. One benefit of involving end users is the possibility to tap the empirical knowledge and practical knowhow that system design engineers might be lacking. The research carried out in this project looks to harness that empirical knowledge and make use of it in the planning process to improve the end result while decreasing the risk of making costly and time consuming mistakes.

## 2.4 The Volvo Trucks Production System as a Product-Service System

In addition to the actor and task mapping conducted in the previous sections, a third model was generated to better understand the setting and current state. It explicitly divides the production organisation of Volvo into Actor, Product, and Service categories. The Product Service System (PSS) is a concept developed for supporting sustainable consumption where the producer retains responsibility of the product throughout the use phase by selling its function as a service rather than the physical product itself (Mont 2002). This model fits well with how a production system is thought within an industrial company. It is an investment bought and sold

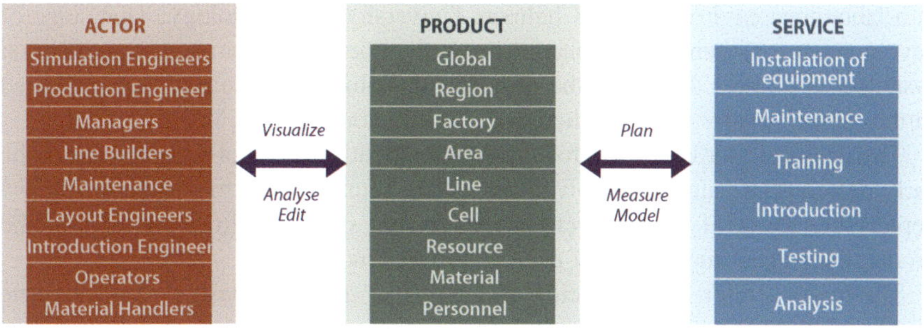


**Fig. 4** Actor PSS model of the production system at Volvo

within the company and both the seller and buyer are equally adamant of keeping the system functional, providing the service of producing vehicles. Thus, the product in the view adopted by the project, are the components of the production system. The APS model was used to infer how a 3D visualisation tool could be linked to the system. The mapping of the Actor PSS that was defined for a general production system for trucks can be seen in Fig. 4.

The actor part includes all the identified actors from Sect. 2.2. The product part concerns the production organisation broken down hierarchically from the global organisational level down to the actual resources on the factory shop-floor. The service part holds a list of the main activities which are carried out by those resources.

# 3 Development and Evaluation of Collaborative Tool

This chapter describes the development of the tool for the industrial case. It exemplifies use cases within the manufacturing development process at an automotive company where a need for this technology has been identified. A demonstrator that was developed is described and finally the results from testing the demonstrator with end users within an industrial company.

## *3.1 Development of the Technical Solutions*

As mentioned in the previous section, the solution should support planning of upgrades and changes to the existing system by providing an accurate current state model and a realistic and intuitive visualization environment to elicit domain expert feedback. The improved current state representation reduces risk of taking decisions based on faulty data. The realistic visualization lowers the threshold to understanding the model so as to make the involvement of stakeholders from different areas of expertise easier. The solution was developed in an iterative fashion, starting in a laboratory environment at Chalmers University of Technology. That stage of development was then implemented using Volvo factory equipment and production system environment. Based on the response the solution was refined and improved further before finally being applied to several factory units at Volvo.

The demonstrator case used for the development of this tool was looking at the early design phase and the involvement of cross functional actors. Figure 5 below depicts the focus of this project, in the context of a simplified version of the production project methodology used at Volvo Trucks.

The demonstrator case chosen was looking at the early design phase and the involvement of cross functional actors.

The demonstrator consists of a virtual model of a Volvo factory in United States. The virtual model is a hybrid using both measurements captured using 3D imaging technology and CAD data. The demonstrator is accessed using a VR kit from HTC. The architecture of the demonstrator is set up according to Fig. 6.

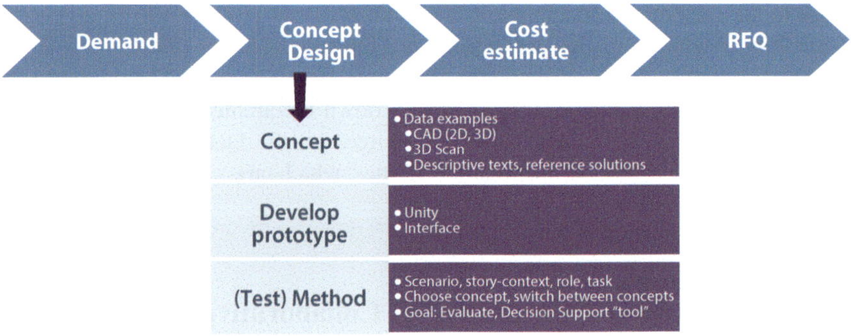


**Fig. 5** Process targeted by the demonstrator, put in context of a simplified version of the production project methodology in use at Volvo

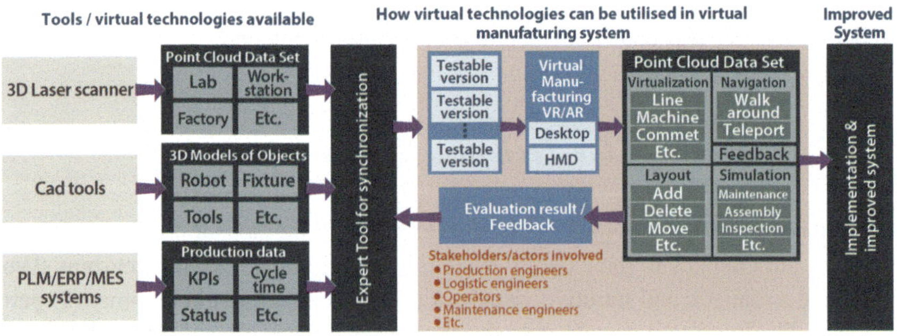


**Fig. 6** Architecture of the collaborative VR tool

**Table 2** 3D imaging data summary

| | Firewall cell | All data collected |
|---|---|---|
| No. scans | 5 | 82 |
| Area coverage | 390 $m^2$ | 6600 $m^2$ |
| Size of raw data (.fls[a]) | 843 MB | 13,840 MB |
| Size of processed data (.off[b]) | 714 MB | n/a |
| | Firewall cell | All data collected |

[a]Native scan data format of FARO laser scanners (www.faro.com)
[b]Object file format a geometric data format that was used to import 3D imaging data into unity 3D

The 3D imaging data was captured by Volvo employees and assembled by researchers from Chalmers University of Technology. The data was then combined with CAD data to form the virtual model in Unity 3D environment. The user goes through a short training scenario and is then presented with the factory model. During the demonstration the user is able to modify the layout and store the changes. He or she can load stored layouts from other users and review them by leaving feedback on selected features in the layout.

The data collection was conducted by Volvo employees on site at a Volvo run plant in the United States. The data collection was conducted during two days and resulted in a total of 82 individual scans, covering a large portion of the main assembly line. The section of the factory that was used for the demonstrator, the firewall subassembly consists of only five scans, but data from surrounding areas were also included to give context to the cell which is a part of the whole. Table 2 gives more details on the data collected in the US factory.

## 3.2 *Implementing the Demonstrator Solution*

The focus of the demonstrator was the design stage for upgrades of existing production system infrastructure. In this process there is an overarching goal of adhering to global manufacturing guide lines, i.e. the Master Process, as well as aligning the different production sites to a more homogeneous manufacturing solution. This can potentially increase consistency in quality and improve the possibility to spread improvements and kaizen work throughout the organization. (e.g. an improvement found in One factory can immediately be introduced also in other factories). This ties back to reaching actors in different location with the concepts. An actor working with the fire wall process in factory A can look at and assess the corresponding fire wall process in factory B, and thereby learn from other company sites.

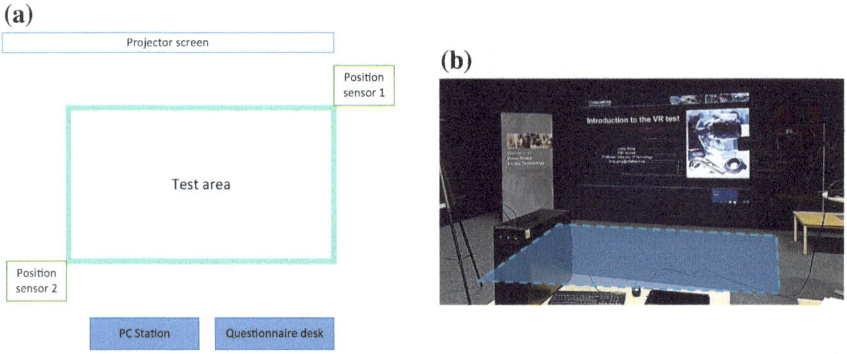


**Fig. 7** Demonstrator setup: (**a**, *left*) schematic illustration, (**b**, *right*) photograph, the outlined rectangle indicates the test area

The demonstrator was set up in Volvo facilities, in an auditorium with a stage area and a back projected screen. The setup consisted of:

- A PC station with demonstrator software
- Positioning sensors on tripods to track the VR space[1]
- Head mounted display (HMD)[2]
- Two hand held controllers for interacting with the VR environment[3]
- Presentation screen used to give instructions before the test and to duplicate the VR user's view for onlookers and researchers during the test

A schematic overview and a photo of the test facility can be seen in.

To the left and rightmost sides of Fig. 7b are tripods holding sensors that continuously tracks the location of the HMD and the two controllers. Near the front of the picture is the PC that runs the software and in the background the back-projected screen is visible. Data extracts from the demonstrator depicting the current conditions of the Fire wall production cell as captured using a 3D laser scanner is shown in Fig. 8.

In total, participating in the demonstrator evaluation were nine persons from different actor groups within Volvo and one senior researcher in the field of virtual production from the research team at Chalmers. The participants where all involved in the engineering side of the organization, working with R&D related to manufacturing. The average age of the group was 38.8 years.

[1]Part of the HTC Vive kit.

[2]Part of the HTC Vive kit.

[3]Part of the HTC Vive kit.

**Fig. 8** 3D laser scan data of the production cell used for the demonstrator

## 3.3 *Conducting the Evaluation*

The demonstrator evaluation was initiated by the researchers introducing the UIW-project, along with its aim and scope. Then a presentation detailing the test procedure was given collectively to the test subjects (the subjects were brought in groups of 1–4 persons). The procedure of the demonstrator was as follows:

In group:

- Overview of the VR application structure—Description of the system and motivation behind it
- Getting started—Theoretical introduction to the VR system and how to interact with the system

Individually:

- Testing the equipment—The participant familiarizes with the interface in a test environment
- System demonstration—The participant conducts a series of tasks in the demonstrator system
- Questionnaire feedback—The participants document their experience by answering a questionnaire

During the individual portion of the evaluation, each of the participants in turn wore the VR gear and conducted a series of tasks in the modelled environment. The tasks consisted of an initial training scenario where the participant is given basic instructions to familiarize with the VR equipment. These tasks include navigating through the environment, interacting with objects by grabbing and moving them, leaving feedback by pointing at objects, and using the menu system to store and load configurations of the environment. This training and introduction was carried out in a model of the Chalmers production system lab, screenshots from the training module of the demonstrator can be seen in Fig. 9.

Once the participant was familiar with the navigation and controls they were asked to proceed to the next step of the demonstration. In the second step the participant is shown a scaled down version of the 3D imaging data of the US factory, positioned on a table. The participant can walk over the model and inspect the layout of the plant. The participant is then asked to locate the highlight area, which is the fire wall cell. By using the hand controller to touch and click the volume of the fire wall cell area the participant is moved into a full sized model of the cell. In this environment the participant was given some time to explore freely, using the navigation controls, before being given a set of tasks. The tasks were a

**Fig. 9** Screenshots from the training environment depicting the menu and pointing activities

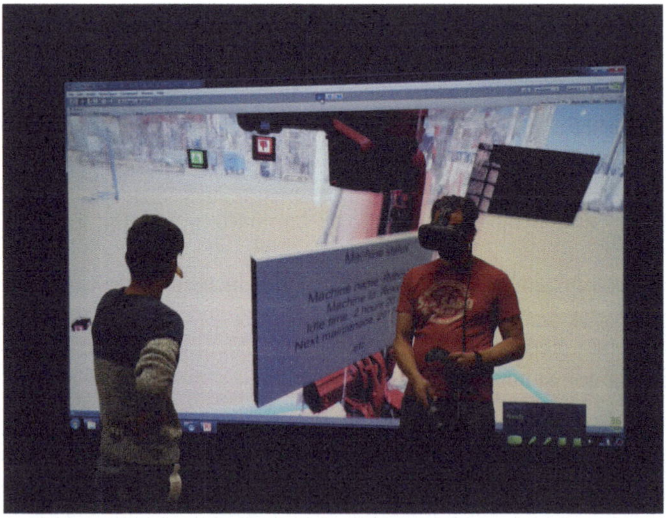

**Fig. 10** Participant (on the *right*) being guided by a facilitator (on the *left*) during the demonstrator evaluation

repetition of the training tasks, but where given in a non-explicit manner, such as move objects to the positions you see fit or leave comments indicating if you like or dislike some feature of the model. The fire wall cell model also included virtual information plates with equipment data. A picture showing one of the participants while interacting in the real sized virtual factory environment is seen in Fig. 10.

After completing the tasks in the demonstrator scenario, each of the participants were given a questionnaire to fill out. The results from the questionnaire are presented in subsequent sections.

## 3.4 *Result from the Evaluation*

The questionnaire had two parts, one qualitative which leaves room for the respondents to express in words their experience, and to motivate their choices in the quantitative part which ask the respondents to rank different aspects of the demonstration and the value of the proposed system to different stakeholders. Figures 11 and 12 below summarises the quantitative responses that were given by the test persons.

From the responses it is clear that a majority of the test persons saw benefits from the system, for the various stakeholders. Most benefit was recognized to the user, in other words the engineers and the factory personnel who would use it to develop better upgrades. While no one disagreed strongly about the benefits of the system, one users was not sure about there being clear benefits to Volvo from using it. However, that same user agreed to the overall benefits to different stakeholders in the second table, Fig. 12.

Table 3 shows the qualitative questionnaire responses from the demonstrator subjects. In the comment sections some reoccurring themes were positive benefits such as easy to use, visually representative of the real factory, accurate and "near" life like experience. Some obstacles that were detected was dizziness when using the HMD (one user), disorientation (one user), and that the tool as such/interfaces took some time to get used to (two users).

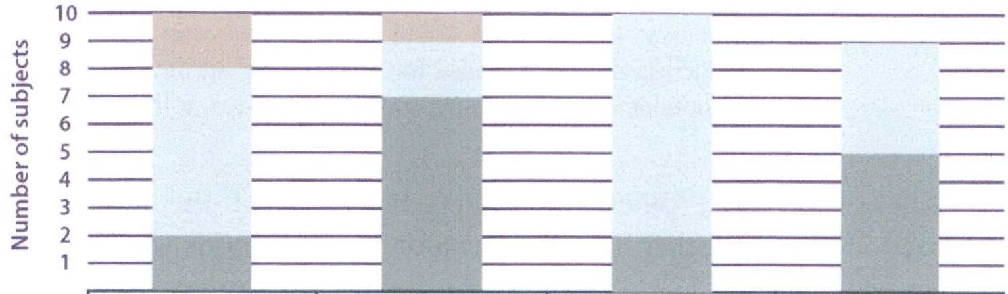


| | Easy to use | Clear benefits | Useful | Recommend |
|---|---|---|---|---|
| Strongly Disagree | 0 | 0 | 0 | 0 |
| Disagree | 2 | 1 | 0 | 0 |
| Agree | 6 | 2 | 6 | 4 |
| Strongly Agree | 2 | 7 | 2 | 5 |

**Fig. 11** User feedback on the collaborative VR tool design concept evaluation

| | to user | to company | to customers | to network | to EU | to society |
|---|---|---|---|---|---|---|
| Strongly Disagree | 0 | 0 | 0 | 0 | 0 | 0 |
| Disagree | 0 | 0 | 0 | 0 | 0 | 0 |
| Agree | 4 | 6 | 8 | 6 | 6 | 5 |
| Strongly Agree | 6 | 4 | 2 | 3 | 3 | 2 |

**Fig. 12** User feedback on the benefits/value of the collaborative VR tool to different stakeholders

**Table 3** Benefits/value at different levels of impact based on questionnaire and interviews

| | Benefits, value |
|---|---|
| End user | The virtual model is easy to understand. Easier than previously experienced models. It is easier to navigate the model in this way. More functions could be implemented dealing with trial and error |
| Company | The system supports giving users the same view of the production system. It gives better understanding. Of course the system could provide value. One user was not sure about the value on a company level, and another stressed the importance of that it should be easy to prepare the input, preferably through integration with the existing PLM platform |
| Customer | The system can provide value to the customers on a long term basis. And that the work and communication with them can work quicker |
| Value network | Respondents stated that this system can make interactions easier. And also that it would be nice with many users sharing the same environment simultaneously |
| EU | On an EU level the respondents felt that the system can lead to better understanding, more interaction, and therefore better decisions. One respondent said: "Will push EU as an enabler of new technology" Generally a lot of focus was placed on faster and easier decision making and communication quality. Ultimately leading to better products delivered |
| Community/society | On the societal level some users saw direct benefits through shifting some processes to the digital world and thus requiring less travel needed and reduction of material used for prototyping. At the same time some of the respondents were not sure about the benefits at this moment |

When asked about other uses and advantages of the system, respondents expressed that they either liked or wanted: Point clouds are good for quickly viewing actual station layout, system can be used to showcase new products/tools with its uses, and manufacturing simulation in VR.

The respondents were also asked in what areas within the manufacturing system that they saw uses for the collaborative VR tool. "In which areas of manufacturing do you think this system can be beneficial for the improvement of current work practice?". The categories that were presented to them are based on the work of Nee

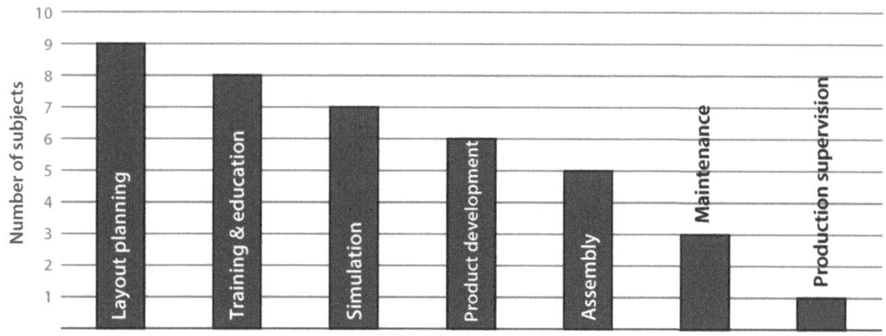


**Fig. 13** Areas of application as selected by the respondents

et al. (2012). The most promising application areas was seen to be layout planning, training and education, and simulation. Figure 13 lists the aggregated results from this part of the questionnaire.

The things that users liked about the experience and system for virtually accessing the factory ranged from smart/easy interaction to novelty and state of the art. In general, the spatial understanding, realism, and the holistic visualisation of the production system was repeatedly stated as valuable. When asked about drawbacks the test subjects lifted that the point density in the Point cloud data was too low, this is a performance issue with the system where points have to be reduced to maintain an acceptable frame rate. For five of the ten respondents this was their first experience using VR systems. Towards the end of the questionnaire the respondents were asked:

"*What challenges do you anticipate if your company is going to implement this VR systems?*"

The answers given can be categorised into three different challenges: *data compatibility*, *organisational attitudes*, and *cost*. The first category is probably most central to the possible implementation at Volvo or any company. Data of the various aspects of the production system resides in many internal systems and in different formats. Accessing all of it seamlessly is a challenge, one that is addressed also in other research projects carried out within the Volvo Corporation. In addition, there would need to be an infrastructure in place to handle the 3D imaging data and making sure it is recent enough for it to be used. The second challenge relates to acceptance within the organisation. This requires education and training of users as well as incorporation into existing work methods. Finally, some of the respondents raised the issue of cost, where should the "burden" be placed on a system that does not exactly fall under any of the traditional department structures?

## 4 Discussion

As with any new tool or technology there exists both benefits and limitations and these will be discussed in the following chapters.

## 4.1 Identified Benefits

3D-imaging provides visually realistic and geometrically accurate snapshots of the physical properties of the real world. The snapshots are stored in a format often called point clouds and can be used for modelling and analysis in virtual planning software. The point cloud data can be overlaid with other models and/or information regarding the various subsystems, separately or in parallel to find, discuss, and analyse issues and changes. Through the natural ease of understanding these models provide, they allow the various actors and experts that are using the system to express their different needs and requirements (Lindskog 2014). In this manner they can provide a valuable discussion ground and act as decision support for a manager, allowing him or her to make informed decisions with an expanded understanding of the consequences. Furthermore, it gives him or her a tool with which to visualize and communicate the decisions in a way that is approachable by all different actors regardless of technical background. By being able to include a broader range of actors and end users there is potential to gather a broader range of inputs and design comments to feed into the decision process.

Simplifying and speeding up the workflow to produce models enables iterative and frequent use of the models throughout the development process. It also means that a higher number of concepts and ideas can be tested and explored. The collaborative virtual reality models allow actors to experience the models in a 1:1 scale. Participants in the evaluation described that this gave them a better sense of the proposed solutions. Furthermore, the ability to share these realistic models with users in other departments or countries within the organisation was stated as a benefit.

Volvo has been working actively with virtual reality in a research capacity for several decades. However, it is only with the recent development and the introduction of VR on the consumer market that the usability and cost has created the conditions for making use of it in large scale, across the organisation. Previously, this technology work was limited to large test facilities and costly fixed installations. The ability to set up and implement solutions at a low cost means that investments in development of technical solutions and work methods can be shared and benefited from on a greater scale than before.

## 4.2 Identified Limitations

3D imaging is still an expert tool. And to introduce another expertize to the existing roles in the manufacturing organisation can prove costly. Furthermore, 3D imaging data capture is still a manual operation which requires users to access the production system at rest. This is costly, either through shutting production down or through accessing the system at night/weekend or vacation time. These requirements can limit the ability to collect new data on the fly or just-in-time as it is needed. At the same time, collecting data at opportune times, might mean that it is incorrect or outdated when it is needed in the decision making process.

Another important aspect is that the 3D imaging models do not replace CAD representation in every aspect. 3D imaging data is a surface representations of the geometries present in the real world. As such they are missing design aspects and construction information that is key for some simulation and analysis activities. So while 3D imaging data is good for some activities there might still be need for high fidelity and detailed CAD representations for other tasks.

## References

Berglund, J., Lindskog, E., Vallhagen, J., Wang, Z., Berlin, C., & Johansson, B. (2016). Production system geometry assurance using 3D imaging. *Procedia CIRP, 44*, 132–137.

Checkland, P. (2000). Soft systems methodology: A thirty year retrospective. *Systems Research and Behavioral Science.*

Johansson, P. E. C., Mattsson, S., Moestam, L., & Fast-Berglund, Å. (2016). Multi-variant truck production—Product variety and its impact on production quality in manual assembly. *Procedia CIRP, 54,* 245–250. doi:10.1016/j.procir.2016.05.062.

Lindskog, E. (2014). *Towards realistic visualisation of production systems.*

Mont, O. K. (2002). Clarifying the concept of product–service system. *Journal of Cleaner Production, 10*(3), 237–245.

Nee, A. Y. C., Ong, S. K., Chryssolouris, G., & Mourtzis, D. (2012). Augmented reality applications in design and manufacturing. *CIRP Annals-manufacturing technology, 61*(2), 657–679.

Volvo Group. Volvo Group Financial Report. (2014). Retrieved on November 16, 2016 from http://www3.volvo.com/investors/finrep/ar14/sv/ar_2014_sve.pdf

# Supporting the Small-to-Medium Vessel Industry

**Nikos Frangakis, Stefan N. Grösser, Stefan Katz, Vassilis Stratis, Eric C.B. Cauchi and Vangelis Papakonstantinou**

**Abstract** The aim of this chapter is to present a methodology for supporting the collaboration between the involved parties and for augmenting the final product with an always up to date digital file. The methodology is based on three support tools, which focus on the life cycle of small craft passenger vessels made of composite materials. The chapter concentrates on FRP (Fibreglass Reinforced Plastics) made vessels with length overall up to 30 m and total capacity up to 150 passengers, for the purposes of cruise ship liners disembarkation, scheduled routes or transportation of professional personnel to offshore sites. The collection of proposed tools consists of the "Vessel Meta-File", a user-friendly, web-based, information rich, technical meta-file that acts as the main knowledge-base between the ship-yard, which is the constructor of the vessel, the classification society, which is the controlling body imposing the restrictions of the vessel and the end-user. The Vessel Meta-File enables the storage of information regarding all

N. Frangakis (✉)
I-SENSE Research Group, Institute of Communication and Computer Systems, Zografou, Greece
e-mail: nikos.frangakis@iccs.gr

S.N. Grösser · S. Katz
Institute for Corporate Development, Bern University of Applied Sciences, Bern, Switzerland
e-mail: stefan.groesser@bfh.ch

S. Katz
e-mail: stefan.katz@bfh.ch

V. Stratis
OCEAN Boatyard Company OE, Attica, Greece
e-mail: vstrat@ocean.gr

E.C.B. Cauchi
SEAbility Ltd., Athens, Greece
e-mail: sea@seability.eu

V. Papakonstantinou
International Naval Survey Bureau, Piraeus, Greece
e-mail: vagelispapakon@gmail.com



S.N. Grösser et al. (eds.), *Dynamics of Long-Life Assets*,
DOI 10.1007/978-3-319-45438-2_15

aspects of a vessel's life cycle; from initial customer requirements, to drawings, material and equipment data, sea-trial reports to post-delivery survey and inspection reports. The Vessel Meta-File provides a collaborative platform for sharing such data among all involved actors across the vessel's life-cycle, reducing costs involved in the design, production and maintenance phases. The proposed methodology introduces the use of two additional tools which can be used in conjunction to the Vessel Meta-File. First, a Dynamic Causal Context Model that describes the mechanisms and variable interactions between the Yard, the Classification Society and the end-user, and enables the three different parties to forecast trends in the behaviour of the small craft passenger vessels market and allow predictive actions and decisions such as the upgrade of a vessel to support and extend its life-cycle. Second, a "Vessel Configurator" system is also proposed to assist the transformation of the business and operational requirements derived from the Dynamic Causal Context Model to technical specifications that comply with current national flag or international regulations for the specific type of vessels.

**Keywords** Naval sector · Small vessels · Business models · System dynamics · Communications · Computational simulation

# 1 Introduction

## *1.1 Introduction of the Cluster Case and the Respective Cluster/Company Challenges*

The aim of this chapter is to present a methodology, based on three support tools, which focus on the life cycle of small craft passenger vessels made of composite materials. The chapter concentrates on FRP made vessels with Length Overall up to 30 m and total capacity up to 150 passengers, for the purposes of cruise ship liners disembarkation, scheduled routes or transportation of professional personnel to offshore sites.

The collection of proposed tools consists of the "Vessel Meta-File", a user-friendly, web-based, information rich, technical meta-file that acts as the main knowledge-base between the yard, the classification society and the end-user. The Vessel Meta-File enables the storage of information regarding all aspects of a vessel's life cycle; from initial customer requirements, to drawings, material and equipment data, sea-trial reports to post-delivery survey and inspection reports. The Vessel Meta-File provides a collaborative platform for sharing such data among all involved actors across the vessel's life-cycle, reducing costs involved in the design, production and maintenance phases.

The proposed methodology introduces the use of two additional tools which can be used in conjunction to the Vessel Meta-File; a System Dynamics Model (Groesser 2012a) that describes the mechanisms and variable interactions between the Yard, the Classification Society and the end-user, and enables the three different parties to forecast trends in the behaviour of the small craft passenger vessels market and allow predictive actions and decisions such as the upgrade of a vessel to support and extend its life-cycle. A “Vessel Configurator” system is also proposed to assist the transformation of the business and operational requirements derived from the Dynamic Causal Context Model (see Groesser, Chapter “Complexity Management and System Dynamics Thinking”) to technical specifications that comply with current national flag or international regulations for the specific type of vessels.

The Cluster’s main actors include (a) the ship yard: OCEAN, (b) the classification society: INSB and (c) the end user representative: SEAbility. Below each actor is described in more detail framing its activities around the Vessel information rich-Meta file.

OCEAN is essentially a boat manufacturing company which specializes in building work boats and passenger vessels made of composite materials. The company is based in Greece, a country with numerous islands and economic activity related to tourism. As with other Greek boat manufacturing companies, OCEAN has its roots in production of coastal fishing boats for professional use. Although production of professional fishing boats is still a major boat market sector for countries like Greece, focusing on product-markets related to tourism and efficient sea-water transportation is essential in times where local economies and demand are hit by global recession. Using its past reputation for tough, over-engineered professional boats, over the past years OCEAN has invested efforts in specializing in passenger vessels for all purposes but mainly tourist transportation. As any other manufacturing process involving complex products, boat manufacturing involves marine specific materials, parts, conformity to marine specific regulations, design patterns, etc. For this purpose, OCEAN is working within a network of marine professionals and marine related companies: Equipment vendors representing foreign manufacturers, local equipment manufacturers, material manufacturers, technical consultants and certification bodies (Shipping Registers or Classification Societies). Each of these companies brings its expertise, experience and innovation into the final product. The boatyard’s task is summarised as the effort to use and concentrate the best options offered by this “network of companies” in order to satisfy customer-specific requirements.

INSB is a non-governmental ship classification society active in the international maritime industry. It promotes ship safety standards by providing customers with reliable technical services for their ships and marine installations, while cost leadership and quality compliance (Certified by ISO 9001: 2008) are embedded in every aspect of its operations. INSB provides proper certification to vessel, according to national and international laws and regulations. Through a sound organisational structure and technically competent human resources, it enjoys worldwide confidence on the part of all major maritime stakeholders. INSB operates internationally via a well-structured expanding network in 50 countries with 6 regional offices, 60 field stations, 200 ship surveyors and auditors supported by professional staff, able to respond timely and effectively in Europe, Asia, Africa and the Americas—wherever ships are being built, repaired or operated. INSB Class aims to be a preferred global technical provider of risk management solutions, enhance its customers’ quality orientation and environmental and business performance. Safety for life and property at sea, quality, sustainability and immense responsibility for environmental protection are the bedrock of INSB's corporate mission. INSB business deliverables and technical services satisfy internationally-recognised safety and quality standards, IMO Conventions, national requirements and general EU criteria.

SEAbility is a private Greek SME, specialising in representing shipping lines, performing vessel port operations as well as consulting to Shipping and Transport Lines. SEAbility is proficient in all aspects of Containerised as well as of RoRo (Roll-On/Roll-Off, as in e.g. ferries, where loading and discharging of wheeled vehicles takes place horizontally) and conventional shipping. It is especially strong in vessel port operations, Logistics and Cost Management, ship operations and efficient handling. Its activities include managing sea transportation services and adding value to them through well-trained and motivated team members interacting with an advanced IT environment. At the same time, it is a consultant to Shipping Lines on issues regarding their introduction to new markets, the handling of their fleet and of their services. These issues comprise operational, scheduling, financial, environmental and marketing aspects and optimisation whilst also taking into account and evaluating possible synergies with existing services loops (of the same shipping line or other lines), aiming at economies resulting from scale and also from scope.

## *1.2 Connection to the UIW-Challenge in Part I*

Via the development of a single rich-metadata file the consolidation of the shipbuilding process, better management of costs and improved maintenance planning, Use-it-Wisely (UIW) will be able to offer extended lifecycle and improved post construction survey and certification processes, hence costs reduction in EUR and environmental costs.

Improving certification of existing and new passenger ships is achieved through the reduced consideration time and approval in accordance with national regulations and any amendments thereto. The digitisation of the relevant law is combined with the initial configuration request of the owner of the vessel and allows the owner to take more informed decisions on the type of the vessel needed and allowed. Two steps will provide the improvement: (1) Standardisation of requests and (2) Combination of the consideration and the rules in conjunction with their amendments and application in the standard requests.

Moreover, unification of standardisation will aid increasing productivity. Decreasing review times and approvals, the time of final certification is reduced, so the society becomes more efficient in handling requests by the owners and the ship owning companies of passenger vessels up to 30 m in length overall and passenger capacity of up to 200 passengers. Improved response times, minimise decision time for shipbuilding and rebuilding by the owners therefore produce more efficient passenger ships "decreasing the operational cost" (lighter ships = decrease in fuel consumption), or possible increase in capacity or a combination thereof. To elaborate more on how each actor benefits from the overall achievements of the UIW-challenges:

Customers will be able to:

- View the final outcome as a whole from day one
- Make decisions based on visualised scenarios which will include information such as physical properties and cost
- View and visualize any change or update
- Track changes during any stage of production or use of product.

The boatyard will be able to:

- Offer and quote to customers with virtual models of the final product
- Make proposals, estimate costs regarding material and parts
- Conform with specifications, rules, guidelines
- Optimize designs
- Validate manufacturing procedures and processes
- Validate changes of design, materials and parts
- Track changes and updates
- Communicate the project and its properties to vendors and subcontractors.

The Classification Society will be able to:

- Offer to the customers an automated consultation tool
- Keep track of the legislation and its changes
- Follow the modifications to the vessel and their conformity with legislation
- Have an overview of previous approved solutions to offer to customer.

### *1.3 Reasons to Select the Tools*

The tools (vessel meta-file application and vessel web configurator) selected to facilitate the communication between the actors are mostly web-based, so as to enable the modern cloud-based approach of software and also to enable various approaches of exploiting their usage, namely software-as-a-service (Dubey 2007). Moreover, business modelling for analysis and prediction has been used for informed decision making and thus it was logical to use such tools for long-lived products, such as vessels.

## 2 Tools and Solutions

### *2.1 Development Process*

The objective of the Cluster 5 model is to link business activities to the objectives of individual market actors and show their impact on the UIW-objectives. To achieve that, individual models for SEAbility, OCEAN, and INSB have been built. Each

| | 2015 | | | | | | | | | | | |
|---|---|---|---|---|---|---|---|---|---|---|---|---|
| | Jan | Feb | Mar | Apr | May | Jun | Jul | Aug | Sep | Oct | Nov | Dec |
| Seability | LS | LS | LS | HS | HS | HS | HS | HS | HS | LS | LS | LS |
| OCEAN | HS | HS | HS | HS | HS | HS | LS | LS | LS | HS | HS | HS |
| INSB AR | LS | LS | LS | HS | HS | HS | HS | LS | LS | LS | LS | LS |
| INSB NR | HS | HS | HS | HS | HS | HS | LS | LS | LS | LS | LS | LS |

**Fig. 1** High season (HS) and low season (LS) for each actor (AR = annual requests, NR = new requests)

model was extensively validated on the level of system structure and behaviour (Groesser et al. 2012). The individual models were subsequently linked together to form the Cluster 5 industry-model. The industry model is driven by the demand from the tourism market which is strongly seasonal. The operators buy boats and try to optimize the purchase so that the boats are ready for service at the beginning of the high season (SNAAM 1985). This is reflected in the model with yearly oscillation patterns for all market actors in customer demand; i.e. tourists for SEAbility, boat orders for OCEAN and INSB respectively. The yearly high season and low season periods for the market actors are shown in Fig. 1.

The touristic high season for operators in Greece typically spans from April to September inclusive, of each year. This means that prior to the period when cruise ships with tourists start their schedules to Greece, the boats have to be operational and to achieve this the boats are built between October and June of each year, a period which represents the high season for the boatyard OCEAN. It is important to note that in the model operators tend to target April for boat delivery times and rather restrictive towards early and late boat deliveries, meaning that they postpone the purchase to the next year, resulting in strong peaks in the purchasing behaviour in the simulation results. Annual requests for INSB are occur between February and July so as to ensure that the boats are ready for that year's operation, while new requests for boats run parallel to the construction of boats and result in a high number of new requests for INSB between January and June.

# 3 Results

## *3.1 System Dynamics Model*

### 3.1.1 Overview of the Integrated Industry Model

The elements of the integrated industry model.

The industry model consists of the three individual models for the market actors which are complemented by a market model simulating the market behaviour of

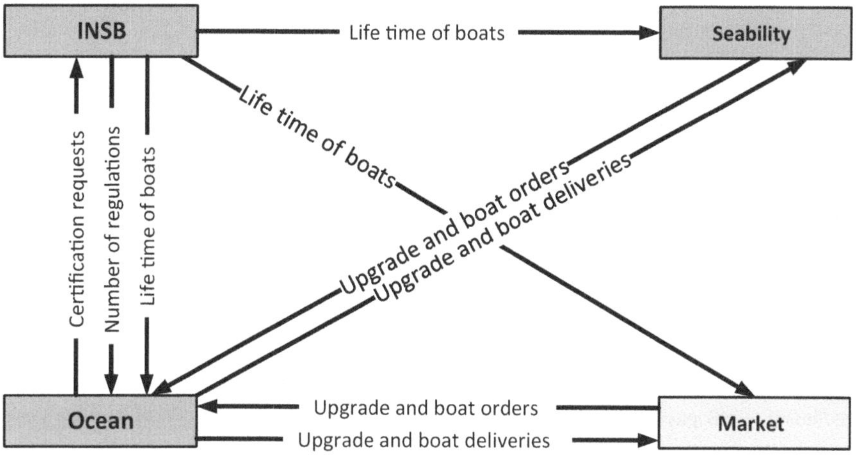


**Fig. 2** Sector diagram for the integrated industry model

SEAbility's competitors. Figure 2 shows the major information flows of the industry model. Due to the size of the model and the number of connections between the individual models, only the most relevant information flows are displayed (for a further example of this approach see (Groesser 2012b). INSB's impact is mostly through the setting of boundaries and constraints such as boat lifetime, i.e. the time that a boat is allowed to operate, which will be evaluated in the policy analysis. Furthermore, INSB identifies the number of changed regulations and that information is passed on to OCEAN. OCEAN sends the certification requests which INSB then handles. In addition, OCEAN receives the boat-building and/or upgrade orders from SEAbility and the market, which in turn lead to construction of boats which are then delivered to the respective operators. The relevant market is divided in two parts (Fig. 3), "*All other markets*", representing the overall tourism-related shipping demand with the exception of Santorini, which is modelled separately as Santorini is the area of operation for SEAbility.

All operators for the market have a decision making structure similar to that of SEAbility, but base their decisions uniquely on the high season, whereas SEAbility also includes low season factors in its decision-making process. Furthermore it is assumed operators always have the financial means to buy boats when it is necessary.

The market in Santorini is depicted to grow as shown in Fig. 3, while the other market are assumed to be constant at 1.8 million passengers per month. The individual models for the three market actors INSB, OCEAN, and SEAbility are described in more detail below.

INSB is the certification society in charge of managing the changing regulations and certifying both boats in operation as well as new buildings. For the purpose of the model, the impact of INSB on the entire model is rather small. The certification

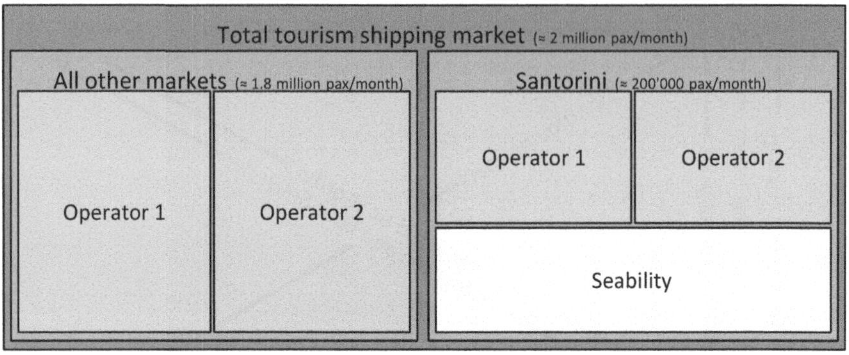


**Fig. 3** Elements of the market, SEAbility competes for customers in the Santorini market, pax/month means passengers/month

society adds a delay when it comes to the construction of the boats through the checking of the boat's design. INSB's importance in the model is in setting the framework for boat operation such as the total time a boat can be used, which we will evaluate in the policy section. One of the most important features of a classification society is to ensure that boats are kept in order and designs for boats are safe. However, for the purpose of this model, individual boat designs have not been modelled and thus this role has no impact in the model. It is assumed in this model that all boat designs are approved. The certification role of INSB is limited to certifying each new construction and the annual certification of each boat. This delays the construction of the boat and removes the boat from use in the low season, which is only applicable to SEAbility.

The structure in Fig. 4 shows the different steps that have to be taken before a new request is complete and is certified. The first two steps "*guidance*" and "*survey*" are done during the construction of a boat while the latter two "*consideration*" and "*certification*" are done upon completion of the construction of a boat, thus extending the boat construction time.

Figure 5 shows the behaviour of handling time for new requests (left) and allocated capacity for new requests (right). INSB's business consists of two separate elements: The annual requests (AR) and the new requests (NR). The annual requests happen during the entire low season when boat operators do not operate their boats (with the exception of SEAbility) while new requests peak towards the end of the low season when boat operators want to put their newly purchased boats to service. This leads to peaks in handling time as seen on the left and peaks in allocated capacity as seen on the right. The boat construction business is cyclical and there are periods without boat construction. However, INSB cannot anticipate that and still provides capacity that then is then underutilised.

OCEAN is the boatyard in this cluster. The company is an important player in the industry, having a market share of 80% in passenger boats. While OCEAN's

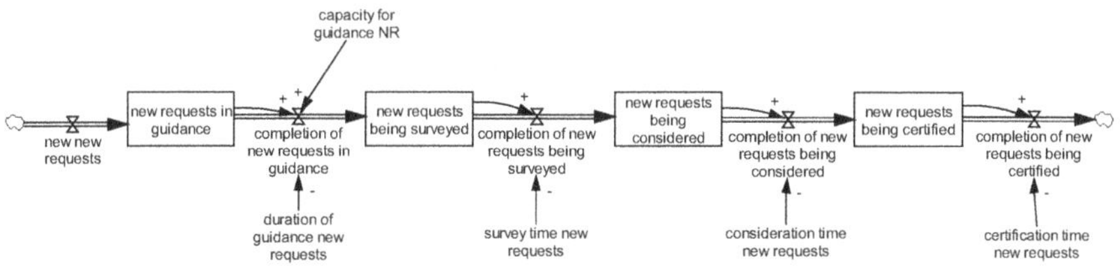


**Fig. 4** Essential structure of the INSB model: handling of new request

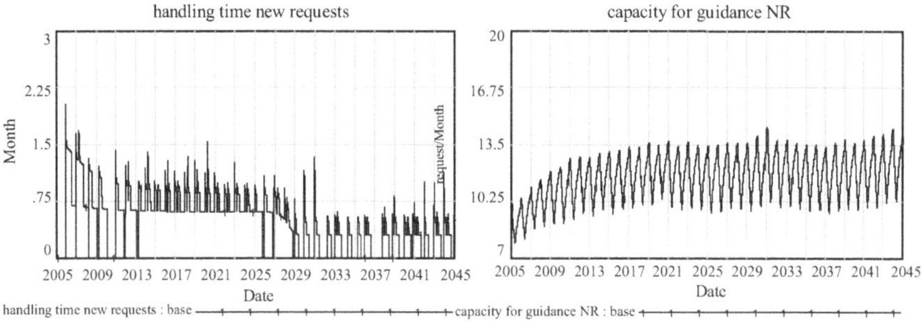


**Fig. 5** Essential behaviour of the INSB model about new requests

portfolio features a multitude of boat designs of various lengths, for the purpose of the model this portfolio was simplified to comprise two categories, viz. small (<10 m) and large (>10 m) boats. To keep the model as simple as possible, newly constructed small boats are used for a single purpose, as utility boats and all small passenger boats have to be converted from utility boats. The resulting difference in the construction of small boats between reality (where only a few small boats are designed as passenger boats) and the model is only marginal and has no impact on the validity of the model results.

OCEAN and its competitors perform three types of boat related services: (1) construction of new boats, (2) conversion of the type of boat, and (3) upgrading of boats. The construction of new boats is the process where a new boat is built from scratch. In the model, this is done for small utility boats and large passenger boats. The construction of a new boat triggers a new request for certification with INSB. The conversion of the type of boat is done by taking the hull of a utility boat and changing the set up to make it usable as a passenger boat. The conversion of a utility boat to a small passenger boat is shorter than the construction of a new boat, but the boat also has a shorter lifetime due to its past use as a utility boat. The conversion of a boat also triggers a new request for certification with INSB. The upgrading of boats does not change their general set up. However, it updates the technical set up of the boat (e.g., efficiency, emissions, attractiveness).

Upgrading is the shortest of the three services, and does not trigger a new request with INSB as the technical set up of the boat essentially remains the same.

The causal structure shown in Fig. 6 shows OCEAN's building process of large boats. The orders come in from the operators (MARKET and SEAbility) and the construction is prepared. Then, the boat is constructed and released to the market. OCEAN experiences the same purchasing behaviour with strong peaks as INSB since the operators try to optimize their purchasing behaviour by having the boats delivered and operational just before the start of the high season.

The construction time for boats are varies and depends on their size (Fig. 7). For small boats the construction time starts at around 4.75 months and decreases slightly to around 4.25 months. This decrease is due to the implementation of the UIW tool (shown in the following chapters) and a reduction of changes in regulations. For large boats, the building time increases from 5.25 to nearly 8 months. This is due to the fact that the average size of large boats is assumed to increase steadily, hence longer construction times. However, the increase is softened by the implementation of the UIW tool for improved communication between the boatyard and the certification society, with the time savings shown in Fig. 19. In Fig. 7, the dotted line is the planned construction time while the solid line shows the actual construction time. The graph shows how the implementation of the UIW tool in 2015 significantly reduces the delays from changes and regulations (from about 0.5 months to a few days) by comparing the planned construction time (dotted line) to the actual construction time (solid line). The purchasing behaviour of the operators of the boats results in large oscillations in the utilisation of OCEAN's

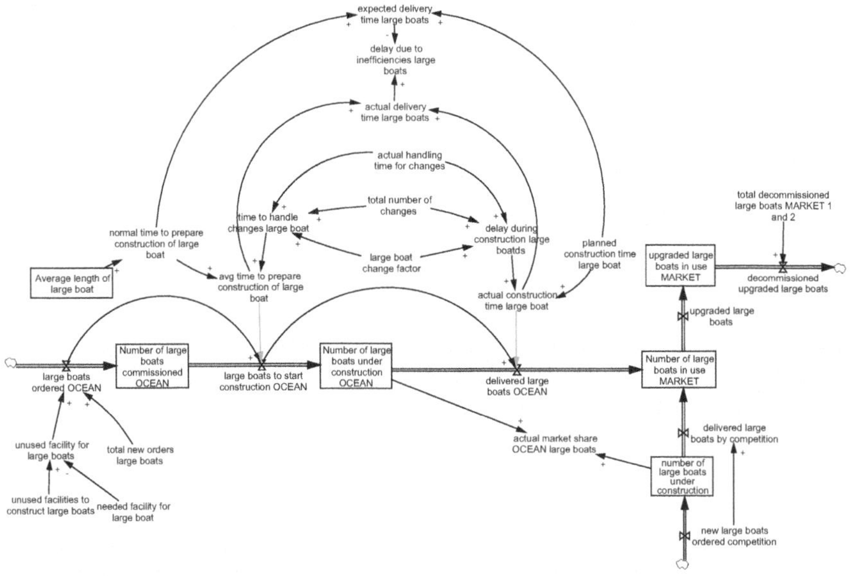


**Fig. 6** Structure for building large boats

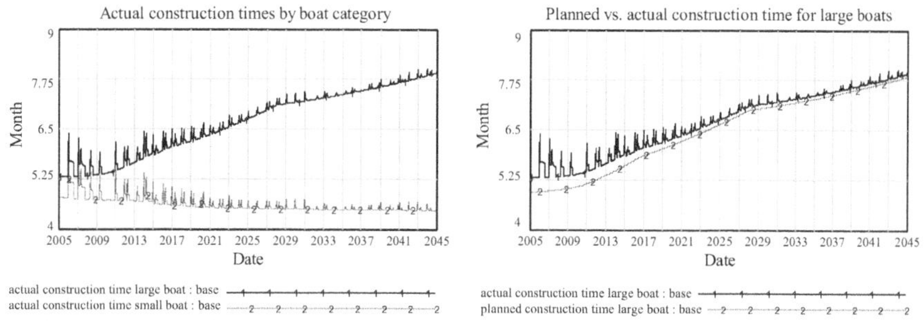


**Fig. 7** Essential behaviour of important indicators for OCEAN

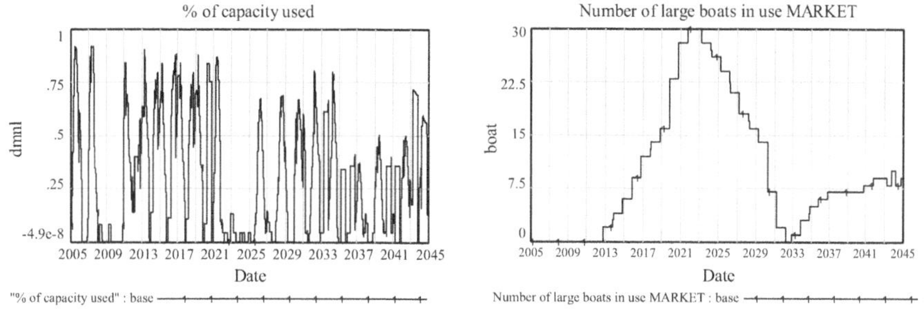


**Fig. 8** Short term cycles in large boat construction (*left*) and long term business cycles for OCEAN (*right*)

capacity. In addition to short term oscillations, OCEAN also experiences long term oscillations in the construction of large boats (Fig. 8, right side). The solid line shows the number of large non-upgraded boats in use in the entire industry. The first period of construction of large boats is from 2013 to 2021, during which 30 large boats are built. Between 2021 and 2032 all of these boats are upgraded (and thus are not counted in this variable anymore), whilst new large boats are built after 2033.

SEAbility represents the operator side in the industry model. Passenger boat operators in Greece mainly operate in the tourism high season and has as a main market the carriage of tourists from cruise ships anchoring at sea near the island harbours to the islands' disembarkation ports and back. SEAbility operates in the market of Santorini, but the essential market and operator dynamics are assumed to be the same for all operators. Other elements of the business model for operators can be additional local boat tours for the tourists that are in the islands (having arrived at the islands both by cruise ships and otherwise) as well as low-season services (e.g., ambulance, longer transport routes, postal), however, only SEAbility has included these services in its model. Operators use a variety of boats for their services. Some boats are converted sail or fishing boats and some are newly-constructed boats. With their demand for boat construction, the operators fuel the business of the other actors. To model this more in-depth, the model features an extensive decision-making structure based on demand and current market share for all operators. There is a bias for large boats in the market as the purchasing decision for large boats has to be made prior to the purchasing decision for small boats as the larger boats take longer to be constructed, if the boats are to be operational at the start of the high season.

The business objective for boat operators is to have sufficient boats profitably to cover the demand. Operators have the choice to build small or large boats (Fig. 9). The newly-built boats subsequently age and become less attractive to tourists and more costly to operate. Eventually and after operating for their entire allowed usage time, the boats are decommissioned, leading to replacement purchases if demand warrants this. For the large boats, the operators have the opportunity to upgrade the boat thus leading to an increase in attractiveness and decrease in operating costs.

In the model, SEAbility starts operation in 2015 in the Santorini market, which is expected to decline in customer demand until 2020, followed by recovery. This development is mirrored in Fig. 10 (left) where the demand is sufficient to trigger the purchase a boat in 2015 and 2026 and a second boat in 2037. Interestingly, the boat purchased in 2015 is decommissioned in 2025, leaving SEAbility with no boat for about a year as the decision making by SEAbility is rather conservative and does not allow for the purchase of a boat to replace the existing boat because the demand is insufficient. Utilisation (Fig. 10, right) is below 100% until 2025, indicating that there are overcapacities in the market that linger until 2026, when demand has picked up sufficiently and capacity is adjusted.

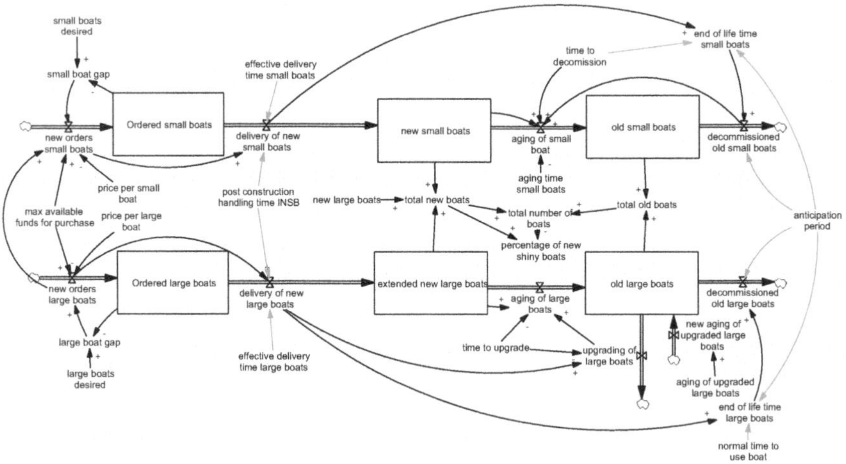


**Fig. 9** Fleet composition for operators (using SEAbility as example)

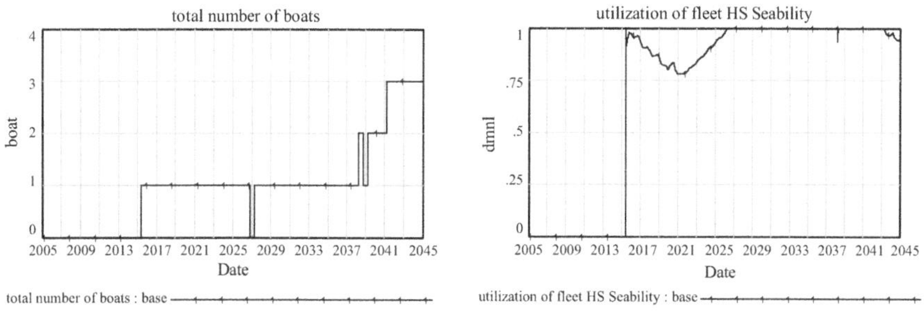


**Fig. 10** Essential behaviour for SEAbility, showing the entire fleet for SEAbility (small and large boats)

| | | | |
|---|---|---|---|
| | 240 months (base) | | 120 months (base) |
| Large boats | Normal boat life time | | Extended life time |
| Small boats | Time utility boats | Time to use small boats | |

**Fig. 11** The different lifetimes in the model

### 3.1.2 Policy Analysis with the Integrated Simulation Model

Policy description and results.

The evaluated policy is one set by INSB for the entire industry in terms of the lifetime of the boat. INSB regulates the normal boat lifetime and it is assumed that the extended boat lifetime is always 50% of the normal boat lifetime (Fig. 11). The extended boat lifetime can be achieved by upgrading large boats. As small boats cannot be upgraded, their life span is entirely defined by the normal boat lifetime. The operational lifetime of small boats is further decreased by the fact that in the model all small boats are converted utility boats and can only be used for the remaining lifetime of the boat. To capture the effects of the boat lifetimes, the time horizon for the simulation has been set to 480 months (forty years) with ten years simulating past behaviour and thirty years simulation time into the future (measured from the base year of 2015).

For the policy analysis of the boat lifetime there are two policies simulated in addition to the base case shown in Fig. 11. The policy "boat lifetime 204" (LT204) simulates the effects of 204 months normal lifetime and 102 months extended and "boat lifetime 276" (LT276) with the values of 276 months normal lifetime and 138 months for extended. The simulated policies show the effects, if INSB chooses to reduce or extend the permissible use time for boats by three years.

As can be seen in Fig. 12, OCEAN profits from a reduced boat lifetime. LT204 (dotted line) performs better nearly throughout the entire simulated period. This can be expected because with a reduced boat lifetime operators need to replace their boats sooner and this leads to more boat orders. Interestingly however the runs only start differing in 2023. The available facilities (i.e., production capacity) stay roughly the same for all scenario until 2033, so the improved financial result after 2023 is mainly due to a better utilisation of the available facilities. The comparison between LT276 (dashed line) and the base case (solid line) is also interesting because over large parts of the simulation period, the LT276 run performs better than the base run. This is counterintuitive since a longer boat lifetime result in fewer boat orders. The cause for LT276 to perform better lies in a better distribution of orders during the multi-year cycle. The difference only changes in around 2037 when many of the large boats need to be replaced and since the lifetime of large boats is more sensitive to any reduction or extension of the normal boat lifetime, the effects can be observed more sharply after 2037. Also, in that time there is a strong clustering of orders in the LT276 run prompting OCEAN to expand its capacity sharply. The fact that both policies fare better over most of the simulated period suggests there are local optima for setting the boat lifetime where OCEAN does not lose revenues but the operators have the possibility to maximize their revenues through longer use of their boats. This does not occur in the current base case where the normal boat lifetime is 20 years.

For the operators, however, the effects are mostly opposite. Naturally, the operators would like to maximize their revenue and use the boat as long as possible. The effects of increasing and decreasing the boat lifetime results in a difference of about 1 million euro of cash flow in the case of SEAbility and a larger increase in spending for "Market 1", one operator in the market representing half of the transport capacity of all the other markets (Fig. 13). "Market 1" is used for illustrative purposes, all other operators experience the same effects. The case of SEAbility is interesting because the cash flow for both policies performs better between 2035 and 2045 although the base run eventually catches up. For "Market 1", however, the spending on boats is higher for both policies, which should only be expected for the LT204 run. SEAbility profits disproportionately from more frequent replacement of their boats because of the small size of their fleet, which explains the better performance of LT204 and saves more money in the case of LT276. In the case of "Market 1", both policies are more expensive because in LT204 boats have to be purchased more frequently and in LT276 the boats are more evenly distributed allowing the operators to purchase more large boats.

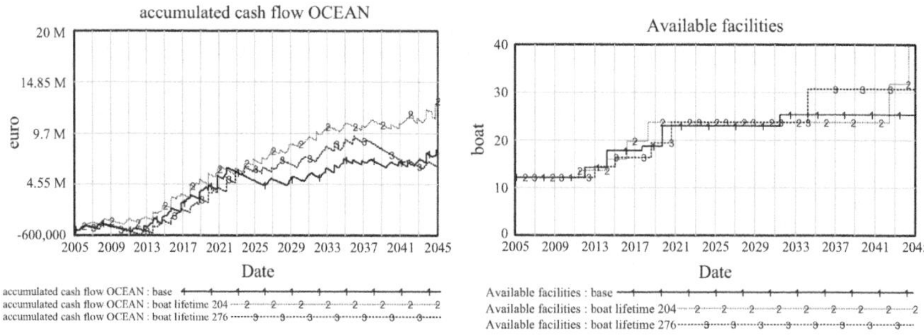


**Fig. 12** Effects on OCEAN for the different policies

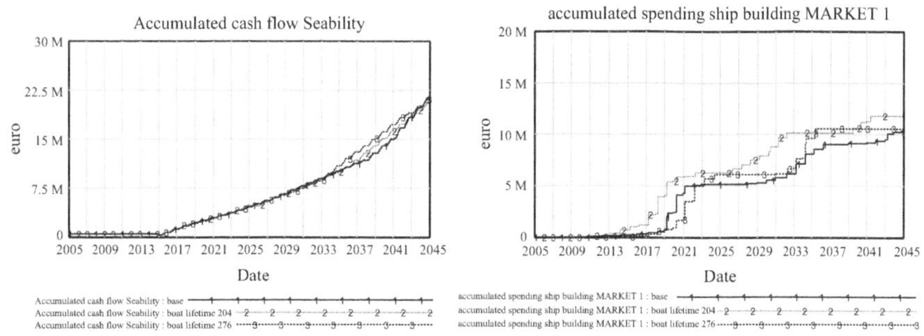


**Fig. 13** Effects of the policy on the operators SEAbility (*left*) and Market 1 (*right*)

Interestingly enough, one could expect that large boats with their longer lifetime would be subject to greater demand, yet this is not the case; this is mostly because the decision-making does not, for planning purposes, take into account the entire boat lifetime but rather a shorter planning period of five years for strategic decisions. Irrespective of the boat lifetimes, the total demand for the entire market (except Santorini) increases steadily and tops of at 40 large boats for the base run. For both LT204 and LT276 however, the number of large boats increases to around 50 as the boatyard's capacity is more evenly distributed over the years, leading to more purchases of large boats as more capacity is available because boat orders are less clustered.

## 3.2 *Information Technology Support Tools*

The shipping cluster is using two distinct information technology support tools. A Redmine based communication hub (Redmine 2006), called the vessel meta-file application (Fig. 14).

And a vessel web-configurator, which includes the relevant legislation (MoMM 1979a, b, 1988, 1996, 2011) (Fig. 15).

In the vessel meta-file application, each actor has assigned a specific workflow, which enables the correct transition of the different procedures from one state to another state.

Currently five different workflows exist:

1. Workflow for the conduction of a survey
2. Workflow for the completion of a technical work
3. Workflow for a document request
4. Workflow for an initial configuration of a vessel
5. Workflow for the initial price quotation for a vessel.

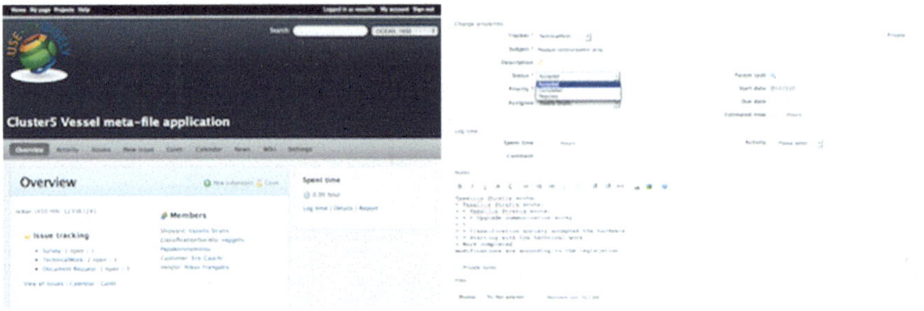


**Fig. 14** Vessel metafile application

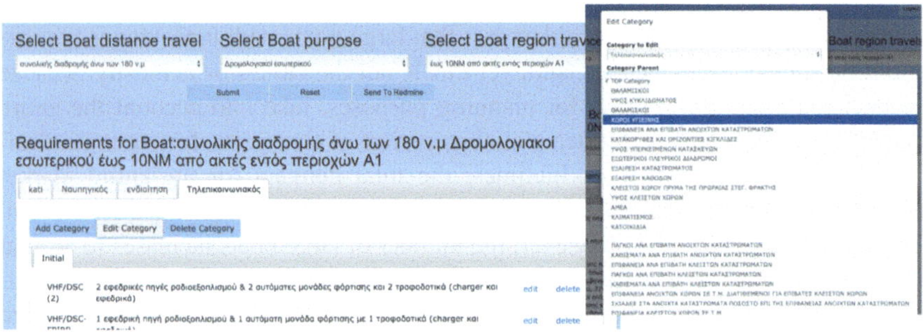


**Fig. 15** Vessel web-configurator

Each actor (Shipyard, Classification Society, Customer, Technical Consultant, National Supervisor and Vendor) is assigned a specific workflow to facilitate the verified procedure.

The states of the workflow include:

1. New: the workflow has just started
2. In Progress: currently some actors are actively working on a task
3. On Hold: the task is on hold for some reason
4. Accepted: the task has been accepted by the appropriate actor
5. Declined: the task assignment has been declined by an appropriate actor
6. Completed: the task has been competed
7. Rejected: the task completion has been rejected by an appropriate actor.

For example, the shipyard is able to start a new task "Technical work" and is able to change its status to in progress, on hold, completed or rejected. For the same task, after the shipyard has marked the task as completed, the classification society should check the outcome and mark the task accepted or rejected based on the results of the survey. Moreover, the customer is able to decline this task if the results are not satisfactory (Fig. 16).

**Fig. 16** Vessel metafile application workflow configuration

Similar workflows exist for all the procedures, ensuring transparency to the activities and collaboration of the actors.

The vessel web-configurator enables a future customer to enter the initial requirements into a web system, which then displays a rough overview of the applied legislation (SECP 2000; SoNaME 1990). This enables the future customer to finetune the initial requirements. The legislation is updated by the classification society and covers all the aspects of the vessel.

# 4 Discussion

## *4.1 Benefits of Using the Tools*

### 4.1.1 Impact of the System Dynamics Scenario on Cluster Objectives

The objectives for the UIW Cluster 5 scorecard have been set as part of the UIW-project. The objectives have then been subsequently added to the model and the simulated results are compared to the set objectives. As part of the UIW-project, Cluster 5 has also developed a tool to facilitate the communication between the boatyard (OCEAN) and the classification society (INSB) in terms of regulations and amendments of regulations. The tool is only applicable to large boats and only those results are reported. For the simulation, the tool and its effects have been modelled and two runs (one with UIW tool, one without) have been executed. The objective of the UIW tool is a shorter construction time through improved communication which means that its impact is negligible in terms of technological progress (objectives 4a and 4b) and therefore only the run with the tool active is reported for these objectives (Figs. 17, 18, 19, 20 and 21; Tables 1, 2, 3, 4 and 5).

A system which will integrate past project experience, boatyard's infrastructure and technical ability, vendor solutions and classification society rules into one system which will produce the best possible solution for one customer's business requirements as a dynamic meta-file with possible visualisation of attributes and specifications. Project attributes will be based on future platform's output which could be dynamically changed according to each actor input. Initial requirements will be pre-validated by the future platform. Pre-validation will be based on data passed by the Classification society. Selection of specific materials and parts will be based on data passed by vendors and suppliers. Any aspect of initial design or change on initial design will be optimised and checked for compatibility with all

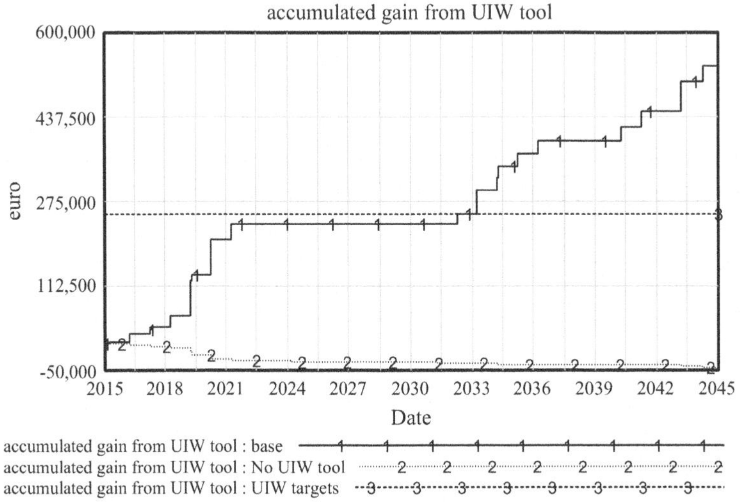


**Fig. 17** Graph for gain from UIW tool

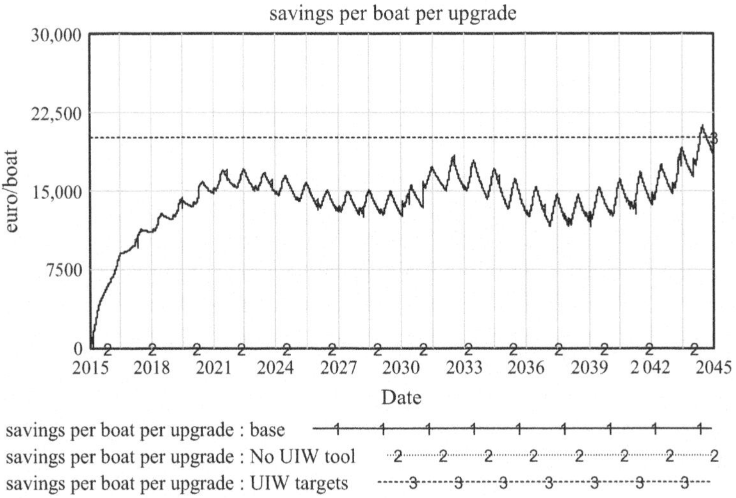


**Fig. 18** Graph for savings per upgrade

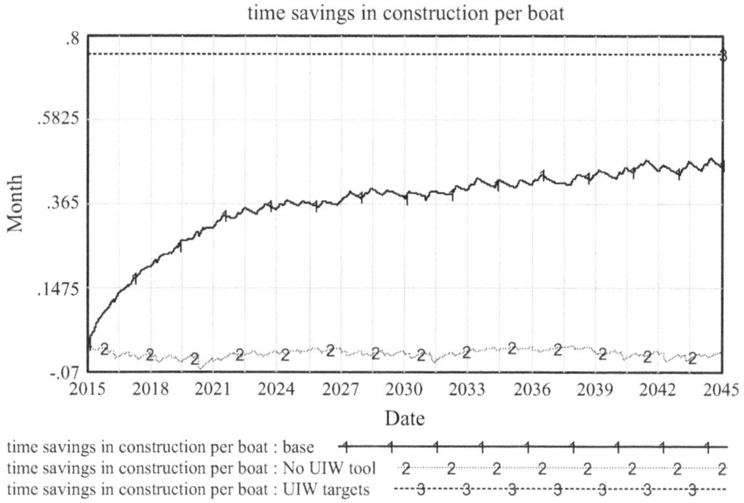


**Fig. 19** Graph for time savings

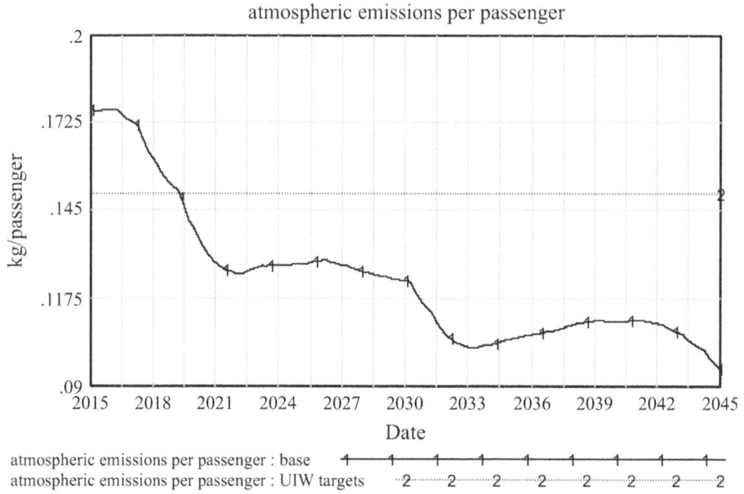


**Fig. 20** Graph for atmospheric emissions

actor's specifications. A system acting as a pool of information for all parties would solve the problem of information flow. A system which would integrate properties such as technical specifications, rules, physical attributes, cost, etc. in a virtualised model would solve the problem of optimizing design to dynamic updates and changes. The final result would be a new process of manufacturing where final outcome is based more on initial design than on continuous design cycles.

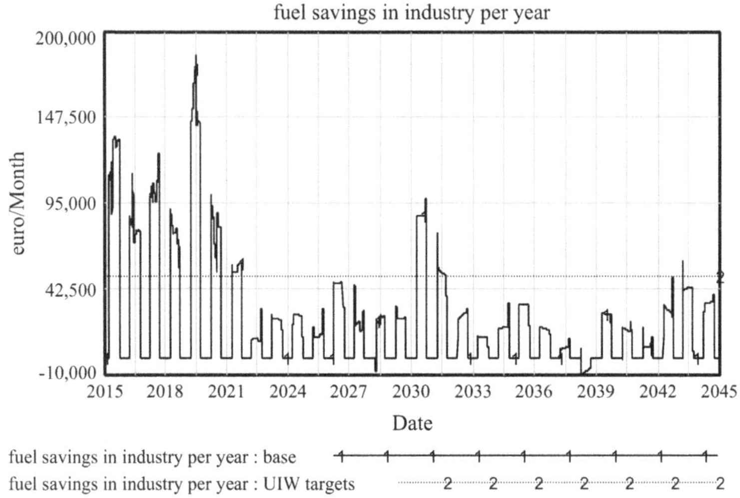


**Fig. 21** Graph for fuel savings

The process of deciding on the construction details can be summarised on the following steps:

1. Boatyard decides on materials, based on project requirements (for example cost and weight) and availability from vendors. Material specifications and data sheets are already embedded into the system. Hence, selection is optimised using initial requirements.
2. Calculations regarding material aspects, structural elements and other construction design elements are made by the system, using predefined Classification Rules.
3. A pre-validated construction plan and engineering analysis is produced.
4. Any change or update during the duration of the project dynamically change attributes of the construction plan.

## *4.2 Limitations of Using the Tools*

The decision-making of operators is highly individual. Factors such as how aggressively is growth pursued and the timing of the boat purchase depend greatly on how individual operators perceive the market. For the purpose of this model, only one decision-making process is modelled, leading to a reduced amount of richness. This decision-making process can be adjusted for parameters of

**Table 1** Objective 1 of the UIW Cluster 5 scorecard

| Objective | Behaviour |
|---|---|
| **Name of the objective**: Economic gain from UIW tool | Figure 17 |
| **Objective definition**: Increased ability to rapidly follow the market dynamics by means of fast production and delivery of personalised final products | |
| **Cluster-specific objective**: Quick reaction to varying service demand, regulation change, alterations requests from the customer through value chain integration (€250–300k for the entire industry) | |
| **Explanation**: The graph above shows the target as a dashed line and the simulated result as 1 and 2. The time horizon reported here is from 2015 to 2045 as the tool is not implemented prior to 2015. There are two large boat purchasing cycles. The first one starts in 2015 and lasts until 2020 and the second one starts in 2030. In both periods, a large amount of the operator's transport capacity is replaced with large boats. The economic gain of the UIW tool consists of two parts: (1) The construction of the boat occupies capacity for a shorter period of time as the exchange of technical information between the certification society (INSB) and the boatyard (OCEAN) is improved. Thus, the boatyard can construct more boats during the same building period. (2) The operators (SEAbility) need to commit fewer financial resources with shorter lead times when purchasing a boat and can therefore react better to market trends. The improvement is due mainly to a reduced time to react to changes in the design of boats as well as improvements in handling times for new requests. The target is reached around 2032. Between 2015 and 2030 there are no large boats built and thus no gains from the UIW tool are obtained. The benefit in this objective is measured for the whole industry and accumulated over time The dotted line shows the comparison run in the case that the tool is not implemented. The reference year is again the year 2015 and the effects are accumulated. The "No UIW tool" run shows an accumulated loss for the industry of about 50,000 Euro. This makes sense given that the tool shortens construction times for large boats. This leads to the operators having to make decisions with larger uncertainties about the utilisation of their fleet. This in turn leads to overcapacity in the market. This can be confirmed as the Market 1 as a sample operator uses two more large boats and has a marginally lower utilisation rate over the simulation period in the run without the UIW tool. Therefore, the benefit derived from the improved information exchange and resulting shortening of construction and order times, not only has financial benefits for all actors but also supports an improved use of resources available, e.g., boat materials that are not used for construction | |

aggressiveness and other factors to more optimally manage an operator's fleet, but it will remain only a guideline on how actual decisions are implemented. Therefore, the market structures are kept as simple as possible. There are just two operators in each market, with the exception of SEAbility being a third, each representing a collection of small operators. The behaviour for many small operators is unlikely to be much different as the model assumes the same decision making process for each operator. Inefficiencies in the purchasing behaviour are, such as an undersupply of available boats, are due to a lack of capacity of OCEAN and of competitors.

Similarly, the topic of upgrading is simplified. For each operator, the upgrading policy can be set individually, but stays uniform for the entire fleet. The operator has no opportunity to change its operating policy from one boat to another. This is obviously a simplification to achieve a manageable model. However, the current

**Table 2** Objective 2 of the UIW Cluster 5 scorecard

| | |
|---|---|
| **Name of the objective**: savings per boat | Figure 18 |
| **Objective definition**: Cost reduction of around 30% by decreasing lead times in product/process development | |
| **Cluster-specific objective:** Reducing time and costs by 30% due to the availability of the vessel technical information (from €50–60k to €40k) | |
| **Explanation**: This objective shows a different aspect of the implementation of the UIW tool. The graph shows the target from the UIW-objective as a dashed line and the result of the simulation as a solid line. The solid line shows the 12 month average for savings in upgrading. While objective 1 concerns the construction of new boats, the implementation of the UIW tool also facilitates and improves the upgrading of existing boats. Upgrading is in general a shorter process than complete construction, as the hull and other elements of the boats remain intact. Regardless, the savings are in the same range as for building on a per case basis. Thus, the tool has a larger impact for the upgrading as it has for building. The objective of €20K is achieved towards the end of the simulation period, when the database in the tool includes nearly 90% of all relevant regulations and amendments. The simulated results oscillate due to the fact that the improved communication between the certification society and the boatyard also depends on the number of amendments. Amendments to existing regulation happen mostly when there are new constructions which in turn take place mostly when fleets are renewed. The renewal of fleets is a cyclical process and causes the oscillating behaviour shown in the graph above<br>The dotted line shows the run simulating without implementing the UIW tool. In the case of upgrading, no capacity issues are expected to matter and therefore there is no loss to be reported. Thus, the run shows a constant 0 | |

**Table 3** Objective 3 of the UIW Cluster 5 scorecard

| | |
|---|---|
| **Name of the objective**: time savings in boat building | Figure 19 |
| **Objective definition**: Set-up and ramp-up time reduction for new processes and plant designs (30%) | |
| **Cluster-specific objective**: Decreased lead time in product modifications by at least 20% (from ca. 90 to 70 days) due to better information about the modifications costs needed to meet new business demands | |
| **Explanation**: Time savings from the implementation of the UIW tool are shown in the objective above. The target (dashed line) is never reached by the simulation result (solid). This is due to the fact that the initial goal was set for larger boats. Larger boats have longer lead times and changes in the design take longer to be amended. In the case of large boats in the simulation, its result shows a reduction of lead times of nearly half a month. The improvement after the implementation of the UIW tool is initially steep as more and more new requests comply with the system and flattens out after around 2021 when the smaller improvements are due to a decrease in amendments necessary in the regulations. The dotted line shows the "No UIW tool" run and shows a small negative time saving of around three days. This is due to the increased construction of boats and the creation of occasional bottle necks for new requests at INSB. The bottlenecks are corrected rather fast and therefore the run is always very close to 0 | |

**Table 4** Objective 4a of the UIW Cluster 5 scorecard

| | |
|---|---|
| **Name of the objective**: emissions per passenger (part a of the 4th objective) | Figure 20 |
| **Objective definition**: Reduction of around 40% in the environmental footprint and resource consumption during the production and use phases of the meta products, together with an increased use of more environment-friendly materials | |
| **Cluster-specific objective**: Ability to consider environment-friendly materials that could expand the life cycle of the product while decreasing the environmental footprint due to better forecast and planning (reduce atmospheric emissions to less than 0.15 kg per passenger per voyage) | |
| **Explanation**: This objective describes the decrease in emissions due to the use of new materials and technologies. The graph shows the emissions per passenger transported. This is calculated under the assumption of a homogeneous set of high season transport routes. A constant load factor for the market is also assumed to be at 80%, meaning that on average for each voyage 80% of capacity is filled. Depending on the load factor, the overall level of emissions per passenger increases or decreases but the general behaviour stays the same. The behaviour is due to two factors of fleet management: (1) There is an overall trend to lower emissions per passenger due to improvements in technology and (2) there are periodical increases of emissions caused by boat aging. It is assumed that due to wear and tear of the engine and other related boat characteristics the older boats operate at a lower efficiency and produce more emissions per passenger. The decreases in emissions comes from the increased building periods we have seen in objective 1. There is no run without the implementation of the UIW tool shown as the differences in the emissions per passenger are only marginal | |

**Table 5** Objective 4b of the UIW Cluster 5 scorecard

| | |
|---|---|
| **Name of the objective**: Fuel saving (part b of the 4th objective) | Figure 21 |
| **Objective definition**: Reduction of around 40% in the environmental footprint and resource consumption during the production and use phases of the meta products, together with an increased use of more environment-friendly materials | |
| **Cluster-specific objective**: Ability to consider environment-friendly materials that could expand the life cycle of the product while decreasing the environmental footprint due to better forecast and planning (decrease of fuel consumption at approx. €50–80k/year) | |
| **Explanation**: This objective addresses fuel savings due to improvements in material usage, technology and designs. The graph shows the UIW-target as a dashed line and the simulated result as a solid line. The simulation results show the comparison of the savings in any month compared to the same month a year ago. The savings are adjusted for market coverage, i.e., show the comparison if all passengers are served. There are some periods where operators do not have enough boats available to serve all passengers (between 2016 and 2021). This is also the period during which the largest yearly savings in fuel are realised. During this period a large number of boats are replaced with boats with a higher fuel efficiency and thus lead to fuel savings while also maxing out on the available capacity for boat construction and a backlog that causes the market to be underserved | |

setting of the model allows among other things to compare the effectiveness of upgrading strategies.

Regarding the Information Technologies (IT) support tools, the main limitations lay in the complexity of the tools (Snabe et al. 2006; Grossler 2004).

## 5 Conclusion and Future Work

Building an industry model generated an important amount of information for strategic thinking and decision making to the cluster members. On one hand, it provided a clear link between the cluster activities, e.g., the development of the UIW tool and the UIW-objectives. On the other hand, it explicated the link between the individual and partially conflicting business objectives of the different market actors. One example is the boat lifetime which can be regulated by INSB. INSB's main concern for regulating the boat lifetime is safety, but at the same time it is a strong tool to manage the industry as a whole. SEAbility and OCEAN, however, have potentially conflicting objectives regarding the lifetime of boats. SEAbility requires the lifetime to be as long as possible as the initial purchase of the boat represents a significant investment. In particular, when it comes to converted small boats, the boat lifetime needs to be above twenty years to allow the effective and remunerative use of the small boats. On the other hand, OCEAN has an interest in shortening the lifetime of boats to increase replacement purchases although local optima exist where this causal relationship is reversed.

Overall, the model depicts the general dynamics of the ship-borne tourism industry in Greece and has been validated by market actors at the level of model structure and model behaviour. However, the lack of available data does not allow for a more in-depth calibration than the expert opinion of the cluster members. The difficulty in getting a clear set of data is that classifications, for example, include many other types of boats besides passenger boats, and thus during the model development it could not be identified which of the built boats are relevant for the model. In the end limited data sets for customer demand in Santorini were available as well as boat construction numbers for OCEAN. While the lack of data did not allow for modelling the actual development in the industry, the model provides value nonetheless by explicating the causal relationships between the different actors and markets and their respective dynamics. This allows users of the model to test possible outcomes of business decisions under any current circumstances.

The trade-off between the different market actors requires more research. In particular, the search for optima and their implications for operational safety will bring important insights for the management of the entire industry. Since this model has a strong focus on allocating the available resources of the boatyard and classification society equally between the different operators, it would be of interest to define more individual building and upgrading patterns for operators to allow for more detailed testing of the individual operator's strategies. Finally, the aspect of sustainability of boat replacements has not been addressed and could potentially alter the attractiveness of policies that shorten the boat lifetime.

## References


Redmine. (2006). http://www.redmine.org

Dubey, A., & Wagle, D. (2007). Delivering software as a service. *The McKinsey Quarterly, 6*, 2007.

Groesser, S. N. (2012a). Mental models of dynamic systems. In N. M. Seel (Ed.), *Encyclopedia of the sciences of learning*. Heidelberg: Springer Science+Business Media.

Groesser, S. N. (2012b). *Co-evolution of standards in innovation systems: The dynamics of voluntary and legal building codes, contributions to management science*. Heidelberg: Springer.

Groesser, S. N., Schwaninger, M., et al. (2012). Contributions to model validation: Hierarchy, process, and cessation. *System Dynamics Review, 28*(2), 157–181.

Grossler, A. (2004). Don't let history repeat itself—Methodological issues concerning the use of simulators in teaching and experimentation. *System Dynamics Review, 20*(3), 263–274.

MoMM. (1979a). Rules Subdivision and Stability of vessels with LOA < 31 m. Survey Department/Ministry of Merchant Marine.

MoMM. (1979b). Rules for surveying tourist passenger vessels. Survey Department/Ministry of Merchant Marine.

MoMM. (1988). Rules for surveying small work-boats. Survey Department/Ministry of Merchant Marine.

MoMM. (1996). Fire safety requirements for ships, Survey Department/Ministry of Merchant Marine.

MoMM. (2011). Rules for Accommodation of passenger vessels, Survey Department/Ministry of Merchant Marine.

SECP. (2000). Passenger vessels for the new Millenunium, Culnane, 2000, SECP Section Papers.

SNAAM. (1985). The small passenger vessel, Cashman 1985, Marine Technology, Society of Naval Architects and Marine Engineers.

Snabe, B., Grössler, A., et al. (2006). System dynamics modelling for strategy implementation—Case study and issues. *Systems Research and Behavioral Science, 23*(4), 467–481.

SoNaME. (1990). Operation and cost of high speed craft, Wright, 1990 Marine Technology, Society of Naval Architect and Marine Engineers.

# Sustainable Furniture that Grows with End-Users

**Tim Bosch, Karin Verploegen, Stefan N. Grösser and Gu van Rhijn**

**Abstract** Economically and environmentally it might be more responsible or even feasible to combine products and services to elongate product lifetime. Gispen, a major office furniture producer in the Netherlands, has embraced circular economic principles to create new business, extend product life time and improve the adaptability of their products. In the Use-it-Wisely (UIW) project two applications were developed. To estimate possible business impacts of adapting a circular economy concept for a company, a dynamic business model simulation has been created by using the system dynamics methodology. And second, Gispen has developed a new Circular Economy Design Framework to support circular product design development. A combination of basic principles to design, upgrade, and reuse products according to circular economy principles are included in the framework as well as a circular life cycle assessment methodology. The development process, non-confidential company results of the tool application and directions for future research are described in this chapter.

**Keywords** Circular economy · Business models · Life Cycle Analysis · System dynamics

---

T. Bosch (✉) · G. van Rhijn
Department Sustainable Productivity & Employability, TNO, Leiden, Netherlands
e-mail: tim.bosch@tno.nl

G. van Rhijn
e-mail: gu.vanrhijn@tno.nl

K. Verploegen
Gispen, Culemborg, Netherlands
e-mail: karin.verploegen@gispen.nl

S.N. Grösser
Institute for Corporate Development, Bern University of Applied Sciences, Bern, Switzerland
e-mail: stefan.groesser@bfh.ch



S.N. Grösser et al. (eds.), *Dynamics of Long-Life Assets*,
DOI 10.1007/978-3-319-45438-2_16

## 1 Introduction to the Company Challenge

The market for office interior design is changing. In the last decade, costs, efficiency, quality, and design were the main drivers for office manufacturers. Nowadays, new market demands and government legislations have an impact on business. Customers have become more environmentally conscious, and the global market for environmental friendly goods and services is estimated at €4.2 trillion (Department for Business, Innovations and Skills 2012). By that, manufacturers of office furniture have to show and prove the circularity of design and manufacturing (e.g., end of life options, sources of material, and sustainability of suppliers). Furthermore, future government legislations require European manufacturers in many industries to assume responsibility for their products after use either for disposal or for reuse, and encourage them to incorporate as many recyclable materials as possible in their products to reduce waste (Communication from the Commission to the European Parliament 2015).

Besides the increased awareness on environmental issues, the market demand is fluctuating and has become more unpredictable, and strongly declined in recent years due to its sensitivity to the economic conjuncture. After a peak in 2007, total industry production has decreased by more than 14% and total sector employment decreased by 20% between 2007 and 2011 (CEPS 2014). Moreover, the market for office interior and furniture has moved closer towards a commodity market with the consequence to strongly compete on prices. Prices and margins have dropped significantly over the past decade. Office furniture has become a substitution good, i.e., multiple goods satisfy the same consumer need and therefore can be replaced by one another and tend to be influenced by cross-elasticity of demand, even though the acquisition value of furniture is still fairly high. Nowadays, employees of most companies work at all sorts of locations and new technological developments effect the way of working dramatically (e.g., virtual meetings, tablets). Moreover, new flexible, customized, and innovative office concepts are required to support the new generation of employees in the best possible way (Vos and Van der Voordt 2002; Vink et al. 2012). Office furniture should be more adaptable to future customer demands, i.e., the furniture should be able to handle better the changes in requirements for functionality, look and feel and numbers, but still guarantee a high level of quality and at a reasonable price. Proved sustainability, flexibility, and upgrades will become crucial elements to office furniture companies to guarantee long-term success. This leads to shorter lifecycles of office furniture due to changing demands on functionality.

Gispen, a major office furniture producer in the Netherlands, is aware of these changes and wants to overcome highly competitive dynamics in the current Dutch furniture market, in a lesser degree in the European market, by developing new product-service combinations (see company profile). Innovative product-service combinations prolong the life cycle time of an asset and thereby avoiding a new purchase incentive. Gispen especially focusses on the innovation of products and services based on circular economy principles (Ellen MacArthur Foundation 2013). Currently, most products in the field of office interior are designed, produced, and sold to the end-user. In case of malfunction, out of fashion, or changing requirements of the end-user, a new product is designed, produced, and sold again. The circular economy concept aims to keep products, components, and materials at their highest utility and value at all times (Ellen MacArthur Foundation 2013; McKinsey 2011). In contrast to a traditional linear economy, i.e., “take-make-dispose”, the circular economy emphasizes reusability of products and raw materials as a starting point and minimize waste in the entire industrial and ecological system. Careful consideration of product design and materialisation may result in longer use of materials. Designing new adaptable and upgradable products is crucial in realizing this circular economy-based new business model.

To implement new product service combinations, aimed at implementing innovations and therefore elongating a products life, a sound business model should be developed. Currently, a strong interaction between Gispen and the customer during the sales and implementation stage (i.e., <1 year) takes place. However, office furniture will commonly be used for more than 10 years and hardly any interaction with customers occurs. Hence, it is currently almost impossible to directly perceive change in customer requirements, and thus benefits of upgrades or lifespan expansion cannot be reaped. In a new, alternative business model, Gispen wants to strengthen the relationship with the customer by more frequent interactions. Only then, Gispen could directly perceive changes in customer needs and consequently adapt or upgrade the products to meet these needs.

Next to product design and an appropriate business model, other crucial elements are, among others, organizing new closed-loop processes such as reverse logistics (Savaskan et al. 2004) or remanufacturing (Allwood et al. 2011). Remanufacturing will be one of the processes to close the loop and restore worn-out products to new-like condition and sometimes superior in performance and expected lifetime to the original new product. The total value of sold remanufactured goods as a share of total sales of all products within the furniture sector was estimated 1.3% in the US (USITC 2012). The Dutch report ‘Remanufacturing HTSM’ indicated that the market size of remanufacturing in the furniture industry in the Netherlands could be estimated at 50 million Euro (Innovatie Zuid 2013).

This chapter describes the developments at Gispen to close the gap: changing from a linear into a circular concept with a special focus on circular economy oriented alternative business models and circular product design. We have selected two methods from the Use-it-Wisely (UIW) platform. First, to estimate possible business impacts of adapting a circular economy concept for a company, a dynamic business model simulation is developed. We use the system dynamics methodology (Groesser, Chapter “Complexity Management and System Dynamics Thinking” of this book) to develop this analysis. The development process, as well as non-confidential company results, are described in Sect. 2.1. And second, Gispen has developed a new design Circular Economy Design Framework to support circular product development. Basic principles to design, upgrade, and reuse products according to circular economy principles are included in the framework (Van Rhijn, Chapter “Fostering a Community of Practice for Industrial Processes” and Pajula, Chapter “Virtual Reality and 3D Imaging to Support Collaborative

Decision Making for Adaptation of Long-Life Assets" in this book). Section 2.2 explains this design framework. Section 3 concludes this chapter and provides avenues for future work.

**Company Profile Gispen** The Gispen Group BV is the second largest office furnisher and designer in The Benelux. Gispen was awarded the greenest company in the Netherlands in 2011 and has a long tradition of working environment friendly, i.e., from 2008 the EMAS certificate (verified environmental management). Gispens' mission statement—Be at your best—is put to practice by Gispens' core values: Sustainability, Innovation, Inspiration, and Design. Gispen as a designer, manufacturer and supplier creates ideal environments that have a positive impact on people. This combination provides all the ingredients needed for a sustainable approach through design, manufacturing principles and taking responsibility for a closed-loop system. Hence, the core value sustainability is increasingly important. In everything Gispen designs and produces they wish to make a positive contribution to the environment in which people live and work. In 2014, 21,000 products collected for repurpose and almost 1800 products have been refurbished, upgraded and brought back into use (sold) by Gispen. Having tools to make sustainable choices and to provide detailed, well-founded information to the end user assuring the necessary accountability has been the motivation to develop the models and tools described in this chapter (Fig. 1).

**Fig. 1** Collecting, disassembly, remanufacturing and reassembling of office furniture at Gispens manufacturing site in Culemborg, The Netherlands

# 2 Detailed Application of the Tools and Solutions to the Company Challenges

To tackle the company challenges as detailed in the introduction, various tools and methods are needed. In the UIW-project the following applications were developed to achieve the goals of Gispen:

- *A System Dynamic (SD) simulation model.* The SD model provides detailed insights into the dynamics of the changing business model. The business model will change from a single transaction model (sale/buy) to a (circular) product-service model. Hence, we develop a multiple transaction model with split payments.
- *A Circular Economy Design Framework.* In order to create awareness among customers and engineers and be able to rank product designs, a Design Framework, including a checklist has been developed. A circular Life Cycle Assessment (LCA) methodology is also part of this framework.

The process of developing these tools is a valuable undertaking by itself. This development requires attention, involvement of key personnel, and disciplines as well as intensive discussions amongst various company disciplines. Awareness and gaining acceptance for and a deeper understanding of choices made out of routine are part of this surplus.

## *2.1 Towards a Circular Economy Business Model*

A business model aimed at sustainability by means of re-use, remanufacturing and recycling depends on products that are returned either to a manufacturer or specialized third parties. The business model needs to have ownership by the manufacturer as a starting point to close material loops. Ultimately, customers will not buy new furniture, but they only pay for use, i.e., changing from ownership to performance-based payment models (e.g., Stahel 2010; Webster 2015; Lovins and Braungart 2013). To investigate a new circular business approach and simulate different circular based service scenarios for different customers and type of products, a dynamic modelling approach has been adopted (Groesser, Chapter "Complexity Management and System Dynamics Thinking" this book). The SD model supports enhancement of the decision-making process by the Gispen management team to develop, implement, and grow a new business model based on a circular economy (i.e., what kind of business model scenario might be successful within the model boundaries and assumptions). We used the software Vensim© (Ventana Systems, Inc., Harvard, Massachusetts) for the development of the simulation software. Vensim is able to simulate dynamic behaviour of systems that are impossible to analyse without appropriate simulation software, because they are unpredictable due to many influences and feedback interrelations.

### 2.1.1 Development Process

An iterative approach has been used to quantitatively model Gispens' new business model. In the group model building sessions (Vennix 1996) the following steps were undertaken:

- Define the most important central KPI's, i.e., business objective variables, for Gispen. A shared definition of the business objective variables was determined to evaluate effects of different tested policies and scenarios. Hence, a common understanding of profit, total turnover, market share, etc. for current and future scenarios was formed.
- Define the relevant variables in the causal-context model (Groesser, Chapter "Complexity Management and System Dynamics Thinking" this book). A management science approach was used to structure discussions on input variables and important outcomes.
- Determine and quantify the relationships between central KPI's and variables in the model. Gispen management was frequently consulted to ensure that the model building proceeds in the right direction. Moreover, the Gispen management was involved in testing the model and evaluating the benefits for Gispen provided by the model. Gispen employees from sales and the financial department were involved to provide data on relevant business parameters which are used as initial values in the model. Macro-economic predictions at an EU level, existing GDP data, market trends for the office furniture market, standard values for cost and time to implement new business models structures and Gispen specific data such as annual reports and branch reports were incorporated (e.g., Cijfers and Trends Meubelindustrie 2013). Not all data required by the model (e.g., the quantitative relationship between product attractiveness and company profit) were known. Expert meetings were used to define best expert estimates for these assumptions in the model (Ford and Sterman 1997). Furthermore, several scenarios in terms of macro-economic conditions were taken into account (i.e., negative, neutral and positive trends) as well as a predefined bandwidth for variables with a high level of uncertainty. Furthermore, the scenario and policy variables with the highest impact on business performance as well as the bounds for the set-up of these variables were defined.
- The model was validated on the level of model structure and model behaviour (Groesser and Schwaninger 2012). The focus was on internal and external validity of the model, for instance, were all relationships correctly modelled and KPI's calculated in a correct manner, and concurrent validity, i.e., does the model give similar results for the model predictions and Gispen historical data.

A circular business scenario was modelled and evaluated. Within this business scenario, office furniture will be leased to an user (who will pay per month) and will get a financial incentive by Gispen after several years of use. In this model, Gispens' current, i.e. linear, as well as the new circular business model were both included (Fig. 2).

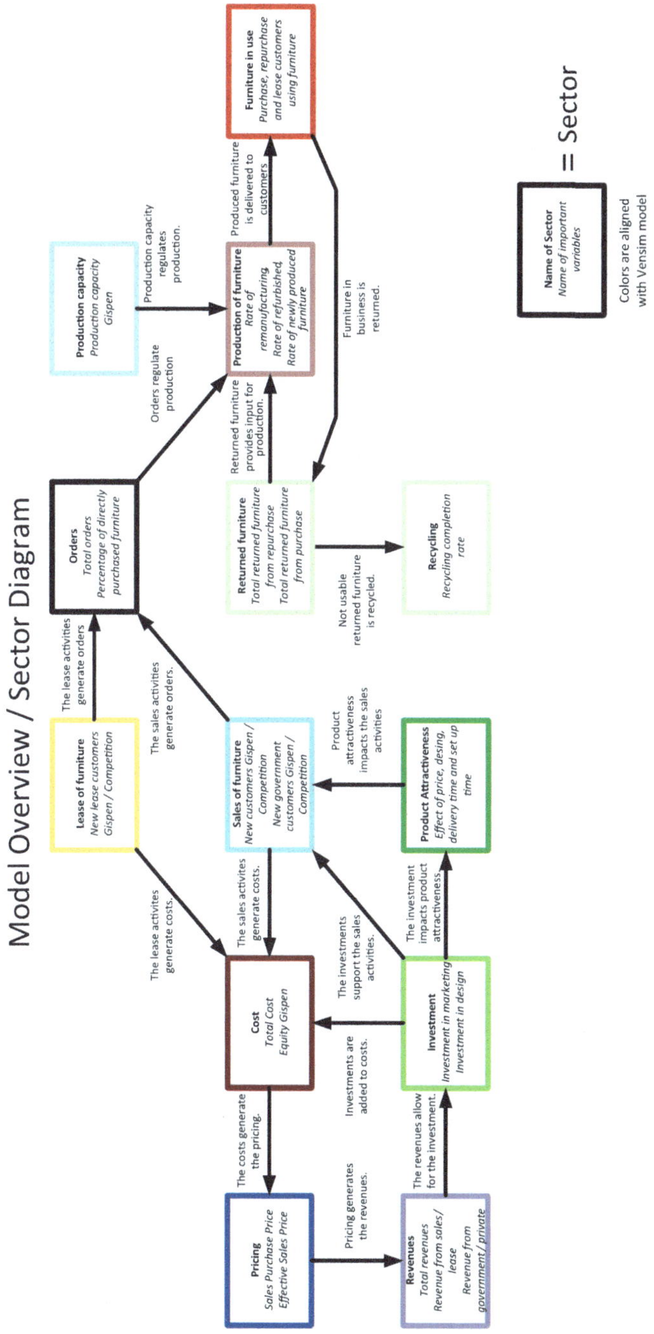


**Fig. 2** A schematic simulation model overview of the first version of Gispen's circular business model

The main learnings from this model were summarized and included in a more simplified SD model to facilitate an easier understanding. Moreover, the simplified SD model has a narrower system boundary and focused only on the new business model (Fig. 3). Following the conclusions of the first model the new business model was treated as a separate business unit with no influence from running businesses, apart from some initial assumptions such as that Gispen already had a customer base. Different model development steps were undertaken to ensure a consistent model in which all relationships were modelled correctly and all KPI's were calculated in a correct manner. Moreover, the structure of the model has been discussed extensively in several workshops and the face validity of the behaviour of the model was evaluated (for validation see Chapter "Complexity Management and

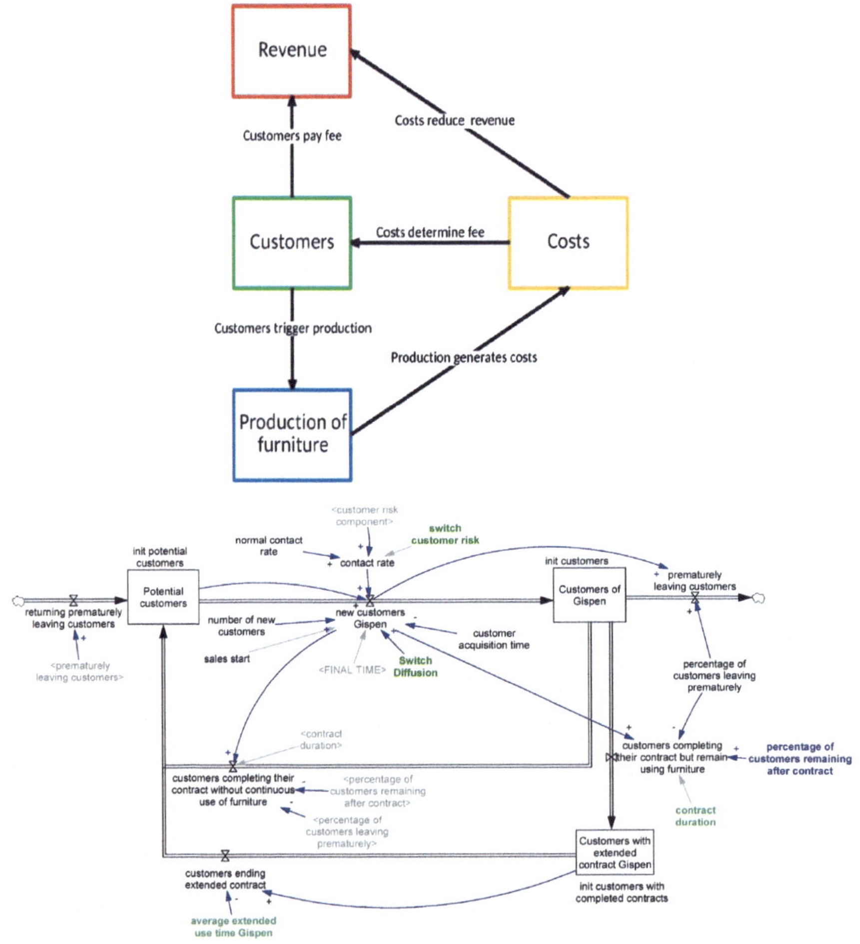


**Fig. 3** High level overview of the final business simulation model (*top*) and a more detailed impression of a part of the SD model (*bottom*)

System Dynamics Thinking"). The initial settings of the models parameters were checked and different scenarios evaluated to see its effects on the most important KPI Gispen was interested in: the break-even point.

### 2.1.2 Results

In this section, the most important outcomes of the simplified model are described. In the final version of the model, historical data of the current business model were used where reasonable. This model included three major loops, the loop of cash, the loop of customers, and the loop of products, i.e., furniture. These three loops were modelled only considering circular economy furniture and not making a difference between refurbished and remanufactured furniture and different types of customers, i.e., new or existing customers in different market segments. Cost structures were implemented in simple terms.

From the simulation model the following conclusions were drawn:

- The implementation of circular economy of assets with a long usage cycles generates long delays with high negative initial cash flows in a pay per use scenario. This leads to the conclusion that lease models, as we currently know and apply, are less usable to drive more sustainable use of products. Integration of service components and solutions to get through the 'first use' period needs to be considered in more detail as this causes a highly negative cash flow (Fig. 4). A possible option, among others, is the intensification of the use of products, i.e., stimulate multiple or serial use (Webster 2015; Stahel 2010). Another option that might be viable is upgrading existing Gispen products, as a service, at the customer site (i.e., move from production to services).
- The business model made it possible to simulate not only Gispen's internal processes, but also their interaction with market and competitors. This also allowed to focus on the adaptation of the market, competitors and own organization, pinpointing the uncertainty of the adaptation speed that is a critical point in the model. Figure 5 shows the accumulated profit for the base run and two alternative scenarios. The base run is simulated with an adoption fraction of 0.008, meaning that 8 contacts out of 1,000 between clients result in a successful client acquisition and an effectiveness of marketing of 0.00025, meaning that 25 out of 100,000 potential clients are attracted every month as new customers. To show the effects of different adaptation speeds the scenarios 'comblow' and 'combhigh' have been created with the settings of 0.004 for adoption fraction and 0.000125 for effectiveness of marketing in the 'comblow' run and 0.012 and 0.0005 for 'combhigh' respectively. 'Comblow' therefore simulates the effects, if the adoption is low in both marketing and word of mouth while 'combhigh' simulates when the new business model is embraced more quickly by the customers. In terms of effects the breakeven point for the business model in the scenarios are 109 (comblow), 147 (base) and 150 (combhigh). Low adoption rates have therefore a positive effect on the time to breakeven, mainly due to the

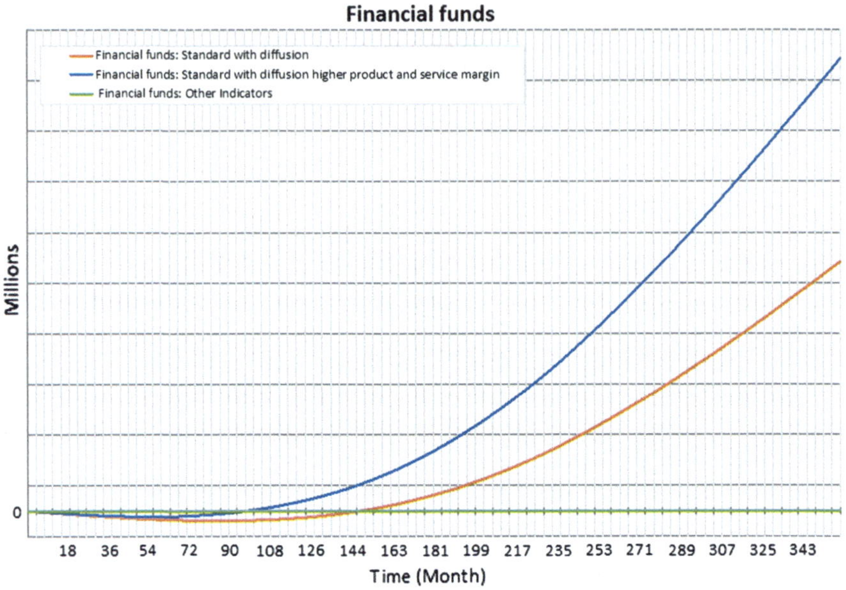


**Fig. 4** Example of system dynamics simulation outcome: two scenarios of how financial funds develop over time given different assumptions for the product and service margins

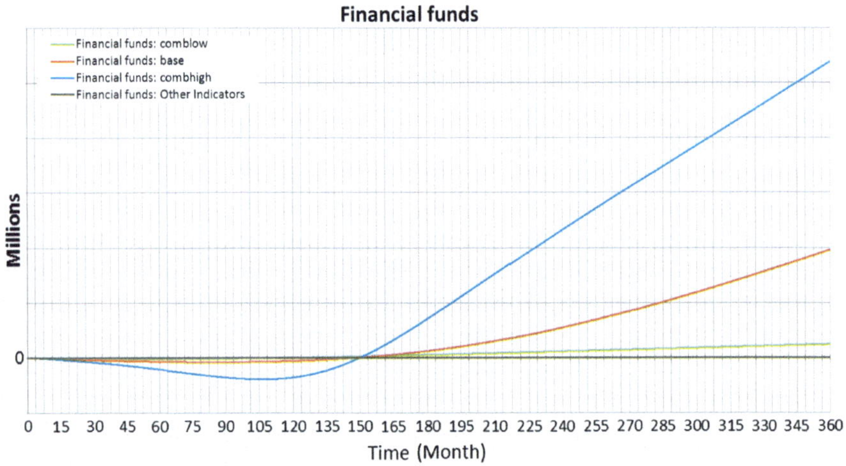


**Fig. 5** Accumulated profit for Gispen for different adaptation rates

fact that investments are low. The challenge for the new business model is that the costs arise at the beginning of a customer contact (production costs), while the flow of revenues is distributed over the entire duration of the contract (breakeven of an individual contract is between 39 and 40 months on a 60 months contract). This is illustrated by the scenario 'combhigh' where many customers are attracted quickly. Once the new business model is implemented however, the higher rate of turnover of furniture (and thus input for refurbishment) also makes the financial funds grow the fastest.
- Main added value of dynamic modelling is the deeper understanding of the mechanisms simulated. The method forces the user to provide well-founded reasoning and data to make the model reliable.

### 2.1.3 Upgrade as a Service

In essence the goal is to waste as little resources as possible. To do so one option is to upgrade or remanufacture existing, client owned furniture. A service is provided by the manufacturer and resources remain at the highest utility value. In practise the process starts with an inventory of the furniture in use and an inventory of the desired requirements for this furniture. These two are matched and additional services are executed, if possible on the customer site to keep transport to a minimum. A proven concept so far is to reuse desks and remanufacture the pieces to 'as new' desks. Visually the remade desk cannot be set apart from newly produced, and warranties are applicable for the remade desk. Since there is no shift of ownership and most of the existing materials are reused, the remade desk is considered a service. Which in turn can be embedded in a pay per use model. Even though the costs are still incurred at one moment in time, whereas the service is payed over a period of time a combination of tools can prevent the extreme dip in cash flow as described above. If at initial delivery a service package, including maintenance and upgrades, is agreed a more stable cash flow can be realized

### 2.1.4 Benefits of System Dynamics Modelling

The current simulation model concentrates on the objectives of Gispen but could also be used as an illustration of added value of business or process modelling for other companies. The development process of a model itself forces participants to create a shared vision/idea of the new business concept. Moreover, it organizes thoughts, concepts and ideas and how these interrelate. To create commitment of management or stakeholders they should be involved in this development. Furthermore, this development process leads to a better understanding of all related aspects and their relationships. A first simulation of strategies ('trial and error') can be done in the model before implementation in the real world takes place. Thereby more successful and durable changes in any business model are supported.

### 2.1.5 Lessons Learned

The lessons learned of the application of system dynamics modelling in supporting the exploration of alternative business models are summarized below.

- To simulate the relevant aspect of reality in detail, a quite comprehensive and thus complex model was developed. The quantification of the resulting relationships is time demanding and challenging, but results in a detailed understanding of the mechanisms involved. After the detailed understanding of relevant system, the extensive simulation model was simplified. The second simulation model focusses exclusively on the new circular economy business model of Gispen. By using this model with lower complexity and details, it was possible to provide relevant information to the management team enabling them to obtain the insights for their decision making. In other words, only after the detailed model was developed it was possible to focus on the relevant mechanisms in the simplified model which then provided better insights in the relevant developments of the business model with concrete results. It is often, not always, beneficial to develop a larger model first to be able to evaluate what aspects of a situation are actually necessary.
- It was possible to demonstrate the robustness of the model through many extreme condition tests and through the consistency of the units of measure. To have a more practical discussion on the feasibility of circular business model scenarios, it is useful to provide detailed information for decision making. A dashboard which shows the assumptions in the model and visualize the input and output could be a helpful means to enable even deeper discussions.
- In certain cases, to show to the management a certain trend, the timescale assumption was set to 2050. This was necessary since the delay times (use periods of the furniture products) in the modelled business system are relatively large and hence, changes in the underlying business model can only be seen, for instance, after several iterations of remanufacturing of furniture. A time horizon of 2050 is long, given that the time horizon for decision-making is regularly much shorter. After determining a trend by using the model with the long time horizon, it would be useful to then relate again to a timescale of 7–10 years. Disparities in business dynamics and decision dynamics are challenges which the SD model could demonstrate. But given the dominant paradigms for decision makers and the strong competition in the furniture industry, the SD model could not influence the decision making processes regarding the time expectations.
- The model is a means to evaluate the business potential. Such simulation models are used a few times during a year when the top management team reflects about its current corporate strategy.
- Group model building turned out to be successful in face-to-face meetings (Groesser, Chapter "Complexity Management and System Dynamics Thinking"). Misunderstandings or decisions taken were easier to understand in these meetings compared to virtual meetings or discussions.

- Involvement of different stakeholders, among others, management representatives during the development process and critical decisions on assumptions of the model will require time, but at least the major and important conclusions of every development step should be evaluated by management. Moreover, the assumptions taken during development process should be shortly described and presented to management.

## 2.2 *Creating a Design Framework for Circular Economy Office Furniture*

Gispen has a high level of customization (i.e., Engineer To Order projects). In the near future Gispen wants to keep this high level of customization in their products, but at the same time a modular product design should allow easy (dis)assembly and adaptability. In order to do so, design guidelines and circular requirements for product design, re-design and remanufacturing are necessary. These guidelines are part of a Circular Economy Design Framework (hereinafter Circular Framework, Fig. 6). The ultimate goals to achieve with support of the Circular Framework are (1) no waste or pollution during the entire life cycle (2) 100% re-use of products, modules and parts, (3) no use of energy from non-renewable resources for producing products or the use of products itself; (4) no use of virgin materials and (5) maintain the highest possible value of the product during the product lifetime and maximisation of product lifetime itself.

The Circular Framework provides an approach including a checklist to sustainable design and aims to support designers and R&D officers within Gispen to develop circular office furniture. Moreover, this approach will support Gispen to

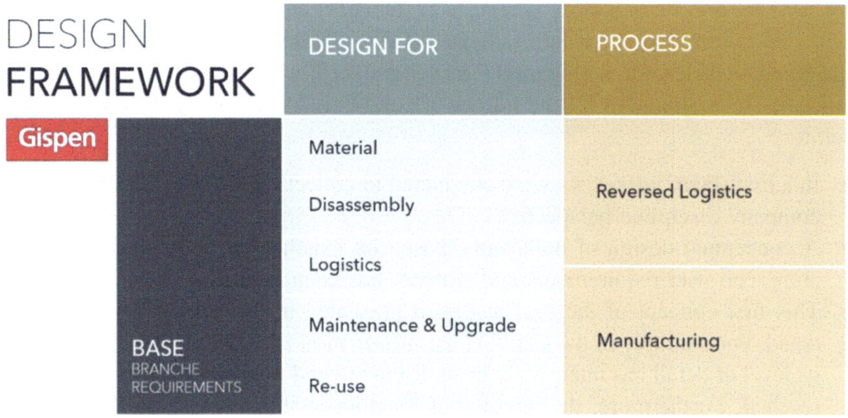


**Fig. 6** The Gispen circular economy design framework

adapt, by upgrading or retrofitting the product at the customer site or remanufacturing at the factory floor, in order to prolong the lifespan of the product and to meet the changing end-user needs. The checklist is based on some of the design principles described elsewhere in this book (Van Rhijn, Chapter "Fostering a Community of Practice for Industrial Processes" this book). All due to improvement of product design, more sustainable actions can be taken in the future. In other words, the lifespan of products and modules can be more easily prolonged. The initial cost trade-off is not incorporated in the Framework which is purely aimed at product design.

Sustainable design choices need to be well-founded. Generally accepted are LCA tools to calculate environmental impact. However, traditionally these tools have a take-make-dispose scenario. Insights in reuse, remanufacturing and the impacts thereof is needed. So the traditional LCA tool needs to be upgraded including new closed-loop scenarios, according to the circular economy concept. Besides a checklist, a Circular Life Cycle Analysis tool (C-LCA) is part of the Circular Framework. The background of this methodology has extensively been described (Pajula, Chapter "Virtual Reality and 3D Imaging to Support Collaborative Decision Making for Adaptation of Long-Life Assets" in this book). This tool aims to support product development and is based on the quantitative LCA methodology (Fig. 9). Besides product development departments, sales representatives should be able to show the effects of a particular circular scenario (e.g., sell, repurchase, and lease back) on environmental impact for different kinds of furniture, materials, and processes. Moreover, the combination of qualitative design requirements and quantitative LCA calculations provide an in-depth product evaluation to support the transition to a more closed-loop system.

### 2.2.1 Development Process of the Circular Framework and C-LCA Methodology

An iterative and participatory design (e.g., Douglas and Namioka 1993) approach was used to create the Circular Framework Checklist and C-LCA methodology. All stakeholders (sales, marketing, and R&D employees) were actively involved in this process. The major steps for the framework and C-LCA development are described below:

- In a first stage, interviews were conducted to collect requirements from different company discipline perspectives.
- A conceptual design of both tools, based on existing methodologies and literature, end-user requirements and experts, has been created.
- This first concept of the tool has been presented to all stakeholders and validated. For example in the C-LCA, the information included in the database and its level of detail has intensively been discussed and finally a consensus has been reached. Furthermore, the degrees of freedom at the scenario definition stage were determined as well as the dashboard information shown to customers (by

sales and marketing representative) and R&D to support design decisions. For the framework major topics concerning product design were discussed as well as the level of detail of the framework.

- Several prototypes have iteratively been tested and evaluated by the company. Typical products were evaluated using several linear and circular life cycle scenarios. Feedback on user interfaces, level of detail and usability of the databases was collected by the development team to improve the final versions of the tools.
- A final version of the tool has been presented to all stakeholders.

The iterative, participatory development approach for these tools was particular useful for several reasons. Firstly, including stakeholders created a shared view on how the tools are going to be used and underline the benefits of the tools for this particular interest group. Secondly, participation required input from all stakeholders and thereby different perspectives. By providing input it becomes clear if and for what reason there is resistance regarding the new approach.

### 2.2.2 Results—Checklist

The Circular Framework contains a checklist for circular product design that results in a circularity score. Availability of design and process information, were the major requirements for the checklist. From a practical perspective, the time spend on the assessment of a product design with the checklist is crucial and should therefore be limited.

Office furniture is subject to various regulatory requirements aimed at health and safety of the products and the office environment (e.g., NEN-EN-1335-2 2009). These requirements remain 'intact'. Moreover, regulatory requirements are always fulfilled and are therefore not part of the final circularity score. The DESIGN block contains design rules and guidelines that are related to product design principles, clustered to main topics (e.g., re-use or maintenance). The PROCESS block contains all principles related to process a product. Each topic in both blocks contains various questions to provide an overall (single) score for a product. Questions in the checklist should simply be answered by clicking (1) = 'Yes' or (0) = 'No'. A clear definition for each aspect in the Circular Framework was determined and has been presented in Table 1.

To rank the different design and process aspects in the design checklist the 'in pairs equations' method (e.g., van Dieën and Hildebrandt 1991) has been applied. All predefined aspects were presented in pairs to experts inside and outside the company. They were asked to indicate which factor in each pair contributes most to a circular product design. Using these scores, frequency proportions and z-values (relative position with regard to the average) were calculated. The z-values were subsequently converted to calibration units, using a standard conversion table (Swanborn 1982) and finally to weight factors.

**Table 1** Definition of framework aspects and typical questions included in the circular framework checklist

| Framework aspect | Definition | Typical statement in the checklist |
|---|---|---|
| Design—re-use | Re-use of products, parts or components for any (other) purpose after a certain use period instead of breaking them down into raw materials. In a closed-loop system maximisation of reuse requires high quality and flexibility as supported by design criteria for product modularity | Each product module has more than one functionality and in case of reuse a secondary functionality is available |
| Design—maintenance and upgrade | Maintenance of products, by taking care of products through (un)scheduled maintenance activities on a regular basis, will extend the product lifetime and retain the product's value | Product modules or components could be replaced or exchanged by one person within 10 min without damaging other parts through the use of dismountable connections |
| | Upgrading a product, by adding or removing parts from the original product leads to a functional or aesthetic improvement of the product without replacing the product as a whole and thereby extends the product lifetime | |
| Design—logistics | By taking into account product packaging and product design itself, volume, weight, waste, etc. will be reduced and thereby environmental impact and product damage will decrease during the transportation of products | The product has been designed to allow flat packed or nested transportation without increasing the risk of product damage during transportation or (un)packing activities |
| Design—material | In order to create a closed-loop system material waste does not exist. Design choices of materials are based on the ability to re-use materials with minimal energy, use of renewable resources and use of non-toxic materials | If available, recycled materials have been used to produce a product |
| Design—disassembly | Products are designed for taking apart (disassembly) complex products into interchangeable modules, parts or components to keep materials at their highest utility and value. In a closed-loop system products should be designed for effective disassembly without losing value in materials, energy and labour | If necessary, every product module could be disassembled into individual reusable components |

(continued)

**Table 1** (continued)

| Framework aspect | Definition | Typical statement in the checklist |
|---|---|---|
| Process—manufacturing | A closed-loop system should avoid any consumption during the manufacturing process. Manufacturing energy must come from renewable source | Residual material and waste during (re)manufacturing will be collected, separated and recycled |
| Process—(reversed) logistics | The environmental impact of the supply of materials and transportation of products has been minimized by optimizing modes of transportation, strong collaboration with suppliers, local sourcing of materials and local (re)manufacturing and recycling of products | Suppliers deliver parts, components or modules in reusable packages which are in proportion to the size of the packaging content |

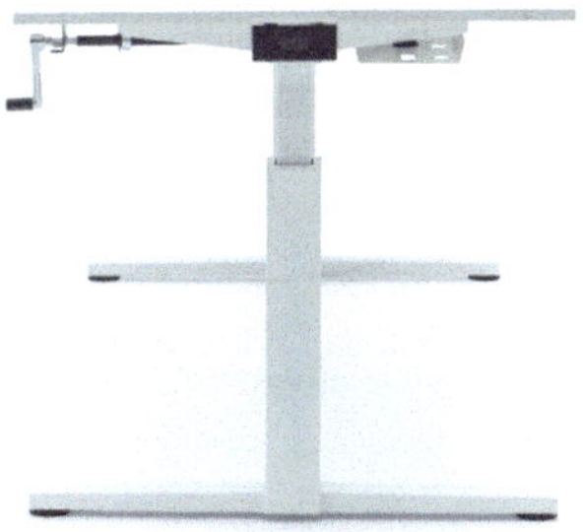

| Design - (dis)assembly | |
|---|---|
| Instructions for (dis) assembly of the product are available and easy traceable | Yes |
| The product can easily be disassembled to logic modules without any damage (i.e. by mechanical connections) | Yes |
| Each module in the product can be dissembled to separate and reusable parts | Yes |
| Modules and parts are stable during (dis)assembly and transportation | Yes |
| If necessary the product or module is transportable during (dis) assembly | Yes |
| Each module can be reached separately for (dis) assembly purposes | Yes |
| No special tools are need for (dis) assembly and the number of different tools has been minimized | No |

**Fig. 7** Product of Gispen (*left*) and checklist scores for some of the (dis)assembly questions

As mentioned in the development approach, by means of several iterations the checklist was tested and adjusted. During this development process the checklist has been used to evaluate several product designs. An example of an assessment has been presented above for one of Gispen's typical office desks (Fig. 7). For this office desk, which was not specifically designed for circular use, about 40% of the questions were answered positive. Using the checklist stimulated a better understanding of design choices and their influence in the circular product life cycle, awareness of the circularity levels of Gispens current products and supported a push towards more creative solutions. A circular product design as shown in Fig. 8 about 65% of the questions were answered positive.

**Fig. 8** Nomi, a highly modular seating system. Upgrades and visual changes are easy due to the flexible design and removable upholstery

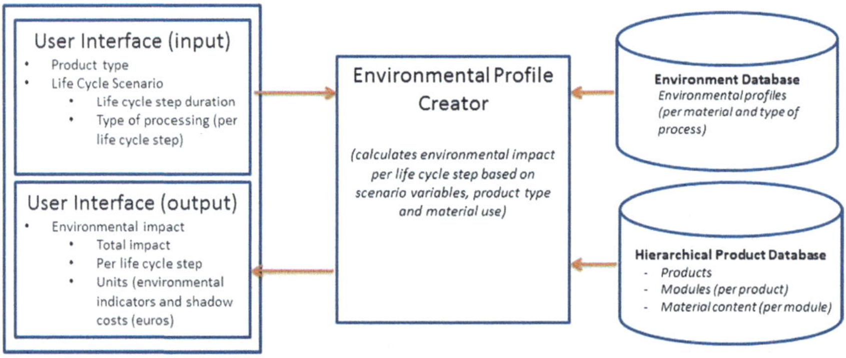


**Fig. 9** A schematic representation of the CLCA methodology to calculate environmental impact of circular product life cycle scenarios

### 2.2.3 Results—C-LCA

The C-LCA tool is able to calculate environmental impact of an industrial product for the entire life cycle including closed-loop thinking (circular economy). A high level representation of the C-LCA methodology has been shown in Fig. 9.

The tool contains two databases:

1. A product definition database which contains relevant product characteristics. Product data are structured hierarchically; products are divided in modules, product modules contain information on material composition (type of material and the amount) and the required (re)manufacturing processes and transport for this product module.
2. An environmental profile database which contains the environmental impact (e.g. climate change) of materials (e.g. steel but also bio-based materials) and manufacturing (e.g., bending, final assembly), maintenance (e.g., cleaning) and transportation processes.

Based on the selected product type, the selected life cycle scenario (e.g. 'linear': Take—Make—Dispose or 'Circular Refurbishment': Take —Make—Use—Clean and repair—Reuse—Remake—Reuse—Dispose) and life cycle duration, the database information is used to calculate environmental profiles for the entire product life cycle. The total impact (expressed in, e.g., euros and kg $CO_2$) for a (circular) product life cycle scenario is calculated and presented to the user. Sales representatives are able to show the effects of different kinds of furniture and materials, and a particular use scenario (e.g. sell, re-purchase and lease back) on environmental impact. Engineers could easily compare the environmental impact of their design decisions and thereby optimise product design from a sustainability perspective.

The C-LCA tool has been used to describe various circular scenarios. For example, for a particular client of Gispen the estimated benefits of reuse were different based on the selected decision criteria. These decisions combined various factors (1) sustainability (2) aesthetic value of the office environment (interior design requirements) and (3) costs. By creating two scenarios where the aesthetic value was similar we were able to demonstrate that a higher percentage of reuse was the most efficient choice, i.e. sustainable wise as well as cost efficiently. Furthermore, by discussing the data it created the opportunity to collaborate on planning and disassembly issues in order to avoid unnecessary transport and thereby save additional costs. C-LCA calculations where performed for the product shown in Fig. 10. It is a normal desk with a table top made out of steel.

As can be seen in the results of the calculation (Fig. 11, right), opting for a refurbishment scenario saves 1.3 kg $CO_2$ emission per year during the total lifespan of the product, here set at 12 years. As is shown in the left graph in Fig. 11, reuse outweighs virgin production vastly. In the right graph of Fig. 11 benefits and additional contribution to the emission of $CO_2$ is presented. Except logistics, as

**Fig. 10** Gispen TM Steel top

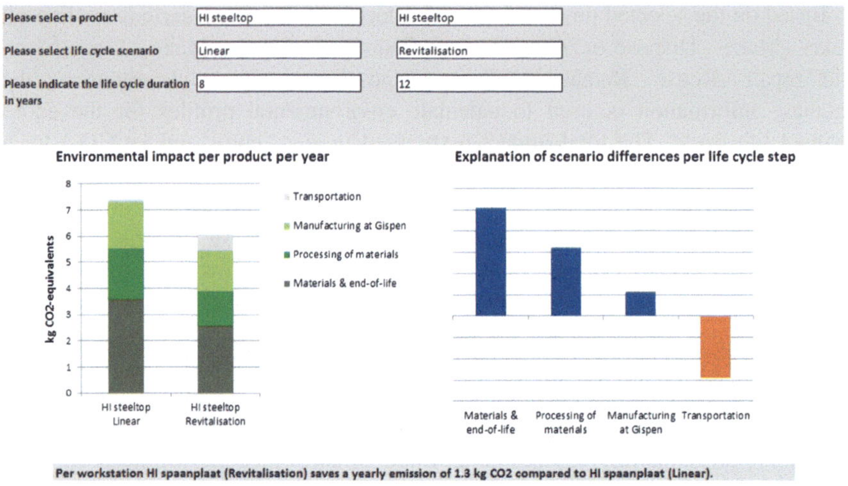


**Fig. 11** Outcomes of the C-LCA calculations for a linear as well as revitalization scenario (*bottom*)

reversed logistics were part of this circular scenario, reuse reduces $CO_2$ emission compared to a linear scenario. Upgrading on site was the most optimal form of product-life expansion in this particular customer case.

### 2.2.4 Benefits of the Circular Framework and the C-LCA

By using the Circular Framework, Gispen could show customers the degree of circularity of their products and the effects of several product life cycle scenarios (i.e., linear vs. circular). A more quantified effect of, for example, design choices in material or packaging on the environmental impact could be visualized. Using the Circular Framework thereby supports a decision making of Gispen and their customers. Furthermore, the framework and C-LCA create awareness of choice of material and process impact amongst designers, R&D and sales employees. The mission and vision of Gispen are translated in realistic objectives and the framework has been aligned to these objectives. Thereby, it contributes to the development of a circular product portfolio.

The framework provides insight in the degree of adaptation to circular principles. By filling out the checklist for each product design, and thereby creating a total score for the product, it is possible to compare one product versus another. This circular product score provides information to monitor progress on circular design and adjust whenever necessary. The checklist is a first attempt to create a tool which is easy to use for designers and on the other hand is covering the broad topics of design for circularity.

### 2.2.5 Lessons Learned

- Involvement of different end-users during the development process requires time and effort but improves the understanding of the methodology and thereby creates the opportunity to deal with resistance against the new methodology. Moreover, user interfaces, are adapted to the different user needs and thereby usability has been improved. However, presenting the data in a way that is easily understood by the various user groups and has the right level of detail is still challenging.
- The Circular Framework checklist and C-LCA are just tools. If these tools are not adequately implemented in current design and sales processes within the company, the benefits of both tools will be marginal.
- Traditionally design for a particular discipline is built up on the creation of rules to be applied during product design in the product development department, or in concurrent engineering between departments within or outside the company. Designing for a closed-loop system is designing for future use, whilst use might change over time. Upgrading a product during its life time and usage will require the product development function to get directly involved in the customer interface. Product development engineers can no longer expect to be given readymade.
- It might be concluded that both tools can be applied in other sectors and companies but the success of the tools will be based on the willingness to embrace the principles and company culture of a closed-loop system.
- In general the C-LCA methodology is fairly technical and detailed product information on materials and processing is needed to make any calculation.
- Maintenance or updating the C-LCA tool with new products, modules, materials and processes can only be done by a few employees of Gispen. A LCA expert outside the company is needed in case alternative materials (e.g., bio-based materials like bamboo, engineered wood), which are not included in the current database, will be used in product designs.
- The C-LCA methodology provides outcome parameters (e.g. environmental costs in euros or $CO_2$ in kg) which could easily be understood by non-expert users.
- The checklist questions have been based on existing literature (e.g., Boothroyd 1980) and if needed, adjusted according to expert opinions. To ensure a similar understanding and interpretation of checklist questions different disciplines have been involved. Nevertheless, in depth knowledge of the aim of questions is sometimes required to get correct answers. A clarification has been added to support the user and avoid misinterpretation. Training of users will be considered in case this seems insufficient.
- The checklist is a qualitative assessment with a limit number of design and process aspects to ensure a limited time effort from engineering perspective and easy understanding from a customer perspective. The checklist has not yet been validated and is a first step to show circularity aspects in furniture to customers.

## 3 Conclusion and Future Work

Although the circular economy is a current issue, the industrial state-of-the-art is that still a limited number of manufactures have shown a shift towards a closed-loop business. Companies exploring these new strategies are primarily focused at servicing at their customers site and not on total efficient and cost effective reverse logistics, disassembly and remanufacturing strategies with their entire supply chain. Primary processes and supporting ICT systems are insufficient developed, neither is the use of alternative bio-based materials sufficiently developed to enable large scale exploitation. Gispen has successfully started working on circular economy projects. Simulated business model scenarios, among others, have been used to establish new business agreements with public and private companies in the Netherlands. To support awareness of designers and engineers the design methodologies will be implemented and updated in the near future. Furthermore, the circularity level of Gispen products can be transparently shown to potential customers by using the scores of the C-LCA and Circular Framework outcomes. By means of this data, customers can be informed by Gispen about the effect of their decisions and choices on product life cycle impact, business wise as well as from a sustainability perspective. A next step will be the transition from successful projects towards a closed-loop thinking company culture. Moreover, Gispen has identified additional needs and will continue the implementation of their circular economy strategy by the following developments in the near future:

- A furniture management system will be setup for monitoring product use and ageing at the customer site. Due to rapid technology developments, we now have access to a wide range of low-cost embedded microelectromechanical systems (e.g. accelerometers or gyroscopes). These sensor data could be useful to monitor product use (e.g., Cheng et al. 2013) and thereby support decision making to follow the best strategy for service and maintenance, disassembly, remanufacturing and recycling.
- To overcome the high labour costs caused by manual disassembly (Duflou et al. 2008), smart disassembly systems with operator ICT support for (manual) operations and semi-automated stations might be a direction for future developments. Moreover, the use of cognitive, vision-based robots for quality control of returned products (Vongbunyong et al. 2012) and for example the use of low-cost collaborative robots looks promising also for SME's.
- A decision support system for remanufacturing strategy on a component level incorporating quality assessment of remanufactured components and products. This would involve new policies based on remanufacturing, reversed supply chains and revenue and cost management fit for these flows.
- Further business model exploration by the development of incentive based methods of contracting, including financial incentives for a closed-loop system possibly within a linear accounting system. Ultimately, Gispen creates sensible alternatives from a financial, fiscal, and legal point of view to ensure closed-loop

systems. This would need not only a pragmatic solution regarding incentives, but more general a systemic change.
- Development and use of new bio-based materials in office furniture. Finding materials that are fit for all the use requirements today, are renewable and of a stable supply. Nowadays, bio-based material is not of a fit quality and is unstable in supply which is devastating for high volume use.

## References

Allwood, J. M., Ashby, M. F., Gutowski, T. G., & Worrell, E. (2011). Material efficiency: A white paper. *Resources, Conservation & Recycling, 55,* 362–381.

Boothroyd, G. (1980). Product design for assembly. Department of Mechanical Engineering, University of Massachusetts, Amherst.

CEPS (2014). The EU furniture market situation and a possible furniture products initiative. DG Enterprise and Industry.

Cheng, J., Zhou, B., Sundholm, M., & Lukowicz, P. (2013). Smart chair: What can simple pressure sensors under the chairs' legs tell us about user activity? In *UBICOMM 2013: The Seventh International Conference on Mobile Ubiquitous Computing, Systems, Services and Technologies* (pp. 81–84).

Cijfers & Trends Meubelindustrie. (2013). https://www.rabobankcijfersentrends.nl/index.cfm?action=branche&branche=Meubelindustrie

Communication from the Commission to the European Parliament, the council, the European economic and social committee and the committee of the regions (2015). Closing the loop—An EU action plan for the Circular Economy. http://eur-lex.europa.eu/legalcontent/EN/TXT/?uri=CELEX:52015DC0614

Department for Business, Innovations and Skills. (2012). Low carbon environmental goods and services.

Douglas, S., & Namioka, A. (Eds.) (1993). *Participatory design: Principles and practices.* Boca Raton: CRC Press.

Duflou, J. R., Seliger, G., Kara, S., Umeda, Y., Ometto, A., & Willems, B. (2008). Efficiency and feasibility of product disassembly: A case-based study. *CIRP Annals—Manufacturing Technology, 57*(2), 583–600.

Ellen MacArthur Foundation. (2013). Towards the circular economy. In: *Economic and business rationale for an accelerated transition, Vol. 1. Ellen MacArthur Foundation.* Available from: www.ellenmacarthurfoundation.org

Ford, D. N., & Sterman, J. D. (1997). Expert knowledge elicitation to improve formal and mental models. *System Dynamics Review, 14*(3), 309–340.

Groesser, S. N., & Schwaninger, M. (2012). Contributions to model validation: Hierarchy, process, and cessation. *System Dynamics Review, 28*(2), 157–181.

Innovatie Zuid. (2013). Hightech systemen en materialen: Remanufacturing.

Lovins, A. B., & Braungart, M. (2013). *A new dynamic—Effective business in a circular economy.* Ellen MacArthur Foundation Publishing.

McKinsey. (2011). Resource revolution: meeting the world's energy, materials, food, and water needs. McKinsey Global Institute; McKinsey and Company Sustainability, Resource Productivity Practice. Available from: http://www.mckinsey.com/mgi

NEN-EN-1335-2. (2009). Office furniture—Office work chair—Part 2: Safety requirements.

Savaskan, R. C., Bhattacharya, S., & Van Wassenhove, L. N. (2004). Closed-loop supply chain models with product remanufacturing. *Management Science, 50*(2), 239–252.

Stahel, W. R. (2010). *Performance economy.* Basingstoke: Palgrave MacMillan.

Swanborn, P. G. (1982). *Scale techniques*. Amsterdam: Boom.
USITC. (2012). Remanufactured goods, overview US and global industries.
Vennix, J. A. M. (1996). *Group model building: Facilitating team learning using system dynamics*. Chichester: Wiley.
van Dieën, J. H., & Hildebrandt, V. H. (1991). Het gebruik van weegfactoren in een ergonomische risicoanalyse. *Tijdschrift Voor Ergonomie, 16*, 15–24. (in Dutch).
Vink, P., Blok, M., Formanoy, M., De Korte, E., & Groenesteijn, L. (2012). The effects of new ways of work in the Netherlands: National data and a case study. *Work, 41*(S1), 5081–5085.
Vongbunyong, S., Kara, S., & Pagnucco, M. (2012). A framework for using cognitive robotics in disassembly automation. *Leveraging technology for a sustainable world* (pp. 173–178). Berlin, Heidelberg: Springer.
Vos, P., & Van der Voordt, T. (2002). Tomorrow's office through today's eyes: Effects of office innovation in the working environment. *Journal of Corporate Real Estate, 4*, 48–65.
Webster, K. (2015). *The circular economy—A wealth of flows*. UK: Ellen Mc Arthur Foundation Publishing.

# Comparing Industrial Cluster Cases to Define Upgrade Business Models for a Circular Economy

**Magnus Simons**

**Abstract** Upgrading is often seen as a means to strengthen customer loyalty between investments in new equipment, but there is more to it. It is a means to introduce innovation in small, but continuous steps keeping both OEMs and their customers at the innovative forefront of technical and business development. Upgrading also improves sustainability and it is a driver in the development of the circular economy. Basically upgrading means transformation of a used piece of capital-intensive equipment to meet the new conditions in the user's business environment, but in practice it can take on a variety of forms depending on what type of added value is provided to the customer. In this article, we define four generic types of upgrade business models based on the industrial cluster cases in the UIW-project. Using a modified business canvas approach, we define the four Upgrade business models and compare how they create value for the customers, how they organise their main activities and how they earn money. A central means of achieving profitable upgrade business is to develop efficient business processes through digitalisation and through the use of modern information technology. Here we identify four areas where technologies such as AR and VR help to create an efficient environment for information management and communication in the upgrade value network.

**Keywords** Upgrading · Business model · Digitalization · Information technology · Value proposition · Value network · Earnings logic · Business process · Circular economy

---

M. Simons (✉)
VTT Technical Research Centre of Finland Ltd., Espoo, Finland
e-mail: magnus.simons@vtt.fi



S.N. Grösser et al. (eds.), *Dynamics of Long-Life Assets*,
DOI 10.1007/978-3-319-45438-2_17

# 1 Introduction

Upgrade is a life cycle service provided to an owner or user of capital-intensive equipment. As such it is one type of service product in a larger service portfolio provided during the life cycle of the equipment in order to enhance its performance. We define commercial upgrade service provided to a customer here as upgrade business. As a business model, the upgrade service differs in many aspects from services like spare part sales or maintenance. To put this new business model into context, we will first have a look at the concepts of circular economy and industrial service business.

Circular economy and industrial service business are slowly becoming common concepts in industry. They are, however, not new as concepts (Roos and Agarwal 2015), but as more and more efforts are put into this area, both by industry and academia, the terminology gets more vivid and the concepts get more comprehensive. In order to understand the role of upgrade business in industry, we start by identifying its context.

Circular economy and industrial service business are interrelated concepts (Roos and Agarwal 2015). However, they represent slightly different views on the same topic. While the concept of a circular economy starts at a system-level view on the industrial ecosystem (Stahel 2016) and material flows (Ellen MacArthur Foundation 2016), industrial service business takes the view of the company. The driver behind the circular economy is to achieve an ideal state resembling nature, where internal cycling of material is complete or nearly complete (Bocken et al. 2016).

Several authors have described business models for combining the drivers of the circular economy with the drivers of single companies (Allwood et al. 2011; Ellen MacArthur Foundation 2016; Bocken et al. 2016; Lacy and Rutqvist 2015). According to Bocken et al. (2016), two major strategies for building circular economy business models can be identified: (1) closing the resource loops, and (2) slowing the resource loops. The Ellen MacArthur Foundation (2016) has distinguished between finite stock and renewable material. They identify several strategies for prolonging these loops. From the Use-it-Wisely (UIW) point of view the finite material cycles are more relevant. Here the economic circles described by the Ellen MacArthur Foundation are to maintain/prolong, reuse/redistribute, share, refurbish/remanufacture and to recycle the finite materials.

Linton and Jayaraman (2005) have focused on different business models (modes) of product life extension for finite materials. The nine business models they have identified and their main focus or objective can be seen in Table 1. In this chapter, we will focus on upgrade, part reuse and remanufacturing which are closest to the cluster cases in the UIW-project.

Business models like recall, repair and maintenance strive to ensure that the delivered products provide the user with the physical and functional qualities they originally invested in as they bought the product. Through these business models the customer can expect to make continuous use of the product over its life time. But these models do not improve on the qualities of the product as technological

**Table 1** Business models for product life extension (adopted from Linton and Jayaraman 2005, p. 1808)

| Business models (modes) for product life extension | Focus |
|---|---|
| Recall | Safety and extend life |
| Repair | Life extension |
| Preventative maintenance | Continuous use |
| Predictive maintenance | Life extension |
| Upgrade | Reduce cost and extend life |
| Product reuse | Life extension |
| Remanufacture | Life extension |
| Part reuse | Reduction of materials and processing inputs |
| Recycle | Reduce material and energy inputs |

development proceeds and, thus, they will not impact the competitive value of a product in comparison to other newer ones. This is the value added upgrade that business is focusing on and, hence, the way to differentiate from other service business models. Product reuse means transferring a product from one owner to another as it gets obsolete to the first one. Recycling is the re-use of materials in a product. This can be seen as the prevailing industrial practice for handling finite materials.

According to Linton and Jayaraman (2005), an upgrade improves the quality, value, effectiveness or performance of a product which has eroded over time as competitors bring new technologies to the market. "Very complex products may also contain components or subsystems with far shorter life-cycles than the product" (Linton and Jayaraman 2005, p. 1814). An upgrade may be conducted by the customer, manufacturer or a third-party vendor. Parts required for an upgrade are typically provided by the manufacturer or a third party. Upgrade involves moderate transformation of the unit. The information value is high, since the product life and/or capabilities are extended with only small amounts of material and labour.

Remanufacture is, by Linton and Jayaraman (2005) defined as the restoration of a used product to a condition close to that of a new one. The restored product "provides the performance characteristics and durability as least as good as the original product" (Linton and Jayaraman 2005, p. 1815). Remanufacture involves a major transformation of a unit, component or part. The value of added material is low, since few new parts are used, but the labour value added is high, since many parts may have to be tested and/or refurbished. Although much of the labour value-added is of a low skill level, low labour costs are an important element for the economic viability of this approach.

Part reuse is defined, by Linton and Jayaraman (2005), as "the use of a part in its same form for the same use without remanufacturing" (Linton and Jayaraman 2005, p. 1815). "The cost of collecting and testing the parts is much less than the cost of manufacturing new parts. Reuse of parts involves a major transformation of the product. It involves the extraction of the desired components from the product. The components may need to be tested and/or refurbished. The information value of this mode is medium, since knowledge of the product and the reuse requirements for the component is required. The material value added of the reuse of parts is high, since the component not only offers the correct material composition, but also the desired shape. The labour value is low, since like many of the other modes, it typically focuses on placement and extraction of the component" (Linton and Jayaraman 2005, p. 1816).

These business models for product life extension, described by Linton and Jayaraman (2005), focus on how to prolong the life span of the product and on what actions the extension will require. Other writers have also included other aspects in the business models. Lacy and Rutqvist (2015) also include the aspect of ownership of products, components and materials in their models. They describe five potential business models related to the circular economy. These business models are:

- Circular Supply-Chain—access to fully renewable, recyclable or biodegradable inputs
- The Product Life-Extension Business Model—making a product's useful life as long as possible and maximised profitability over the lifecycle
- Recovery and Recycling—every by-product and waste stream is optimised to maximise its revenue potential
- The Sharing Platform Business Model—provides a platform to connect product owners with individuals or organisations that would like to use them
- The Product as a Service Business Model—selling access to—and the performance of—an item on either a short or long-term basis.

In the UIW-project, we have focused on the upgrade of durable goods, which in traditional transaction based business models require big upfront investment. In this chapter, we will examine the experiences from the six industrial cluster cases in the UIW-project. Although most of them were at a very early phase of upgrade business development, each cluster had a shared vision of what kind of business activities they were aiming at. We will see from these cases how they consider closing the loops, prolonging the loops or how ownership of the durable goods could affect the business models for upgrading of them.

## 2 Upgrade Business Models

In this chapter we analyse the business models explored by the six cluster cases of the UIW-project in order to get a more detailed understanding of how these models work, what the drivers of these models are and what challenges related to these business models were identified during the research project. To compare the business models of the cluster cases, we used a simplified version of the business model canvas developed by Osterwalder and Pigneur (2010). We focus our analysis on the value proposition, the main resources and value network, the earnings logic of the business models used in the cluster cases and on the information management in main business processes. The analysis also raises the question of how the main actors in the value network have to transform their business model to create synergy between original equipment production and upgrading. In the next section we look at how upgrade processes can be made more efficient through the use of modern information technology.

The *value proposition* to the customer is a central part of the business model. It tells us what added value our service offering can provide to the customer. In the case of capital intensive equipment and machinery, the value of additional after-sales services is related to the use of this equipment. In an industrial business-to-business situation, a basic value for the customer is return on investment—invested capital should be used as profitably as possible over the span of the life cycle of the equipment. In practice, this can mean different things in different situations.

In the upgrade *value networks*, we can identify a set of basic roles occurring in slightly different ways in the different clusters. These are the user of the equipment, the main designer, the producer or provider of the equipment—here called the original equipment manufacturer (OEM), the upgrade service provider and provider of supporting services. The UIW-clusters are at an early stage of development of upgrade business and in most clusters, the final operational organisation has not yet been set up. Yet, from the organisation of the cluster cases we can see which actors the core companies in the clusters have identified as central partners and resources in their upgrade network.

Based on the cluster cases, we can say that the main *earnings logic* of the companies involved in upgrading is to improve their competitive situation and to earn more through improvement of added value for the customers. In most cases, upgrade business is focusing on and improving on already existing customer relationships. Upgrading can, however, also bring new customers through the added value of the upgrade service. To understand how the cluster cases aim to profit from the new upgrade services, we look at how this new service increases sales directly through sales of innovative upgrade services or indirectly through improved customer loyalty, and how costs are managed through the introduction of efficient service processes supported by new innovative digital information management solutions.

In the upgrade business, many business processes differ from processes used in original equipment manufacturing. There are also completely new processes like the reverse logistics process in remanufacturing. For many of these processes, a central feature is low volume and little repetition, customisation and a whole lot of information to be managed. In the UIW-project focus was on *information management* issues. We will in this chapter look in more detail at how this issue was met in the business models explored during the UIW-project.

Based on analysis of the cluster cases in the UIW-project, we can distinguish between four generic upgrade business models among the six clusters. We call these the ***Customized Upgrade***, the ***Modular Upgrade***, the ***Remanufacturing*** and the ***Service Upgrade*** business models. These models differ in the type of added value with which the customer is provided, but also in how this value is produced. Our study also shows that the different business models stress the need for development of digital means in different areas.

## 2.1 Customised Upgrade

The first business model is the Customized Upgrade. This model is based on the experiences from Clusters #3 and #5—the Italian and Greek the clusters (see Chapters "Space Systems Development" and "Supporting the Small-to-Medium Vessel Industry") in the UIW-project. Here the provider of a capital intensive physical product provides services aimed at upgrading the performance of the product, owned and used by an external customer, to meet new requirement from the customer or user of the equipment. In this business model, the service is initiated by the need of a specific customer and the service is customised to meet these needs. Central challenges in this business model are identification and management of customer needs in all phases of the service process, and to manage cost and time of the customised service performance.

### 2.1.1 Value Proposition for Customised Upgrade

In the Customised Upgrade business model, the proposition made to the customer is to adapt the original equipment to new needs of the customer. These needs may occur due to changes in the business environment of the customer, like new needs of the customer's customers or changes in equipment and services provided by competition.

Cluster #3 is looking at developing a new business model providing space services, using the Space Tug concept as an example in the project. A space tug is a type of spacecraft used to transfer payloads between orbits or to escape trajectory. Thales Alenia Space is studying this concept and related technological research in a parallel project (Pasquinelli et al. 2016). This was felt as the best disruptive example to study the UIW-methodology with respect to a new type of business. Moreover, it is a good example in the space domain where there is not a final customer who buys a spacecraft and related services, but there are multiple potential customers who can profit from a multi-mission spacecraft. This example is very complex, and the methodology may also be applied to conventional programs (institutional or commercial). In case of Cluster #5, customers are provided the opportunity to adapt the vessel from one type of shipping business into another as market demand shifts. Requirements for the new business activities are defined with the customers and they are implemented through technical or other changes to the vessel. Improved sustainability of the vessel is often an objective for the upgrade.

In Cluster #5, the aim is to upgrade the vessel according the needs of the owner. As market focus shifts from one segment to another, the vessel has to be adjusted to meet the requirements in the new market segment. This process also involves having the classification of the vessel checked and perhaps changed.

### 2.1.2 Roles in Customised Upgrade

In Customised Upgrade, the key players are the owner of the equipment and the OEM responsible for production of the original equipment. The customer initiates the upgrade process by presenting new needs and the OEM is responsible for providing the upgrade service. Due to the complexity of the customised upgrade process and the information management involved, the main roles like customer needs management, upgrade engineering and manufacturing are typically managed internally by the OEM. Supporting functions can be outsourced to expert organisations.

In both Clusters #3 and #5, the OEM is responsible for a majority of the roles involved. They are the provider of the solution, engineer, part or component manufacturer as well as coordinator of the final integration as part of the upgrade service. In Cluster #3, the responsibility for managing information related to the customer request is outsourced to Vastalla—a company offering IT consulting services, software development and IT systems activities emphasising especially on IT security. In Cluster #5, the boat manufacturing company OCEAN acts as both original equipment producer and as provider and producer of the upgrade service. Here the non-governmental ship classification society INSB, responsible for ship classification, survey and statutory certification and engineering approvals is a central actor in the value network. It plays an important role in the approval of the new, upgraded vessel construction, and it is involved as a partner in the early phase of the upgrade process.

Based on these two cluster cases, we suggest that in Customised Upgrade the control of the information flow requires the OEM to take a central role in the operative work. The mode of operation is vertically integrated, leaving only support functions and specialist functions to outside partners. Innovative development of core technology to support the upgrade business is done in a close network of partners (Fig. 1).

### 2.1.3 Earnings Logic in Customised Upgrade

Offering a customised upgrade requires unique input from the service provider and it is typically done at a high cost level. Due to this customised upgrades can only be offered if the price of the service is high enough or the costs can be returned otherwise. Then again, a high price requires high added value to the customer. This is typically achieved through the provision of unique service characteristics provided only to the customer in question. This can be seen in the case of Cluster #3,

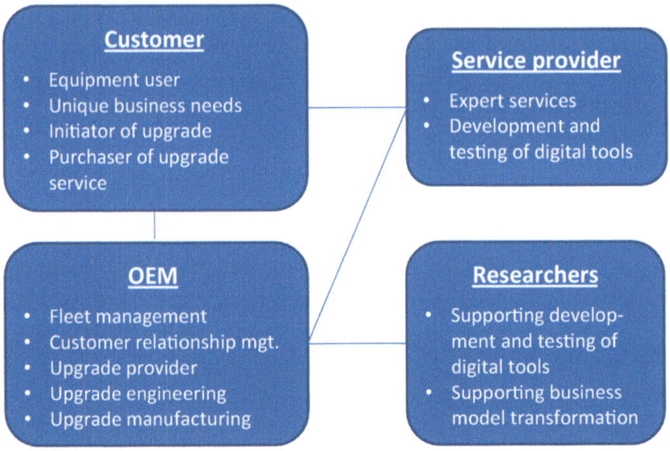


**Fig. 1** Actors, roles and connections in the Customised Upgrade business model in the UIW-project

where the goal is to present a totally new, unique value adding service to the customer or user of the space equipment. Changing the use of a space unit in orbit was earlier done from a space shuttle, but today there is no infrastructure available for this task.

In Cluster #5, the upgrade service is aiming to transform the vessel from use in one business area to another. This can be profitable to both customer and service provider as long as the upgrade service is less expensive than options like buying a new vessel, but still the price is high enough to give the provider a good margin. Limited and less profitable customisations can be done, for instance, for the sake of customer loyalty.

Customised upgrade involves some extent of disassembly and reconfiguration of the existing equipment. In some cases this is done in the field, in other it is done at a factory. Since this involves activities not part of the original equipment manufacturing, it is likely to require some extent of dedicated resources, infrastructure and facilities. Since customised upgrade is based on initiatives from the customer, information management is crucial for cost management. Also management of critical skills and functions is likely to require in-house resources.

### 2.1.4 Information Management in Customized Upgrade

In Customised Upgrade, a major challenge in the actor network is the collection and management of customer-specific information. Customisation means deviations from standards and from previous activities, which again means that existing data and information is no longer up-to-date. Instead, customisation requires specification, documentation and management of new information. Since the generation of new data and information is a manual and often not a well-structured task, it is prone to mistakes and delays. Checking that all necessary information exists and is available is a major challenge in customisation. This is also true for the quality checking and the dissemination of correct and up-to-date data and information to all parties concerned. These challenges are reflected in the pilots made in Clusters #3 and #5.

Cluster #3 developed a system to enhance communication between stakeholders (including customers) in all communication-sensitive phases of the service lifecycle, from initial choice among design solutions, to choice among alternative configurations before service executions also supporting general decision-making processes during Space TUG operations. This cluster focused on developing a reference data model (meta-model) that can serve as standard for storing and interchanging industrial information. Cluster #3 is also developing a Web Configurator to enhance communication between stakeholders in the service lifecycle, modelling the application using the meta-model that makes use of software called the Web Environment.

Cluster #5 developed a system to support upgrades of small passenger boats. The upgrades can be driven by changes to regulation or variation in service demand, which have to be balanced with reductions in cost and lead-time of product modifications. Within UIW, Cluster #5 developed an information system to support upgrading activities in this context, through giving stakeholders access to an information-rich technical metafile for the vessel that includes all aspects of the vessel. The meta-file is accompanied by a vessel web configurator that is the customer's entry tool to the application suite of Cluster 5.

## 2.2 Modular Upgrade

The second business model, used in the Finnish Cluster #2 (see Chapter "Rock Crusher Upgrade Business from a PLM Perspective"), we call Modular Upgrade. As in the previous business model also in this model, the OEM of a capital intensive physical product provides services aimed at upgrading the performance of the equipment, owned and used by an external customer. In this business model, the service is not defined by the needs of a single customer or end user. In this business model, the service provider defines the characteristics of the upgrade based on input from the market. In the Finnish case, the upgrades are changes to the physical machine predefined by the product development in the OEM. A modular structure of the machine enables the company to develop the features of the machines piece by piece. As the new modules are fitted to old machine constructions, they become upgrade options for the fleet of machines in use in the field.

### 2.2.1 Value Proposition for Modular Upgrade

In this business model, the upgrade service is predetermined by the service provider. Equipment owners or users are provided leading edge performance through predefined and productised modular upgrading of their equipment. Increased sustainability in use of original equipment can be part of added customer value. The added value depends on how the customer can utilise it in order to increase competitiveness or to move into new areas of business. In Cluster #2 crushers are, for instance, adapted for use in urban areas through additions of noise and dust-reducing modules. This gives the operator of the crusher improved opportunity to compete for sustainable urban crushing contracts.

### 2.2.2 Roles in Modular Upgrade

In Modular Upgrade the OEM plays a central role as the provider of the upgrade service to the owner or user of the original equipment. The OEM also takes the responsibility for the defining and engineering of the upgrade module. Modular upgrade sets the emphasis of efficiency of operative execution and thus requires specialised resources. A forward integrated role of the OEM creates a close relationship to the end users and customers, and through a thorough productisation of the upgrade service, operative functions like module production, customer interface design and production, and final assembly can be outsourced to a network of specialised actors.

In Cluster #2, Metso—the OEM—is concentrates on designing the modular upgrades based on thorough understanding of the technology and the market needs. The operative responsibilities for producing the upgrade service can be outsourced to a partner company. Since the modular upgrade, projects are limited in scope, they are not always suitable for the business processes of the OEM or for the organisations focusing on these processes. This is why Metso is considering outsourcing the production of the upgrade service to an external company such as RD Velho—a smaller and more agile partner organisation.

In the Cluster #2 case example, part of the operative information management is also outsourced to the network partner. In this case, RD Velho is responsible for collecting information on the machine as it is used in the field. This information is compared to the original geometry of the machine and to the geometry of the upgrade module to see how it can be fitted to the machine (Fig. 2).

### 2.2.3 Earnings Logic in Modular Upgrade

The Modular Upgrade business model strives to provide the customer with new, but not unique, functionality in order to improve customer competitiveness. Restricting the upgrade to single modules in the equipment limits both the effect on the performance improvement, but also the resources needed for performing the upgrade.

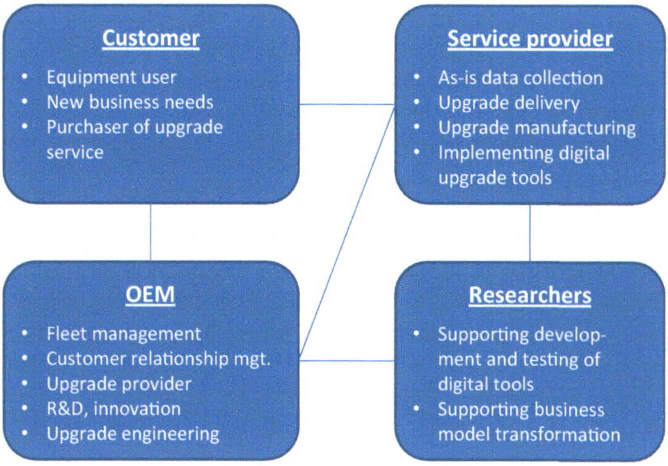


**Fig. 2** Actors, roles and connections in the Modular Upgrade business model in the UIW-project

Basing the upgrade on design and plans from product development ensures that the efforts put on developing the module are re-used both in new products and in upgrades for other customers.

The modular design also means that the production of the physical module and its parts is repeated. This makes batch production possible and enables economies of scale in production of the modules. The experience from Cluster #2 shows however that the upgrade business is in many other areas quite different from the original equipment manufacturing and can benefit from separation between the two business models. For instance, the management of a modular upgrade project is much more limited than the management of an original equipment project. Also assembly of the module to a machine in the field differs significantly form new equipment production in the factory. Here, dedicated upgrade resources—in-house or external—can be necessary.

In the case of Cluster #2, an upgrading business already exists, but to improve profitability of this activity, a new mode of upgrade business is developed. In the new mode, the modular upgrade business model, Metso is to some extent reducing the customers' options from a completely customer needs-based mode to a modular, innovation-based mode. They are balancing added customer value with internal efficiency, cost, control and profitability.

### 2.2.4 Information Management in Modular Upgrade

In Modular Upgrade the challenges in information management are reduced significantly compared to the Customised Upgrade. Since it is a major part of development work and thus, also of information management, it is handled in-house in the OEM's product development organisation, the main information management challenges are related to what goes on outside this organisation. A major information challenge is to collect and keep up to date on what is happening to the fleet of equipment in use in the field. Machines change owners and they are transferred from one location to another. At the same time they are maintained, changed or upgraded by their owners or by third parties. Defining the interface between the upgrade modules and the equipment in the field can be considered a bottleneck of information management in this type of business model.

In Cluster #2, where Metso is already providing customised upgrades, the aim of the development process in the UIW-project was to improve profitability of this business. A central objective was to build and develop a dedicated business network to perform the upgrade activities. Presently, Metso designers and workshop personnel do upgrade activities in parallel with the development and production of new machines. Since the upgrades are generally small, unique projects, they are difficult to fit into the main activities. In the UIW-project, the role of the upgrade producer has been planned for RD Velho—today a subcontractor in engineering to Metso. This organisation can in the future be responsible for module interface design activities, and of the coordination of partial production and installation of upgrade modules. Through the support of an outside partner, Metso can free their own resources to focus on the main business.

Cluster #2 has in the UIW-project-tested 3D scanning technologies for creating digital data and information about the target machine including 3D geometry. This was used especially to document changes made to the machine during use. A central objective of creating new information about the machine is to enable fast design of the interface between the upgrade module designed by Metso and the machine in operation. Having complete information on the state of the machine during upgrade design, enables a fast upgrading process, especially when the upgrading is taking place in the field where the machine is used. Cluster #2 also tested VR- and AR-based review tools to envision upgrade solutions to engineers and customers. These tools were tested in design reviews with Metso engineers. The design object used in the test was a maintenance platform attached to a mobile rock crushing machine that was part of the upgrade for the already existing machine. The virtual reviews enable engineers to evaluate upgrade solutions before they are realised as physical elements of the upgrade module. This reduces the need for iterative behaviour in downstream functions like purchasing, component manufacturing, upgrade assembly and installation.

## 2.3 Remanufacturing

The third business model we call Remanufacturing. This business model has close resemblance to what Linton and Jayaraman (2005) call remanufacture, but it also has elements of the part reuse model. In this business model original equipment is disassembled into parts which are re-used in the production of new equipment. The new equipment can fulfil the same or similar functions as the original equipment, or it can have completely new functionality. A main objective of reusing parts is to create a sustainably produced piece of equipment through reduced use of material and energy resources in the production of the new equipment.

In the Dutch case, Cluster #6 (see Chapter "Sustainable Furniture that Grows with End-Users"), the core company is collecting furniture sold to external customers in order to re-introduce them as parts of new furniture. Collecting of furniture can either mean that the parts are bought back from customers willing to get rid of old furniture and selling upgraded furniture to new or repeat customers, or it can mean that the equipment is leased to the customer and parts of the old equipment are used as input for new equipment, thus reducing the cost of materials in the new delivery.

### 2.3.1 Value Proposition for Remanufacturing

Remanufacturing is typically driven by the values of the end user and by the OEM. The value proposition to the customer or end user of equipment is that sustainable and ecological values are endorsed in the production of the new equipment through prolonging of the life cycle of parts of the equipment. Hence, the material loops are secured through collaboration benefiting both the end user and the OEM.

In Cluster #6, the Dutch company Gispen is adding new customer value through sustainably remanufactured furniture. They provide the users new furniture, and at the same time they add new ecological value for the customer as they build the furniture from used parts, thus reducing the need for use of materials and energy in production.

### 2.3.2 Roles in Remanufacturing

In Remanufacturing, the OEM is typically in a central position. It manages the equipment design and business, and it has control of what parts have been used in what products and of the design and production information of these parts. In this position, it can be well positioned to also be a provider of remanufactured equipment. Forward integration for better control of the equipment fleet will for many OEMs become a necessity as they go into this area of business. Remanufacturing also involves other processes that are not needed in original equipment manufacturing. These are for instance, reverse logistics, disassembly of the original equipment and quality checking of reusable parts. These processes can be outsourced to dedicated expert organisations.

In Cluster #6, the OEM—Gispen—looked into the Remanufacturing model in order to gain insight in the effects and requirements for changing business. Close contact to the customers is crucial in order to tailor furniture to customer needs and in order to manage the fleet of furniture in use. This will also require management of a totally new operation like reverse logistics, the disassembly of old furniture and the quality control of used parts. Where the scale and duration is different between the OEM and the upgrade process, it is natural to look for new ways to organise the activities and sometimes this mean involving external partners to perform tasks and activities not suitable for own processes and organisation.

In the different scenarios explored in the UIW-project, Gispen is considering several alternatives for management of ownership of the furniture and components. One way is to buy back used furniture; another is to own the furniture and lease it to the user.

In Cluster #6, Gispen has chosen to cooperate mainly with the research organisation providing support in defining and analysing the new business model (Fig. 3).

### 2.3.3 Earnings Logic in Remanufacturing

The earnings logic of remanufacturing rests on the values of the customer. In remanufacturing, a product is produced through the reuse of parts, thus reducing the use of virgin materials and energy to form a new part. Often, but not always, this is lower than the price for new products. Since the reuse of parts involves reverse logistics, disassembly of the used product, and quality control, the production of the remanufactured part includes additional costs not included in the production of original parts. In Cluster #6 Gispen is providing the end user a new offering—sustainably produced furniture. This can be seen as an addition to their existing product portfolio.

As mentioned before, remanufacturing requires a whole range of new activities including management of the use base, logistics for the collection of used products, disassembly and so forth. This will require a dedicated workforce and infrastructure capable of performing at high productivity and low costs.

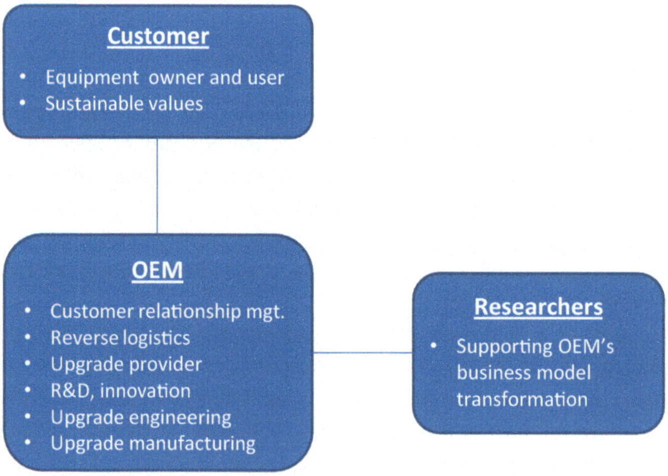


**Fig. 3** Actors, roles and connections in the Remanufacturing business model in the UIW-project

A central challenge in remanufacturing is the management of the installed base. How can the service provider ensure that used parts are available as they are needed in the process of remanufacturing? One option for the service provider is to keep the possession of the goods and only rent or lease it to the user (see Lacy and Rutqvist 2015). This business model, however, also includes challenges. In Chapter Sustainable Furniture that Grows with End-Users, a scenario based on leasing of the furniture to the users, showed that a long usage cycles generates long delays with respect to cash flows for the provider and producer of the remanufactured product.

### 2.3.4 Information Management in Remanufacturing

As in most areas of the circular economy, a central idea of Remanufacturing is to ensure that efforts and materials included in an existing machine or equipment are used and reused as much as possible in order to reduce creation of waste and use of energy. This is a primary driver behind remanufacturing. Reusing components of equipment provides the customer with an ecologically more sustainable product, but productivity and profitability in this business requires strict control of both the flow of material and of information.

Cluster #6 focused on the development of a circular economy design strategy. To do this, the cluster developed tools and methods that speed up and improve the efficiency of the design information flow in the communication between customers, manufacturers and designers to design, upgrade and reuse products according to circular economy principles. In the UIW-project, Cluster 6 evaluated a Design Framework, a checklist approach to circular product design using a recently developed lifecycle analysis tool (LCA+) for circular economy scenarios. The aim of the task was to describe the development of a lifecycle analysis tool (LCA) and evaluate the usefulness of this tool.

## *2.4 Service Upgrade*

The fourth business model is called Service Upgrade. Here new, innovative digital tools are introduced as part of a service in order to radically improve the added value provided for the customer. Using new, innovative digital solutions, the customer is offered an information service, which significantly improves critical business processes and the use of capital intensive equipment. This model offers unique business opportunities for service providers. This can, for instance, be a service supporting other upgrade activities either in-house or as a service to external customers. In the Swedish Cluster #4 (see Chapter "Adaptation of High-Variant Automotive Production System Using a Collaborative Approach"), the owner of the production equipment is planning and performing the upgrade of the equipment themselves. The original provider of the equipment can be involved in this process, but this varies from case to case. Services are also procured from outside service providers, but the main responsibility for the upgrade is with the owner. In the Spanish cluster—Cluster #1 (see Chapter "Collaborative Management of Inspection Results in Power Plant Turbines")—a service provider is improving its capabilities to provide a service to an external customer who owns the capital-intensive equipment. The information provided through the service can be used by the owner to maintain the equipment or as input for planning an upgrade to meet new needs.

### 2.4.1 Value Proposition for Service Upgrade

The value for the customer in the Service Upgrade business model is the improved efficiency of service provision and more valuable results.

Cluster #1 is striving to improve service performance in the turbine inspection process. Through the improved service, the customer gets better information on the condition of the equipment and can make better decisions on how to operate and maintain the equipment.

In Cluster #4 the production line for trucks is adapted to changed market needs. The changing demand for different types of trucks requires changes in technology and in layout in the production line. Another example of adopting to change market needs is when new legislation forces users of stone crushers to improve the safety of the operator to meet the new standards. The upgrade necessary to do this can be added as a module to the machine operating in the field.

### 2.4.2 Roles in Service Upgrade

In Service Upgrade, the focus is on the network actors providing services to the equipment owners.

In Cluster #1, the service providers are not providers of the original equipment, but specialise in providing high level, focused service for a specific market segment. The competitive edge for this company is based on managing the service task. In Cluster #4, where the customer is internal, the service provider is not the producer of the original equipment, but the service provider has been involved in designing and building the manufacturing system, and thus also has a thorough understanding of the system and its components. In both clusters outside research partners were involved in the development of new tools and technology for improving the service operation.

In the Service Upgrade the OEM of the equipment in use is not directly involved in the service, but the core actor in this value chain providing the service to the end user is the service provider. This actor is responsible for both planning and executing the service. External actors like research partners support the development of service technology (Fig. 4).

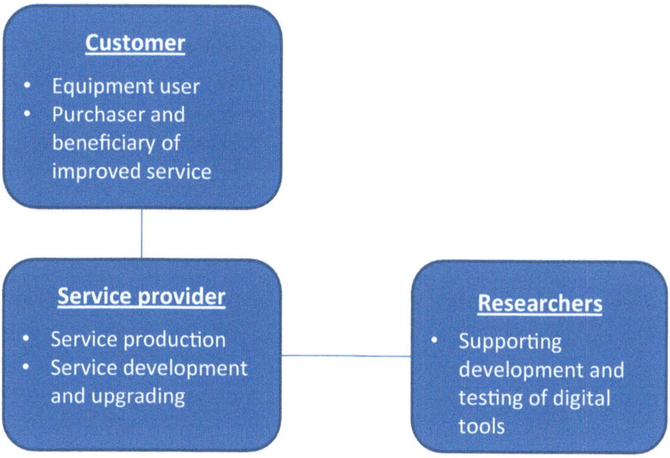


**Fig. 4** Actors, roles and connections in the Service Upgrade business model in the UIW-project

### 2.4.3 Earnings Logic in Service Upgrade

In the Service Upgrade business model, the objective is to improve an existing service in order to improve customer value or to improve the efficiency of the service process. The first option will offer an opportunity to distinguish from competition and to charge a higher price for the service. The second option cuts cost for the service provider.

In Cluster #1, Tecnatom focuses on improving internal processes in order to meet the needs, not of a specific customer, but of the market as a whole. The new solution developed and piloted in the UIW-project enables Tecnatom to provide the customer more elaborate information on the condition of the power plant's equipment. This enables better and faster understanding for the customer of what has been done during maintenance and what still required.

In Cluster #4 information on the state of the Volvo production plant is collected through scanning. This enables efficient planning for upgrading the process to meet the new market needs.

### 2.4.4 Information Management in Service Upgrade

In Service Upgrade, a central objective is improving the value added provided by the service to the customer. This added value can be achieved through new digital means for creation of data or from new means to combine and bundle data to useful information, thus, making it easier for the customer to acquire and use the information. This can be seen in the pilots developed in Clusters #1 and #4.

Cluster #1 developed value-added turbine inspection services for the fossil power industries. The aim was to develop collaborative environments that make all available and relevant information accessible to all stakeholders taking part in the post-inspection decision-making processes. The ultimate goal was to reach faster decisions that minimise outage duration and better decisions that prolong the turbine service life by several years. Within the UIW-project, Cluster #1 developed a system that integrates 3D visualisation of the turbine with all inspection related data. From the upgrade process point of view, this tool is combining original design data with data from the equipment in use in order to enable efficient decision-making on what needs to be done to ensure continuous operation of the power plant.

Cluster #4 is focused on developing applications to store technical information of the production system and improving current work activities centred in a collaborative view. Through the system developed in the UIW-project, measurement data collected with a 3D laser scanner and CAD data of the production cell can be combined. The goal is to improve the communication between the actors from different departments in order to make technical decisions using this information. In the UIW-project Cluster #4 tested the system in an industrial setting supporting the decision-making of different actors in the manufacturing change/upgrade process. The test was based on a 3D laser scan of a part of the manufacturing which was due for an upgrade. The users were able to see the cell as-is in the first phase and then in the concept design phase they were able to visually compare alternative design solutions for the upcoming change.

# 3 Comparing the Business Models

In this chapter, we look at some common challenges related to the development and implementation of the four business models as well as some differences between these models.

## *3.1 Common Features and Challenge in Implementation of Business Models*

All cluster cases in the UIW-project focused on developing existing customer relationships and the main focus of all OEMs in the clusters is on the customers owning original equipment produced by them. This forms the market basis for their upgrade business activities. Building a confidential relationship with a customer is an investment of time and effort, and it should be re-utilised as far as possible. This is true for all the business models. As the designer of the original machines, equipment or systems, the OEM possesses the information on how it was originally designed and built. This is also an asset for reuse. In practice, introducing a service business into an OEM organisation is not straightforward. There are challenges related to identification of the present owners of previously delivered products, understanding the upgrading needs of the customer, defining the state of the machine or system in operation, etc.

In general, we can say that the roles of the actors in the upgrade business are different from the roles these companies have in original equipment production. Upgrade projects are typically smaller in scope and shorter in duration than the original equipment production, and the original business processes are most likely not suitable for handling these new types of upgrading projects. Despite this difference to the original manufacturing process, the OEMs are in a central position in most of the upgrade business models presented in this chapter. Only in the Service Upgrade cases are the OEMs of the equipment not involved.

In all cluster cases in the UIW-project, the customer of the OEM is the owner and user of the equipment. In all but one case, this is an external party. Only in Cluster #4, the customer is internal—a separated department within the same company. In four of the cluster cases, the providers of the upgrade services are OEM companies responsible for designing and manufacturing the original equipment. They have a good understanding of the technology and how it works, and based on this they provide solutions to new customer needs emerged after the original piece of equipment was delivered. This is their competitive advantage as upgrade service providers. The service activities are also, in general, based on existing customer relationships.

A common challenge for most of the Cluster cases and to the business models relates to the role of the new service business as part of the company's overall business portfolio. To some of the companies in the UIW-project introducing an upgrade service meant adding a new service to the existing portfolio of services. To others it was more a question of improving on existing services. Although the objective of adding a new service is improved customer service and increased sales, the introduction of the new life cycle service is also connected with a sense of risk that it might endanger the success of existing business activities. The synergy (or sometimes the lack thereof) between the old and the new activities affects how the companies can benefit from introduction of new upgrade business activities.

For the customer or the user of the equipment, the introduction of an upgrade service offers a new alternative means of ensuring the continuity, quality and competitiveness of their activities and the use of the equipment in their possession. An alternative would be to buy completely new equipment specially built for or originally constructed more suitable for the new situation. For the OEM, finding a balance between original equipment production and upgrade life cycle services is a central challenge when considering entering the upgrade business. Defining the scope of the upgrades and the upgrade business, as well as, pricing of upgrades are important decisions in this phase. A sense of risk for cannibalising of existing business was discussed in several of the UIW-cluster. In this chapter, we have seen that prolonging the lifetime of a boat—a central goal of the circular economy business models described earlier in this chapter—is from an economic point of view not trivial for the companies. In the simulated scenario, OCEAN—the boat manufacturing company—generally benefits from a reduced boat lifetime, but this was not true for all situations. Additionally, the boat operator Seability seems to profit from a shorter life cycle, which can be considered counterintuitive.

Based on the analysis of the Cluster cases, we identified three areas of cost control through the creation of efficient business processes. These areas are:

(1) reuse of resources and components
    (a) original equipment as market base
    (b) materials and components
(2) developing dedicated resources and service infrastructure,
    (a) business network for upgrade production
    (b) service equipment as business platform
(3) streamlining processes through improvement in information management and communication

## 3.2 *Main Differences Between Business Models*

A primary distinguishing factor between the business models is the clear difference in the value proposition offered. While the Customised Upgrade focuses on uniqueness and customisation, the Modular Upgrade s owners of old equipment to reach leading edge performance level typically offered by new equipment through as a low-cost alternative. Remanufacturing offers sustainability as its main value proposition. Service Upgrade is as such not a novel business model, but an improvement on an existing life cycle service.

We can also see some differences between the roles of the OEMs in the different business models. While they are not heavily involved in the Service upgrade cases, they are at the centre of the three other business models. Here again there are some differences in what roles they manage in-house and what they can outsource. Based on the UIW-cluster cases, it seems that in the Customised Upgrade and Remanufacturing business models the OEM performs all major activities in-house and outsource only highly specialised tasks. In the Modular Upgrade network, partners can play a central role also in the realisation and delivery of the upgrade service.

In Table 2, we have summarised the main features of the four upgrade business models.

**Table 2** Upgrade business models

| Business model | Customized upgrade | Modular upgrade | Remanufacturing | Service upgrade |
|---|---|---|---|---|
| Value proposition | Enables equipment owners or users to capture unique, innovative business opportunities through an upgrade service tailored to their needs. Increased sustainability in use of original equipment can be part of added customer value | Provided equipment owners or users leading edge performance through predefined and productised modular upgrading of their used equipment. Increased sustainability in the use of original equipment can be part of added customer value | Providing sustainable equipment designs through reuse of component from used/existing equipment | Providing equipment owners unique, productised and digitally supported services to improve utilisation of capital-intensive equipment and to enhance end-customer service. Increased sustainability in the use of original equipment can be part of customer value |
| Market base and customers | Original equipment in use and its owners/users | Original equipment in use and its owners/users | Reusable components of original equipment in use | Original equipment in use and its owners/users |
| Upgrade task | Upgrading parts of the original equipment to meet new purposes of use | Adding upgrade module or replacing existing module with upgraded module | Reusing components of original equipment in new products | Information management to support upgrade and other service activities |
| Key actors and roles | **Customer**: equipment owner, initiator of upgrade process, purchaser of upgrade service **OEM**: fleet management, CRM, upgrade provider, engineering, manufacturing, development of upgrade business process **Service provider**: provider of outsourced expert services | **Customer**: equipment owner, purchaser of upgrade service, **OEM**: fleet management, CRM, upgrade provider, R&D, product development, productisation, development of upgrade business process **Service provider**: as-is data collection, upgrade delivery and installation, | **Customer**: equipment owner, purchaser of remanufactured equipment **OEM**: designer and producer of original equipment, designer and producer of remanufactured equipment, reverse logistics, **Researchers**: developing and testing of innovative digital technology, | **Customer**: equipment owner, purchaser of improved service **Service provider**: provider of improved service, service process development, testing and implementation of innovative digital tools **Researchers**: developing and testing of |

(continued)

**Table 2** (continued)

| Business model | Customized upgrade | Modular upgrade | Remanufacturing | Service upgrade |
|---|---|---|---|---|
| | **Technology provider**: provider of digital tools, technology development and manufacturing **Researchers**: developing and testing of innovative digital technology, supporting business model transformation | management of upgrade process, testing and implementation of innovative digital tools **Researchers**: developing and testing of innovative digital technology, supporting business model transformation | supporting business model transformation | innovative digital technology, supporting business model transformation |
| Earnings logic | Improved sales through innovative capturing of customer needs and value Dedicated upgrade service infrastructure and resources Integrated information management in business network Value-based pricing | Improved customer loyalty, Added turnover per customer, Productised modular upgrade services Dedicated upgrade service network and resources Focusing in-house product development efforts on innovative modules and product features | Providing customer with sustainable equipment based on reused components Control of market base Reverse logistics process Remanufacturing process | Improved customer loyalty through improved service performance Improved productivity of service work Value-based pricing |
| Cluster cases in UIW-project | Cluster #3 Cluster #5 | Cluster #2 | Cluster #6 | Cluster #1 Cluster #4 |

## *3.3 Similarities and Differences in Information Management*

Since the focus of the UIW-project was on information management in the upgrade business, we will look more closely at the similarities and differences between the pilot solutions developed for the different business models in order to see if we can identify special information management challenges related to these business models. The pilots are listed in Table 3.

**Table 3** Information management pilots in the UIW-project

| Business model | Cluster case | Pilot | Abbreviation (see Fig. 5) |
|---|---|---|---|
| Customised upgrade | Cluster #3 | Reference data model<br>Request Web Configurator<br>Web environment | CU1<br>CU2<br>CU3 |
| | Cluster #5 | Reference data model<br>Vessel configuration tool | CU4<br>CU5 |
| Modular upgrade | Cluster #2 | Testing of 3D scanning technologies<br>AR-based review tool | MU1<br>MU2 |
| Remanufacturing | Cluster #6 | Circular design framework | RM1 |
| Service upgrade | Cluster #1 | Webb app for managing inspection results using 3D environment. | SU1 |
| | Cluster #4 | Combination of measurement data collected with a 3D laser scanner and CAD data of the production cell | SU2 |

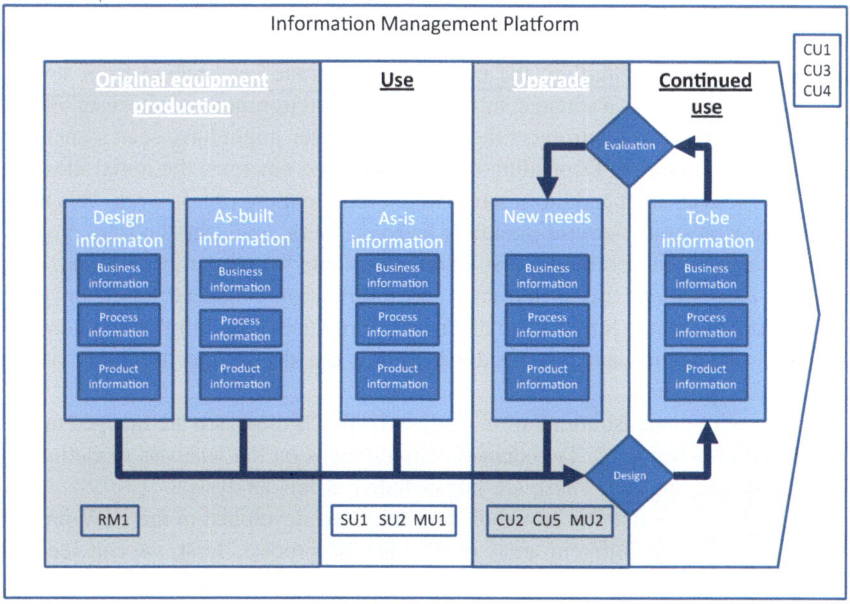


**Fig. 5** Upgrade information management process

In Fig. 5, we have described a rough model for information management in the upgrade business. The starting point is the original equipment production and the design data created in this phase. In this model, we have divided the information in business-related data or information, process-related information and product information. While product data and information is stored in formal formats in CAD and PLM systems, process information and business information can take a variety of forms and the quality and completeness of stored data varies.

*Designed information*: reusing the original design information is a central factor in the business model of upgrading. This information is stored in the OEM's archives in different formats. Today, most of it is in electronic format, but for very old equipment or systems there may still be a need to look for this information on paper. Additionally, the electronic formats have changed over the year, so making use of old information might require updating the information to a newer format.

*As-built information*: in complex products like machinery and equipment there are often steps that are not documented fully during the design process. This so called as-built information is not always documented, but modern means like digital cameras have for some time been used to document this information.

*Use-information*: during the use of the equipment, changes are made for several reasons. Worn out or broken components are replaced, smaller or larger additions or upgrades are made, etc. Often these types of changes are not documented, or some of the information can be stored by the organisation responsible for the changes. In order to perform an upgrade, as-is information is often needed, and needs to be collected in one way or another. Formally stored information can be requested from the user or other actors, or information can be created from scratch.

*Upgrade need information*: the need for an upgrade can emerge from several root causes. It can be a change in the business environment of the user of the original equipment which triggers the need, or the user might have seen something similar somewhere else. Depending on how this need emerges, the initial idea can be more or less abstract and the solution might require more or less work. When the initial idea is abstract, several iterations between users, engineers and the production team can be needed before a solution acceptable for all parties is found.

*To-be information*: this is the data and information produced based on prior information, re-created information and new information. This information needs to be stored, maintained and managed for further use during the life cycle of the machine or equipment.

Twelve pilot demonstrations were made in UIW. Of these, ten are mapped on the upgrade process in Fig. 2. Two demonstrations focus on the business modelling in Cluster cases #5 and #6. These are not included in this analysis.

In Fig. 5, we see that the new tools and solutions developed in the UIW-project are focusing on four different areas in the upgrade process. First, we can see that two clusters have developed tools and methods for general information management in the upgrade process. Secondly, one group of tools developed by the clusters focuses on creating and evaluating information on new customer needs. Thirdly, three clusters have focused on as-is information; creating it through 3D-scanning, combining it with original design data and visualising it to support dialogue and decision-making among several actors involved in the process. Fourthly, one cluster focuses on the original equipment design process.

### 3.3.1 Pilots for Customised Upgrade

The tools and methods in the first area developed for general information management can be divided into two categories; one is the creation of a reference data model—a meta-file—for storing and managing all the life cycle information of the machine to be upgraded. The information stored concerns a specific piece of equipment, not a machine type or class. Without this system, the information is scattered around in the network of actors or even non-existing in formal sense. The second category of tools and methods in this group is the communication infrastructure between independent actors in the business network for the management of common meta-files. The meta-files and communication network tools were in the UIW-project developed especially by Cluster #3 and #5, and although similar tools can also be useful in other upgrade business models, the need for collecting and managing information on single customer needs and for transforming this information into new upgrade solutions makes a tool like this crucial in this business model.

The second area of tools development in the UIW-project focused on creating and evaluating information on the new needs of the single customer looking for an upgrade. This is crucial in the cases of customised upgrading. Understanding the needs of the customer, documenting it and evaluating it with different stakeholders is an essential part of the upgrading process. Mistakes in this phase of the process mean that everything done before the mistake is realised has to be reconsidered and possibly redone, and this costs both time and money. In both the Italian and the Greek cluster cases, the focus is both on documenting the customer's initial ideas for the upgrade, but also on evaluating and comparing different upgrade design solutions with the customer's needs and ideas.

### 3.3.2 Pilots for Modular Upgrade

In the Modular Upgrade business model, a great deal of information is dealt with internally by the OEM, and the special development needs were found in the customer interface in the management of as-is information. This represents the third area of tool development in the UIW-project. Comparing it with original design information and visualising the changes that have taken place in the equipment during use support dialogue and decision-making in a network of actors planning and designing the upgrade solution for the customer. Creating digital as-is information is essential in situations where this information does not exist or is not available to the actors performing the upgrade. In the Metso case, the machines have typically been in use for years and the user might have made changes to the machine without systematic documentation. 3D models of the used equipment were in Cluster #2 created using a set of 3D scanning techniques.

Also the evaluation of upgrade design solutions was considered important in Cluster #2. Here the focus was, however, more on visualisation for engineers and customers of how a predefined upgrade module would fit the customer's machine and to demonstrate how it would function with the new upgrade. To do this, virtual design reviews were held in a virtual reality environment that also made use of augmented reality solutions.

### 3.3.3 Pilots for Remanufacturing

The fourth area addressed in the development of the tools and methods in the UIW-project bring into focus the design of original equipment. As we saw earlier, Gispen focused on developing a circular economy Design Framework and demonstrated the use of a checklist for circular product design. This list was used for evaluating how well original equipment designs supported remanufacturing and circular design. In this case, the market base consists of re-usable components of furniture available and fit for recycling. The better the recycling already planned in the original design phase, the faster the market base of recyclable components will grow and the bigger the market base will become.

### 3.3.4 Pilots for Service Upgrade

The Service Upgrade pilots can be divided into two groups. First, one pilot focuses on creating the as-is information in an environment including several machines and equipment as well as infrastructure, in this case the building. The second pilot in this group documents and presents data on what has been done during maintenance of equipment.

In Cluster #4, as-is information of the Volvo factory is created through 3D scanning. In this case the object—the factory—consists of a wide range of equipment, the building, products, components, material, etc. Original information on the building or equipment can exist in a digital format, but most likely scanning the necessary information is faster than collecting original data from external sources.

In Cluster #1, a software tool is storing information on inspection and testing tasks, procedures and plans, information on results of inspections, as well as 2D drawings of the inspected equipment. A 3D model based on the 'as-is' turbine was created after 3D scanning the turbine. This 3D model is used to visualise the turbine and the inspection results in order to easily understand the overall situation and allow for the decision making of the stakeholders to take place in a collaborative manner and with all of the necessary information.

## 4 Conclusions

In this chapter, we have described four generic upgrade business models based on the six industrial Cluster cases in the UIW-project. These business models provide opportunities for producers of capital-intensive goods or equipment to strengthen the contact with their customers and to provide the customer valuable services aimed at improving their competitiveness under changing market conditions. The four business models all provide their own, specific added value for the customer. These business models can be added as part of the life cycle service portfolio in a company, but some of the business models can also have the potential to achieve more profound changes in how manufacturing companies operate in the future. For instance, remanufacturing has the potential to take manufacturing into a new cycle of material and energy flow, where existing physical parts become the raw material for the production of similar or even totally new products. Modular Upgrade can revolutionise how we see the connection between innovation and the product life cycle.

In the analysis of the business models, we realised that circular economy drivers were present in most of the cluster cases, but not necessarily in the way that they have been presented in academic work. Closing the material loop (Bocken et al. 2016) and thus, providing the customer more sustainably produced products was a driver mainly in the Remanufacturing case of Gispen in Cluster #6. Prolonging the loops (Bocken et al. 2016) was considered a challenge or even risk for the OEM companies in Clusters #2 and #5. Instead, these companies offered more sustainable operation of the original equipment as an added value for the customer. This can enable the customer to perform business activities in areas of high sustainability standards.

To the companies in the clusters, the upgrade business provides opportunity for added sales and turnover through the addition of new customer offerings, or through improvement in or replacement of existing services. To the OEMs providing upgrade services, it is also a means of improving the competitive edge in the original equipment market.

We also learned that, while providing existing customers with upgrade services can improve sales, profitable execution of this business requires efficient management of the business processes. While the circular economy business models focus on the reuse of finite or renewable materials, the business model used in the cluster cases are all centred on what could be called reuse of intangible resources. Development or strengthening of the long-term customer-supplier relationship was the main objective in most of the UIW-clusters. To the users of the equipment, prolonging of the economic life cycle of the equipment is a central objective, but to the OEM companies, this plays a secondary role. Among the companies in the six clusters, only Gispen was looking to directly close the material loop through remanufacturing.

The second means in creating efficient processes in the cluster cases was the use of dedicated resources. While the object of the upgrade activity is the same as in original equipment manufacturing, the process is not the same. Upgrading results in limited changes to the equipment and is thus a separate process. Depending on the case, the roles in the upgrade network can be managed in-house or by external partners. Dedicating special resources for upgrading activities gives a stronger focus to both the original equipment manufacturing and the upgrade activities.

Thirdly, the role of information management is emphasised in the upgrade value network since detailed information has to be collected from several sources using several different means. From the cluster cases, we identified four areas where modern information technology can improve information management in the upgrade business process. Firstly, it helps to create as-is information on equipment in use in, and in comparison to, this information with information from the original equipment design and production. Secondly, it can be helpful in creating, documenting and evaluating the upgrade needs of the customers or users. Being able to do virtual tests on new design solutions with the customer needs in a virtual environment is a central means for reducing iterations during design and implementation of the customer-specific upgrade.

Fourth, there is a need to consider upgrade business issues already in the original equipment design and manufacturing. This was demonstrated in the remanufacturing case of Gispen, but it will most likely also be of importance in cases of modular upgrading, where the feature of the product is upgraded by adding or changing specific modules.

Fifth and finally, upgrading is, by its nature, a process of information management in a networked environment. Joint information management and information sharing are crucial for the success of the upgrade business and, therefore, a common information management platform plays a central role in these activities. A central focus of the UIW-project was initially on technologies like VR and AR. These technologies are used for visualisation of electronically stored data. The work done in the UIW-project shows that there are several areas in the upgrade process where visualisation of information is needed. Visualisation of data and information can be a means to get a better understanding of three-dimensional models used for planning upgrades, and as such it can be a means for people of different backgrounds to communicate whit each other about the upgrade. These are central means in developing a dynamic upgrade process where data is collected from several sources and several actors have to understand and approve it.

A final conclusion of the findings from the UIW-project is that, although there are signs of the growing importance of environmental sustainability in the activities of companies in the durable goods area, in most cases the main objectives driving the companies to adopt upgrade business are still in line with more traditional service business objectives. Sustainability becomes a driver in business as a demand for sustainable products develops. This can be clearly seen in the crusher market in Cluster #2 and the boat market of Cluster #5. The different cycles in the circular economy will also compete with each other. Recycling of materials is already a huge business and for some raw materials like copper, a significant part of the material is already recycled (European Copper Institute 2016). Thus, upgrading is not only competing with virgin materials, but with recycled materials and from an environmental point of view, the benefit of using upgrades is the prolonging of the cycle. For the OEM companies the role of upgrading business alongside the original equipment manufacturing will change as margins from upgrading outperforms margins of original equipment manufacturing. In this situation, production of new equipment aims mainly at growing the market base for upgrading. In remanufacturing, the difference from recycling is the saving of energy as part are reused without heavy processing.

For OEM companies focusing on original equipment manufacturing changing to an upgrade business model based on ownership of the equipment, major changes in the capital structure are required. Building and owning the original equipment absorbs huge capital, while inbound cash flows will initially be low and gradually increase as business grows. In many companies, especially SMEs, these changes are likely to require renewal of the funding structure and possibly also the ownership of the company.

## References

Allwood, J. M., Ashby, M. F., Gutowski, T., & Worrell, E. (2011). Material efficiency: A white paper. *Resources, Conservation and Recycling*, No 55. pp. 362–381.

Bocken, N. M., De Pauw, I., Bakker, C., & van der Grinten, B. (2016). Product design and business model strategies for a circular economy. *Journal of Industrial and Production Engineering, 33*(5), 308–320. http://dx.doi.org/10.1080/21681015.2016.1172124

Ellen MacArthur Foundation. (2016). *Circular economy system diagram*. Retrieved May 31, 2016, from https://www.ellenmacarthurfoundation.org/circular-economy/interactive-diagram

European Copper Institute. (2016). Resources: The sources of copper. Retrieved September 29, 2016, from http://copperalliance.eu/about-copper/resources

Lacy, P., & Rutqvist, J. (2015). Waste to wealth : The circular economy advantage. Basingstoke, GB: Palgrave Macmillan. ProQuest ebrary. Web. 31 May 2016

Linton, J. D., & Jayaraman, V. (2005). A framework for identifying differences and similarities in the managerial competencies associated with different modes of product life extension. *International Journal of Production Research, 43*, 1807–1829.

Osterwalder, A., & Pigneur, Y. (2010). *Business model generation. A handbook for visionairies, game changers, and challengers*. New Jersey: Wiley.

Pasquinelli, A., Chico, L., Pasquali, L., Bisordi, C., Lo Gerfo, A., Fabbrini, M., et al. (2016). Gly482Ser PGC-1alpha gene polymorphism and exercise-related oxidative stress in amyotrophic lateral sclerosis patients. *Front Cell Neuroscience (April), 10*, 102. https://doi.org/10.3389/fncel.2016.00102

Roos, G., & Agarwal, R. (2015). Services innovation in a circular economy. In R. Agarwal et al. (Eds.), *The handbook of service innovation*. London: Springer.
Stahel, W. R. (2016). Circular economy. A new relationship with our goods and materials would save resources and energy and create local jobs. *Nature*, 03/2016, *531*(7595), 435–438.

The manufacturer's authorised representative in the EU is Springer Nature Customer Service Centre GmbH, Europaplatz 3, 69115 Heidelberg, Germany. If you have any concerns regarding our products, please contact ProductSafety@springernature.com

Printed and bound by CPI Group (UK) Ltd, Croydon, CR0 4YY
30/09/2026
02225657-0009